Activities Handbook

for the

Teaching of Psychology

VOLUME FOUR

Edited by

Ludy T. Benjamin,

Barbara F. Nodine,

Randal M. Ernst, and

Charles Blair Broeker

AMERICAN PSYCHOLOGICAL ASSOCIATION
WASHINGTON, DC

Typeset in Trump Mediaeval by EPS Group Inc., Easton, MD
Cover designer: Oring Creative Marketing, Gaithersburg, MD
Printer: Data Reproductions Corp., Rochester Hills, MI
Project Manager: Debbie K. Hardin, Reston, VA

Library of Congress Cataloging-in-Publication Data
(Revised for vol. 4)

Activities handbook for the teaching of psychology

　　Vol. 4 edited by: Ludy T. Benjamin, Jr. . . .
[et al.].
　　Includes bibliographies and index.
　　1. Psychology—Problems, exercises, etc.　I. Benjamin,
Ludy T., 1945– .　II. Lowman, Kathleen D., 1948–
BF78.A28　　1981　　　150′.7　　　　81-1648
ISBN 0-912704-34-9　　(v. 1)
ISBN Volume 2: 1-55798-030-6
ISBN Volume 3: 1-55798-081-0
ISBN Volume 4: 1-55798-537-5

Published by American Psychological Association
750 First Street, NE
Washington, DC 20002

Copies may be ordered from
APA Order Department
P.O. Box 92984
Washington, DC 20090-2984

Printed in the United States of America
First edition

TABLE OF CONTENTS

V LEARNING **161**

VI MEMORY **187**

VII COGNITION AND EMOTION **209**

PREFACE

Teachers of psychology—from those who teach introductory-level to upper-level courses, from experienced veterans of the classroom to beginners, from instructors in experimental courses to courses on the abnormal, from faculty in small classes to those facing large lecture halls— all find that adding activities to their lessons makes the course a more effective learning experience. Activities that give students something to do with the material learned in lecture and from the textbook make the course material more accessible, more memorable, more integrated into their understanding. Faculty members understand that activities not only make their courses more interesting, but they also contribute to the depth of understanding that their students gain. With those outcomes in mind, we present the fourth volume in the series of activities handbooks, published over two decades by the American Psychological Association. Volume 4 is similar in many ways to the previous three volumes, but has some differences. A circle has been completed in that Ludy Benjamin was an editor of the first volume and is again on this volume. The authors of these activities are teaching faculty members in a wide range of institutions, as has been true of the previous three volumes. In fact, two of the authors included have contributed activities to all four volumes. In most cases, the activities are useful for the beginning course in psychology; however, a number of activities would also be useful for a course in a particular content area, such as developmental psychology or psychology of women.

These activities have been organized to offer maximum usefulness to teachers. The activities are grouped by the topics of general skills and critical thinking, research methods and statistics, biopsychology and animal behavior, sensation and perception, learning, memory, cognition and emotion, developmental psychology, human diversity, social psychology and personality, and psychological disorders and treatments. As you can imagine, some activities could have been placed in more than one topical area. Thus, depending on the organization of the course, teachers might find that an activity is useful but fits a category different from the ones designated in the table of contents. This is especially true of the activities found grouped together as general skills and critical thinking, research methods and statistics, and human diversity.

All of the activities are described with a common format that instructors will find easy to use. Each activity begins with a brief abstract, followed by a concept section that provides the teacher with enough information to decide where to place a particular activity in his or her syllabus. Once a teacher has decided to use a particular activity, he or she can check the materials-needed section to identify what items are necessary to use the exercise in a classroom setting; often all that is needed is a handout that can be duplicated for the class. The next two sections, instructions and discussion, tell how to conduct the activity. These activities have been used numerous times by the authors, so their experience with them provides the teacher using them for the first time with an idea of how they will be received. Next, in most activities, is the writing component section, new to this volume, which suggests ways to incorporate writing into the activity. The final sections, references and suggested reading, may reflect a particular source that the author found useful. In some cases, the references show the original theoretical or empirical work on which the activity was based.

Activities differ along many dimensions other than topical content. Teachers will select the types of activities that work in their individual classes, depending on the number of students, expectations of the students, physical layout of the classroom, and the time frame for activities. We respect teachers' experience in making a judgment about what types of activities are useful for their courses, but we urge you to try something a little different. The experience of the authors gathered in this volume suggests that a very wide range of activities will contribute to the richness of students' learning. The activities differ in the following ways: the amount of class time necessary to conduct the activity; the amount of time the student will spend outside of class, as well as in class; the amount of time the teacher will need to organize the materials and prepare the activity; the types of student groups needed for the activity, from students working individually to working in pairs, small groups, or as a class; and the background level of the students in the course. We respect the fact that courses differ in how students will receive each of these dimensions and in how comfortable a fit a particular type of activity is for each teacher. In addition, this volume's activities have included, wherever possible, a cross-cultural component. Faculty members have shown that they wish to broaden their students' cultural horizons, so we have tried to embed in the activities a wider perspective.

What does it mean to say that teachers are incorporating active learning in their courses? A definition of active learning is not simple; we assume that active learning is the opposite of passive learning:

> Active learning connotes an array of learning situations in and out of the classroom in which students enjoy hands-on and "minds-on" experiences. Students learn through active participation in simulations, demonstrations, discussions, debates, games, problem solving, experiments, writing exercises, and interactive lectures. (Mathie et al., 1993, p. 185)

Even a formal lecture class can be an active learning experience if the students are engaged with the material, so note the activities in the general skills section. Whether the whole class is hearing a lecture or viewing a video or demonstration, it becomes active learning when the student is personally engaged with the material. That engagement can be obtained with some fairly simple activities, such as asking students to respond in writing to questions. Mathie et al. (1993) and Benjamin (1991) have discussed the varieties and roles of active learning in the classroom in greater depth.

In this volume you will find that we can infer a definition of active learning from the kinds of participation in which the students will engage. Activities may require students to engage in role play, taking on a particular persona or perspective; participate in a debate or symposium in which they present a point of view; gather data or observations on each other or on a wide range of subjects in the world outside of the classroom; summarize the observations or data in a very formal manner, in some cases even calculating statistical summaries, or in a less formal, but organized manner; and finally, write about the experiences to reflect their own learning or to summarize the content of the activity. Thus the nature of involvement across activities is quite variable. What is important is that students get involved in their own learning and that the instructor welcomes them into the learning process through the inclusion that active learning demands.

A statement regarding authorship is warranted here. It is the nature of teaching activities and classroom exercises that they are passed from teacher to teacher and friend to friend. In this sharing process, the source of original materials is often lost or forgotten. If the material was never printed, the creator of the activity is often never known. We have made every effort to locate the original authors and copyright owners, and we hope that appropriate credit has been cited for each activity. However, in the event that an activity has been published previously and not appropriately cited, we ask that you call this to our attention. We apologize for any oversights of this kind.

We thank our many colleagues (listed after this preface) who served as reviewers on the articles included in this book. Their efforts clearly enhanced the quality of these activities. Our gratitude is extended especially to Sherilyn McLemore, who was responsible for much of the correspondence involved and who worked long hours to make many different word-processing programs speak one language. Finally, we thank the authors of these activities for their commitment to excellence in teaching. Some of the authors were inspired to design and write up the activities because of their successful use of activities from the earlier handbooks. We also acknowledge the APA's continued commitment to a publication that serves teachers effectively and enriches students.

REFERENCES   Benjamin, L. T., Jr. (1991). Personalization and active learning in the large introductory psychology class. *Teaching of Psychology, 18,* 68–74.

Mathie, V. A., Beins, B., Benjamin, L. T., Jr., Ewing, M. M., Hall, C. C. I., Henderson, B., McAdam, D. W., & Smith, R. A. (1993). Promoting active learning in psychology courses. In T. V. McGovern (Ed.), *Handbook for enhancing undergraduate education in psychology* (pp. 183–214). Washington, DC: American Psychological Association.

LIST OF REVIEWERS

The editors gratefully acknowledge the following individuals who assisted in the review of the articles in this book:

William Addison
Mary Beth Alum
Ruth Anderson
Winfred Arthur
Bernard C. Beins
Lynn Blair-Broeker
Charles L. Brewer
William Bryant
Samuel M. Cameron
Janet F. Carlson
Timothy A. Cavell
Judith C. Chrisler
Carol Jo Dean
Dana S. Dunn
Ann Elliott
Martha M. Ellis
Sherri A. Ernst
Stephanie Farnsworth
Clifford L. Fawl
John Finch
Diane Finley
Christina Frederick
James E. Freeman
Angela R. Gillem
Perilou Goddard
George D. Goedel
Ernest Goetz
James Grau
Nancy Grayson
Deborah Green
Nancy P. Grippo
Craig Gruber
Chris Hakala

Jane S. Halonen
Bruce B. Henderson
Paul I. Heittich
David K. Hogberg
J. Roy Hopkins
David E. Johnson
Wesley Jordan
Deborah Kashy
Kenneth Keith
Nicholas C. Kierniesky
Cindy Kremer
Kyra Kulik-Johnson
Rebecca A. Lafleur
Janet D. Larsen
Judith R. Levine
Cynthia R. McDaniel
Rob McEntarffer
Lance McMahon
Laura Maitland
Mary Meagher
Dennis Miller
Marianne Miserandino
Henry Morlock
Jack Nation
Tony Pacquin
Benton Pierce
Thomas W. Pierce
Greg Pool
Tom Pusateri
Chris Randall
Kelly Reene
Randy Refsland

Nancy Rhodes
Steven J. Robbins
William Rogers
Karen Roper
Carolyn Rosenfeld
Diana S. Rosenstein
Jack Rossmann
Wayne Shebilske
Cynthia Sifonis
Jeffry A. Simpson
Jeffrey M. Smith
Randolph A. Smith
Steven M. Smith
Mary Spilis
Brian Stagner
Steven Stern
Michael Sullivan
Thomas Thieman
David G. Thomas
James H. Thomas
Douglas Trimble
Frank Vattano
Linda Walsh
Jamie Ward
Thomas Ward
Catherine Wehlburg
Paul Wellman
T. Baird Wiehe
Judith G. Wiley
Mary M. Winn
Wendy Wood
Kris Woolley

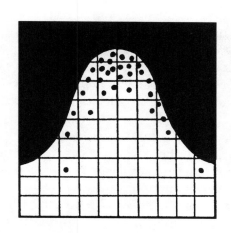

CHAPTER I
GENERAL SKILLS AND
CRITICAL THINKING

The 13 articles in this chapter emphasize active learning via critical thinking activities and writing exercises. In addition, there is an activity for class review, a capstone activity for the introductory course, and two activities that teach history of psychology. The chapter begins with an activity that introduces students to a variety of services offered by college and university libraries, including CD-ROM databases such as PsycLIT. Activity 2 describes a method for getting feedback from students about their understanding of course material throughout a course using 3-by-5-in. cards.

The next four articles describe various critical thinking activities. Activity 3 uses a murder scenario to teach students about the costs and benefits of being a critical thinker. Activity 4 describes three critical thinking exercises designed to teach students about the principle of parsimony in science. Urban legends are used in Activity 5 to teach students about epistemology—that is, ways of knowing. The last of the articles on critical thinking, Activity 6, uses "psychic" demonstrations to help students understand the similarities of critical thinking and scientific method.

The next three articles describe several ways to use writing exercises to learn psychology. Most of these are in-class writing assignments, but one emphasizes writing outside of class. Activity 7 uses writing assignments to deepen students' understanding of the concepts presented in class. Activity 8 emphasizes writing about psychology via a letter to a friend or parent. Activity 9 involves students writing to psychologists whose work is of particular interest to them.

Activity 10 is a capstone exercise in which students are asked to develop a novel approach to deal with some important societal problem based on what students have learned in the course. The quiz bowl procedure described in Activity 11 encourages students to review for exams. The competition can be within a class, between classes, or even between classes at other schools or colleges.

The final two articles in this chapter examine the history of psychology and are largely intended for use in that course, although the procedures could be modified to apply to any course. Activity 12 describes a survey used to assess how much students know about the history of psychology when they begin the course. Activity 13 describes a newspaper exercise that allows students to learn about psychology in the broader historical context of which it is a part.

1 Learning to Use the Contemporary Library: A Laboratory Exercise

Charles I. Abramson, Donald P. French, and Steven M. Locy
Oklahoma State University

This exercise acquaints students with various services provided by an academic library. The exercise can be used in elementary and advanced psychology courses and is designed to teach students how to use new library technology and to sharpen such basic but underused skills as using interlibrary loan, ordering dissertations, using Science Citation Index, and finding information about graduate programs, grants, and fellowships.

CONCEPT

Efforts to provide students with a quality education that will equip them with basic research skills useful in school and life begin, in our view, at the steps of the library. Students who are proficient in the use of the library can make better use of directed research experiences, use their study time more efficiently, help themselves by finding scholarships and fellowships, and make better graduate students. Students with library skills are better prepared to enter academic and nonacademic careers than are those who lack such skills.

In this activity we will describe an active learning exercise in which students engage in a library treasure hunt. It consists of 25 tasks roughly divided into three sections: (a) databases, (b) general library search skills, and (c) self-education (i.e., what the library can do for the student). These sections were designed to correspond in part to the minimum training guidelines for library instruction for psychology majors recommended by Merriam, LaBaugh, and Butterfield (1992). The instructor can assign any or all of the sections. Suggested replies to a subset of questions follow each section.

MATERIALS NEEDED

Students will need access to a research library, a handout of the library exercise, a formatted computer disk, copy card, and access to a word processing program. The activity was originally developed for a laboratory course in experimental psychology and can be completed in approximately 2 hr. Individual tasks are presented as models that can be easily modified to fit the needs of an instructor, course, and academic institution. Reed and Baxter (1992) provided a useful guide that presents information on reference sources, journals, and computer-based material. The information in this and other guides (Baxter, 1993; McInnis, 1982) can be used to modify the assignment.

INSTRUCTIONS

The activity should be assigned during the first week of the semester and prefaced by a lecture that addresses the importance of a research library and the type of skills necessary to retrieve information effectively. College librarians are often glad to deliver such lectures. As Baxter (1986) and Parr (1978, 1979) have discussed, librarians, because of their contact with students, are in a unique position to anticipate questions and offer practical suggestions. Moreover, as Merriam, LaBaugh, and Butterfield (1992) suggested, students feel less intimidated when entering a library to begin the assignment (and on subsequent visits) when they have a contact person who understands their frustrations and fears in using library technology.

Before students begin the assignment, it is important to work closely with a library staff member whether or not a librarian presents the library lecture. The instructor should give a librarian a copy of the assignment (with answer key) and alert the library staff to expect many anxious students often asking the same questions. If the class contains a laboratory component, the laboratory instructor should accompany and assist both the students and librarian.

Section I: Database Use

The first section covers the use of various CD-ROM databases. Because of the interdisciplinary nature of psychology and the opportunity to develop a laboratory exercise that would teach skills useful for any course, it is important for students to learn not only how to use PsycLIT but how to use other databases, such as Medline, available at many libraries. This section also teaches students how to use the Institute for Scientific Information's Science Citation Index.

To complete this section, students should perform each of the tasks and be prepared to answer each of the questions that follow.

1. How many CD-ROM database systems does the library offer?
2. What steps are necessary to conduct a CD-ROM search? Include in your answer the use of search operators.
3. What are the limitations and drawbacks of a CD-ROM search?
4. What are the benefits of a CD-ROM search?
5. Conduct a literature search on your assigned topic using each of the following databases: Agricola, Biological Abstracts, GeoRef, Medline, PsycLIT. Download the results of your search onto a floppy disk. Using a word processing program, upload your literature review. Turn in both the floppy disk and a printout of your review.
6. What is Science Citation Index?
7. How do you use Science Citation Index?
8. Why would you use Science Citation Index?
9. Use Science Citation Index and describe how you did this.

The answers to many of these questions rely, to a great extent, on the facilities of the library. For example, Oklahoma State University has more than 14 networked CD-ROMs and 40 separate CD-ROM database systems. Each system contains the standard search operators, such as *With, And, Near, Not,* and allows students to output the results of their searches to a printer or floppy disk. The floppy disk can be uploaded to the student's personal computer for later integration into literature reviews and other writing assignments. In conducting a CD-ROM search, students will note in their answers limitations that focus on the use and location of the databases (e.g., CD-ROMs that must be manually loaded, machines dedicated to a single database, difficulty in gaining access during peak hours), an inability to access material prior to 1970, and issues of accuracy. With regard to accuracy, students might be surprised to further learn that there is no guarantee that a journal abstracted in one CD-ROM issue will be abstracted in the next and that there is no guarantee that the entire issue will be abstracted, leading to what is known as *selective indexing*. These limitations are offset somewhat by such advantages as speed and the ability to download information. The advantage of speed is readily apparent when students are required to use paper abstracts. The remaining questions focus on Science Citation Index. Students should note in their replies that the index is an alphabetical listing (by author) of all citations found in footnotes and bibliographies of journal articles and is a valuable source for tracing the evolution of an idea, determining the popularity of a research area, estimating the publication record of a potential faculty advisor, and verifying an article citation.

Section II: General Library Search Skills

The second section covers such routine, yet rarely used, tasks as locating and ordering doctoral and master's theses, finding an address of a publisher, and converting an abbreviated journal title into American Psychological Association (APA) style. Knowing how to acquire theses is important for students engaged in historical research. We also believe that students should know how to use paper versions of abstracts. As mentioned previously, relying solely on computerized databases to conduct literature reviews is not only dangerous but does not allow students access to the pre-1970 literature (Abramson, 1994).

Ask students to perform each task and be prepared to answer each of the questions that follow.

1. What is Dissertation Abstracts?
2. How would you use Dissertation Abstracts?
3. Use Dissertation Abstracts and photocopy or printout the abstracts describing one of the following:
   - The instructor's thesis
   - Charles I. Abramson's dissertation
   - Donald P. French's dissertation
4. How would you acquire the preceding dissertations?
   - from University Microfilms
   - from Interlibrary loan
5. What are the steps necessary to obtain a dissertation written at a foreign university?
6. How do you acquire a master's thesis?
7. The following are several abbreviated titles of scientific journals. Find the full names and explain how you did it.
   - *J. Exp. Bio.*
   - *Sitz. Ber. D. Akad. Wiss. Wien. Math. Naturwiss.*
   - *Zool. Jb.*
   - *J. C. P.*
8. How do you find the address of a book publisher? What is the address of K.D.V.H. publisher in Illinois?

9. You are about to submit a manuscript to *Journal of Comparative Psychology*. Find and attach the "Instructions to Authors" for the current year.
10. What is the difference between microfilm and microfiche?
11. Using microfilm or microfiche, find the school catalog for the college of your choice and list the chair of the psychology department.
12. Using the paper version of Psychological Abstracts, locate the abstracts and photocopy the information associated with the titles of each of the following.
    - Skinner, B. F. (1935)
    - Thurstone, L. L. (1930)
13. Find one book and one article that the library does not have. Fill out (*do not send*) an interlibrary loan form for each and attach it to the rest of your material.

Students should note in their answers that Dissertation Abstracts is a database containing abstracts from all doctoral dissertations completed at more than 1000 accredited colleges and universities worldwide. The database dates back to 1861 and is useful for identifying trends, locating comprehensive subject bibliographies, reviewing the dissertations of famous psychologists, and, when purchased through University Microfilm or borrowed through interlibrary loan, provides a wealth of unpublished material that is useful in conducting research. Master's theses can also be borrowed from interlibrary loan. The answer to Question 3 concerning the titles of the Abramson (1986) and French (1985) dissertations are, "Aversive Conditioning in Honey Bees (*Apis mellifera*)" and "The Dynamics of Behavior During the Formation and Maintenance of Social Systems in Bluegill Sunfish, *Lepomis Macrochirus*," respectively. The full title of a journal can be obtained from *Periodical Title Abbreviations* published by Gale Research Company (Detroit, Michigan) and should be available at the library reference desk. The complete titles of the journals mentioned in Question 7 are (a) *Journal of Experimental Biology*, (b) *Sitzungsberichte der Akademie der Wissenschaffen in Wien, Mathematisch—Naturwissenschlaftliche Klassee*, (c) *Zoologische Jahrbücher*, (d) *Journal of Comparative Psychology*. The address of the publisher mentioned in Question 8 is K.D.V.H., P.O. Box 6788, Chicago, Illinois 60680 and can be found in the *Publishers Directory*, published by Gale Research Company. Instructions to authors are commonly found in the January issue of a journal and are often available in each issue. In Question 10, the primary difference between microfilm and microfiche is ease of use. The rectangular design and individual sheets make it easier to find material on microfiche. The answer to Question 12 is B. F. Skinner, "A Discrimination Without Previous Conditioning" and L. L. Thurstone, "The Mental Growth Curve for the Binet Tests."

Section III: Self-Education

In the final section of the exercise, students use library resources to find information on a potential faculty advisor, grants, fellowships, and potential graduate schools.

Ask students to perform each task and be prepared to answer each of the questions that follow.

1. You are interested in attending graduate school but do not know with whom you might like to work. What library resources would be helpful?
2. You plan to apply to graduate school. You know the name of someone who might interest you, but you have no other information. How do you use the library to find additional information. (To answer this question you must have an idea what information is important.)
3. You are interested in scholarship and financial aid programs at both the undergraduate and graduate level. Where do you look to obtain the information? List the names and addresses of several private and public sources where you may obtain funding.

Students should note in their replies that they can use any of the CD-ROM databases to select a potential advisor. One strategy is to conduct a literature search to learn about the work of an individual who excites them. The popularity of the research can be estimated with Science Citation Index; the publication record can be estimated by conducting, for example, a PsycLIT database search or by using the library Internet site to visit the homepage of the potential advisor. The amount of successful grant activity can be estimated by reading the author notes of papers published by the potential advisor. A subsequent Internet search of the granting agency will determine the amount and duration of the grant. Students should also be aware that many libraries contain college catalogs (or CD-ROMs) describing the programs of other universities. A library Internet workstation can also be used to "visit" potential campuses. Students will note that a limitation of an Internet visit is that the quality of the university and departmental homepages varies widely and may not contain all the information available in the university catalog. Students will also be aware that they can use the Internet to search for various government databases containing information on student grants and fellowships. They will note in their answers that books such as the *Foundation Directory* (Gale Research Company) describe funding opportunities offered by private foundations, as does a CD-ROM (e.g., Knight-Ridder OnDisc Grants Database) that covers government and private sources of funding.

DISCUSSION We have used the library research laboratory with great success in advanced courses such as the psychology of learning and in introductory psychology. The exercise was especially effective for students engaged in directed research. Such students receive the exercise prior to the first laboratory meeting and on its completion begin their directed research project. It is our experience that such students become more effective and productive members of the laboratory. The exercise can also be used to evaluate a student's critical thinking ability (e.g., how efficiently the student conducts a computerized on-line search) and persistence.

The library exercise can also be used by colleges and high schools that have limited library resources. If necessary, interested students or classes can visit a local university library that has the necessary facilities. High school teachers can use this exercise by arranging a tour with the local university library that will enable their students to learn library skills before enrolling in college. To further encourage high school students to learn library skills, instructors can contact teachers of high school psychology courses and arrange a visit to conduct at least portions of the exercise through the university office or high school relations. In addition, many universities conduct enrichment camps for high school students, and this exercise can be made available as part of their camp activities. A copy of the exercise can also be placed on file in the local public library.

REFERENCES

Abramson, C. I. (1994). *A primer of invertebrate learning: The behavioral perspective.* Washington, DC: American Psychological Association.

Baxter, P. M. (1986). The benefits of in-class bibliographic instruction. *Teaching of Psychology, 13,* 40–41.

Baxter, P. M. (1993). *Psychology: A guide to reference and information sources.* Englewood, CO: Libraries Unlimited.

McInnis, R. G. (1982). *Research guide for psychology.* Westport, CT: Greenwood.

Merriam, J., LaBaugh, R. T., & Butterfield, N. E. (1992). Library instruction for psychology majors: Minimum training guidelines. *Teaching of Psychology, 19,* 34–36.

Parr, V. (1978). Course-related library instruction for psychology students. *Teaching of Psychology, 5,* 101–102.

Parr, V. (1979). On-line information retrieval and the undergraduate. *Teaching of Psychology, 6,* 61–62.

Reed, J. G., & Baxter, P. M. (1992). *Library use: A handbook for psychology* (2nd ed.). Washington, DC: American Psychological Association.

SUGGESTED READING

Feinberg, R. A. (1981). Positive side effects of on-line information retrieval. *Teaching of Psychology, 8,* 51–52.

Gardner, L. E. (1977). A relatively painless method of introduction to the psychological literature search. *Teaching of Psychology, 4,* 89–91.

Joswick, K. E. (1994). Getting the most from PsycLIT: Recommendations for searching. *Teaching of Psychology, 21,* 49–53.

LeUnes, A. D. (1977). The developmental psychology library search: Can a nonsense assignment make sense? *Teaching of Psychology, 4,* 86.

Lewis, L. K. (1986). Bibliographic computerized searching in psychology. *Teaching of Psychology, 13,* 38–40.

Mathews, J. B. (1978). "Hunting" for psychological literature: A methodology for the introductory research course. *Teaching of Psychology, 5,* 100–101.

Schilling, K. L. (1983). Teaching psychological issues in context: A library exercise. *Teaching of Psychology, 10,* 57.

Sutton, E. D., Feinberg, R., Levine, C. R., Sandberg, J. S., & Wilson, J. M. (1995). Bibliographic instruction in psychology: A review of the literature. *Reference Services Review, 23,* 13–22, 44.

2 KEEPING IN TOUCH WITH YOUR STUDENTS BY "CARDING" THEM

Margaret A. Lloyd
Georgia Southern University

This activity describes the use of index cards for a variety of pedagogical purposes and can be used in any psychology course. The only classroom-required materials are index cards, which the instructor or students can supply. Index cards provide an inexpensive, flexible, and easy way to assess the quality of teaching and learning in a course and can also be used to provide writing opportunities for students.

CONCEPT

This activity, usable in any psychology course, uses index cards as a means to obtain a wide variety of course-relevant information from students. Essentially, students regularly provide course feedback to teachers on index cards. Student feedback, in turn, can be put to numerous pedagogical purposes.

MATERIALS NEEDED

Students will need index cards and a writing utensil. If you decide to use cards infrequently, you may want to provide them; with frequent use or with larger classes, consider asking students to purchase their own. Index card size is determined by the amount of information required or nature of your request (see the following instructions).

INSTRUCTIONS

Tell students what information you would like from them. Be sure to indicate whether you want names on the cards. (If the information is confidential in nature, ask students to use only one side of the card and to turn it over before passing it in for collection.) Depending on the assignment, students may complete the cards in or outside of class.

Index cards may be used for a variety of pedagogical purposes:

1. to ascertain which concepts, theories, and so forth are confusing, either by asking students to summarize the major lecture/discussion points or by asking for questions;
2. to facilitate and evaluate students' understanding of important issues and to explore how these issues are related by having students construct a concept map, which is a graphical overview of concepts and their interrelations (discussed by Ault, 1985);
3. to elicit questions about sensitive topics (for example, prejudice, discrimination, sexuality, or gender-role issues);
4. to solicit timely and honest feedback about specific aspects of the course (lectures, papers, projects, exercises, discussions, exams, etc.);
5. to facilitate class discussions by having students write down their thoughts about an issue before discussing it;
6. to encourage students to keep up with and think about the reading assignments (e.g., by asking them to describe something new learned from the

reading or to answer one or two objective questions at the beginning of class; awarding response points is usually helpful if cards are used for this purpose); and

7. to award credit for participating in special class activities without the need for the instructor to take attendance

DISCUSSION

Using index cards in the classroom is a low-cost/high-benefit pedagogical device. This highly flexible technique is useful for a wide variety of purposes, is very simple to use, and requires little preparation or class time. Moreover, it permits easy classification of students' responses because each student uses a separate card and enables the instructor to obtain anonymous or personalized feedback. Carding also allows timely student feedback about exams, lectures, papers, guest speakers, and so forth. Finally, it keeps the instructor in touch with students and helps students feel that the instructor is relating to them.

I have used index cards to good effect in a variety of ways and in a variety of courses. For example, several days before an exam, I distribute index cards and give students about 15 minutes to review their notes and textbook and to list up to five concepts, theories, or experiments about which they have questions. I limit the number to five to force discriminating choices. The next day, I review the most frequently listed concepts. If students want clarification on points I do not cover in class, I encourage them to see me during my office hours.

I have also used index cards to obtain student feedback after the first exam. I ask students to rate (on a 5-point scale) how well they feel the exam covered the assigned material and how fair they feel the questions were. Then I ask them to offer one or two specific suggestions as to how the exam could be improved and one or two steps they can take to improve their performance on the next test.

Another way I have used index cards is to evaluate the effectiveness of class exercises, activities, and speakers. In this case, I ask students to indicate on the index cards what they learned from the experience, whether I should use the activity again, and why or why not.

WRITING COMPONENT

The adaptability of index cards makes it easy to incorporate a variety of writing opportunities into classes, and the opportunity to practice writing on a regular basis improves writing skills. Index card writing exercises can be planned in advance, but you can also assign them on the spur of the moment as an issue arises in class. When you need to make written responses on students' cards, you need to remind students to leave some blank space on their cards.

REFERENCE

Ault, C. R. (1985). Concept mapping as a study strategy in earth science. *Journal of College Science Teaching, 15*, 38–44.

SUGGESTED READING

Briscoe, C., & LeMaster, S. U. (1991). Meaningful learning in college biology through concept mapping. *The American Biology Teacher, 53*, 214–219.

Conderman, G. J. (1993, March). Note cards promote discussion. *The Teaching Professor, 7*, 5.

3 THE COSTS AND BENEFITS OF CRITICAL THINKING

Randall E. Osborne, Judy Laws, and Ken Weadick
Indiana University East

This activity can be used with small to medium-size classes (up to about 50), although the ideal size would be between 15 and 35. No prior understanding of critical thinking is necessary, although the demonstration should be prefaced with information about critical thinking that the students can use as they work in groups. You will need at least a 75-minute class period, although the activity could be completed over two smaller class periods if presentations and judging are done on a second day. This is an effective demonstration for fostering work within groups, encouraging students to think critically about information, connecting general psychology course content (especially the biological bases of behavior), and aiding understanding of the costs and benefits of being a critical thinker.

CONCEPT
This activity demonstrates the relationship between the amount of effort spent (illustrated in this activity as money) and the benefits gained in terms of critical thinking (illustrated in this activity as assignment points earned). This is accomplished by allowing student groups to purchase information about a case and then using the information purchased to present a critical analysis of the case to the class. Students earn assignment points for how much money they have left and how "sophisticated" (or critically thought through) the judges rate their analyses to be.

MATERIALS NEEDED
A summary of Bloom's (1956) taxonomy of educational objectives (included at the end of this activity), enough Monopoly (or play) money for each group to have $240, and additional case information that groups can purchase are needed (sample lists we have used are included at the end of this activity). Each piece of information can be written on a notecard and stacked according to monetary value.

INSTRUCTIONS
Present a brief lecture on Bloom's taxonomy: knowledge, comprehension, application, analysis, synthesis, and evaluation. Make sure that students understand each of the cognitive objectives. After students understand these objectives, they should relate these objectives to critical thinkers. The discussion should center on the fact that a critical thinker goes beyond the simple facts (knowledge), makes it a point to know the meaning of the information (comprehension), can generalize the knowledge (application), is able to break the information down into subparts and recognize how those subparts might interrelate (analysis), can put the information back together into a form that now has more meaning (synthesis), and can critically evaluate the strengths and weaknesses of the conclusions drawn (evaluation).

Students now listen to a short case history about Rick Donlan, a man who climbed a tower and shot and killed or wounded multiple persons. The following case information is read to the class:

> On April 1, 1988, Rick Donlan took a sniper rifle, and climbed to the top of a clock tower on the campus of a major university in the United States. Slowly, over the next 4 hours, he killed and wounded many students before a SWAT team stormed the tower and Donlan himself was killed.

Each group is then given the following four pieces of information about the case:

1. Donlan killed 14 persons and wounded 11.
2. He had a protruding forehead.
3. His favorite movies were those that starred Jean Claude Van Damme.
4. His favorite magazine was *Guns & Ammo*.

Students are told that they can purchase from the instructor additional information about the case and Donlan's history. There are three cost categories ($25, $40, and $75) of information (see appendixes A, B, and C), and the more expensive the information is, the more informative it will be.

Students then take 30 min to devise a strategy for purchasing information, analyzing that information, and preparing a presentation for the class on why they think Donlan did what he did. At the end of 30 min, groups make brief (3- to 5-minute) presentations to the class (and a panel of judges the instructor can bring in as volunteers from other classes) about why they think Donlan committed these murders. Students are told that they will earn assignment points based on money left over and the judges rating of how well they used Bloom's objectives in building their case. If you have five groups, the group with the most money receives 5 points, then the next highest amount of leftover money receives 4 points, and so on. The groups earn points for their analyses the same way.

A few important things to note for the students:

1. Once a piece of information is bought, no other group can buy the same information. This is included to help illustrate the fact that some groups will be more successful with their critical thinking because they have better information. Discussion focuses on the relationship between the quality of the information one possesses and the quality of one's thinking.
2. Students must present the cards with the information they purchased to the judges before making their presentation (this allows the judges to determine whether the students are drawing conclusions that go beyond their data, etc.).
3. Students can use information from the textbook and lecture to support their arguments. (If they discover, for example, that Donlan had severe damage to his amygdala, they may turn to their textbook and discover that the amygdala has been linked to aggression and fear.)
4. The costs of critical thinking include the following. It is
   - more time consuming,
   - requires acquisition of more information, and
   - may reveal one's own biases and assumptions.

The benefits of critical thinking include the following: It allows

- more sophisticated analyses of information,
- more flexibility in thinking,
- use of more logical inferences, and
- more rational conclusions based on an examination of evidence.

DISCUSSION

After the students have made their short presentations to the class, the judges retire to the hallway and reach their decisions about the sophistication of the groups' analyses. Provide judges with a list and description of Bloom's objectives (appendix D) and have the students give the judges a written summary of their analysis to use in their considerations.

Once the judges have made their decisions and groups have tallied their points (remember they will earn at least 1 assignment point for amount of money left over, even if they have none, and at least 1 point for their analysis), we focus the discussion on critical thinking. Students are told that it is important for them to be able to present an argument that demonstrates all of Bloom's cognitive objectives. Because educators are encouraged to teach these skills, it would be valuable for students to use those same objectives in doing their work. It is quickly obvious to students that there is a relationship between the cost of doing critical thinking (in this case spending more money to gather more information and evidence) and the benefits reaped (in this case a higher rating of their analysis leading to more points).

Discussion about this activity is usually quite animated and in our experience student feedback about it has been overwhelmingly positive. Because the students are earning assignment points just for trying, it is also a very nonthreatening way to encourage them to use their critical thinking skills, to draw connections between pieces of information, to use their lecture notes and textbooks as supplemental resources, and to encourage groups to brainstorm.

This activity has been used in introductory psychology courses but by varying the scenario it could fit virtually any course and any topic.

WRITING COMPONENT

We build our discussion of critical thinking around effective thinking and communication, so important components of this activity are the oral presentation and the written analysis students turn in. Judges use information from the oral presentation to evaluate the sophistication of the groups' analyses. In addition, students write a reflective behavior on Bloom's cognitive objectives and this activity. Students are required to suggest how they can use an understanding of these objectives in other courses and in their careers. The written analyses and oral presentations are critiqued but not graded. The major goal of the activity is to demonstrate the connection between the costs and benefits of critical thinking so students earn assignment points for their efforts.

SUGGESTED READING

Bloom, B. S., Englehart, M. B., Furst, E. J., Hill, W. H., & Kratwohl, O. R. (1956). *Taxonomy of educational objectives: The classification of educational goals. Handbook 1: The cognitive domain.* New York: Longman.

Smith, R. A. (1995). *Challenging your preconceptions: Thinking critically about psychology.* Pacific Grove, CA: Brooks/Cole.

Appendix A

$25 Information

He was single and has never been married.
He was 38 years old.
He was a security guard at an Avon Factory.
His mother had blond hair.
He was the oldest of nine children.
He is shy.
He prefers to be alone.
He often saw puppies in Rorschach inkblots.
He had rubella when he was 4 years old.
He was allergic to penicillin.
His father was an alcoholic.
He placed first in his fourth-grade science fair with a project on electricity in the home.
He was the youngest of three children (he had two older brothers).
His mother occasionally worked as an exotic dancer (but only when the family really needed the money).
His first car was a beat-up, black Ford Pinto.

Appendix B

$40 Information

When he was little his mother sometimes dressed him like a girl.

Of the 14 people he killed, 9 were women.

He sometimes suffered from severe migraines.

The morning of the murders he suffered three blackouts.

Twice as a child he was evaluated by psychiatrists.

He was an ex-marine who hated country music.

He was an expert marksman who practiced on the firing range.

He flunked out of medical school.

He meticulously stands his rolled pairs of socks on end in the sock drawer by color.

His father died in a freak accident when he was 14 years old.

Early IQ and achievement tests suggested competency well beyond his level of performance.

He was not allowed to receive a driver's license until he was 18 years of age because he was caught joy riding in a stolen car at age 15.

Despite extremely poor attendance and what teachers labeled as lack of motivation, he graduated high school in the top 15 percent of his class.

Appendix C

$75 Information

At the age of 7, he skinned his cocker spaniel alive.

He was repeatedly molested by a mentally retarded uncle, an incident that was covered up and denied by the few family members who knew about it.

He was passed over four times for a promotion at the post office.

He bred Doberman puppies as a hobby.

He often took his female dates to see dogfights.

His only true love left him for a singer in a country band.

He has "Macho Man" tattooed on his left forearm.

He heard voices telling him to kill.

He was hospitalized twice because of seizures.

All the women he killed had blonde hair.

He left a note behind saying, "This is the only way I could stop the voices."

An autopsy revealed major damage to his amygdala.

Appendix D

Bloom's Objectives

knowledge	= specific facts
comprehension	= understanding of those facts
application	= can generalize those facts to other situations
analysis	= can break problem down, recognize connections between subparts
synthesis	= can assemble parts into a more meaningful whole
evaluation	= critically uses information to make (reasonable) judgments

4 PARSIMONIOUS EXPLANATIONS OF APPARENT MIND READING

James W. Kalat
North Carolina State University

A key point in scientific thinking is parsimony, the preference for simple explanations over those requiring new or unnecessary assumptions. The three easy demonstrations used in this activity allow an instructor to display apparent mind-reading (skills similar to those used by stage psychics) and then to present parsimonious explanations. Although we should not expect to turn students into skeptics after one or two lectures, we can at least plant some seeds that may eventually alter their thinking.

CONCEPT

Surveys indicate that many students believe in extrasensory perception, ghosts, UFOs, alien abduction, astrology, precognitive dreams, the Loch Ness monster, and a wide variety of other phenomena for which no convincing evidence exists. An important goal of a course in psychology is to teach students to evaluate evidence and to apply the principle of parsimony, the preference for simple explanations over those requiring new or unnecessary assumptions. The principle is also known as Occam's razor ("Do not multiply entities beyond necessity") or as Lloyd Morgan's canon (Morgan, 1896).

MATERIALS NEEDED

The first and second demonstrations require no materials. For the third, cut out a few one-column newspaper clippings. The best articles are at least several inches long, have both right- and left-justified margins, and include no photographs, bold text, or subheadings. Ideally, the article should have a photograph, advertisement, or column of statistics rather than text on the back. Cut each article between the first and second lines. Then take the bottom part, turn it upside down, tape it to the top part with transparent tape, and trim it so that from a few feet away it appears to be normal. For each article, determine what is the on last line of the article—that is, the one at the bottom of the upside-down part, farthest from the title. Write out that line on a card or piece of paper and seal it in an envelope. You will need one sealed envelope for each article. Be sure to label which is which. You will also need a pair of scissors for this demonstration.

INSTRUCTIONS

Lecture Background

Clever Hans, the horse that appeared to be doing mathematics, is an excellent example of the search for parsimonious explanations. Begin your class period by describing this episode to your students. The horse's owner, Mr. von Osten, asked Hans questions and Hans would tap the correct answer with his foot. Hans, it seemed, could count, add, subtract, multiply, divide, do simple algebra, convert fractions to decimals or decimals to fractions, tell time to the minute, and so forth with better than 90% accuracy. He could answer questions put to him by other interrogators, including skeptics, even in von Osten's absence. Eventually,

Oskar Pfungst discovered that Hans could answer correctly only if the questioner knew the correct answer and only if Hans could see the questioner's face during the tapping. Pfungst demonstrated that Hans was responding to subtle, unintentional facial cues that many questioners gave when Hans reached the correct number of taps (Pfungst, 1911). The key point is that psychologists prefer the facial-cues explanation to the genius-horse explanation because it is more parsimonious.

Today, stage psychics and others often claim to have abilities that appear incompatible with our current understanding of both psychology and physics. The following demonstrations show how easy it is to display what appears to be an amazing ability for which there is a more parsimonious explanation. All three can be completed within a class period.

First Demonstration

This demonstration requires advance preparation. The instructor must learn something about two or more students in the class that the students do not expect the instructor to know, such as their names (if the class is large). In a smaller class, the instructor could look up the students' addresses, telephone numbers, or middle names.

Announce something like the following: "The Clever Hans trick still works today, and with a little practice you can use it to make it appear that you can read minds. I'm going to demonstrate. I want everyone to concentrate on the first initial of your last name. I shall call out letters of the alphabet while I scan over a section of the class looking for subtle changes in facial expression. Not everyone gives good signals, but sooner or later someone will flinch when I get to their letter. Ready? *A* ... *B* ... *C* ... *D* ... *E* ... *F* ... *G* ... *H* ... (Pause.) You ... (gesturing): Does your last name begin with *H*? It does? Okay, now let me see whether I can get your first initial. Concentrate on your first initial. *A* ... *B* ... *C* ... *D* ... *E* ... *F* ... *G* ... It's *G*, isn't it?"

Then repeat the demonstration with another student, looking at a different part of the class. Students will be impressed with your abilities. Go on to the other demonstrations and at the end of class come back to explain: "Remember earlier when I identified two students' initials by the Clever Hans trick? If I had never mentioned Clever Hans and I had told you that I was reading minds, would you have believed me? (Most students shake their heads no.) Why did you believe it was a Clever Hans trick? Because I told you so. Can you think of a more parsimonious explanation?"

The actual explanation is that you had already learned those students' names. I have a seating chart and I simply look up names on the seating chart. Amazingly, students who know they put their names on a seating chart in a previous class meeting never suspect that I might have consulted it. If you do not have a seating chart, use whatever other devices you have to find people's names. For example, before class you might ask one student whom you know to tell you the name of another student whom you do not know.

Incidentally, a similar trick was once used at a national convention of skeptics, the Committee for the Scientific Investigation of Claims of the Paranormal (Steiner, 1986). No one in the audience expressed any doubt that the demonstrator was actually using the Clever Hans method! You can reassure students that even if this demonstration fooled them completely, they are in good company. We all sometimes let down our guard.

Second Demonstration

The Amazing Kreskin is an outstanding performer who does not claim to be using any psychic power but who certainly allows the audience to believe that he might be. He has described how he performs some of his tricks (Kreskin, 1991). Here is a slightly modified version of a mind-reading demonstration, based on a description by Marks and Kammann (1980).

Announce, "Now I am going to project my thoughts and give you a chance to read my mind. First, I am thinking of a number between 1 and 50, but both digits are odd and they are not the same. For example, 13 or 15 would be fine, but not 11. Everyone have a number? Okay, my number was 37. Did anyone think of 37? (Many hands go up.) Actually, I started to think of 35 and then switched to 37, so some of you may have gotten the 35. Anyone?" (Many other hands go up.)

The explanation here is that students have fewer choices than they realize. If both digits must be odd, the first must be 1 or 3, and the second 1, 3, 5, 7, or 9. That leaves only 10 numbers. Students eliminate 11 and 33 because both are the same. Most will choose numbers far away from the examples, 13 and 15, without choosing the extreme, 39. Thus, 35 and 37 are by far the most likely choices.

Next say, "Draw a picture of a large object, such as a tree, sailboat, or house. Please draw something now. (Pause.) Okay, I was thinking of a car. How many read my mind?" Many hands go up. The explanation: When simply asked to draw a large object, the four most common objects are tree, sailboat, house, and car. By listing three of those as examples, you bias people to draw the fourth one, a car.

Finally say, "Write down something that you have been thinking about or worrying about recently—something that has been bothering you. Now I'm going to try to read your minds. Ah, I'm getting something. Someone in this room is worrying about his or her course work and grades for this semester." No one will be especially impressed with this case of finding a straw in a haystack, but at least it is worth a laugh. (In fact, more students write that they are worrying about boyfriend, girlfriend, or sex problems. However, if you ask for a show of hands for how many wrote down such concerns, few if any will raise their hands.)

Third Demonstration

This is a procedure I first saw demonstrated by Doug Bernstein, who learned it from Dennis Coon, who in turn learned it from the magician James Randi.

Announce, "Here is a clipping from the newspaper. I'm going to slide these scissors up and down the article. I want a volunteer to tell me where to cut. I will cut where you tell me, and the bottom part will fall to the floor. I shall then ask another volunteer to retrieve it and read the top line of the part that has fallen off. In this sealed envelope I have written a prediction of that line. It certainly appears that you have a lot of choices about where to cut, but maybe one choice is more likely than the others. The only restrictions are that you cannot ask me to cut above the top line or below the bottom line."

Because you have prepared the article in advance, the "prediction" turns out to be correct. Students will think you have manipulated them into saying "now" at a particular time. Do the demonstration once or twice more, letting vociferous skeptics be the new volunteers. At the end, repeat one more time, this time letting a student cut the article. However, you cannot let the students examine the article closely. Either blindfold the student who is cutting, or cover the article with a piece of paper.

This demonstration works because you have specially prepared the articles as is described in the Materials Needed section. Unless students get very close, the most they can see is the headline, and they of course assume that the rest is also right side up. When you or anyone else cuts the article, the bottom part falls to the table or floor. Whoever picks it up orients it right side up and reads what appears to have been the top line. Actually, from the way you were holding it, it was the bottom line. The prediction in the envelope merely states the line that was upside down at the bottom of the article.

DISCUSSION

The debate over psychic phenomena offers a particularly clear opportunity to discuss parsimony, although the principle applies broadly whenever we are comparing a simple explanation with one that has new or untested assumptions. Advocates of extrasensory perception claim that at least some people gain information that they could neither have inferred logically nor received through any sense organ. The alleged ability to read minds and so forth reportedly does not decrease as a function of time or distance between the sender and the receiver, as we should expect from the inverse-square law of physics. Thus, a belief in such phenomena would require a major revision of theories in physics, not just psychology. In fact, it would seem to require rejection of the idea that we live in a universe of matter and energy.

Class discussion of this topic ordinarily includes explanation of why scientists insist on extraordinarily strong evidence for extraordinary claims, why anecdotal evidence is scientifically weak, and why scientists do not trust evidence that is hard to replicate. The demonstrations described enable the instructor to go beyond the statement "let's be skeptical" to show how something that appears to be amazing can have a simple explanation.

Sometimes the data force us to revise our worldview drastically and to substitute new theories for old ones. Science, however, is a conservative enterprise and we rightly resist making major changes until and unless the data force us to replace one worldview with another (Kuhn, 1970).

REFERENCES

Kreskin. (1991). *Secrets of the amazing Kreskin.* Buffalo, NY: Prometheus.

Kuhn, T. S. (1970). *The structure of scientific revolutions* (2nd ed.). Chicago: University of Chicago Press.

Marks, D., & Kammann, R. (1980). *The psychology of the psychic.* Buffalo, NY: Prometheus.

Morgan, C. L. (1896). *Habit and instinct.* London: Edward Arnold.

Pfungst, O. (1911). *Clever Hans.* New York: Holt.

Steiner, R. A. (1986). Confessions of a magician. *Skeptical Inquirer, 11,* 10–11.

5 THE USE OF URBAN LEGENDS TO IMPROVE CRITICAL THINKING

Alva Hughes

Randolph-Macon College

Critical thinking involves an assessment of how we determine the truthfulness of information we encounter. As they evaluate urban legends, this activity encourages students to think critically about the way they make decisions about truth. The activity can also be used to launch a discussion of the value various cultures place on ways of knowing. This activity is useful for introductory students and students in research methods classes.

CONCEPT

Although methods of assessing truth have been given a variety of labels, four basic approaches are usually covered in research methods texts: intuition, authority, rationalism, and empiricism (e.g., Graziano & Raulin, 1993). When we use intuition to make decisions about truth, we rely on the use of nonrational, nonconscious abilities. We go with our gut feeling. When we use authority to make decisions about truth, we rely on someone else's knowledge and expertise. When we use rationalism to make decisions about truth, we rely on the rules of logic or on reason. Finally, when we use empiricism to make decisions about truth, we rely on objective observational techniques. Introductory psychology texts also emphasize critical thinking and ways of knowing. They typically focus on contrasting intuition with empiricism (e.g., Myers, 1995).

The information on methods of knowledge testing could be conveyed to students using the traditional lecture format; however, critical thinking is an active rather than a passive skill. The most effective way to teach students to use critical thinking is to have them actually apply each of the four methods of evaluating knowledge. The following assignment allows students to practice the four methods of knowing by evaluating a series of claims described as urban legends. Urban legends are stories that the storyteller believes to be true. The events in the story happened to "a friend of a friend" or were reported in the media and heard by someone once or twice removed from the teller (Brunvand, 1981). The stories include a high level of detail and often have a moral. Students use the ways of knowing to decide if the claim is valid or if it is an urban legend. These claims listed in Table 5-1 were taken from two Internet news groups. An alternative would be to select claims from collections of urban legends (e.g., Brunvand, 1981, 1989), talks shows, or tabloids.

MATERIALS

1. Definitions of the four ways of knowing.
2. Urban legends or other claims. Table 5-1 presents a list of sample legends based on those under discussion in the Usenet newsgroups alt.folklore.urban and alt.folklore.college. Some of the statements should be true so that students cannot assume that all of the claims are false.

Table 5-1. *Claims to Be Evaluated*

1. Aspirin can cause cerebral hemorrhages when taken with alcohol.
2. A large comet will pulverize the midwestern United States next month.
3. An old chemistry professor at Clarkson University invented Jell-O and Teflon.
4. Kilroy, of "Kilroy was here" fame, was an irritating inspector of some type.
5. If at least three fifths of a bank note is still readable the federal government will reimburse you for the full face value.
6. Forty-five percent of the $20 bills in circulation in the United States are contaminated with cocaine.
7. Bubonic plague still exists in the western United States, but it does not cause epidemics.
8. Prozac is prescribed for depressed dogs.
9. The stereotypical American image of Santa Claus originated in a Coca-Cola advertising campaign.
10. Tattoos laced with LSD are used to hook children on drugs.

INSTRUCTIONS

Present the students with a 20-minute lecture on the four methods of knowing. Following the lecture, assign the students to work in groups of two. Give each group the description of an urban legend, and ask the students to discover the truth about the legend using each of the four methods of knowing. Inform students that some legends cannot be tested empirically for ethical or practical reasons. If some students are assigned a legend that they cannot actually test, ask them to describe an experiment that could be used to validate the claim. Give students 1 week to complete the assignment.

DISCUSSION

After listening to the presentations from each team, the class can discuss the usefulness of empiricism in validating claims. The discussion can include the fact that science uses all four ways of knowing. As scientists, we use intuition to generate hypotheses, and we often use authority by basing our decisions on reviews of existing research findings. We use logic and empiricism in designing experiments and in interpreting the results. The discussion can also include the fact that there are cultural differences in the value placed on empiricism and on authority. Traditional societies often place more emphasis on authority, whereas technological societies often emphasize empiricism and ignore the logic, intuition, and authority that also underlie science. Finally, the discussion can show students they now have the tools to validate information that they encounter as part of their daily lives. The assignment can help students to see why psychology is a science. It can also help them to see how the methods of psychology are related to life.

WRITING COMPONENT

Have a member of each student team write a one-page paper. The paper should include the way in which the team members used the ways of knowing to collect information, the information they found, and an assessment of the usefulness of each method. Each team should also be prepared to give a five-minute oral report to the class on the team's findings.

REFERENCES Brunvand, J. (1981). *The vanishing hitchhiker*. New York: Norton.

Brunvand, J. (1984). *Curses! Broiled again!* New York: Norton.

Graziano, A., & Raulin, M. (1993). *Research methods: A process of inquiry* (2nd ed.). New York: Harper Collins.

Myers, D. (1995) *Psychology* (4th ed.). New York: Worth.

Usenet newsgroups alt.folklore.urban and alt.folklore.college.

6 Research Methods and Critical Thinking: Explaining "Psychic" Phenomena

Sandra S. Goss and Douglas A. Bernstein
University of Illinois

■───■

Rather than lecturing about research methods, this activity attempts to motivate students to learn about these methods so they can understand "psychic" phenomenon. After presenting a set of easy-to-perform, but impressive, magic tricks as demonstrations of "psychic power," students are challenged to explain how the tricks were done.

■───■

CONCEPT

This classroom exercise introduces research methods by exploring a phenomenon of interest to students. Students are challenged to use critical thinking in explaining how the phenomenon occurred. Those who are skeptical about "paranormal" phenomena are eager to debunk these demonstrations, and those who are convinced of the reality of such phenomena are challenged to think scientifically about them, to prove they could not have been done through trickery.

MATERIALS NEEDED

For Demonstration 1 you will need an overhead projector, blank transparencies, and a marking pen. For Demonstration 2 you will need a cardboard box or a clean wastebasket, a pad of paper, and a pen. For Demonstration 3 you will need two identical telephone books (white pages), a large piece of poster board, a heavy black marking pen, and an accomplice.

INSTRUCTIONS

Pose as a psychic or get a colleague to pose as a "guest psychic." We usually do one or more of our "psychic" demonstrations in the first class of the term, after lamenting the fact that the course schedule allows us time only to mention and quickly demonstrate one of the more important topics in psychology: ESP and other paranormal phenomena.

Demonstration 1

This is basically a warm-up activity. Ask all of the students to (a) silently choose a number between 1 and 10, (b) a color, and (c) to draw a picture. Then ask them to concentrate on their chosen number and try to "send" it to you telepathically. Research on prototype suggests most people are likely to choose the number 5 or 7; the color red or blue; and to draw either a tree or a house. As you begin to "receive" the students' messages, write the number 7 on the overhead, then mark it out and write 5 instead. Say something like, "I first thought it was a 7 but then I got a really strong perception of 5." Having received the choice of the majority of the audience will be moderately impressive. You can do the same feat with their chosen color or drawn object. As an alternative, you can send mental messages to the class, asking students to write the number, or color, or image they receive. Again, on base rates alone, most of your students will write down the stimulus you claim to send.

Demonstration 2

Stand at the front of the room with a pad of paper and a pen and ask your students to name some European cities. Paris will eventually be mentioned. You should appear to write each city name on a separate sheet of paper, wad it up, and throw it into the wastebasket. However, write "Paris" on every sheet. By the time Paris is actually mentioned, you will have a wastebasket full of crumpled papers, all of which say "Paris," but which your students assume are all different. (If Paris is named at the beginning of the demonstration, keep going until you appear to have plenty of different cities in the basket.) Now ask a student to choose one of the crumpled balls (holding the wastebasket high so the student cannot see into it), open it, and concentrate on the city name. Students are again amazed when you say "Paris." Requests from the same class for a repeat performance with a second wad of paper should be denied for obvious reasons.

Demonstration 3

Position your accomplice out of the students' sight (in the hallway or at the back of a large room, for example) with a telephone book, a black marker, and a piece of cardboard. Now "randomly" choose a student to whom you will give the other copy of the same telephone book. It is best to choose a student who is sitting where students looking at him or her will be looking away from the accomplice's position. Ask this student to choose a page number of the telephone book. Then ask another randomly selected student to choose a column on that page, and ask another student to choose a telephone number in that column (counting down from the top). Each of the students should announce their selections aloud. Ask the student holding the telephone book to locate and concentrate on the telephone number thus identified. Your hidden accomplice should locate the same number and, using a black marker, write it in large numerals on the cardboard. Be sure the accomplice is located so you can see the cardboard but your students cannot. Also be sure to clearly repeat the page, column, and line numbers as they are chosen by your students; this will help your accomplice write down the correct telephone number. (You can do so as if you are mentally focusing on this information: "Okay, we are on page 341, in the second column from the left, and the 14th number from the top.") The class will be stunned when you correctly "read your student's mind." (To make the demonstration more dramatic, turn off the overhead projector, write down the "received" number on the overhead transparency, then turn it on so the class can see the number you wrote.) *Warning*: Be sure to practice these tricks with colleagues or graduate students before you present them in class.

DISCUSSION   Following these demonstrations, many of your students will be convinced that you really do have psychic abilities. Tell them that these were simple magic tricks and that their assignment for the next session is to try to figure out how they could have been performed without psychic power.

At the next class, students are usually eager to begin their research. Ask them for possible explanations of the trick that interests them the most. It is very easy at this point to include the proper experimental terminology, such as "Your hypothesis then is that I memorized the telephone book." As students attempt to explain how they might test their hypotheses, concepts such as independent variable, dependent variable, and other components of experimental design will arise, though the terms themselves may not be used. This makes it easy for you to label them ("OK , in scientific research terms, whether or not I am blindfolded would be the independent variable because . . ."). Students will challenge other students' designs and point out the need for control groups and double-blind designs, as well as the problems posed by confounding variables, sampling errors, and experimental bias. A lively discussion about experimental methods will probably occur, and the students will better appreciate their value in critical thinking.

Inevitably, your students will ask how you did each trick. If you ever want to use the trick again, you cannot tell them. Our solution to this problem is to say something like, "Some of your hypotheses were very close to the truth. However, scientists never know for sure when they have found the truth; they can only eliminate plausible alternative hypotheses and reach a conclusion with a statistically significant, but not absolutely certain, likelihood of being correct. Like scientists, you will have to be satisfied with this situation." If this does not satisfy them, just remind the students that magicians cannot reveal their tricks.

WRITING COMPONENT

Require students to submit a written explanation of how any of the demonstrations could have been performed without psychic abilities. Students could even meet in small groups, based on which demonstration they want to explain, and share their written explanations. Each group could then generate hypotheses, design experiments for testing them, and report back to the entire class. This latter approach would not only require students to write, but would also allow them to share their ideas in the small-group setting.

REFERENCES

Morris, S. (1981). *Believing in ESP: Effects of dehoaxing.* In K. Frazier (Ed.), *Paranormal borderlands of science.* Buffalo, NY: Prometheus Books.

Smith, R. A. (1995). *Challenging your preconceptions: Thinking critically about psychology.* Pacific Grove, CA: Brooks/Cole.

7 READING, WRITING, AND THINKING BEFORE EACH CLASS

William J. Lammers

University of Central Arkansas

This activity encourages students to prepare for each class by reading assigned sections in the textbook, writing a brief summary of the section that most interests the particular student, and writing their own thoughts on the section chosen. These writing assignments are brief and frequent. A variable ratio schedule of grading can be used in large classes to provide consistent effort by the students without increasing the instructor's grading time.

CONCEPT

This activity involves frequent writing assignments to prepare the students for class, to encourage writing as a means of summarizing information, and to motivate students to think at a deeper level about how the information provided in their textbook affects their own beliefs and behaviors. The assignments provide a relatively easy way to include a writing across the curriculum (WAC) component in what is typically a large class. Additional class time and excessive grading time are not necessary.

MATERIALS NEEDED

No special materials required.

INSTRUCTIONS

Provide a brief description of the nature, purpose, and grading of the reading/writing assignments in the course syllabus. Reiterate these points when you make the first assignment (often the second day of class). Tell students that on most class days a reading assignment will be posted on the chalkboard (e.g., "for Tuesday, pages 55–72"). Students are to read the assignment and pick one section from the assigned pages that most interests them. They are to write, *in their own words*, a one-half page summary of that section. In addition, the second half of the page should be filled with their own thoughts on the topic. This may include a critical analysis of the information, how the information applies to their own life, what questions are raised by the information, and so forth. The instructor will look for evidence that the student spent some time thinking about the topic and expressed those ideas clearly in writing. As students enter the classroom, they should turn in their summaries. Throughout the course, randomly choose five of the assignments to grade and return to the students.

DISCUSSION

Incorporating this reading/writing activity into the introductory psychology course serves several important functions. It is a relatively easy way to enhance the writing component of a course that typically has a large class size. It helps the students avoid procrastination and prepares them for the next class. This preparation leads to better informed students in the classroom, which results in more active participation (comments/questions/discussion) by the students. The nature of the activity also permits the students to have some control over the topics that they will be graded on and permits students to express their own ideas and opinions without doing so in a large group of people. The instructor can use these assignments to discover students' interests and current beliefs.

The variable ratio schedule of grading elicits consistent efforts and leads to nearly perfect attendance at class meetings. This occurs when only five assignments are graded throughout the course and the total value of the five assignments is equal to 7% of the students' course grade. It is recommended that the instructor grade and provide extensive feedback on either the first or second assignment so that expectations are clear.

WRITING COMPONENT

The primary objective of this activity is to provide introductory psychology students with experience summarizing information and writing to express their own thoughts. This activity provides a relatively simple way to substantially increase the writing component in a large class without excessive demands on the instructor or class time. Further, because the writing is done outside of class, the students can write at their own pace.

SUGGESTED READING

Davis, B. G. (1993). *Tools for teaching*. San Francisco: Jossey-Bass.

Erickson, B. L., & Strommer, D. W. (1991). *Teaching college freshmen*. San Francisco: Jossey-Bass.

White, E. M. (1994). *Teaching and assessing writing: recent advances in understanding, evaluating, and improving student performance*. San Francisco: Jossey-Bass.

8 LETTERS HOME: WRITING FOR UNDERSTANDING IN INTRODUCTORY PSYCHOLOGY

Kenneth D. Keith
Nebraska Wesleyan University

This activity uses letter writing as an assignment in introductory psychology. Students write four letters, each one explaining or reacting to recent material in the course. Letters are written to a friend, relative, or parent; reflect the student's voice and style; and discuss material the student finds interesting, confusing, disappointing, or surprising in the unit. Assessment suggests that students find the course helpful in development of writing and thinking skills and regard the assignment as more interesting and less intimidating than traditional writing assignments.

CONCEPT

Writing assignments in psychology often serve one of two purposes: to learn psychology or to learn to write like a psychologist (Nodine, 1990b). The former notion, that writing can improve knowledge of content, has proven fruitful not only in psychology but in other sciences as well (e.g., chemistry, botany, nutrition; Broughton, 1986). This teaching activity uses letter writing to enhance student understanding of introductory psychology. It is based on the premise that writing actively engages the learner in such a way as to improve both disciplinary understanding and engagement with the learning process (Fulwiler, 1988).

MATERIALS NEEDED

No special materials are required for this assignment, but the instructor will benefit from review of previous work on the effects of psychology assignments on writing skills (Madigan & Bosamer, 1990), the influence of writing on students' perception of scientific psychology (Friedrich, 1990), the use of writing to connect the personal experiences of students with material they are studying (Nodine, 1990a), and writing as an aid to personal discovery (Murray, 1986).

INSTRUCTIONS

During the course of a semester each student is required to write several letters (I use four). Students are given the following instructions: Each letter should explain or react to current material in an interesting, individual way. Address the letter to a friend, parent, relative, and so forth, and make that person (*not* a psychology professor) the audience for the letter. It should be written in your own voice and style and should *not* be a simple listing of what you have read. Talk about what was most interesting, most disappointing, most surprising, or whatever, in the unit. Your letters should be prepared on a computer or typewriter. Submit *two* copies, along with a stamped envelope (*not sealed*) addressed to the recipient. I will read and grade one copy and return it to you; I will mail the other copy, along with a note from me. All four of your letters should be written to the same person. The letters are graded on three dimensions, each receiving roughly equal weight: factual/conceptual content, interest/originality, and grammar/structure. Grades on the letters constitute approximately 30% of the course grade. I suggest that students select a topic that is particularly interesting, frustrating, or surprising, in an effort to capitalize upon the integral role of audience and motivation as aids to writing (cf. Vipond, 1993).

DISCUSSION

As Vipond (1993) noted, it is important not only that we teach students how to write, but *why* they should write as well. Many writing assignments convey the notion that the topic belongs to the instructor more than the student (Zemelman & Daniels, 1986), thus stifling the writer's effort to communicate. Although the letter-writing assignment provokes initial anxiety in some students, most find it an interesting alternative to more typical term paper assignments. In particular, they like having the opportunity to choose the subject matter for their writing and to do it in their own voices. Sometimes students preface the psychology portion of their letters with personal messages, and attempts to deal with material in humorous ways are common. Although it is not necessary to specify a particular length for the letters, the typical letter is three to four typewritten pages.

Try to provide feedback that encourages good questions, critical judgments, and clear, accessible writing. Course evaluations suggest that students believe the assignment is helpful in the development of effective writing skills and the ability to reason logically. Occasionally, I receive letters from the recipients of the students' letters. When this has happened the responses, without exception, have been positive, usually mentioning the pleasure derived from seeing evidence of the intellectual growth of the relative or friend in the course.

Integration of writing with teaching may help students to discover what they know and to have more fun when they write (Murray, 1986). At the least, it can help teachers to become more flexible and diversify their instructional skills. At best, it may give students an opportunity to improve their ability to develop, organize, and communicate important knowledge.

REFERENCES

Broughton, L. (1986, Winter). Writing across the curriculum. *Vermont*, 11–13.

Friedrich, J. (1990). Learning to view psychology as a science: Self-persuasion through writing. *Teaching of Psychology, 17*, 23–27.

Fulwiler, T. (1988, April). Computers promote writing across the curriculum. *The University of Vermont Computing Newsletter, 11*(7), 2.

Madigan, R., & Brosamer, J. (1990). Improving the writing skills of students in introductory psychology. *Teaching of Psychology, 17*, 27–30.

Murray, D. M. (1986). One writer's secrets. *College Composition and Communication, 37*, 146–153.

Nodine, B. F. (1990a). Assignments in psychology: Writing to learn. In T. Fulwiler & A. Young (Eds.), *Programs that work: Models and methods for writing across the curriculum* (pp. 146–148). Portsmouth, NH: Boynton/Cook.

Nodine, B. F. (1990b). Psychologists teach writing. *Teaching of Psychology, 17*, 4.

Vipond, D. (1993). Social motives for writing psychology: Writing for and with younger readers. *Teaching of Psychology, 20*, 89–93.

Zemelman, S., & Daniels, H. (1986). Authorship and authority: Helping writing teachers grow. *English Education, 18*, 219–230.

SUGGESTED READING

Boice, R. (1990). Faculty resistance to writing-intensive courses. *Teaching of Psychology, 17,* 13–17.

Chamberlain, K., & Burrough, S. (1985). Techniques for teaching critical reading. *Teaching of Psychology, 12,* 213–215.

Fulwiler, T., & Young, A. (Eds.). (1990). *Programs that work: Models and methods for writing across the curriculum.* Portsmouth, NH: Boynton/Cook.

Willingham, D. B. (1990). Effective feedback on written assignments. *Teaching of Psychology, 17,* 10–13.

9 THE USE OF CORRESPONDENCE IN THE CLASSROOM

Charles I. Abramson and Douglas A. Hershey
Oklahoma State University

In this activity students write to eminent psychologists in order to increase their understanding of the field. Students find the activity both creative and engaging, and instructors can use the exercise to accomplish multiple learning objectives. The activity comprises two different classroom-tested letter-writing exercises, in addition to a number of variations on the basic theme. The activity can be effectively adapted for students at all academic levels, from introductory psychology students to graduate students.

CONCEPT   The ability to clearly express one's ideas in writing is a key training objective at both the undergraduate and graduate levels. This letter-writing activity can be presented to students as a clearly structured task (e.g., requiring each student to write a psychologist to ask a specific series of questions) or it can be presented as a more involved and creative task (e.g., requiring an entire class to develop its own minisurvey as a group and then devise a plan to solicit opinions from a representative sample of psychologists). The activity can be adapted for use as an individual or group assignment.

MATERIALS NEEDED   The materials needed for this activity are modest and will depend on the scope of the project as defined by the instructor. In the simplest case the exercise requires only an envelope, a sheet of paper, a postage stamp, and access to some type of professional directory such as the membership directory of the APA. Alternatively, an e-mail version of the exercise could be employed, which would require students to have access to an end-user terminal with word processing capabilities, an e-mail account, and a server with a connection to the Internet.

INSTRUCTIONS   The general goal of the activity is for a student to open up a dialog with an individual whose work excites the student. Ideally the student has been exposed to the individual's work in the course of the class. The letter-writing exercise can be assigned at any time during the semester, and it can be used as a formal component within the class or as an extra-credit assignment. Students can generate their own questions or, alternatively, receive some assistance from the instructor. If the responses to the letters are to be compared, at least some of the questions must be similar from student to student.

Once the student has identified the individual(s) he or she is interested in corresponding with, the student can readily obtain the person's address from any number of sources such as from the APA or Society of Neuroscience directories or from reprints of articles. Students who have access to electronic mail can use a number of on-line search engines available on the World Wide Web that are designed to locate an individual e-mail address.

What follows are two examples of the letter-writing exercise. The first was designed as an exercise in comparative psychology in which students wrote open-ended letters containing questions on a variety of topics (note that other branches of psychology could be substituted as well). The second example is a survey-style version used in a course on cognitive aging.

Case 1: The Individualized Letter Approach

In this approach the student makes up his or her own questions. To encourage comparisons among letters we suggest, however, that a core list of questions be common to all letter writers with the addition of several questions unique to the student. Core questions that have proved useful include the following: What is your main area of focus? What do you consider your most significant contribution? Who do you consider your greatest influence? What is your prediction for the field? Would you recommend that I enter this field of psychology? What are the job prospects? What tool or apparatus do you find most useful? What type of research design do you typically use? With what species have you worked?

Questions that are unique to students have included the following: What classes do you teach? Does working in this branch of psychology influence your social life? What do you enjoy most about practicing this type of psychology? What is the most valuable advice you can give a future graduate student? What one person do you think has exemplified this field the most, and why? What are the job prospects for those interested in this branch of psychology? Is there a particular animal species you like to work with the most?

Case 2: Multiple Mailings

Instructors can also use a survey-style version of the activity, in which a small group of undergraduates are assigned the exercise. For example, we once assigned students to take on the task of contacting a number of the top researchers in the subfield of cognitive aging. These researchers were identified using a conference proceedings program from the biennial Cognitive Aging Conference. The student's goal was to solicit the opinions of these researchers regarding important developments in the field—past, present, and future. The initial step in the project involved directing the students to develop a small set of carefully worded questions. After a week of deliberation they arrived at the following set of questions:

1. Briefly, what do you see as the two most significant challenges facing the field of cognitive aging in the foreseeable future?
2. What do you consider to be the most significant advances seen in the field of cognitive aging in the past 50 years?
3. What do you see as the most significant issues to be addressed in training young researchers entering the field of cognitive aging?
4. Who do you consider to be the three most influential researchers (living or deceased) in the field of cognitive aging in the past 4 decades?

5. What research areas do you feel should receive more attention in the next 20 years?

Variations of Correspondence in the Classroom

This activity has many possible variations and can be used with any type of course (e.g., abnormal, comparative, developmental, experimental, history, learning, neurobiology, and personality). It can be aimed at obtaining information of a personal nature (e.g., why did you join the field?), of a retrospective nature (e.g., what do you think have been the most important developments in your field?), of a prospective nature (e.g., what trends do you foresee?), and of an informational nature (e.g., what do you see as the best way to select a graduate program?). One of our colleagues, for example, used the exercise in his history of psychology class by requiring students to write to psychologists located in institutions outside of the United States. His goal was to have students explore a different cultural perspective on psychological issues.

DISCUSSION

Students generally find this activity not only informative but fun as well. At first, many students are hesitant in writing to eminent psychologists, especially with the individualized letters approach. This initial reluctance is readily forgotten when students begin to receive replies. In some cases students have received detailed responses including reprints and offers of assistance. Students are excited to receive a reply from someone they have come to respect and admire through the course of their studies.

This activity does have some limitations. First, it is best if the exercise is assigned early in the semester to allow adequate time for students to receive responses. Approximately half of those in the multiple mailing are likely to respond. Letters that contain a few questions rather than many questions are more apt to get a response. Students will be disappointed if they do not receive a reply and should be encouraged to try again. Second, some students will need guidance on how to obtain an address or an e-mail address and how to write a polished letter. Third, there is always the possibility that a student will receive a negative letter. Fourth, the instructor should be aware that several students may seek a reply from the same individual. Although this need not be viewed as a problem, the instructor can easily avoid such duplication by assigning students to write to specific individuals.

This correspondence activity can stimulate the development of many spin-off lectures and hands-on exercises. For instance, instructors who elect to take the minisurvey approach can use the activity to discuss issues of representative sampling and response rate problems. Students can also perform content analysis of the replies and other comparative qualitative research techniques.

WRITING COMPONENT

One of the clear strengths of this activity is that it fosters formal written communication of a scientific nature. The instructor can encourage the student to compose and turn in more than one draft of the letter before mailing. Students should explain to the correspondent that the letter is part of a course assignment. Students can also be asked to critique drafts of letters composed by their peers. Finally, students should be encouraged to write thank you notes on receiving replies.

SUGGESTED READING

Barrass, R. (1978). *Scientists must write: A guide to better writing for scientists, engineers, and students.* New York: Chapman & Hall.

Gottschalk, L. A. (1995). *Content analysis of verbal behavior: New findings and clinical applications.* Hillsdale, NJ: Erlbaum.

Rosengren, K. E. (1981). *Advances in content analysis.* Beverly Hills, CA: Sage.

10 APPLYING PSYCHOLOGY TO ISSUES IN SOCIETY

William J. Lammers
University of Central Arkansas

This activity uses principles taught in the introductory psychology course to help students develop a novel and innovative approach to deal with an important problem in society. After working in small groups, students present ideas and the psychological principles used through both written summary and oral presentation.

CONCEPT
This activity provides an opportunity for students, at the end of the introductory course, to consider the knowledge they have gained in the course and to apply that knowledge creatively to issues in society that are important to them.

MATERIALS NEEDED
No special materials required.

INSTRUCTIONS
Sometime during the week prior to the actual activity, ask the students to list (anonymously) what they consider to be the three most important problems in society today. Outside of class, tabulate the responses and create a Top 10 list, as determined by the students.

During the last week of regular classes, put the Top 10 list of problems in society on the chalkboard and be sure to note that the list was derived from the students' responses. With approximately five students working in a group, each group should (a) pick an issue to address from the list, (b) develop a new and innovative program or policy to deal with the issue, with the ideas based on principles they have learned in the course, (c) prepare a one-page written summary outlining the program or policy and the psychological principles used, and (d) be prepared to present its plan to the entire class. Allow approximately 40 min for the groups to develop ideas and write one-page summaries. Allow approximately 3 min per group for presentation to the class.

DISCUSSION
During an introductory psychology course, it should become apparent to students that the principles they are learning can be, and often are, applied to problems in society. Many of the issues typically discussed in the textbook and lecture (and revealed in their own Top 10 list) include crime, violence, gangs, child abuse, drug addiction, divorce, war, teenage pregnancy, spread of AIDS, discrimination, and many others. The learning activity presented provides students with an opportunity to creatively apply what they have learned in the course to a particular issue that concerns them. Because students choose the issue themselves, they are often very passionate in their discussions. It is recommended that the instructor observe the groups to be sure that they are actually applying psychological principles and not simply basing their ideas on personal opinions.

Grading the activity may or may not be necessary, depending on your class policies. In regard to class size this activity has been effective in class sizes up to 70. For very large classes or classes in which only one day can be devoted to this activity, the instructor could opt to eliminate the oral presentations and simply require the one-page summary.

WRITING COMPONENT

The writing component consists of one-page summaries developed by the small groups. As such, the exercise requires collaborative writing by the groups of students. Although atypical, collaborative writing has distinct benefits. The ideas of several students must be merged into a coherent and accurate description. As the groups attempt to summarize their ideas in writing, individual students receive immediate feedback as they offer sentences that might be used. It is common to hear expressions such as, "Yes, that's a good way to say it," "I think that's good, but we might also include . . . ," and "How about if we write . . ." As each group writes the last sentence for the summary, there is often a sense of accomplishment that can be clearly seen in the group members' expressions.

SUGGESTED READING

Cooper, J. L., Robinson, P., & McKinney, M. (1994). "Cooperative learning in the classroom. In D. F. Halpern (Ed.), *Changing college classrooms: New teaching and learning strategies for an increasingly complex world* (pp. 74–92). San Francisco: Jossey-Bass.

Davis, B. G. (1993). *Tools for teaching*. San Francisco: Jossey-Bass.

Erickson, B. L., & Strommer, D. W. (1991). *Teaching college freshmen*. San Francisco: Jossey-Bass.

Goodsell, A., Maher, M., Tinto, V., Smith, B. L., & MacGregor, J. (1992). *Collaborative learning: A sourcebook for higher education*. University Park, PA: Pennsylvania State University, National Center on Postsecondary Teaching, Learning, and Assessment (NCTLA).

Johnson, D. W., Johnson, R. T., & Smith, K. A. (1991). *Cooperative learning: Increasing college faculty instructional productivity* (ASHE-ERIC Higher Education Rep. No. 4). Washington, DC: George Washington University, School of Education and Human Development.

11 ACADEMIC CHALLENGE: A REVIEW ACTIVITY

Margie Cole
Kellam High School, Virginia Beach, VA

Betsy Fuqua
Princess Anne High School, Virginia Beach, VA

Lisa Kopacz
Salem High School, Virginia Beach, VA

Kathleen Self
Green Run High School, Virginia Beach, VA

David Weiss
Tallwood High School, Virginia Beach, VA

This review activity allows psychology students to participate in an academic challenge competition twice a year. School teams are asked psychology questions in a "College Bowl" format, and the winning team or school is determined by total points gained throughout the game.

CONCEPT

This review activity is designed to prepare students for cumulative evaluations such as midterm exams, semester or final exams, or the Advanced Placement (AP) examination. We developed this activity as a way to help our high school students get ready for the AP Psychology Exam, and what started as competition between three schools has now expanded to a much-publicized biannual event involving seven high schools in Virginia Beach. This activity, however, is clearly adaptable to many other academic settings. It could involve competition among students from several local colleges, among students in different psychology classes within the same college, or among students in the same psychology class. The activity described reflects our own situation; however, instructors should feel free to modify the activity to fit their own needs.

MATERIALS NEEDED

A set of questions from each area of psychology covered on the exam, a buzzer system, a scoreboard, and a stopwatch will be required. An amplification system may also be necessary.

INSTRUCTIONS

Generating and Selecting Questions

The participating teachers should meet well in advance of the competition to generate the question bank. Questions should be designed as objective recall questions with clearly defined responses, and they should be proportionately representative of the content areas to be evaluated. Each question and answer should be placed on an index card. The question bank should then be divided into packets of 20 questions with topics equally represented within each packet. Each packet represents one round in the competition.

Team Selection

Each school fields two teams of four students. Team members may be selected based on academic average, willingness to participate, or any other criteria deemed appropriate by the teachers. Once teams are selected, students may participate only with the team for which they were selected. The only exception is in the event of a tie at the end of the competition. In this case, the schools involved may choose any four of their players to participate in further competition.

Roles for Participating Teacher

- *Moderator*: One of the participating psychology teachers should read the questions for each round. This person will determine the accuracy of the response given by the student.
- *Judges*: In the event of a questionable response, the moderator will defer to a panel of psychology teachers who will confer and determine whether or not to award points. All decisions of the judges are final.
- *Timer*: One teacher will recognize which student buzzed in first and enforce time restrictions.
- *Scorekeeper*: One teacher will maintain a record of accumulated points during each round and post the score at the end of the round.

Scoring

Each round consists of 20 questions. Teams receive ten points for each correct answer. Five points are deducted for each incorrect answer. If one team answers incorrectly, the other team is not given an opportunity to answer that question. The winner of the entire challenge is the school that accumulates the most points in its four rounds. In the event of a tie, the two schools will play a tiebreaker round.

Administration

Round-by-round matchups may be designated according to a round-robin format (see Table 11-1). A student from either team will randomly select a packet of

Table 11-1. *Sample Round-Robin Pairings for Competition Between High School Teams*

Rounds 1–6	Rounds 7–12
Salem 1 vs. Tallwood 1	Kellam 1 vs. Green Run 1
Kellam 1 vs. Princess Anne 1	Tallwood 1 vs. Kempsville 1
Green Run 1 vs. Kempsville 1	Princess Anne 1 vs. Salem 1
Kempsville 2 vs. Princess Anne 2	Princess Anne 2 vs. Tallwood 2
Salem 2 vs. Kellam 2	Salem 2 vs. Green Run 2
Tallwood 2 vs. Green Run 2	Kellam 2 vs. Kempsville 2

questions for that round. Each of the eight students competing will be in command of a buzzer attached to a light. Our apparatus is designed so that the first student to buzz blocks out all other students. The teacher serving as the timer will recognize the student whose light indicates a first response. This student must wait to be recognized before answering or the answer will be counted as incorrect. If the student buzzes in before the question is completed, the moderator will stop reading the question, and the student who buzzed first must answer based on what was read to that point. The student has 5 s from the time he or she is recognized to begin answering. During this time, he or she may confer with teammates but the student who buzzed must be the one to respond. Failure to begin a response within 5 s will constitute a wrong answer. The moderator will supply answers to all incorrect or unanswered questions in the interest of review for the teams and the audience.

DISCUSSION   The Advanced Placement Psychology Academic Challenge is held in Virginia Beach for the purpose of using competition to encourage students to review the material. The first challenge is held at the end of January to review the students for the midterm exam. During this event, only questions from material covered during the first semester are used. The second challenge is held immediately before the AP exam in early May and includes questions from the entire year. To involve all AP students and not just those selected to compete, the audience for the competition is composed solely of AP psychology students from the participating schools. This way all students hear the questions and answers and can use the event to review the material.

The bank of questions used for the two challenges was developed by the AP psychology teachers in Virginia Beach with the intention of reflecting information that students are expected to know for the AP exam. The competition described in this activity uses a multitextbook approach to developing the questions rather than a specific-text approach. It is also helpful to have the chapter or area of psychology from which the question is drawn noted in the top corner of the index card. This information enables teachers to mix questions to ensure content validity in each round, and it facilitates the moderator's job as well.

Student reaction to this activity has been positive. Students have been competitive and forgiving of the temporary anxiety produced. The precompetition study groups have fostered a sense of community and camaraderie. Although winning the interschool event certainly engenders a rise in self-esteem among participants, even those who do not win report feeling good about their performances. The students sometimes view the event from a win–lose perspective, but the teachers tend to focus on the review benefit. In fact, only five correct answers separated the first- and fourth-place winners in our last competition. To quote one student in an advice letter to a future AP psychology student, "Prepare for the AP exam by joining the psychology team. That was the best review for me and will be for you, too. Enjoy yourself. I did."

The additional benefits of networking among the participating psychology teachers who spend considerable time together preparing and revising questions and organizing the event are tremendous. These teachers now share teaching ideas, materials, and even guest speakers to a much greater degree. Other AP disciplines in Virginia Beach have also adopted this format as a means of review.

We have involved the community in our competition by inviting parents and members of the school administration to participate in the audience, by soliciting scholarships for student participants among local psychiatric/psychological practices, by involving our Adopt-A-School business partners, and by publicizing the event to enhance psychology's reputation in our community. We are currently in the process of proposing multilevel competitions with local universities and district competitions with nearby school systems, and we might someday go statewide.

12 Have I Heard That Name Before?: A Survey of Historical Figures in Psychology

Charles L. Brewer
Furman University

Stephen F. Davis
Emporia State University

This activity results in a survey that measures students' familiarity with important persons in the history of psychology. This survey can be used to diagnose the level of students' knowledge on beginning a course, to evaluate postcourse improvement, and as a general assessment tool.

CONCEPT   According to McKeachie (1994), "Since students' previous knowledge determines how they will learn what we teach, an important part of effective teaching is to analyze students' existing structures of knowledge as well as the learning tasks we are asking them to perform. Effective teaching is as much diagnosis as presentation" (p. 286). Nowhere is the importance of this advice more clearly seen than in the history and systems course. Because this course typically comes toward the end of the undergraduate program, instructors may assume expertise and knowledge that their students do not possess.

Many instructors consider individuals included in the history and systems course to be almost like old friends. Likewise, we may be tempted to assume that our students view these individuals in the same way. This assumption arises because history and systems is typically taught as a capstone course. Thus our students have completed most of their psychology program and should be familiar with many of the persons covered in this course. Are these valid assumptions? What information do students bring to the history and systems course? Are our lectures falling on deaf ears? This easy exercise addresses these questions by providing pre- and postcourse measures.

Bunnell (1992) asked psychology students and faculty in New Zealand to rate their knowledge of 53 famous persons in the history of psychology (see also Duncan, 1976; Punches & Viney, 1986). Bunnell reported very poor recognition by students in her sample. Curiosity prompted us to replicate her study. Our first attempts, which employed Bunnell's original list, yielded comparable results; American students beginning the history and systems course are no better at recognizing psychology's historical figures or their contributions. Subsequently we expanded the list to include notable women and minorities. The next logical step was to conduct a posttest for comparison, and ratings improved appreciably. The final modification involved the addition of space for students to write the contribution for each individual. (Previously students simply indicated that they could list such accomplishments.)

MATERIALS NEEDED   Individuals listed on the present form appear in appendix A. As noted, Bunnell's (1992) original list was expanded to include other notable psychologists, especially women and minorities. We drew these additions from contemporary history of psychology textbooks. (Instructors may change this list to suit their own needs in a particular course.) Students rate each individual according to the following scale: 0 *(do not recognize this individual)*, 1 *(recognize this name)*, 2 *(recognize this name and the person's contribution to psychology)*, and 3 *(recognize this name and can describe the person's contribution to psychology)*. Space is left beside each name for students to describe the individual's contribution to psychology.

INSTRUCTIONS   The written instructions, which appear at the top of each sheet of the survey, are as follows: "For each of the following names, circle one of the choices and, if you can, write a brief phrase or sentence indicating the person's main contributions to psychology."

DISCUSSION   Two principal uses of this survey are to (a) allow teachers to make a precourse diagnosis of students' knowledge and (b) evaluate the value added at the completion of the course by assessing students' familiarity with psychology's important individuals and their contributions. Data gathered with this instrument can be used to answer many related questions. Are students less familiar with female psychologists and their accomplishments than with male psychologists and their accomplishments? Are students as familiar with the names and contributions of historical figures as they are with those of contemporary psychologists? The number of such questions may be limited only by your imagination.

Students' numerical responses (i.e., each student's *overall* score) allow you to calculate descriptive statistics, such as measures of central tendency and variability. Likewise, tests of significance can be conducted on pre- and postcourse ratings.

Although we have used this questionnaire only with students in the history and systems course, it can be used in various courses, especially capstone courses, to ascertain students' entering and exiting knowledge of relevant individuals. For example, appropriately modified lists can be developed for courses in abnormal, personality, learning, developmental, cognitive, and so forth. Obviously, such lists do not have to be limited to historical names; major concepts also can be included. Results of such diagnostic evaluations have the potential to modify course content and students' progress substantially.

Similarly, in this age of accountability and documentation, this survey can be added to the department's regular assessment battery. Fortunately, all our students have claimed to know more at the end of the course than at the beginning. Students' direct comparisons of pre- and postcourse results provide compelling and reassuring evidence that they have learned a lot. The fact that they can readily quantify their learning with this survey makes them feel good about the hard work they have done.

REFERENCES   Bunnell, J. K. (1992). Recognition of famous names in psychology by students and staff. *Teaching of Psychology, 19,* 51–52.

Duncan, C. P. (1976). Recognition of names of famous psychologists. *Journal of the History of the Behavioral Sciences, 12,* 325–329.

McKeachie, W. J. (1994). *Teaching tips* (9th ed.). Lexington, MA: Heath.

Punches, A., & Viney, W. (1986). A note on the historical literacy of first-year graduate students in psychology. *Journal of the History of the Behavioral Sciences, 22,* 64–65.

Appendix A

List of Psychologists Appearing on the Survey

Alfred Adler, Gordon Allport, Anne Anastasi, James Rowland Angell, Richard Atkinson, Marian Breland Bailey, Albert Bandura, Vladimir Bekhterev, Ludy T. Benjamin, Jr., Alfred Binet, Janis S. Bohan, Horace Mann Bond, Josef Breuer, Percy W. Bridgman, Paul Broca, Jerome S. Bruner, Mary Whiton Calkins, Walter Cannon, Harvey Carr, James McKeen Cattell, Auguste Comte, Jean-Martin Charcot, Kenneth B. Clark, Mamie Phipps Clark, Charles Darwin, Rene Descartes, Florence L. Denmark, John Dewey, Knight Dunlap, Hermann Ebbinghaus, Erik Erikson, Gustav Fechner, Anna Freud, Sigmund Freud, Laurel Furumoto, Francis Galton, Luigi Galvani, John Garcia, Lillian Moller Gilbreth, Florence Goodenough, Edwin R. Guthrie, G. Stanley Hall, David Hartley, Hermann von Helmholtz, Edna Heidbreder, Mary Henle, Johann Herbart, Ewald Hering, Ernest R. Hilgard, Leta Stetter Hollingworth, Karen Horney, Carl Hovland, Clark L. Hull, David Hume, William James, Pierre Janet, Ernest Jones, Mary Cover Jones, Carl Jung, Immanuel Kant, Wolfgang Köhler, Kurt Koffka, Emil Kraepelin, Thomas Kuhn, Oswald Külpe, Jean-Baptiste Lamarck, Carl George Lange, Karl Lashley, Kurt Lewin, John Locke, Jacques Loeb, Elizabeth Loftus, Thomas Malthus, Abraham Maslow, William McDougall, Maude Merrill, James Mill, John Stuart Mill, George Miller, Neal Miller, Jill Morawski, Christiana Morgan, Conwy Lloyd Morgan, O. H. Mowrer, George Elias Müller, Johannes, Müller, Hugo Münsterberg, Henry Murray, Ulric Neisser, Ivan Pavlov, Karl Pearson, Oscar Pfungst, Jean Piaget, Henri Pieron, Walter Pillsbury, Adolph Quetelet, Rosalie Rayner, Carl Rogers, George John Romanes, Julian Rotter, Edgar Rubin, Nancy Felipe Russo, Elizabeth Scarborough, Walter Dill Scott, Charles Sherrington, B. F. Skinner, W. S. Small, Charles Spearman, Kenneth W. Spence, Herbert Spencer, Roger W. Sperry, Carl Stumpf, Francis Cecil Sumner, Lewis Terman, Edward L. Thorndike, Louis L. Thurstone, Edward B. Titchener, Edward C. Tolman, Charles Henry Turner, Edwin Burket Twitmyer, Margaret Floy Washburn, John B. Watson, Ernst Weber, Max Wertheimer, Lightner Witmer, Robert Sessions Woodworth, Helen Bradford Thompson Woolley, Wilhelm Wundt, Robert M. Yerkes, and Bluma Zeigarnik.

13 READ ALL ABOUT IT! WUNDT OPENS PSYCHOLOGY LAB: A NEWSPAPER ASSIGNMENT FOR HISTORY OF PSYCHOLOGY

William H. M. Bryant
Benjamin Cardozo School of Law

Ludy T. Benjamin, Jr.
Texas A&M University

The newspaper assignment that makes up this activity is an active learning exercise for use principally in a history of psychology class, but it could be used in any class to have students explore the history of that field (e.g., cognition, social psychology, or memory).

CONCEPT This research and writing activity requires students to produce their own issue of a "newspaper" from an earlier time in psychology's history. They do this by combining the history of psychology with American and world history.

INSTRUCTIONS Prepare students for this project by talking about the kinds of published resources that are available to them to locate the books and journals that make up the literature of psychology's past. The *Cumulative Subject Index for Psychological Abstracts* and the *Cumulative Author Index for Psychological Index* and *Psychological Abstracts* are excellent finding aids. The former covers the literature from 1927 through 1983, and the latter covers 1894 through 1983. Further, the APA recently put on-line all American psychology journals from 1887 to the present. Warren Street's (1994) book, which lists important events in psychology by year, is a particularly excellent source for this project.

Students can find nonpsychology materials from past times via newspapers on microfilm or through indexes (such as *Poole's Indexes* or the *Reader's Guide to Periodical Literature*) that allow students to search the popular magazines of the nineteenth and twentieth centuries.

Randomly assign students a year, typically before 1950, by having students select a 3-by-5-in. card from a prepared deck. Each card should list a different year. The student is to use published materials from that year as a basis for creating a four-page newspaper on 8½-by-11-in. paper. Require that half of the content of the paper be about psychology and half be composed of nonpsychology materials. Encourage students to include a number of shorter items as opposed to a few lengthy ones. In any year selected, the possibilities for items to include in one's newspaper are virtually limitless. Thus the student has the opportunity to select items that are of personal interest. Any kind of material may be included, such as photos, charts, cartoons, or advertisements. Students should rewrite the text from these old books, magazines, or newspapers in their own words. The instructor should encourage students to be creative and even make up advertisements that psychologists might have created for the time, touting the advantages of a particular discovery or theory.

As an example, consider some of the items that might be included in a newspaper for the year 1912. The *Titanic* sunk on its maiden voyage. The Cracker Jacks Company added prizes to its boxes of caramelized popcorn. Robert Scott reached the South Pole, only to discover that Roald Amundsen had been there a month earlier. Native American Jim Thorpe, arguably the greatest athlete of the twentieth century, won both the pentathlon and decathlon at the Olympic Games in Sweden. The heating pad was invented. Eva Braun, Adolf Hitler's significant other, was born in that year, as was Wernher von Braun (no relation; he was a rocket scientist; she, obviously, was not).

In psychology, Walter Cannon and Margaret Washburn published their classic study on hunger in which human research participants swallowed balloons that could be inflated in their stomachs. Freud, while on vacation in Switzerland, failed to visit Jung, an affront that added to their forthcoming nonamicable separation. Inez Beverly (later Prosser) graduated from high school in Yoakum, Texas; she would become the first African American woman to earn a PhD in psychology. A new American journal appeared, titled *Studies in Linguistic Psychology*. Max Wertheimer published the article, "Experimental Studies on the Perception of Movement" in which he defined the phi phenomenon and established a new approach to psychology known as Gestalt psychology. And the annual meeting of the APA was held in Cleveland where President Edward L. Thorndike delivered his address on ideomotor action in which he argued that situations and responses could be connected without ideas intervening.

In constructing their newspapers, many students today make use of some kind of desktop computer publishing system. Those programs can produce some pretty fancy newspapers, but it is a good idea to make it clear to students that they will be graded on content and not how glitzy the newspaper is. A follow-up to this exercise is to have a poster day in which the newspapers are displayed on a classroom wall (two copies of each may be needed if they are printed back-to-back) so that the students can see what other students selected for their years. If the instructor would like to provide refreshments for the poster day, that is always a popular addition.

DISCUSSION

This extra-classroom exercise is very popular with our students. It gives them experience with library research in the history of psychology, exposes them more broadly to American and world history, and involves them in a writing exercise. The assignment also gives students the chance to demonstrate some individuality, and perhaps creativity, in choosing what to include in their newspapers.

For the instructor, these newspapers typically make for interesting reading. The creativity and individuality displayed are a bonus. Some students have burned the edges of their newspapers to age them (we trust they had back-up copies in case the flames got out of hand). Some students have added information about important events in their family's history. Others have written self-help columns from the perspectives of eminent psychologists or psychoanalysts such as John Watson or Sigmund Freud.

REFERENCE   Street, W. R. (1994). *A chronology of noteworthy events in American psychology.* Washington, DC: American Psychological Association.

SUGGESTED
READING   Cushing, H. G., & Morris, A. (Eds.). (1944). *Nineteenth century reader's guide to periodical literature, 1890–1899.* New York: Peter Smith.

Hellemans, A., & Bunch, B. (1988). *The timetables of science: A chronology of the most important people and events in the history of science.* New York: Simon & Schuster.

Hilgard, E. R. (Ed.). (1978). *American psychology in historical perspective: Addresses of the presidents of the American Psychological Association, 1892–1977.* Washington, DC: American Psychological Association.

Osier, D. V., & Wozniak, R. H. (1984). *A century of serial publications in psychology, 1850–1950.* Millwood, NY: Kraus International.

Poole's index to periodical literature, 1802–1881. (1938). New York: Peter Smith.

Psychology Library, Columbia University. (1960). *Author index to Psychological Index (1894–1935) and Psychological Abstracts (1927–1958)* (five volumes). Boston: G. K. Hall. (Note: 1959 to 1968 supplements were published by G. K. Hall; 1969 to 1983 supplements were published by the American Psychological Association.)

Psychology Library, Columbia University. (1960). *Subject index to Psychological Abstracts (1927–1958)* (two volumes). Boston: G. K. Hall. (Note: 1959 to 1968 supplements were published by G. K. Hall; 1969 to 1983 supplements were published by the American Psychological Association.)

Reader's guide to periodical literature. (1900 to date). New York: H. W. Wilson.

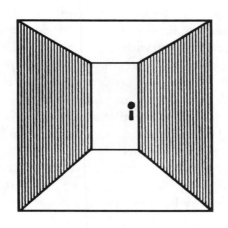

CHAPTER II
RESEARCH METHODS
AND STATISTICS

The ten activities in this chapter focus on issues common to courses in statistics and research methods. Most of the activities deal with elementary concepts of the kind that are treated in many psychology classes, such as observation, sampling, and reliability.

Activity 14 has students counting fidgets in an exercise designed to teach the complexities of naturalistic observation. In Activity 15, students learn about operationally defining behaviors and the assessment of such definitions by examining interobserver reliability. Activity 16, which teaches Galileo's distinction between objective and subjective reality, could be used in a history of psychology course, but it is appropriate in any course to help students understand one of the most fundamental issues of psychology as a science.

Using snack-size bags of M&M's as samples to estimate population characteristics is the subject of Activity 17. Continuing in the "let's give candy to students" approach, Activity 18 shows instructors how to use jelly beans to teach random assignment, to interpret main effects and interactions, and to generate alternative explanations for research outcomes.

Activity 19 uses gender differences in the number of shoes students own to generate a data set for a discussion of sample size and power, operationalization of variables, meta-analysis, and the validity of self-report measures. Activity 20 focuses on the binomial distribution and is appropriate for classes in introductory psychology, social psychology, or statistics. Intended for a research methods course, Activity 21 shows students the relationship of suppressor variables and multiple regression.

Activity 22 not only teaches students how to construct a good survey but describes how this exercise can be used to gather useful information in the school or college setting, such as attitudes toward smoking, satisfaction with academic advising, and so forth. Activity 23 uses a standardized feminism survey to teach students about measuring reliability and validity.

14 COUNTING FIDGETS: TEACHING THE COMPLEXITY OF NATURALISTIC OBSERVATION

Bernard C. Beins
Ithaca College

The research tradition in psychology typically involves controlled laboratory settings. Nonetheless, naturalistic observation can generate important information. Unfortunately, most research methods textbooks devote only a single chapter to all of the descriptive techniques. This 5-min activity uses classroom observers to record fidgeting behavior and outlines a simple classroom technique that successfully conveys to students some of the complexities of naturalistic observation.

CONCEPT

Naturalistic observation can play a significant role in the study of social behaviors. However, students may not appreciate the complexities of this approach. In the activity, students count the number of fidgets they observe in classmates and discuss reasons why different observers in the same situation report different numbers of fidgets. Students then decide how, as researchers, they would solve the problems they identify.

MATERIALS NEEDED

The only implements required for this activity are an ordinary watch or a classroom clock with a second hand and a sheet for tallying the fidgets in each of five 1-min segments.

INSTRUCTIONS

Preparation

Solicit two student volunteers to participate in an as-yet undefined task. They need to have either digital watches or watches with a second hand, or they can borrow these items for the demonstration. It is helpful to know the volunteers because you can then select people who are likely to respond quite differently in the task; such variation enhances the pedagogical effectiveness of the activity. Selecting one student who is energetic and another student who is calmer often leads to very different reports from the observers, which is the point of the exercise.

After choosing the two students, take them into the hallway briefly so you can explain their roles as student observers (see appendix A). Even though the directions are simple, the observers may have questions. Try to avoid answering questions about definitions of fidgets because that is part of the later discussion. In fact, I have found that it is best not to let the observers ask any questions at all. Now return to the classroom.

Table 14-1. *Student Activity and Purpose for the 1-Minute Demonstration Period*

Minute	Activity During the 1-Minute Period	Purpose
1	I talk about a topic unrelated to systematic observation.	This generates a baseline period for number of fidgets.
2	I tell students that I want them to close their eyes and imagine that insects are crawling on their skin.	This prepares them for the period in which the number of fidgets is likely to increase.
3	Students close their eyes and imagine the insects are present.	Students can concentrate on the insects without distraction. It helps generate fidgets.
4	We begin a discussion in which students speculate on the reason for the activity and the role that the student observers played.	This creates a cooldown minute in which fidgets begin to decrease in number.
5	The discussion continues.	This provides another postinsect baseline.

The Demonstration

The students in the class still do not know what is going on. They follow the directions as indicated in Table 14-1. The observation period consists of five 1-min segments. During the observation time, the two observers are really the source of data to be discussed later. In general, the two observers will record very different numbers of fidgets within each 1-min period across the entire time span. I have never failed to achieve notable differences between observers' counts. Often one student will record two or three times as many fidgets as the other. The discrepancy between observers illustrates the difficulty associated with monitoring a behavior as simple as fidgets. Trying to document more complicated psychological phenomena is enormously more difficult.

DISCUSSION   Students are often not aware of the difficulties associated with naturalistic or systematic observation. During the discussion following the demonstration, ask them what could be done to improve data collection in observation studies.

I typically identify the following problems with the present methodology specifically and with observation techniques broadly; if the students do not generate these possibilities, note them and ask students to solve the problems.

1. The concept of a *fidget* although intuitively clear, does not have a clear operational definition. Observations would be more reliable with a set definition.
   - Even though an operational definition would help, such a construct leads to missing some fidgets, whereas some movements that intuitively do not seem like fidgets would be recorded simply because of the definition used.
   - Training people until they are consistent would raise the low interrater reliability.
   - Creating a videotape of the scene to be recorded would allow observers to discuss their criteria so that all observers are recorded in similar ways.

2. The method of recording data might differ across observers. For example, some students log a fidget with every occurrence, taking their eyes off the class, whereas other students tally the movements in their heads and only enter them onto the data sheet when the 1-min segment ends. Students in the latter group are less likely to miss movements while recording data.
3. The student observers may be sitting on different sides of the room, so their vantage points are not the same. As a result, they may not really be recording the same scene because of the possibility of partially blocked viewing conditions or differing perspectives.
4. Students in the class know they are being observed, even if they do not know the purpose. As a result, they may try to figure out the purpose and change their behaviors either to be helpful or to resist intrusive observation of their behaviors. Depending on the student's conclusion, that individual's behavior may not resemble that of the person in the next seat.

This activity is well received by students and generates meaningful discussion. Afterward, they are better able to recognize the pitfalls that arise during even simple observational techniques and to appreciate the difficulties inherent in this approach.

WRITING COMPONENT   Prior to the discussion of problems associated with observational research, students can generate their own list of pitfalls and the means to solve them. As a rule, any single student can produce a few of the problems, but the class discussion extends the listing greatly. As a final writing exercise, students can try to identify some of the strengths of observational research compared to experimental research. To complete the picture, they can also identify some of the limitations of the controlled experimental approach.

SUGGESTED READING   Babbie, E. (1995). *The practice of social research* (7th ed.). Belmont, CA: Wadsworth.

Goodwin, C. J. (1995). *Research in psychology: Methods and design.* New York: Wiley.

Judd, C. M., Smith, E. R., & Kidder, L. H. (1991). *Research methods in social relations* (6th ed.). Fort Worth, TX: Holt, Rinehart, & Winston.

Appendix A

Directions to Student Volunteers

I would like you to record the number of fidgets that the students in the class emit for a 5-min period. Break the 5-min period into separate 1-min segments and keep a count of the number of fidgets in each segment. Keep a written record of the number of fidgets in each segment. You will need to scan the entire class, so sit at the front, facing the class.

When we go back into the classroom, take your observation seats and when I say "begin," start recording the number of fidgets. For the first minute, I will be talking; for the second minute, I will explain that I want the students to sit with their eyes closed and imagine that insects are crawling on their skins. During the third minute, they will actually sit there with their eyes closed, imagining the insects. During the fourth minute, they will begin a discussion of what they think is going on. The discussion will continue into the fifth minute.

Make sure you keep track of the time as accurately as you can and record the fidgets separately for each minute.

15 DISCOVERING THE RELATIONSHIP BETWEEN OPERATIONAL DEFINITIONS AND INTEROBSERVER RELIABILITY

Angela H. Becker
Indiana University Kokomo

This activity is designed for students in research methods and behavior modification classes or the methods section of other content courses. Students observe a brief videotape and collect data on the occurrence/nonoccurrence of a series of six behaviors. The main purposes of this activity are to help students (a) understand the importance of having clear operational definitions, (b) learn to calculate interobserver reliability, and (c) think about ways to improve a study that has low interobserver reliability. In addition, students gain practice in using time sampling and come to realize that observation as a data collection technique is more complex than casual observation.

CONCEPT

This exercise helps students realize that observation as a data collection technique is more complex than casual observation. It introduces students to the use of time sampling, the calculation of interobserver reliability, and the importance of having clear operational definitions.

MATERIALS NEEDED

You will need a 10-min videotape of human or animal behavior, a VCR and monitor for showing the tape to the class, a watch with a second hand, and enough copies of the handouts described later for each student in the class. Students will need pencils and will probably want calculators.

To be most effective, the videotape should be of a group of humans or animals that are active enough to produce several different types of behaviors. If at least some of those behaviors occur quite frequently and in several individuals at a time, students will come away with a better understanding of why time sampling is useful. My tape is of a group of white geese at a local park. (I would be happy to provide a copy of this taped segment to anyone who sends me a blank videotape.) There are many other possibilities for footage that will meet the previously described requirements. For example, you could videotape small children performing at a school program or playing at a birthday party, or you could get some footage of one of the livelier species at your local zoo. If you or someone you know is planning to visit another country, you may be able to obtain a tape of a festival or other group event from another culture. The videos that some universities make of their graduation ceremonies could also be used. If you have access to a VCR, you could tape a segment of an appropriate televised event. Although many television programs show groups engaging in behaviors that meet the criteria identified at the beginning of this discussion, most do not show this activity, uninterrupted by close-ups of individuals or pans to scenery and other locations in the story line, for more than a minute or two. There are exceptions, however, that would make good tapes for this activity: Televised New Year's Eve bashes usually show quite long segments of partyers, sporting events such as basketball or volleyball also show fairly long segments of activity on the court, and dance club shows on cable channels run segments of couples dancing for the duration of a complete song.

Prepare three handouts. The first should contain a data collection sheet with a row for each observation interval and a column for each behavior students are to record (see appendix A). The second should contain a list of behaviors (I recommend no more than six to eight), their operational definitions (some of which are purposely clearer than others), and a simple formula for inter-rater reliability (see appendix B). The third handout should contain a set of postobservation questions (see appendix C).

INSTRUCTIONS   This activity should be prefaced with a lecture on the use of observation techniques, including the advantages and disadvantages of time sampling in relation to other observation techniques (e.g., event sampling and narrative recording) and the concept of interobserver reliability. Although the basic observation techniques described in methods textbooks are much the same, the labels given to particular techniques vary. The following definitions of observation techniques are provided to facilitate gathering background lecture material and to prevent misunderstanding.

Time sampling is a technique in which the observer defines several target behaviors, divides the observation period into short intervals, and then alternates from observing to recording every other interval. In contrast, in *event sampling* the observer defines a target behavior and records every instance of that behavior as it occurs throughout the observation period. A *narrative recording* is a running description of behavior in which everything that is said or done during the observation period is recorded. The following are particularly useful sources for lecture material: chapter 6 from Bordens and Abbott (1996); chapters 6, 7, and 8 from Martin and Bateson (1993); and chapter 19 from Martin and Pear (1996).

Give each student all three handouts, and allow them a few minutes to read through the list of behaviors and operational definitions and become familiar with the layout of the data collection sheet. Have students work in 15-s intervals—alternating between 15 s for observing and 15 s for recording observations completed in the previous 15-s interval. For each observation interval, they simply look for whether or not each target behavior occurs. If the behavior occurs *at least once* in the observation interval, they are to place a tally mark in the appropriate column on the data sheet during the recording interval. Rather than having students keep track of their own intervals, use a watch with a second hand to time intervals for them. It works best if you simply call out "observe" or "record" at the beginning of alternate 15-s intervals. Explain to students that data collection will last for a total of 10 min. Each minute represents an observation period and is divided into 30-s sessions. During each 30-s session, students will have a 15-s interval to observe the behavior on the videotape and a 15-s interval to record their observations. It is important for students to understand what they are observing and recording; be sure to explain that they are recording the occurrence of target behaviors. That is, they are looking for whether or not a behavior occurs; they are *not* looking for the number of times a specific behavior occurs.

After 10 min, have students stop observing and work on the postobservation questions (see appendix C). As appendix C illustrates, students will first answer several questions individually, then compare those answers with a partner, and finally calculate interobserver reliability with their partner for each of the target behaviors.

DISCUSSION Follow up with a class discussion of students' responses to the postobservation questions. Focus on those questions where partners' responses differed most often and on those behaviors that had the highest and lowest interobserver reliability. Then discuss possible reasons for these trends. With my tape of geese and set of behaviors, for example, students generally have very high interobserver reliability for displays and for tail shakes and low reliability for feeding and submission. When exploring possible reasons for these findings, student comments tend to focus on the importance of careful operational definitions and on problems with observation. For example, students notice that my operational definition of display behavior is much more concrete than my definition of submission, that the definition for feeding was too narrow to encompass much of what they wanted to be able to code as feeding behavior, and that several of the behaviors were difficult to identify accurately because of the distance from which the videotape was shot. For example, one student declared that she wanted a better definition of feeding, because "sometimes I thought they might be, but I couldn't see if they really had food in their mouths or not."

Next ask students to offer possible solutions for the reliability problems they have encountered. We talk about clarifying operational definitions. For example, several students decided that "touching beak to the ground several times in a row" would have defined feeding in a way that would have allowed them to record what they thought was feeding behavior. Students also brought up the possibility of reviewing the tape and discussing discrepancies between observers in order to resolve disagreements or practicing with sample tapes to improve reliability before viewing actual data tapes. This second idea was an elaboration on one student's comment that he "wished we could have watched the whole tape first while reading the definitions and *then* done the recording part." The students also decided that the value of a high-power zoom lens should not be underestimated if one wants to observe detailed behaviors and remain unobtrusive. Overall, students' responses to the activity indicated that not only did they learn a great deal, but that they enjoyed the activity as well.

A minor variation on this activity could allow students to discover for themselves that one of the pitfalls to time sampling is that there will always be lost data (i.e., behaviors that occur during recording intervals rather than observation intervals). Instead of having the entire class observe and record during the same intervals, divide the class in half, and have each half observe and record during opposite intervals. Have each half of the class pool their data and calculate the mean number of intervals in which tail shakes, feeding, grooming, display, aggression, and submission were observed by their group. Students should find that for behaviors that occur frequently, there will be little difference between the means reported by each half of the class. For example, the two halves of the class should be quite similar on mean number of tail shakes, simply because this occurs almost continuously among geese. However, for relatively infrequent behaviors, such as displays of aggression, students are likely to notice differences between reports by the two halves of the class. This can lead to a discussion of the relative usefulness of time sampling versus event sampling for observing infrequent behaviors. (Obviously, if you use this alternative procedure and you still want students to calculate interobserver reliability, they must do so by pairing up with someone from the same half of the class.)

WRITING COMPONENT Instructors who want to provide their students with an opportunity to do more writing than the small amount required to complete appendix C may add one of the following writing components to the activity.

1. Have students reflect on their expectations of observation in general and time sampling in particular. After giving students a brief description of the exercise they are about to engage in, ask them to respond to the question, "What do you think will happen when we do this time sampling observation?" After the exercise is complete, have students reread their earlier expectations and write a response to the following two questions: (a) "Which of your earlier expectations were met and why do you think this happened?" and (b) "Which of your earlier expectations were *not* met and why do you think this happened?" As a follow-up, students could construct a list on the chalkboard of the group's most common expectations, identify those that were not met, and then discuss whether those unmet expectations would make them more or less likely to want to use this method in their own future research.

2. Have students write a report to the researchers who set up the study. In that report, students should point out the strengths and weaknesses of the study and suggest improvements. This writing component could be followed by a small-group discussion in which students compare the strengths and weaknesses they noticed and try to identify the most methodologically sound and practical suggestions for improvement. You could also ask the students to use this small-group time to rewrite the operational definitions that they found lacking.

3. Instructors who have their students keep journals might consider having them include an entry about this observation activity. Students could be asked to respond to the question "What do you feel you learned from this observation exercise?" If content analysis is covered in your course, you could have students use these journal responses as data and attempt to code them into categories.

REFERENCES
Bordens, K. S., & Abbott, B. B. (1996). *Research design and methods: A process approach* (3rd ed.). Mountain View, CA: Mayfield.

Martin, G., & Pear, J. (1996). *Behavior modification: What it is and how to do it* (5th ed.). Englewood Cliffs, NJ: Prentice Hall.

Martin, P., & Bateson, P. (1993). *Measuring behavior: An introductory guide* (2nd ed.). Cambridge: Cambridge University Press.

Appendix A

Data Collection Sheet for Time Sampling

Minute	Tail Shake	Feeding	Grooming	Display	Aggression	Submission
1						
2						
3						
4						
5						
6						
7						
8						
9						
10						

Each cell represents a 15-s observation interval. Recording intervals are not shown on this sheet.

Appendix B

Target Behaviors and Operational Definitions

Tail shake	Flicking tail back and forth rapidly several times in succession
Feeding	Actually taking food in beak
Grooming	Preening—using beak to fluff or pick at feathers
Display	Full (or almost full) extension of wings accompanied by several flaps, a slight lift in body posture, and a slight extension of neck—usually done when standing or when walking very slowly
Aggression	Nipping or threatening (by chasing or quickly swinging head toward another individual)
Submission	Running from or obviously avoiding close contact with another individual

* *

Formula for Calculating Interobserver Reliability When Doing Time Sampling

$$\text{reliability} = \frac{\text{agreements}}{\text{agreements} + \text{disagreements}} \times 100$$

(Agreements = number of intervals in which you both marked that the behavior occurred, and disagreements = number of intervals in which only one of you marked that the behavior occurred.)

* *

Appendix C

Postobservation Instructions

1. Individually, tally the number of intervals in which each behavior occurred. Then, answer the following questions:
   - Which behavior occurred *most* often?
   - Which behavior occurred *least* often?
   - Are there any behaviors that at least *appear* to be highly correlated? (That is, are there any behaviors that seem to always, or almost always, occur during the same intervals?)
2. Pair up with another student and compare your answers to the preceding questions. Did you disagree on any of them? If so, which one(s)? *Why* did you disagree?
3. Calculate the interobserver reliability between you and your partner for each behavior category. Identify the category that has the highest interobserver reliability and the category that has the lowest interobserver reliability.

   Tail shake =   Display =

   Feeding =   Aggression =

   Grooming =   Submission =

16 A Classroom Demonstration of Galileo's Distinction Between Objective and Subjective Reality

Ann N. Elliott
Emory & Henry College

This activity demonstrates Galileo's distinction between objective and subjective reality. It can be used in psychology courses to help students gain an intuitive understanding about how beliefs concerning the relation between objective and subjective reality influenced the emergence of psychology as a discipline. This demonstration promotes discussion about the status of psychology as a science and how subjective phenomena can be studied scientifically.

CONCEPT

The question of whether subjective phenomena are amenable to scientific inquiry has a long tradition. In the 1600s, Galileo drew a sharp distinction between *objective* (physical) *reality* and *subjective reality* (later referred to as primary and secondary qualities). He suggested that objective reality (e.g., quantity and shape) is absolute, unchangeable, and capable of precise mathematical description (Hergenhahn, 1997). Subjective reality, on the other hand, is created by the sensing organism and is relative and fluctuating. Galileo indicated that psychological (sensory) experiences (e.g., color, taste, and temperature) have no counterparts in the physical world and thus cannot be studied scientifically (Hergenhahn, 1997). This demonstration provides students with firsthand experience about Galileo's distinction between objective and subjective reality.

MATERIALS NEEDED

You will need room-temperature milk, room-temperature coffee, and two small disposable cups for each member of the class. Students are given the following rating sheet for each beverage: Which of the following statements best describes the first (or second) beverage?

    1. It was hot.
    2. It was warm.
    3. It was cool.
    4. It was cold.

INSTRUCTIONS

Approximately two hours prior to class, pour the beverages into cups and allow them to adjust to room temperature. Before beginning this activity, determine whether any students have a medical or religious reason for not participating (e.g., allergy to milk). To prevent students from knowing in advance what they will be drinking, list five or six common beverages and ask students to indicate if there are any reasons that they should not consume one of these liquids.

    With eyes closed, students drink an unnamed beverage (milk or coffee). They then rate its temperature on a 4-point scale ranging from 1 (*hot*) to 4 (*cold*). To rule out possible order or practice effects, half of the class may consume the milk first while the other half receives the coffee first. With eyes closed, students drink a second unnamed beverage (milk or coffee). They then rate its temperature on the same 4-point scale. Finally, students indicate in writing whether they think the drinks were the same temperature.

DISCUSSION

Although both drinks are the same temperature, most students will rate the coffee as cool/cold and the milk as warm. Their perceptions are subjectively determined by their past experience with and expectations about milk and coffee. Their perception of temperature illustrates subjective reality, which is relative and unfluctuating, rather than objective reality, which is absolute and unchangeable.

After reviewing their ratings for each beverage, students can discuss the principle demonstrated by the activity and why this principle may have been important to the emergence of psychology as a discipline. Next the instructor can introduce Galileo's distinction between objective and subjective reality. This demonstration can then be used to generate discussion about various topics relevant to psychology, such as (a) can consciousness be studied by the objective method of science, (b) can systematic mathematical relations between the physical and sensory (i.e., subjective) world be established, (c) how did this distinction influence Descartes's dualism, (d) is psychology a science, and (e) can other sciences, such as physics, objectively study the physical world independently of the subjective (sensory) world?

Students describe this classroom demonstration as both interesting and thought provoking. It provides a simple and concrete personal experience that generates an intuitive understanding of an abstract, yet conceptually important, distinction. This demonstration is particularly useful as an introduction to psychophysics, which challenged the claim that the subject matter of psychology was incompatible with scientific investigation. It can be used with other standard demonstrations of psychophysical principles as well (e.g., absolute and difference thresholds).

WRITING COMPONENT

Although a writing component is not essential for this activity, after the demonstration and before the class discussion, instructors may ask students to write a paragraph in which they discuss the principle illustrated by the demonstration and explain why this principle may have been important to the emergence of psychology as a discipline.

REFERENCE

Hergenhahn, B. R. (1997). *An introduction to the history of psychology* (3rd ed.). New York: Brooks/Cole.

SUGGESTED READING

Watson, R. I. (1979). *Basic writings in the history of psychology.* New York: Oxford University Press.

Watson, R. I. (1997). A prescriptive analysis of Descartes' psychological views. In L. T. Benjamin, Jr. (Ed.), *A history of psychology: Original sources and contemporary research* (2nd ed., pp. 34–48). New York: McGraw-Hill.

17 A Tasty Sample(r): Teaching About Sampling Using M&M's

Randolph A. Smith
Ouachita Baptist University

This tasty demonstration exposes students to the concept of sampling and gives them a real-life sampling problem. Each student receives a small package of plain M&M's and quantifies the sample by color. Students use these data to hypothesize the population's color distribution. By pooling samples, we achieve closer approximations of the population distribution. Students (and faculty) find this demonstration compelling.

CONCEPT

One concept that causes psychology students some difficulty is sampling. Students do not always understand the need for sampling or the relationship between a sample and its associated population. This knowledge is vital to understanding the research and inference process psychologists use.

MATERIALS NEEDED

Teachers will need a small package of plain M&M's for each student. If students have calculators, the activity will be easier for them. Teachers can design a data sheet if they desire. (Note that students who are on special diets or who have food allergies may want to abstain from this activity.)

INSTRUCTIONS

This M&M sampling demonstration enlivens the presentation of sampling and makes it more relevant to students. Buy large sacks of fun-size packs of plain M&M's and allow each student to choose an "intact random sample" (one pack) from the population of samples. Students examine their data, making a simple frequency distribution of the six M&M colors (blue, brown, green, orange, red, and yellow) on a data sheet you will provide (see appendix A). Scratch paper will also suffice. (You may need to caution your students to complete their data collection before any premature subject mortality occurs!) Because sample sizes typically vary somewhat (you can raise quality control as another interesting concept *and* practical application) and because you will want the students to make some inferences about the population based on their sample, have them convert their raw data into percentages.

Ask each student to generate a hypothesis about the distribution of M&M colors in the population based on the student's sample. These estimates generally vary considerably. Students then form pairs to pool their data (not literally, of course) and generate a joint hypothesis. Finally, we pool the data for the entire class to generate an overall hypothesis.

DISCUSSION

Students learn some valuable lessons about sampling from this exercise. You can increase the sample size of M&M's (e.g., by using larger individual packages or 1-, 2-, or 3-lb bags) and demonstrate how larger samples typically yield better estimates of the population. Students gain an appreciation of statistics applied to real-life situations.

Because students individually generate hypotheses from small samples (usually about 24 M&M's in a fun-size pack), the hypothesized population parameters are usually low in accuracy. However, as the students pair and combine their M&M's into larger samples, their estimates of the populaton proportions decrease in variability and more accurately approximate the population figures. When we combine the data for the entire class, variability decreases markedly, the samples become even better estimates of the population, and the hypotheses generally become more accurate.

Mars, Inc., appears to be a stickler about the percentages of colors for M&M's. Mars, Inc. (1993) published an "encyclopedia" that authoritatively states that plain M&M's are 30% brown, 20% each for red and yellow, and 10% each for green, orange, and blue (originally tan). (Should you wish to use peanut M&M's, you should expect 20% each for blue, brown, red, and yellow, with 10% each for green and orange). If you wish, you can compare the fit of your sample data to the population parameters using the chi square statistic. I have collected large samples of data (more than 1000 M&M's in each sample) on three different occasions. Interestingly enough, two of the three samples showed significant departure from the expected data ($p < .001$ in each case).

Students react quite favorably to this technique, especially in light of the fact that I teach statistics immediately before lunch. I can also report that this class session is probably the most lively of the semester.

WRITING COMPONENT

If you wish to use a writing assignment with this activity, I suggest having the students write a letter to Mars, Inc., that describes the outcome of the class's findings. It is always challenging for students to attempt to communicate statistical findings in plain and easy to understand language. Such an assignment will help both the teacher and students discover whether they truly understand the concepts of sampling and of drawing inferences from samples.

REFERENCE

M&M/Mars. (1993) *A little illustrated encyclopedia of M&M/Mars.* Hackettstown, NJ: Author.

SUGGESTED READING

For more information about sampling, samples, and populations, consult any introductory-level statistics textbook.

Appendix A

Frequency Distribution Data Sheet

Record your sample data and make a prediction of what you think the population of M&M's looks like:

	Blue	Brown	Green	Orange	Red	Yellow
Observed f						
Predicted %						

18 USING JELLY BEANS TO TEACH SOME CONCEPTS IN RESEARCH METHODOLOGY

Hank Rothgerber and Eric Anthony Day
Texas A&M University

This activity is a simple and relatively fast way to illustrate the following important concepts in research methodology: random assignment, interpreting main effects and interactions, and generating alternative explanations. The professor serves as the experimenter with students as the participants in a 2-by-2 between-subjects design that involves rating how much a jelly bean meets taste expectations. After the results have been collected, the instructor should display them in a graph or table and initiate an instructive class discussion.

CONCEPT

Students in a research methodology course need a thorough understanding of the following concepts: (a) *random assignment*, choosing members of a group so that each member has an equal chance of being selected; (b) *main effects*, the effect of one independent variable averaged across levels of the second independent variable, along with *interactions*, which occur when the effect of one variable depends on the level of another variable; and (c) *alternative explanations*, other explanations that are consistent with a study's pattern of results. This activity involves the whole class in an interesting experiment that will explain or review these important concepts. The experiment uses a 2 (typicality of the jelly bean: cherry versus buttered popcorn) by-2 (prior information of flavor: given versus not given) between-subjects design. Students are asked to rate the degree to which the jelly bean tasted like they expected it to taste. The exercise is most appropriate for a research methods course but could be used to illustrate an experiment in introductory psychology.

MATERIALS NEEDED

You will need an adequate supply of two flavors of jelly beans. One flavor should be very typical (we recommend cherry), and the other flavor should be unusual and not easily identifiable even after tasting it (we recommend buttered popcorn or cappuccino). Each student will also need envelopes and pieces of paper to be used as information sheets. Use a box to hold the envelopes. The only other materials needed are an overhead transparency asking students to rate the extent to which the jelly bean met taste expectations and a calculator to compute the results.

Caution: Note that some jelly beans are made with gelatin, which comes from animals. Strict vegetarians or students who are following a kosher diet may want to abstain.

Background

Randomly assign the entire class to one of four conditions (i.e., cherry-identified, cherry-unidentified, buttered popcorn-identified, buttered popcorn-unidentified). Although you can use any acceptable method for random assignment, we suggest that you assign the conditions using the following method: place each jelly bean in an envelope along with a blank information sheet or an information sheet that notes the flavor of the jelly bean. Before filling the envelopes, mark each information sheet with a *C* for cherry or a *B* for buttered popcorn, so that you can later identify each student's appropriate condition. Once the envelopes are filled, place them in the box and allow each student to pick an envelope out of a box.

In Class

Explain to students that you are going to conduct a taste test using various jelly beans. Each student will taste one jelly bean and then indicate whether it meets his or her expectations. Explain that you will provide more information about the different jelly beans when the experiment is completed.

Call students to the front of the classroom one at a time, and let them pick an envelope out of the box. Ask students to remain quiet, not discussing their information with anyone, and ask them to wait before eating the jelly bean. In addition, tell students not to smell their jelly bean. As soon as all students have received their jelly beans and information, tell them to read the information (if any) silently to themselves and then eat the jelly bean. Next, ask students to indicate on the information sheet the extent to which the jelly bean tasted like they expected using the scale anchors (1 = *very little*, 5 = *very much*) presented on the overhead. Collect the papers and compute the means for each condition. This should only require a few minutes for a medium-sized class, but having an assistant available might make the process more efficient. Before presenting the results to the class, give them some background about the experiment.

Explain that an individual's perceptions are not only influenced by the physical properties of stimuli but also by an individual's prior knowledge of the world (Bruner & Postman, 1949). That is, a person's prior knowledge of the world creates a bias in how one interprets incoming stimuli. For instance, the ability of individuals to identify objects in a scene is influenced by the context of the scene (Biederman, 1981; Palmer, 1975). When presented with a picture of a kitchen, one would be able to identify a loaf of bread more quickly than a mailbox. In the present experiment, individuals' taste perceptions are not only influenced by the physical properties of the jelly bean but also by expectations about how a jelly bean should taste. In this case, the typical jelly bean is sweet and fruity, not salty or bitter. Therefore, it was hypothesized that individuals would report a jelly bean that was sweet and fruity (i.e., cherry) as meeting their expectations to a greater extent than a jelly bean that was less sweet and more salty and bitter (i.e., buttered popcorn or cappuccino). Announce that some students in the class ate cherry jelly beans, a typical jelly bean flavor, and that others ate buttered popcorn, an atypical flavor.

Explain that some students were explicitly told the flavor of their jelly bean, whereas others were not. By providing information as to the flavor of the jelly bean, the context of the situation was altered in such a way that participants relied less on their preconceived notions of what a jelly bean should taste like. Moreover, the influence of prior information should have been greater with respect to participants who received the atypical flavor (buttered popcorn).

DISCUSSION At this point, you can ask the class several questions. What is the design of the experiment? As soon as it is correctly identified as a 2-by-2 between-subjects design, draw the design in a table. Ask students how they were placed into a condition. Have someone explain why the method of random assignment is so important. For example, what if all the females were assigned to taste cherry jelly beans and all the males were assigned to taste the buttered popcorn flavor? What if a disproportionate number of individuals who were familiar with atypical jelly bean flavors were assigned to taste buttered popcorn? How would these situations compromise the results? Next, ask students what they would predict based on the background information that you provided. Have them phrase their predictions in terms of main effects and interactions. They should realize that two main effects and one interaction are hypothesized. First, it is hypothesized that the cherry flavor will meet taste expectations more than the buttered-popcorn flavor. Second, it is hypothesized that taste expectations will be met to a greater extent when prior information about the flavor of the jelly bean is provided compared to when no prior information is provided. Finally, an interaction is predicted where the effect of providing information on expectations of flavor will be influenced by the flavor of the jelly bean. When the flavor is typical, prior information will not influence expectations of flavor; however, prior information will lead to a higher degree of meeting expectations of flavor when the flavor is atypical.

Put the class results in the table and graph the relationship. Table 18-1 and Figure 18-1 are examples of hypothetical results. Before interpreting the results in terms of main effects and interactions, ask the class what the results seem to indicate. Were the initial predictions supported? After discussing the results, formally present them to the class in a fashion similar to that in the following paragraph.

As seen in both Table 18-1 and Figure 18-1, the main effect of flavor is indicated in that, overall, the cherry jelly bean matched expectations ($M = 4.10$) better than buttered popcorn ($M = 2.90$). Likewise, the main effect of prior information is indicated in that, overall, when prior information was provided ($M = 4.00$), expectations were more closely met compared to when prior information was not provided ($M = 3.00$). The interaction between flavor and prior information, as depicted in the figure, is indicated in that providing information as to the flavor of the jelly bean prior to tasting led to a higher degree ($M = 3.80$) of meeting expectations of taste for the buttered-popcorn flavor compared to when no prior

Table 18-1. *Cell and Main Effect Means of Taste Expectations as a Function of Jelly Bean Flavor and Prior Information*

Flavor	Prior Information		Main Effect (flavor)
	No	Yes	
Cherry	4.00	4.20	4.10
Buttered popcorn	2.00	3.80	2.90
Main effect (information)	3.00	4.00	

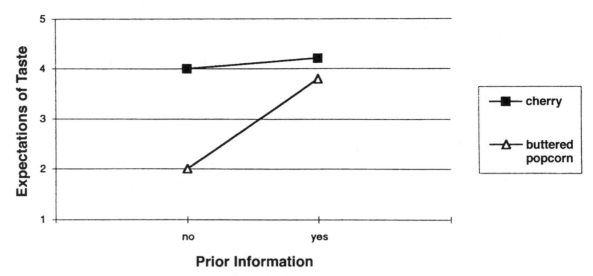

Figure 18-1.   Expectations of taste as a function of jelly bean flavor and prior information.

information was provided (*M* = 2.00). On the other hand, providing information about the flavor of the jelly bean prior to tasting did not lead to an appreciably higher degree (*M* = 4.20) of meeting expectations of taste for the cherry flavor compared to when no prior information was provided (*M* = 4.00). In general, the effect of providing information on expectations of flavor is influenced by the flavor of the jelly bean. When the flavor is typical, prior information does not influence expectations of flavor; however, prior information does lead to a higher degree of meeting expectations of flavor when the flavor is atypical.

WRITING COMPONENT

After discussing the results of the experiment, explain that you would like each student to write a brief (1- to 2-page) paper for the next class that summarizes the experiment. What was predicted? Why? What procedure did the experimenter follow? What were the results? Were the results consistent with the hypotheses?

Finally, ask the students to generate any alternative explanations for the results. How else might the results be explained? Once students have identified an alternative explanation, they should develop an experiment to test the alternative explanation against the hypothesized explanation. For example, a possible alternative explanation is that receiving any information, meaningful or not, about a food product (e.g., the brand or where it was purchased) increases the tendency for one to respond that the product tasted as expected. That is, people will be motivated to demonstrate that they were able to make use of the information even if the information was not actually useful. To test this explanation, one could conduct the same experiment, but instead of providing information about the flavor of the jelly bean, one would provide information that should not be useful in increasing a participant's understanding of how the jelly bean should taste (e.g., the location where the jelly bean was purchased).

Discuss any plausible alternative explanations that the class correctly identified, along with how to test them. Also, mention any inappropriate alternative explanations that the class produced and explain why they are not viable alternative explanations.

REFERENCES   Biederman, I. (1981). On the semantics of a glance at a scene. In M. Kubovy & J. Pomerantz (Eds.), *Perceptual organization* (pp. 213–253). Hillsdale, NJ: Erlbaum.

Bruner, J. S., & Postman, L. (1949). On the perception of incongruity: A paradigm. *Journal of Personality, 18,* 206–228.

Palmer, S. E. (1975). The effects of contextual scenes on the identification of objects. *Memory and Cognition, 3,* 519–526.

SUGGESTED READING   Huck, S. W., & Sandler, H. M. (1979). *Rival hypotheses: Alternative interpretations of data based conclusions.* New York: Harper & Row.

19 THE EFFECT OF GENDER ON THE NUMBER OF SHOES OWNED: GATHERING DATA FOR STATISTICAL AND METHODOLOGICAL DEMONSTRATIONS

Steven E. Stern
University of Pittsburgh at Johnstown

This activity illustrates that the number of pairs of shoes owned by a sample of males and females can be a useful data set for statistics and methods classes. The effect of gender on shoes is large and practically guarantees statistically significant effects with small sample sizes. This exercise facilitates discussion of topics such as the impact and treatment of outliers, sample size and power, meta-analysis, operationalization of variables, and the validity of self-report measures. A discussion of ethical issues is included.

CONCEPT
The difference in the number of shoes owned by women compared to that owned by men can provide an effective way to demonstrate several statistical and methodological issues. Using a survey, students collect data on the number of shoes owned by friends and acquaintances. Unlike many data sets provided in textbooks, the data are genuine, behavioral, and easy to comprehend. The effect is robust, and most students find a statistically significant effect in a data set with a sample size of 20 (10 males and 10 females). Data from four students and a professor during a summer class showed that females owned a mean of 16.82 pairs whereas males reported a mean of 6.42, $t(98) = 7.80$, $p < .0001$, $r = .62$.

INSTRUCTIONS
During the first week of class, have each student collect data from 10 males and 10 females (the ethical considerations of such data collections are discussed later). Students record the number of shoes owned by each participant. The target question ("How many pairs of shoes do you own?") can be easily embedded in a shoe-ownership questionnaire. Instruct students not to ask both members of a couple (e.g., spouses) as this would violate the assumption of independence associated with some statistical tests. The instructor should also encourage uniform wording of the target question if data are gathered orally.

ETHICAL CONSIDERATIONS
This activity requires students to collect data from human participants. It is imperative that ethical issues be taken into consideration. Instructors need to adhere to their institutions' procedures for conducting research on human participants. In many cases, this will simply require the instructor to submit a proposal to the institution's Institutional Review Board (IRB) that would cover the activity for the entire class.

Although this activity basically presents no risk to those involved, all human participants are entitled to informed consent. This can be done verbally, with a script developed in the class that would let participants know the purpose of the study and the confidentiality of their data. The consent procedures should also be approved by the institution's IRB.

DISCUSSION   With samples of 20 participants, most students will find a large and statistically significant ($p < .05$) effect for gender on number of shoes owned, with females owning more pairs of shoes than males. This difference should be obvious when students graph the data set (e.g., frequency histograms, box plots), calculate measures of central tendency, and test for differences between the means. If the entire class aggregates their data, students should be able to see clearly the effect of an increased sample size on p values.

Use this activity to discuss additional statistical and methodological issues. Some of these issues are discussed next.

Effect and Treatment of Outliers

Unlike many of the data sets students routinely collect in a classroom setting (e.g., height), this data set is likely to produce outliers. Students can detect outliers in their data sets by constructing box plots. Once the outliers are detected, students can calculate summary statistics as well as the actual t test on data sets with and without the outliers. Comparisons will illustrate the effects of outliers on data analysis. Discuss the practice of removing outliers from data sets.

Effect of Sample Size on Statistical Power and Effect Size

When students collect data from 20 participants and aggregate the class data, the students see how the larger sample size leads to more statistical power and a smaller p value. They also see how sample size relates to effect size (e.g., point-biserial r, Cohen's d).

Operationalization of Variables

Teachers of research methods courses can use this activity to help students understand the challenge inherent in operationalizing even the simplest of variables. "How many pairs of shoes do you own?" seems like a simple question, but what constitutes a shoe? Are boots included? How about galoshes, sandals, or flip-flops? Do shoes owned but no longer worn count? Teachers facilitate appreciation of this issue by having students work together to shape the wording of the research question.

Validity of Self-Report Measures

Teachers can also use this demonstration to illustrate issues surrounding self-report measures. Discussion should be aimed at evaluating how the data might have differed if people had counted their shoes instead of estimating the number. This thread can lead to discussions of selective memory, social desirability, evaluation apprehension, self-presentation, exaggeration, and other biases that affect participants' answers to both sensitive and nonsensitive questions.

Meta-Analysis of Results

In an advanced methods course, the teacher can choose to have the students view their data as separate studies. The results of these studies can then be combined meta-analytically.

Use the following formula for combining significance levels of three or more studies (Rosenthal & Rosnow, 1991): $Z = (\Sigma\ Z_i)/(\sqrt{K})$; where Z is the standardized score associated with each student's result and K is the number of studies. (Individual findings disagreeing with the general hypothesis should be given negative Z scores.)

The students need to transform each of their p values (one-tailed) into a Z value (e.g., if $p = .05$, then $z = 1.645$). These Z values are summed for the entire class. The students then divide this sum by the square root of the number of studies being combined (K). The resulting Z statistic can be interpreted with a standard table for converting Z scores into p values.

Discussion of Gender Differences

Students generally find this demonstration amusing. It can, however, provide the opportunity for a serious discussion of what seems to be a trivial gender difference. Much of what has been found to differ between the sexes has been pinned on biological differences. Is shoe ownership biological? Students should hypothesize reasons (e.g., norms, personality differences) why women tend to own more shoes and suggest research that could test these hypotheses.

Students should also be able to discuss this topic in terms of potential cultural differences. Is this difference found only in this country? Would we find this gender difference in all segments of our own country?

WRITING COMPONENT

Because the data are easy for the students to understand, the effect of gender on number of shoes owned makes a good topic with which to introduce APA style in a statistics course. For their individual data sets, students should be able to construct sentences such as "There was a significant effect for gender on the number of shoes a person owns, t (18) = 5.57, $p < .001$."

In a research methods course, expand this data collection exercise into a small laboratory paper. Include a discussion section addressing methodological caveats such as the use of self-report measures and any possible difficulties related to how the variable was operationalized.

REFERENCE

Rosenthal, R., & Rosnow, R. L. (1991). *Essentials of behavioral research: Methods and data analysis* (2nd ed.). New York: McGraw-Hill.

20 PROBABILITY DISTRIBUTIONS WITH REAL SOCIAL JUDGMENT DATA

Jane A. Jegerski
Elmhurst College

This activity is suited for a general psychology, social psychology, or statistics class. It presents a concrete way to demonstrate the binomial distribution, which in this case is a close approximation to the normal curve. Students generate the data for the distribution from a memorable class exercise on overconfidence in detecting classmates' lying.

CONCEPT

Instructors often use coin tosses or dice games to introduce probability to students in statistics classes. Probability distributions that have only two event classes (e.g., heads or tails, odd or even number) are the simplest and easiest to plot and can be constructed with data generated in class by students tossing coins or rolling dice. Although students (who may be prompted to think of alternative career paths) usually greet such exercises enthusiastically, there is the risk that students will forever associate the binomial distributions generated by these processes only with games of chance, not real-world psychological events.

Social psychology has demonstrated to us many times that, in general, the accuracy of our social judgments is usually poor to mediocre; sometimes they are no more accurate than random guessing, and we would do just as well tossing a coin to make social decisions. This can be demonstrated by modifying a Bolt (1996) class exercise for social psychology. The exercise is based on the highly reliable overconfidence phenomenon (Dunning, Griffin, Milojkovic, & Ross, 1990) and uses student judgments of truthfulness of a class peer. I have discovered from years of conducting the Bolt exercise that undergraduates are not only reliably overconfident in this task but they can judge truthfulness with the same success, or distribution of outcomes, as they would have using a coin toss strategy (heads she's lying, tails she's telling the truth). Thus this exercise can be used to generate meaningful social data to demonstrate a close approximation to a normal distribution (or, actually, a binomial distribution where the probabilities of success or failure are equal and *n*, or number of students in the class, is equal to or greater than 10).

If the students are familiar with the theoretical underpinnings of the normal curve, this exercise is ideal for extending students' knowledge to another probability distribution, the binomial. If, however, the students have had less experience with statistics, this exercise can increase understanding of the theoretical basis of probability distributions using the more familiar normal curve.

MATERIALS NEEDED

You will need five slips of paper labeled "T" or "*Truth*" and five labeled "L" or "*Lie*," folded and placed in a container or envelope.

Start the exercise by asking students, "How can we tell when a person, someone we know about as well as the other students in this class, is lying?" Students will volunteer answers like "the person will not make eye contact, will fidget," and so forth. I added this part of the exercise to serve as public commitment for the belief that people *are* able to detect when others are truthful or not.

Solicit 10 volunteers, 1 each for the 10 nonembarrassing topics (Bolt suggests favorite meal, grade-school experience, favorite vacation, earliest memory, high-school experience, favorite professor, influential person, surprising talent, geo-graphical living preference, and something interesting about a family member). Each volunteer is given a topic and invited to draw a slip of paper to determine if she or he is to be truthful or not. Then each student gets to tell his or her personal anecdote (truth or lie) after which the class members write down their guesses of whether it was a truth or lie. The audience members also record to what percent they are confident that their guess is correct. After all the student volunteers have told their anecdotes, they reveal which were truths and which were lies. Then all students compute the percentage correct; for volunteers, the score is derived by multiplying the number correct by 11%; for all other students each correct answer is worth 10%. Also, have the students compute their average confidence score (dividing by 10 or 9, depending on whether or not the student was a volunteer).

To demonstrate overconfidence, get a count of how many students were more correct than confident (*few*) and how many students were more confident than correct (*many*). The few students who were highly correct will persist, however, in believing that they are skillful in detecting liars and will fail to appreciate that chance can account for their high scores (and their classmates' low scores). To demonstrate that a distribution of chance events can predict the students' scores, have students call out their percentage correct, one at a time, while you plot them above a line on the chalkboard (see Fig. 20-1).

Ask students, "How many would you expect to get right if you were flipping a coin? How does this distribution compare with one we would get if we had flipped a coin to let heads determine truth and tails to determine lie? What do the results of this exercise tell us about our ability to detect lying?" (Be sure to tell students that the normal curve is a theoretical curve and that if we did this exercise an infinite number of times we would acquire the theoretical curve.)

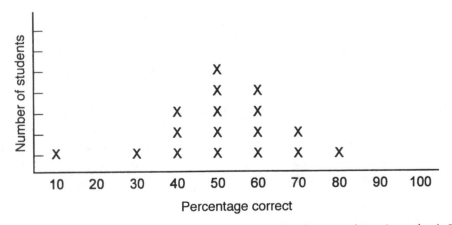

Figure 20-1. Sample plotting of student accuracy scores for detecting lying (one class). Students whose scores are in multiples of 11% should round up or down to the nearest multiple of 10%.

DISCUSSION Even for smaller classes, the distribution turns out to look fairly normal, or what would be expected to happen with a chance process (like tossing a coin). As Lowry (1989) has pointed out, distributions of this type approximate the normal curve when *n* is about 10 or higher. Even small classes of about 15 usually generate a fairly normally shaped curve. (Once, the class distribution was skewed toward the higher percentages. Since then I have made a point of keeping sets of data from several previous classes with me to demonstrate what *usually* happens in case I get another aberrant class result.) This exercise could be used to present some basic probabilistic concepts in courses taken before statistics. Or it can be used in statistics or other advanced courses to introduce the idea of binomial distributions.

WRITING COMPONENT To check students' comprehension of the concepts introduced in this exercise, have them write on one or both of the following statements:

1. Write a definition and description of the overconfidence phenomenon for a high school senior who may or may not have had psychology.
2. Some researchers have made attempts to debunk ESP by demonstrating that precognitive or telepathic responses from individuals reputed to have ESP ability are identical to responses generated by chance processes. Would such evidence convince you that ESP was a sham? Why or why not?

Students can discuss their answers in pairs for 2 min and then share the consensual answers in the large group involving the entire class.

REFERENCES Bolt, M. (1996). *Instructor's manual to accompany Myers' social psychology.* New York: McGraw-Hill.

Dunning, D., Griffin, D. W., Milojkovic, J. D., & Ross, L. (1990). The overconfidence effect in social prediction. *Journal of Personality and Social Psychology, 58,* 568–581.

Lowry, R. (1989). *The architecture of chance.* New York: Oxford University Press.

SUGGESTED READING Hays, W. L. (1981). *Statistics* (3rd ed.). New York: Holt, Rinehart & Winston.

Myers, D. (1996). *Social psychology* (5th ed.). New York: McGraw-Hill.

21 PETS AND PREDICTION: UNDERSTANDING SUPPRESSOR VARIABLES

Kristin K. Woolley
Texas A&M University

Understanding suppressor variables and how they operate in multiple regression analyses is crucial in reporting accurate research results. However, many researchers are unfamiliar with the influences and importance of these variables. Suppressor variables tend to appear useless as separate predictors, but may in fact change the prediction value of other variables and considerably alter research outcomes. This activity allows instructors of research design courses to demonstrate the concepts of multiple regression and suppressor variables.

CONCEPT

Social scientists are interested in the elements that explain or predict certain human behaviors. Predicting behavior is often accomplished by assembling a set of traits, attitudes, test scores, and so forth and testing their relationship to the behavior in question. Multiple regression is a statistical method for studying the separate and collective contributions of one or more predictors to the variance of a dependent variable. Because regression is primarily based on the correlations between the predictor variable and the dependent variable, a simple demonstration using students and what they have in common can be used to explain the basic concept of the correlational nature of regression. In addition, this activity can be used to encourage students to discuss the strength and meaningfulness of relationships among variables and to introduce suppressor variables to the class.

MATERIALS NEEDED

You will need an overhead projector or chalkboard.

INSTRUCTIONS

Choose one volunteer to act as the dependent variable. This person should own *one* house pet, and secretly find out what kind (let's say a dog) as this characteristic will be used later to demonstrate suppressor effects. Choose one or two students to serve as "researchers." If you wish, you can provide them with lab coats to identify them. Have the volunteer come to the front of the class and list on the chalkboard approximately four characteristics about him- or herself (e.g., I own a car, I play a team sport, *I own a house pet*, or I have a sister). Try to avoid general identifiers that apply to everyone (e.g., I like music, I am a male/female) as these will confound the groups. The job of the researchers is to organize the rest of the class into groups that fall into the four categories or independent variables identified on the chalkboard.

Begin by having the groups uncorrelated. Instruct the students to choose *one* of the four categories that they actually have in common with the dependent variable, even if they belong to two or more of the four categories. Have the students in each group form a circle with their members. Students who do not belong to any of the four categories should form a single group. They can represent other independent variables that are interesting, but not correlated with the dependent variable. Quietly inform this group that they will act as a suppressor variable and that their special group characteristic is that they own a different type of house pet than the dependent variable (let's say a cat). Once the four groups are organized, have each group announce how it relates to the dependent variable and its group size.

Draw the uncorrelated groups on the chalkboard making the circles the same size, but vary the amount of overlap between the dependent variable (X) and each of the uncorrelated predictor variables (A, B, C, D). The size of the overlap represents the number of students (n) that share the characteristics of the volunteer as presented in Figure 21-1. The remainder of each circle that does not intersect the student volunteer's circle represents part of the independent variable that does not help explain the dependent variable (i.e., students who own a car and also own a bike or a skateboard). Explain that the differing amount of overlap of each of the four groups also describes the *strength* or *value* of the independent variable as predictor of the dependent variable. This large overlap means that all of the independent variables chosen, owning just a car (not a car and a bike or skateboard) is the characteristic in the population that is most related to the student volunteer. Also, you can have students talk about what problems they see in organizing the variables this way (e.g., Are traits in reality this clear-cut? What if there are many variables? How do you decide which variables should be chosen to describe the dependent variable in question?).

Next, ask the dependent variable (volunteer) to announce to the class that

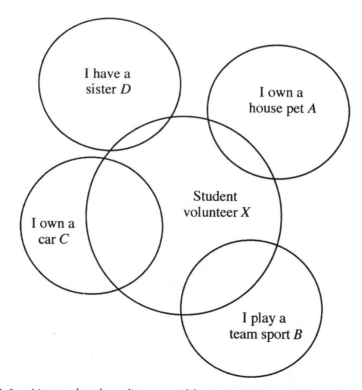

Figure 21-1.   *Uncorrelated predictor variables A, B, C, D, and dependent variable X.*

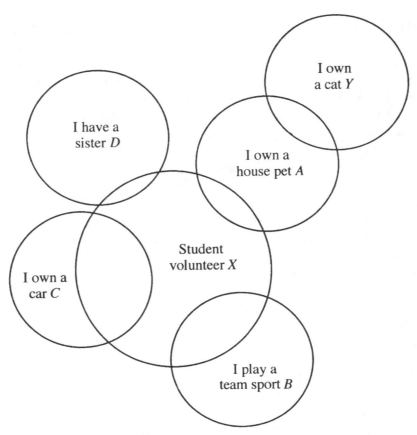

Figure 21-2. Uncorrelated predictor variables A, B, C, D, dependent variable X, and suppressor variable Y.

she or he is a dog owner. Ask the suppressor group you previously identified to announce what characteristic it represents that is uncorrelated with the dependent variable (i.e., these group members are cat owners). Have the researchers rearrange the original house pet owner group into a combined dog owner and other house pet owner group and instruct this rearranged group to stand in a circle. Have the cat owners from the original house pet owner group more into a new circle with the suppressor group so that all cat owners stand in their own circle close to the house pet owner group. Explain how the introduction of the cat owner group removed the measurement artifact or "cleaned up" the original house pet owner group and now only those that own house pets that are dogs explain the dependent variable. This occurs because the new suppressor variable group (cat owners) more accurately represents the variance in the independent variable (house pet owners) and, in turn, more clearly explains the variance in the dependent variable (student volunteer) even though the suppressor variable group is not *directly* related to the dependent variable. An example of this new configuration is depicted in Figure 21-2.

DISCUSSION   Go over the different parts of the multiple regression model (DV, IV, correlations, etc.). *Dependent variables* represent the construct the researcher is trying to measure, such as the characteristics of an "A" student. *Independent variables* are the factors that the researcher uses to predict the construct, such as the number of

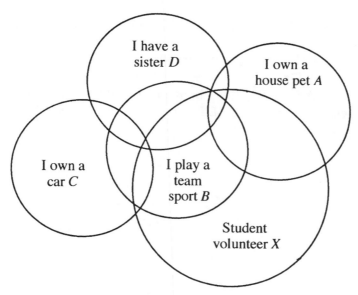

Figure 21-3. Correlated predictor variables A, B, C, D, and dependent variable X.

hours a student studies. Some independent variables are better predictors than others, and researchers use correlations to measure how well the independent variables explain the dependent variables. Simply put, multiple regression analyses determine the best set of independent variables that describe the dependent variable.

Discuss how the first part of the experiment showed uncorrelated independent variables. Have students imagine how much more complicated the analysis of the dependent variable would be if the predictor variables were correlated with each other as depicted in Figure 21-3. Highly correlated predictor variables may make it more difficult to pinpoint how the predictor variables represent the variance of the dependent variable. Explain how important it is to identify clearly and accurately the independent variables that are used in research. In this example, it is more accurate to say that *dog ownership* explained the dependent variable, not just *house pet ownership*.

To further enhance this activity, have the students write down all the predictors they can think of that would represent an "A" in the course (e.g., paying attention during class). Have them identify any possible suppressor variables (e.g., getting enough sleep the night before class) that may not be directly related to getting an "A," but would more accurately represent the predictive value of paying attention in class. Conclude the discussion by going over how suppressor variables can change the way predictor variables explain the dependent variable by removing the contaminating influences within the predictors (see Conger, 1974).

REFERENCE   Conger, A. J. (1974). A revised definition for suppressor variables: A guide to their identification and interpretation. *Educational and Psychological Measurement, 34,* 35–46.

SUGGESTED   Holling, H. (1983). Suppressor structures in the general linear model. *Educational*
READING   *and Psychological Measurement, 43,* 1–99.

Horst, P. (1966). *Psychological measurement and prediction.* Belmont, CA: Wadsworth.

Pedhazur, E. J. (1982). *Multiple regression in behavioral research: Explanation and prediction* (2nd ed.). New York: Holt, Rinehart & Winston.

Smith, R. L., Ager, J. W., & Williams, D. L. (1992). Suppressor variables in multiple regression/correlation. *Educational and Psychological Measurement, 52,* 17–29.

22 SURVEY CONSTRUCTION AND ANALYSIS

Howard F. Gallup
Lafayette College

This is a laboratory activity, used in a course in research design and analysis, that will occupy the students for several weeks. Working as a team, students selects their own topic, write survey items, construct the survey form, and administer it to an anonymous, convenience sample of the population. All responses are scored and collected in a data file for statistical manipulation. Students write a report in APA style based on analyses of some portion of the items, using demographic variables to predict responses.

CONCEPTS

Several concepts are inherent in this activity: writing items that can be interpreted clearly, using statistical analysis of data, interpreting results, obtaining a sample and assessing how representative it is of a population, dealing with ethical issues with human respondents, and writing a report.

MATERIALS NEEDED

You will need a word processor or typewriter, copy machine for mass producing survey forms, and a computer with a statistical package, such as SAS or SPSS.

INSTRUCTIONS

Selecting a topic can be done in several ways. Students can be permitted to brainstorm and select the topic, advisably with a veto power by the instructor, or the instructor can suggest or mandate topics. The former option has the advantage of built in interest in the outcome, but the latter option may encourage students to cover more important problems or perform a service for the institution. After selecting a topic, students should be asked to write items independently and to bring them to the next class meeting where they can be merged. A handout on good Likert-type item construction (we used values from 1 to 9 with verbal anchor points) can be read and discussed before students construct their items. The pool of items can be culled by discarding duplicates and items not deemed to be usable, such as those with double negatives or those too complex for a single response. (I discussed the selected items with the students, usually choosing not to challenge one or two items that were problematical, leaving them for the students to deal with later.) Discuss the use of demographic areas as predictor variables and for comparison of the sample of respondents with the population. Most of our scales had six to eight demographic items (sex, college class, fraternity/sorority/independent status, division of the college [natural science, social science, etc.], or major, depending on the survey topic) and scales were kept to about 25 to 30 response items. It may be more efficient to let a class choose a subcommittee for final preparation of the scale.

Collect data by requiring each member of the class to administer the survey during the next week to 16 people: two men and two women from each of the four college classes. (Our sections usually had from 16 to 20 students, providing from 256 to 320 respondents. Although neither sex nor class size is evenly distributed at Lafayette College, both are fairly close. This made for two demographic variables with equal ns in all subgroupings, an advantage when an interaction effect is significant and analytic comparisons are performed.) Keep respondents anonymous by having them slip their completed surveys into a manila envelope. My students were honor bound not to look at the surveys until time to score them.

All completed surveys are then scored and brought to the computer lab where each student, working with the instructor, can enter the data into a SAS or SPSS file. The complete file is then copied onto the students' floppy disks. The students, working in teams of two, are responsible for selecting some minimum number of response items to be analyzed using two-way analysis of variance, the major topic in statistics in the course. They can also be encouraged to look at the data in other ways, such as using chi-square and correlation coefficients and constructing tables and figures. Require each team to write a research report in APA style, although students could separate at this point and work alone.

DISCUSSION

Discussion of the results depends partly on the topic chosen. However, I make it a point to gather demographic data for the entire college population and to talk with my students about the representativeness of a stratified convenience sample as compared to a random sample and the problems involved in drawing any conclusions about the population. (Lafayette College has about 2100 undergraduate students, close to 50% men and 50% women, and with nearly 25% in each of the four years. With lab sections from 16 to 20, our sample sizes ranged from 256 to 320 respondents, 12% to 15% of the student body. On all demographic items, our samples were within 3 percentage points of the population.) In class we discussed ethical issues, including the necessity for protecting anonymity of respondents, especially in a small residential college where everyone knows or recognizes most of the respondents. We also talked about how research design and statistical analysis can be of use to society.

Table 22-1 lists the topics covered by my students. Most of the topics were student selected, but several were not. After our reputation had been established through reports by me to the college newspaper, I offered our services to various administrators. Several changes were made in health and counseling services, in

Table 22-1. *Survey Topics From a Course in Research Design and Analysis at Lafayette College*[a]

Issues in sorority/fraternity rush	Attitudes toward smoking
Satisfaction with Lafayette	Attitudes toward drugs
Social life at Lafayette	Relationships at Lafayette
Body image and sexual behavior	Advising at Lafayette[b]
Counseling services at Lafayette[b]	Medical services at Lafayette[b]
Attitudes toward an honor code	Attitudes toward alcohol consumption
Career planning and placement[b]	Political attitudes and poll (election year)
University/gown relations	Rape and sexual assault
Relationships and homophobia	Academic stress and social life

[a] Copies of the surveys are available on request.
[b] These surveys were conducted for Lafayette College administrators and all data, analyzed and presented in tables, were shared with them in a complete report written by me.

career planning, and in the meal plans (part of the health services survey) based on our reports; academic advising was not modified after this survey.

Students explore research design in field settings and two-way analysis of variance for this activity in an exercise that requires them to perform in a professional manner with their colleagues in the course as well as with those outside it. Given the close matching of samples to population on demographic variables assessed, the results provide some insight into attitudes of the students at the college. The modification of college services, based on our results, will gain the students the increased respect of their colleagues across the campus. The students also learn that research design and statistical analysis can be useful in the real world.

SUGGESTED READING

Davidson, F. (1996). *Principles of statistical data handling.* Thousand Oaks, CA: Sage.

Goddard, R. D., III, & Villanova, P. (1996). Designing surveys and questionnaires for research. In F. T. L. Leong & J. T. Austin (Eds.), *The psychology research handbook: A guide for graduate students and research assistants* (pp. 85–97). Thousand Oaks, CA: Sage.

Keppel, G., Saufley, W. H., Jr., & Tokunaga, H. (1992). *Introduction to design & analysis* (2nd ed.). New York: W. H. Freeman and Company.

Ray, W. J. (1997). *Methods: toward a science of behavior and experience* (5th ed.). Pacific Grove, CA: Brooks/Cole.

23 CHECKING A TEST'S RELIABILITY AND VALIDITY

Harold Takooshian
Fordham University

This hands-on activity uses a standardized feminism survey to show students how to convert an attitude or trait into a score, then statistically check the reliability and validity of the scale.

CONCEPT

How do we determine the reliability and validity of a test? This simple activity spans two class meetings and is designed to give undergraduates some hands-on experience on how an attitude or a trait is converted into a score and then statistically checked for reliability and validity. This exercise is suitable for any course in which students can learn to calculate a Pearson correlation—testing, methods, statistics, or even introduction.

MATERIALS NEEDED

You will need the Feminism Survey, scoring grid, and reliability worksheet (see appendixes A, B, and C) and, if convenient, the section on test validity/reliability from a related textbook (e.g., Anastasi & Urbina, 1997, pp. 95–97).

INSTRUCTIONS

During Class 1

The students' first step in the activity is self-scoring one test. Give students 10 min in class to complete the Feminism Survey (Takooshian & Stuart, 1983), which assesses one's belief in the equality of women and men (see appendix A). Once students have completed the survey, show them how to hand-score their own scales. To do this, give them 10 min to overlook the five embedded items (10, 13, 16, 19, and 20), which actually measure authoritarianism, and score the remaining 15 items ("2" for every response on the far left, "1" for every *N*, and "0" for every response on the right). The total for these items will give them a feminist score ranging between 0 and 30. (The mean feminist score for a representative group of adult women in New York was 17.2 in 1983 and 17.6 in 1997.)

Next you will have students pair off into two-person teams and assign each team to distribute at least 10 Feminism Surveys by the next class—five should go to expected feminists and five to expected antifeminists (e.g., high/low education, political liberals/conservatives, younger/older women)—to see if the scores turn out as expected. (*Note:* Students unable to pair up can work alone.) Give each student 10 Feminism Surveys plus the two assignment sheets—the scoring grid and the reliability worksheet (see appendixes B and C)—to be completed by the next class meeting. Take another 15 min to explain step by step (outlined in the following section) how to complete the grid, the reliability scatterplot, and Pearson *r*.

Before Class 2

Once students have collected their 10-plus completed surveys, the students should enter each response as a 2/1/0 score in the scoring grid. The Feminism Survey is structured so all responses on the left (regardless of D or A) are scored 2 points as profeminist, 1 point for neutral, and all right-column responses are coded 0 as antifeminist. On the scoring grid, each respondent gets one column. Be sure to group the expected feminists in the first 5-plus columns to the left, then the antifeminists in 5-plus columns to the right.

After eliminating the filler items (10, 13, 16, 19, and 20), students should calculate an odd-score for each column by adding the odd-numbered items (1 + 3 + 5 + 7 + 9 + 11 + 15 + 17) and then an even-score by adding the even-numbered items (2 + 4 + 6 + 8 + 12 + 14 + 18). They can then arrive at a total feminist score by adding all 15 items. Write these O, E, T scores in the space below each column.

To check the validity of the scale, students should calculate the mean feminist scores of the expected high and low columns, to see if the expected high scorers did indeed score higher than the expected low scorers.

To determine if the scale is reliable, have students use the test reliability worksheet to answer items 1, 2, and 3 by scatterplotting all 10 pairs of odd–even scores. They can then calculate the Pearson correlation.

During Class 2

Review students' findings. Take 15 min to list each team's high versus low means and reliability *r* results on the chalkboard. With the class, try to discern a pattern across the teams' results.

Optional Additions

If time and interest permit, consider a few added exercises: (a) To complete the fifth item on the reliability worksheet, show students how to apply a Spearman–Brown correction to their obtained *r*, using the short formula

$$rsb = 2r/1 + r$$

found in many textbooks (e.g., Anastasi & Urbina, 1997, pp. 95–97). (b) Shuffle the assigned sheets, so each team double-checks another team's submission for the following class, particularly if one or more teams had findings that were highly discrepant from the others. (c) Pages 471 to 473 in Carole Beere's (1990) handbook on gender roles reviews psychometric data on the Feminism Survey; distribute this so students can compare their findings with published validity and reliability data. (d) The five-item authoritarianism scale (10, 13, 16, 19, and 20) by Janowitz and Marvick (1973) can also be scored with the same 2/1/0 method, to yield an authoritarianism score ranging from 0 (*low*) to 10 (*high*). Students who want extra practice computing a correlation can score their 10 authoritarian scales, then correlate this with the corresponding feminism scores—which normally correlate negatively, about $r = -.40$.

Several issues concerning validity and reliability make effective discussion topics. For example, ask students to consider whether the Feminism Survey is high in face validity. If students answer yes, ask them whether faking and the need for approval affect respondents' scores. Students might also be asked to think about how the reliability worksheet can be used to check the test–retest and alternative form reliability of the Feminism Survey.

Many students will undoubtedly notice that the *A*s and *D*s on the Feminism Survey are occasionally reversed. This reversal is meant to reduce response set as well as simplify hand scoring. Students should be asked to consider whether the reversal is likely to affect the accuracy of one's scores. Lastly, the feminism scale was standardized in 1983, and it is possible that certain terms, such as *unisex* fashions (Item 4) and *women's liberationists* (Item 14) are outdated. Students could be asked to consider whether a test's value is reduced when possibly dated terms are not updated.

REFERENCES

Anastasi, A., & Urbina, S. P. (1997). *Psychological testing* (7th ed.). Upper Saddle River, NJ: Prentice-Hall.

Beere, C. A. (Ed.). (1990). *Gender roles: A handbook of tests and measures.* New York: Greenwood.

Janowitz, M., & Marvick, D. (1973). Authoritarianism and political behavior. In J. P. Robinson & P. R. Shaver (Eds.), *Measures of social psychological attitudes* (Rev. ed.). Ann Arbor, MI: Institute for Social Research.

Takooshian, H., & Stuart, C. R. (1983). Ethnicity and feminism among American women: Opposing social trends? *International Journal of Group Tensions, 13,* 100–105.

Appendix A

Opinion Survey

Americans seem to have divided opinions about the feminist movement. We are research-ers who would appreciate your frank opinions on the statements below. For each item, circle whether you agree (A), disagree (D), or have no opinion (N). This survey is anony-mous. Thank you.

1. D N A Women who do the same work as men should not necessarily get the same salary.
2. D N A A woman should have more responsibility than a man in caring for a child.
3. D N A Women should have more responsibility than men in doing household du-ties.
4. A N D Unisex clothes are a good idea, so men and women can dress more alike.
5. D N A By nature, women are more emotional than men.
6. D N A By nature, women enjoy sex less than men.
7. D N A When I meet a woman for the first time, I prefer to call her Miss or Mrs. rather than Ms.
8. D N A I would prefer to call myself Miss or Mrs. rather than Ms.
9. D N A A woman should adopt her husband's last name when they marry.
10. A N D Human nature being what it is, there will always be war and conflict.
11. A N D Married women with young children should work outside the home if they wish.
12. A N D I'd say it's perfectly all right for a husband to stay at home while the wife supports the family.
13. A N D People cannot be trusted.
14. D N A I'd say women's liberationists rock the boat too much.
15. D N A Many women who deny their femininity are actually confused people.
16. A N D A few leaders could make this country better than all the laws and talk.
17. D N A The use of obscene language is more unbecoming for a woman than for a man.
18. D N A The needs of a family should come before a woman's career.
19. A N D Most people who don't get ahead just don't have enough willpower.
20. A N D An insult to one's honor should not be forgotten.

21. What is your general feeling about the feminist movement? (more space on back)

_____

22. Age: ____under 20   ____20–29   ____30–39   ____40–49
    ____50–59   ____60+

23. Schoolwork: ____Grammar school   ____High school
    ____Some college   ____College graduate   ____Grad school

24. Marital status: ____Single   ____Married   ____Widowed
    ____Separated   ____Divorced

25. Are you now employed outside the home? ____No   ____Yes, part time
    ____Yes, full time.   If yes, what is your occupation: _____

26. I am ____female   ____male

27. (Optional:) Any comments to add here? (more space on back)

Appendix B

Psychological Test Scoring Sheet

Name: _____

Scale: _____

Respondent #

Item 1
2
3
4
5
6
7
8
9
10*
11
12
13*
14
15
16*
17
18
19*
20*

Odd: _ _ _ _ _ _ _ _ _ _ _ _ _ _ _ _ _ _

Even: _ _ _ _ _ _ _ _ _ _ _ _ _ _ _ _ _ _

Total: _ _ _ _ _ _ _ _ _ _ _ _ _ _ _ _ _ _

Appendix C

Test Reliability

Name: _____   /   /
Worksheet Scale: _____

How reliable is the attitude scale our class completed this month? Compute this here.

1. Type of reliability you are checking here is _____.
    Explain.

2. Scatterplot the two scores per person. Be sure to clearly mark the two axes.

3. Direction. Is the apparent relation of the two sets of scores negative, 0, or positive?
    Explain.

4. Magnitude. What is the correlation of the two sets of scores above?

$$r = \frac{N\Sigma XY - (\Sigma X)(\Sigma Y)}{\sqrt{[N\Sigma X2 - (\Sigma X)2][N\Sigma Y2 - (\Sigma Y)2]}}$$

5. Significance. Is this a reliable scale, according to your data? Explain.

CHAPTER III
BIOPSYCHOLOGY AND ANIMAL BEHAVIOR

The first two exercises in this chapter use fingers and toes to teach about the human brain. Activity 24 uses a toe-touching exercise to challenge students' views of the brain as "hard wired," whereas Activity 25 has students use their hands to learn about brain anatomy.

In Activity 26, students learn about circadian rhythms and arousal by recording their body temperature at regular intervals over a 72-hr period and, at the same time, they rate themselves on a sleepiness–alertness scale.

The last two exercises focus on animal behavior in extra classroom activities. Activity 27 involves studying the flight distance of birds in relation to manipulations made by the students. Activity 28 uses the animals in pet stores for two student projects. Both projects require library research and contain observational/research components.

24 OBSERVING NEURAL NETWORKING *IN VIVO*

Douglas L. Chute
Drexel University

Philip Schatz
St. Joseph's University

Most students have difficulty not thinking that the central nervous system constitutes a set of point-to-point wirings. In other words, they think the brain has hard-wired functioning like a light switch; you turn on the switch and the light goes on. This belief impedes students' ability to grasp complex cortical functions such as perception, thought, and memory that result from neural pools and nodal probabilities. This activity introduces a simple toe-touching phenomenon that can be used to investigate empirically a number of hypotheses about somatosensory organization and learning plasticity. The phenomenon provides concrete experience that challenges the typical student's common-sense view of a hard-wired brain.

CONCEPT

Repeated direct electrical stimulation of the motor or sensory cortex yields similar but not identical movement or sensations. Neurons in the cortex participate in large probabilistic pools, and thus a single neuron does not always produce the same outcome—in other words the brain is not absolutely hard-wired. This probabilistic notion regarding cortical connections is the underpinning for many psychological studies in cognitive and neuroscience, ranging from computer models of artificial intelligence to recovery of function following brain trauma. It is the nature of our brain, however, to be quite certain of the truth of our sensation and the consistency of our thoughts. Thus in the absence of simple experiential evidence, it is difficult to understand that neuronal interactions do not always lead to a predictable and certain outcome. For example, if someone were to touch your second, third, or fourth finger without your being able to see, you would normally tell with 100% certainty which was being touched. The same is not true of your toes! The challenge for students is to think of reasons why.

MATERIALS NEEDED

You will need bare toes and a blindfold. A ballpoint pen makes a good stylus and allows the operationalization of a touch by leaving a mark on the pad of the toe. Use the same pen to keep score on a sheet of paper that has been set up according to various experimental parameters that can be investigated. A calculator or spreadsheet program might be useful if you intend to use a complete research protocol beyond the simple demonstration level we typically employ in introductory psychology teaching. May we suggest that the first time you try this, get your significant other to be a guinea pig before you do it in class.

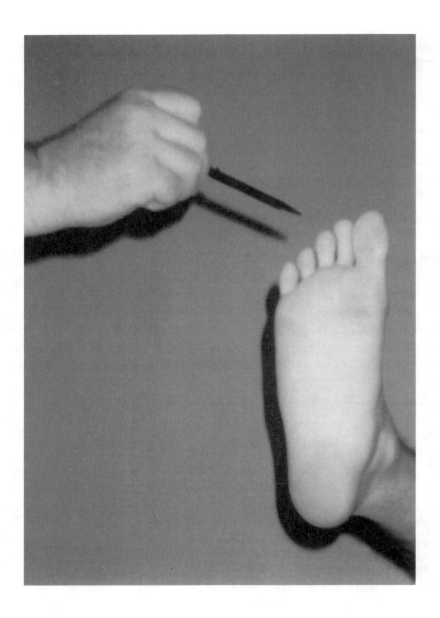

As a simple lecture demonstration, describe the experiment (this is a good time to mention informed consent and related ethical issues), ask for a volunteer, and seat him or her comfortably at the front of the class. The procedure allows many opportunities for a little light humor. (As a cautionary note, remember that some Asian subcontinent cultures consider the foot an erogenous zone.) Have the participant take off his or her shoe and sock and put on the blindfold. Students in the front row can keep a record of which toe was touched and the accuracy of the report. Only touch the second, third, or fourth toes (counting from the big toe out). Touch them gently with the tip of a stylus or pen, not sufficient to move the toe but enough to make a mark or depress the skin. Pause briefly between each touch. (In the classroom demonstration we do not provide any immediate feedback as this leads to very rapid learning.) Participants will be surprised that their accuracy is typically only 80 to 90%. (For the purposes of demonstration you can decrease accuracy by touching slightly to the left or right of midline on each toe, deviating from random by perseverating on errors, touching medial aspects of the second and fourth toes, and so forth. Presumably one might want to decrease accuracy so that the demonstration is seen to work, but we think it is better for students to see acceptable scientific procedures.) With practice and feedback over trials, accuracy will improve. If the first or fifth toe is touched, these references will greatly increase accuracy as well. This presumably happens because these toes experience discrete and regular tactile stimulation, even with shoes. An empirical question that can serve as a variation or assignment is to determine how much the touching the first or fifth can affect overall errors. However, for class demonstrations in introductory psychology we only touch the second, third, and fourth toes. At the end of the demonstration, so that the participant also believes what the rest of the class has clearly seen, we wait until the participant makes an error and, keeping the stylus in place, ask him or her to remove the blindfold and witness the result personally.

This procedure can easily be expanded to include a take-home research experiment in which all class members collect data for group averages. We would typically deal with such data in a recitation or lab section, but this technique also can be used in lecture. By calculating a mean and standard deviation as a class norm you can then determine a z-score for any individual's percentage correct. This anticipates core concepts in psychometrics and individual differences and reinforces the key notion of probability in neural function. The basic phenomenon of localization of sign in toe touching can also be used in more advanced research protocols. The rate of learning is such that performance following feedback reaches asymptote at about 98% correct after as few as 10 trials. For shoe-wearing young adults, performance returns to baseline in a few days. Using a within-subjects design, students could plot learning and forgetting curves to further reinforce notions of neuroplastic phenomena. The big toe and the small toe have different enervation than the middle toes. Their performance is typically much better. A lengthy, carefully planned study can use errors to detect the dermatome boundaries. In the suggested reading section we have included sample Web sites for enervation of the foot and dermatome regions. There appear to be no gender differences, age differences, or left/right foot differences.

DISCUSSION   Students have a natural inclination to use metaphors for understanding the central nervous system and its organization that rely on the notions of electrical wiring between centers of function—a variation of phrenology that is only partially informed by research data. Most students understand the implications of the toe-touching demonstration, and we solidify the discussion by referring to central concepts in the neurosciences, such as plasticity, neural networks, development, memory, motor action schemas, and rehabilitation. On occasion you may have a student who denies the data and maintains a very concrete view. We normally recommend that such students conduct the experiment themselves with a friend or relative and report back. If this empirical approach for a doubting student is not convenient, you might want to come prepared with a file card where a dot and cross are marked so that they are suitable for illustrating the blind spot. The blind spot is demonstrated and then the fact that we do not normally notice it is interpreted as perception in the absence of any neural wiring. Toe touching activates sensory neurons, but their integration and interpretation require experience. The toe-touching phenomenon shows that the nervous system does not come with sensory relationships prewired but that these relationships can be learned and forgotten. If nothing else, this phenomenon provides a justification for attempting rehabilitation following neurotrauma, an important field in which psychologists work.

Related Phenomena

A conceptually similar phenomenon that most students will spontaneously recall derives from a children's game in which the individuals cross their arms in front of them, the palms clasped with fingers interlaced in either left-over-right or right-over-left order. Most people report one way of interlacing is more comfortable, and this can provide another potential variable for investigation.

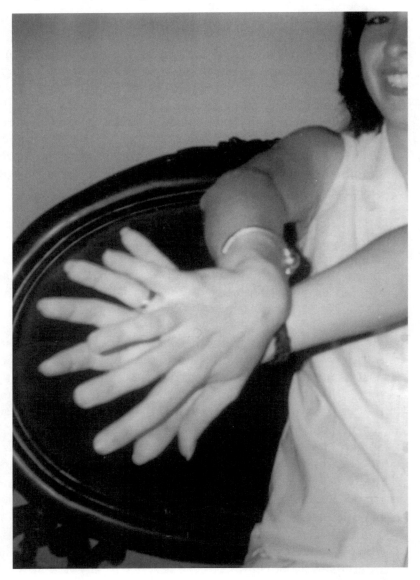

The interlocked arms are then rotated in toward the body. The experimenter then indicates a finger to be moved (without touching it). Most subjects will report an increased latency to respond and they will sometimes make errors by moving the finger from the wrong hand. Requiring a rapid succession of movements for a number of fingers randomly across hands usually results in more errors. If the experimenter actually touches the individual's fingers, there are seldom errors in movement.

In this example, the students should be thinking about cognitive maps or body schema that are being disoriented in their visual-motor mode by the contortion, but not of course in their somatosensory-motor mode. Even persons suffering from mild concussions note that disturbances in such schema result in left–right confusion. For example, in a mental status examination (say on the bench at a football game) it is typical to ask about person, time, and place as well as the individual's left and right orientation for self and others. Errors of perception and

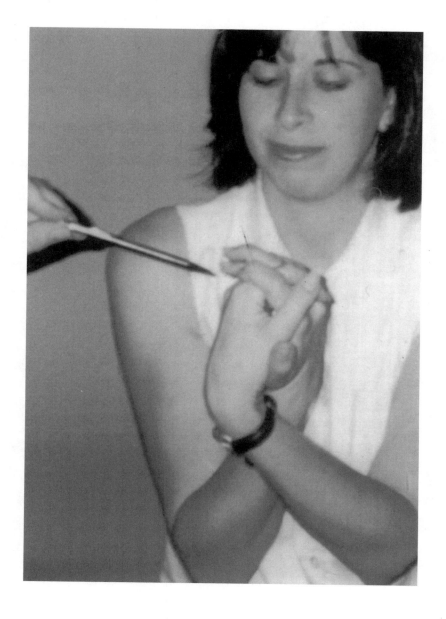

action seen in more serious neuropsychological situations, such as dementia, are conceptually similar to the sensory and motor phenomena illustrated.

This toe-touching phenomenon was first described in an undergraduate research paper. It seems encouraging to students to know that it is possible at their level to make unique empirical observations, in this case derived from thinking about children's games.

WRITING COMPONENT

Have students create an annotated Web bibliography. They put graphics and text they discover at relevant sites on the Web, along with their own critical commentary, into their word processor. This forms a simple laboratory notebook for a number of class exercises. For the toe-touching exercise, students might want to look at the Podiatry Today site as an example of how an annotated bibliography might look (http://www.footdoc.com/footman/medlinks.html).

SUGGESTED READING

Chute, D. L. (1968). *Localization of sign in toe touching.* Undergraduate paper presented in Sensation and Perception. University of Western Ontario.

Students may consult the following websites for more information:

Anatomy of dermatomes
http://www.anatomy.wisc.edu/sc/Text/p1/DEFICITS.HTM

General neuroanatomy
http://www.nan.drexel.edu/nandistance/nanneuro/index.html

Neuroanatomy of the foot
http://www.anes.ccf.org:8080/PILOT/ORTHO/anklanat.htm

25 THE ULTIMATE PORTABLE BRAIN MODEL

Susan J. Shapiro
Indiana University East

■ ────────────────────────────────────── ■

Understanding the three-dimensional nature of brain structures is difficult when given only two-dimensional diagrams. For this activity, the students' hands can be used to provide the framework for a three-dimensional model of the human brain. Mnemonic devices can be included in the activity to assist students in remembering the names and functions of brain structures.

■ ────────────────────────────────────── ■

CONCEPT This in-class demonstration assists students in understanding the three-dimensional nature of the brain and in learning labels for brain structures and locating areas of the brain with specific functions.

MATERIALS NEEDED You will need transparencies or text illustrations labeling brain structure and function.

INSTRUCTIONS This activity should take place after the class has discussed the structure and function of a neuron. Most of the students will have looked at the chapter on biological bases of behavior in an introductory psychology textbook.

Students have the material for an excellent brain model—their hands. I use a description, similar to the example given next, to assist students in using their hands as brain models. The demonstration includes several examples of mnemonics to assist students in remembering structure names or functions. I refer to a projected diagram of the brain as we work with our brain models.

Although hands cannot substitute for the opportunity to examine either real brain tissue or a detailed atlas with a variety of sections, using hands as models helps students understand the three-dimensional relationship among brain structures. This demonstration will also give you the opportunity to discuss brain structure and function in a more interactive manner.

The following example is meant to convey a general impression of the demonstration. The interaction between the instructor and the class determines the detail presented and sequence of the topics covered in the demonstration. The vocabulary that I try to include is in boldface type.

Description of the Ultimate Portable Brain Model

Your brain is made up of billions of **neurons**. These neurons are arranged and grouped to produce identifiable structures, which have different functions. Neuron **cell bodies** tend to be grouped together in locations where they have access to fluids, such as blood and cerebrospinal fluid. These fluids provide food in the form of glucose and oxygen. These fluids also remove waste products from the cell. The **axon** of the neuron extends away from the cell body. The narrow tube-like axon, with its insulation made up of the white **myelin sheath**, carries information to the glands, muscles, and other neurons. Even though neurons are very small and cannot be seen without magnification, their axons are sometimes long enough to carry information all the way across the brain or down the entire length of an arm or leg.

Your brain has two halves or **hemispheres**. Each half controls sensation and movement for half of your body. Sometimes the cells responsible for a particular skill or ability may be located in only one hemisphere. Complex behavior, such as finding and eating food, is usually controlled by many different parts of the brain working together, and both hemispheres may be involved.

We are going to use our hands as a model for the organization of the brain. This is a very portable model. You can always have your brain model with you when taking a test or answering a question.

Hold your hands out in front of you with the back of your hands toward you. Think of the skin on your hands as the **cortex**, the outer layer or surface of the brain. This is sometimes referred to as your "gray matter," because the tissue is slightly grayer than the layer under it. The cell bodies of the neuron make up the cortex of your brain and control much of your behavior and thought.

The muscles in your hands will represent the white matter, or the inner part of the brain tissue. Most of the white matter is made up of the neuron's axons and myelin sheath. These parts of the neuron carry information from one part of the brain to another.

With your hands spread out, a lot of skin (or cortex) makes contact with the air. Air includes oxygen just as the fluid surrounding the brain includes oxygen for the cell bodies. (Remember that cell bodies need oxygen and food to survive.)

Your brain cannot be as spread out as your hands. It must fit within the small box of your skull. Curl your fingers down and bring your thumbs in close to your hands to make fists. Many of the structures inside of the brain are C-shaped because the brain tissue has been curled, just like your hands, to fit in the skull. Even curled up, there is so much cortex that it still will not fit into your skull. Pinch the skin together on the back of your hand. Notice that as the skin moves to fit in a smaller area, it develops wrinkles. Like a landscape, you have mountains and valleys. We call the high points (or mountains) of these wrinkles **gyri** (or a **gyrus** for one hump) and the valleys between the gyri are called **sulci** (or a **sulcus** for one). The cortex of the brain needs to be as large as possible, because it is the location of most of the cell bodies. More cells means more possibilities for processing information. The cortex of your brain is curled and wrinkled to make it fit inside your skull.

To make your two hands correspond more accurately to the two hemispheres of your brain, cross your wrists and put your hands next to each other with the outer edges touching and your thumbs on the outside. Now your *right* hand is on the left side and represents the **left hemisphere**, and your *left* hand is on the right side and represents the **right hemisphere**. (This position can help you remember that the *left* hemisphere controls movement and sensation in the *right* side of your body, including your *right* hand.)

Your wrists represent the **brain stem**. Neurons from both hemispheres reach to the rest of the body through the brain stem and **spinal cord**. Imagine that you are wearing bracelets that have charms dangling down from them. These charms are in the shape of Egyptian pyramids. The points where neurons cross from one side of the body to the other are in the brain stem and are called the **decussation** (pronounced *de kus sa'shun*) **of the pyramids**.

Your arms represent the neurons that send and receive information from the rest of your body. These neurons travel down the spinal cord until they reach about the level of the organ that receives the nerve information. They they branch out into the body to locations such as your heart, lungs, fingers, or toes.

Let's look at your left hemisphere model (your right fist). Your fingers form the **frontal lobe**. The neurons in the frontal lobe are responsible for the brain's complex and abstract abilities, such as judging right from wrong and solving problems.

To move a finger you need to move muscles from the mountain (gyrus) at the base of the fingers. At about this location in the cortex of the frontal lobe is a gyrus that controls most of the voluntary movement of your body. This area of cortex is called the **motor strip**.

The central sulcus (a deep valley) divides this lobe from the parietal lobe. From your knuckles, to a point about halfway back on your hand represents the **parietal lobe**. This takes up just part of the back of your hand. The parietal lobe is responsible for combining sensory information. The areas around the parietal lobe bring in sensory information from the rest of the body. At about your knuckles, just behind the motor strip and in the parietal lobe, is another area of cortex, the **sensory strip**. This small portion of the parietal lobe is responsible for awareness of things that you feel, such as touch, temperature, and pain.

The lower part of the back of your hand represents the **occipital lobe**. Picture two eyes, one on the back of each hand. These imaginary eyes can help you remember that the occipital lobe is responsible for receiving visual information from the eyes.

We still have not talked about your thumb. Look at what your thumb can do. It can lift away from the rest of the brain model, but it remains attached at the base. This is very similar to the structure of the **temporal lobe**. The back section of the temporal lobe is connected to the parietal and occipital lobes, but the front section can be lifted away from the rest of the brain.

Remember, we are looking at the *right* hand, which is a model for the *left* hemisphere. The hand side of the thumb represents the area of brain cortex responsible for hearing or **audition**. Around this area in the parietal lobe are cells responsible for the different aspects of language, such as speaking, understanding speech, reading, and writing. Slightly back toward the occipital lobe (eyes) is the area of cortex needed for one to be able to read. Slightly up into the parietal lobe are areas needed for one to understand language and to be able to speak meaningfully. Closer to the frontal lobe, but still near the auditory area, are areas responsible for the motor movements necessary to talk and write.

Your *left* hand (the right hemisphere of the brain) is more responsible for your ability to know where you are and how to get somewhere else and your ability to manipulate three-dimensional objects rather than words. The right and left hemispheres have slightly different functions, but both work together to provide us with an understanding of our experience.

The lobes that we just labeled are the major areas of the cortex, or surface of the brain. There are also structures underneath these lobes (or areas of cortex) just as there are bones and muscles inside of your hand. It would be difficult to stand up or to move if we did not have a skeleton. Our bones provide a base for the rest of our body. Unlike bones, the internal structures in your brain are not hard, but these structures are important and often very basic in their function. Inside of the brain and the brain stem are clusters of cell bodies (**nuclei**) that have some very important functions. Many of these functions take place without your awareness, but they provide a basis for the more conscious functions of the brain.

Inside both temporal lobes (represented by your thumbs) are the **hippocampus** and the **amygdala**. The amygdala is an almond-shaped structure inside the tip of the temporal lobe (under your thumbnail). This nucleus is involved when you have emotional reactions such as love and anger or you need to decide if something is important. The hippocampus lies inside, along the length of the temporal lobe (like the bone in your thumb). The hippocampus is an essential part of the group of structures that help you to remember and learn.

Inside the brain stem (represented by your wrists) are nuclei called the **medulla** and the **reticular formation**. The medulla is responsible for your heart rate (you can find your pulse at your wrist), breathing, and reflexes such as coughing and sneezing. The reticular formation is responsible for general arousal. Activity in the reticular formation determines whether you are asleep or awake.

If you picked up a cluster of small objects, such as marbles, and held them in your closed hand, they would be in about the same location as the brain nuclei called the **basal ganglia, thalamus**, and **hypothalamus**. These nuclei are responsible for abilities essential for your survival.

The basal ganglia are involved in beginning a movement and in controlling fine movements. People with Parkinson's disease have damaged basal ganglia. They have tremors that they cannot control, but they become unable to move voluntarily.

The thalamus is a relay station for all sensory abilities (except your sense of smell). Messages from your ears and eyes go through the thalamus on the way to the cortex of your brain.

The hypothalamus is involved in a variety of functions: your ability to know that you are hungry or thirsty, your sexual behavior, and the regulation of the function of the systems in the body that communicate through hormones.

Hormones and the **endocrine system** are somewhat similar to **neurotransmitters** and the **nervous system**. Both allow communication to take place in the body. Nerve messages are more direct. The nerve sends information directly to the source for which is it intended, much like sending a letter to a specific person. Hormones are more like articles in the daily paper. Everyone gets the message, even people (organs) who are not interested, but not everyone reads the article or does something with the information.

Although this is only a simplified explanation of the structure and function of the central nervous system, we have covered enough information to help you to begin to understand not only structures described in your textbook, but also the functioning of your own brain and nervous system.

DISCUSSION   Introductory and biological psychology courses introduce a tremendous number of new terms to describe the location and function of brain structures. This extensive vocabulary can be threatening to beginning college students. Yet the understanding of brain structure and function does not need to be in detail for the student to be able to discuss and understand the biological components of behavior. The information needs to be presented in a manner that promotes the retention of basic concepts and with a vocabulary that can be refined in later classes.

Mental models (images) are necessary as we try to understand unfamiliar material. This is even more important when a structure or its behavior cannot be directly observed. Even with the excellent diagrams available in contemporary texts, students often have difficulty labeling regions and understanding the three-dimensional relationship between the different areas of the brain. Three-dimensional models are helpful, but often they are expensive, inconvenient to transport, and cannot be made available to everyone in a large lecture or laboratory class. Animal brains are also expensive for a large class, and introductory courses are seldom assigned to facilities appropriate for dissection. Student disgust associated with working with real brain tissue can also be a barrier.

I have found that this hands-on model is a useful starting point for students struggling with the initial vocabulary and a basic understanding of brain structure. It appears to help students to focus on the relevant locations. Although diagrams are useful, students often fail to pay attention to the appropriate cues and later cannot tell a frontal lobe from a brain stem. Sometimes the cues that distinguish structures from one another are not apparent on a diagram. When a three-dimensional model is used, attachment of structures at a particular point is more apparent. The activity also gives you the opportunity to see which of your students are with you in your discussion. You will often be able to tell who is having difficulty as you look out over the sea of waving hands.

Encourage students to move their hands along with you as you refer to each area. This gives them a chance to try the activity without feeling that everyone is watching. Later, when students take exams, you may see them moving their hands as they try to remember the names and concepts.

The model can be referred to later in the course when students are having difficulty visualizing structures or functional locations, and it can be easily tied to the later use of other models, dissections, or to more advanced explanations. (It can also be used as an example of a mental model when you discuss cognition.)

SUGGESTED READINGS

When it comes to illustrations, more is better. Many excellent books are available with drawings of the brain and nervous system. Some are out of print, but are often available at discount bookstores. Not all are intended for anatomy classes, but they are still valuable sources for illustrations of nervous system structures. Keep an eye out for children's books on the nervous system as they are usually well illustrated and have the essential points in an easy-to-understand format. Look over these books before you use them. Some have inaccuracies that may confuse students.

Alexander, H., & Costa, D. (1990). *Look inside your brain: A poke and look learning book.* New York: Putnam and Grosset Group.

Diamond, M. C., Scheibel, A. B., & Elson, L. M. (1985). *The human brain coloring book.* New York: Barnes & Noble Books.

Ornstein, R., & Thompson, R. F. (1984). *The amazing brain*. Boston: Houghton Mifflin.

Vannini, V., & Pogliani, G. (Eds.). (1994). *The color atlas of human anatomy*. New York: Harmony Books.

West, D., & Parker, S. *Brain surgery for beginners and other major operations for minors*. Brookfield, CT: Millbrook Press.

26 CIRCADIAN RHYTHMS IN BODY TEMPERATURE

Michael J. Renner
West Chester University

This activity allows students who have already discussed circadian rhythms in their introductory psychology course to gather and graph data by recording their body temperature over a 72-hr period. Students also rate themselves on an alertness scale each time a temperature reading is recorded, examining how a psychological variable fluctuates in comparison to body temperature.

CONCEPT

Several biological and behavior variables fluctuate spontaneously in a circadian rhythm (from the Latin words *circa*, meaning "about," and *dies*, meaning "day"). This activity allows students to collect data concerning the circadian variation in their body temperature and correlate this variation with changes in a psychological variable. Students will record a self-assessment of sleepiness or alertness followed by measurement of body temperature every 2 hr for 3 days.

MATERIALS NEEDED

Each student will need an oral thermometer, readable in increments of 0.1°F; a reliable alarm clock; and a data-gathering chart (see appendix A).

INSTRUCTIONS

Read the following statement to your students: To gather the data needed for this investigation, you will record two items of data about yourself every 2 hr for 3 consecutive days. You may vary the time of observation for individual measurements up to 20 min before or after the scheduled time (to accommodate classes, etc.). Be sure to record the actual time you collected the data in the appropriate column of the data table. Try to minimize variations from the schedule and take the thermometer with you wherever you go.

At the appropriate time, subjectively assess your state of alertness on a scale of 1 (*asleep, meaning that the alarm clock woke you to make your observation*) to 10 (*hyper-aroused*) and fill in the rating on the data table. After you have made your rating, record your body temperature to the nearest 0.1°F on the same line of the table. In the Notes column, record what you were doing at the time you gathered the temperature and alertness data and any circumstance that may have affected the reading (e.g., if you engaged in any strenuous physical activity before the reading).

Do not eat or drink anything for at least 15 min before taking your temperature; eating and drinking change the temperature in the mouth so that it does not reflect actual body temperature. Take your temperature only while sitting still; do not take your temperature while driving, walking, running, or engaging in any activity that could result in your biting into the thermometer or having it forced too deeply into your mouth. This could injure you. Female students should schedule data collection so that it does not include the day of ovulation, because a woman's body temperature increases 1° to 2°F at that time. This would both invade your privacy and disrupt your data collection.

DISCUSSION   In my experience, nearly every student detects a variation in body temperature of 1° to 2°F, with a peak temperature between 1:00 and 8:00 p.m. and a minimum temperature between midnight and 7:00 a.m.

Most organisms show changes with patterns that repeat in time. These changes vary from long cycles such as seasonal weight fluctuations in many animals to short cycles such as electrical activity in the brain. Most people who do research in this area focus on circadian rhythms (Rosenzwieg & Leiman, 1989). Many biological systems show circadian rhythms, including the circulating amounts of many hormones, body temperature, and sleep and dreaming.

The functional reason animals have circadian rhythms is not known. One popular hypothesis is that animals coordinate body functions and behavior to cyclical changes in the environment such as night and day. For example, periods of darkness may be dangerous for some animals, because their senses are less able to detect predators.

This exercise is ideal for graphing data. If you simply assign students to draw a graph of their body temperature across time, you will get highly variable student performance. A more structured approach, which has worked well in my classes, is to describe the format of the graph, with the x-axis representing midnight to midnight, and the y-axis representing body temperature. Comparison is facilitated by graphing the data from all three days on the same graph. To structure the exercise further, prepare a graph template to be handed out with the assignment (a range of 95° to 101°F will encompass nearly all observations).

Students have difficulty obtaining thermometers calibrated in degrees Celsius. Given this difficulty and the lack of intuitive understanding in some students of metric temperatures, I advise making an exception to the APA's "Policy of Metrication."

Because of the restriction due to the female ovulation cycle (mentioned in the instructions), you will need to allow more than the usual amount of time to complete the exercise. Also, excuse students with significant health problems from the exercise. Students may report a sense of mild sleep deprivation after three nights in which they do not sleep more than 2 hr without interruption.

WRITING
COMPONENT   Have students write responses to the following questions:

1. Did you find evidence of a circadian rhythm in your body temperature? Describe what you found.
2. Was there a consistent time of day during which you had a lower body temperature compared to other times? A higher body temperature?
3. Were there any unusual data points? Were there any environmental or behavioral factors associated with those observations (e.g., you had been exercising or were caught in the rain immediately prior to taking the temperature reading)?

REFERENCE   Rosenzweig, M. R., & Leiman, A. L. (1989). *Physiological psychology* (2nd ed.). New York: Random House.

SUGGESTED READING

Dement, W. (1972). *Some must watch while some must sleep*. San Francisco: W. H. Freeman.

Kleitman, N. (1963). *Sleep and wakefulness* (Rev. ed.). Chicago: University of Chicago Press.

Wever, R. A. (1979). *The circadian system of man*. Heidelberg, Germany: Springer-Verlag.

Appendix A

Alertness Rating Scale Form

Asleep	Drowsy	Relaxed	Alert	Intense	Manic
1	2	4	6	8	10

Planned Time	Actual Time	Altertness Rating	Body Temp	Notes:

27 FLIGHT DISTANCE IN SMALL BIRDS

Michael J. Renner

West Chester University

This exercise demonstrates the concept of flight distance in small birds and its relationship to anti-predator behavior in prey species. Students leave the classroom to observe the behavior of small local birds, measuring the influence of two factors (approach speed and movement direction) of a potential predator on flight distance.

CONCEPT
One of the mechanisms prey species use in avoiding predators is flight distance. Flight distance is an imaginary circle of space around the animal, such that animals of other species entering this space will trigger flight. Many factors control the size of this space. In this exercise, students determine the flight distance of the red-breasted robin (*Turdus migratorius*) and whether it is affected by the (a) walking speed and (b) direction of movement of a potential predator.

MATERIALS NEEDED
Each student will require a small beanbag or other small object that will not bounce when dropped, a metric tape measure or a string marked off in 10-centimeter increments, and a portable cassette tape player with headset (optional).

INSTRUCTIONS
Data gathering typically takes about an hour, but the length of time required is dependent on the students' relative ease at finding subjects. The exercise has two parts, but part 1 can be used without part 2.

If you do not live in a region of the country where the American robin is plentiful, identify a locally abundant species of small bird that students can readily identify. Visually distinctive species (e.g., cardinals, jays) are less likely to be misidentified by students. These instructions to students have been written for robins.

Part 1

For each trial, find a robin standing on the ground. Look directly at the bird and, while holding the beanbag by your side, walk directly toward it. When the robin flies away, drop the beanbag to mark your location and keep your eyes fixed on the spot from which the robin took off. Measure the distance from the departure point back to the beanbag. Enter your data (to the nearest 10 cm) in the provided table (appendix A). Conduct 20 trials, alternating a slow pace (described next) with a quick pace. Do not use the same bird for all trials.

The bird may hop away. If this occurs, adjust your direction (if necessary) and keep walking until it takes flight. It is important to use consistent walking speeds. If available, try using a portable cassette player with headphones and a favorite song to give you a steady walking beat. Use one fast song and one slow song. Walk at a rate of 60 to 80 steps per minute for slow walking and 110 to 120 steps per minute for fast walking.

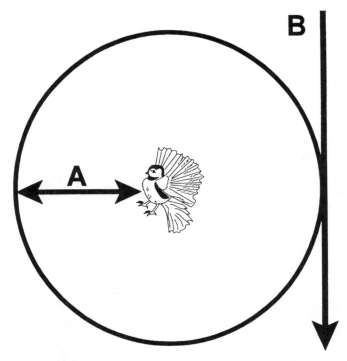

Figure 27-1. Procedural diagram for part 2 of the exercise. Students are to visually estimate a circle around the target bird with a radius equal to the mean slow-walk flight distance (indicated at A), and walk so that their path is tangential to that circle (e.g., the path indicated by B).

After gathering all data, calculate the mean flight distances for fast and slow walking speeds. Enter your calculations in the table provided (appendix A).

Part 2

On each trial, imagine a circle around the bird, the radius of which is the mean slow-speed flight distance determined in part 1. Walk at the slow-walking speed used in part 1, so that your path touches the edge of the circle, as shown in Figure 27-1. Record whether the robin takes flight (appendix B). Repeat this for a total of 10 trials.

DISCUSSION In my experience, students will always get longer flight distances when walking quickly than when walking slowly. If appropriate for the class you are teaching, require a statistical test of significance.

When observing the second part of the exercise, we would expect the bird to take flight on fewer than half of the trials, as the birds are relatively insensitive to the potential predator's tangential (to the outer limit of the flight distance) movements, as long as he or she does not invade the flight distance. In my classes, most students record flight on one to four trials in part 2, with very few students reporting that the birds flew away on more than half of the trials. They will probably conclude that birds are sensitive to direction of movement, but this conclusion will be less clear-cut than the effect of approach speed. Use this discrepancy to begin a discussion on the utility of statistical tests in assessing experimental data.

Students enjoy the exercise, and it has been used successfully when assigned for completion out of class. Students often return with additional observations and hypotheses beyond the required data.

WRITING COMPONENT

Ask students to provide written responses to one or more of the following questions:

1. Compare the mean flight distance for trials during which you were walking slowly and quickly. If the means appear different, how would you determine whether this difference was reliable?
2. If the flight distances for slow and quick walking were different in part 1, what function might be served by this difference?
3. In part 2, what results would you expect if your direction of movement (directly at the bird versus tangential movement to the outer limit of the flight distance) were irrelevant to the bird's flight distance?
4. In part 2, what did the results indicate about the influence of your direction of movement on the bird's flight distance?
5. What is the purpose of the instruction in part 1 to look directly at the bird?
6. What are some of the possible confounds that could have had an effect on your data? How could you control these confounds?

SUGGESTED READING

Drickamer, L. C., Vessey, S. H., & Meikle, D. (1996). *Animal Behavior: Mechanisms, Ecology, and Evolution*, (4th ed.). Dubuque, IA: William C. Brown.

McFarland, D. (Ed.). (1981). Predation. In *The Oxford Companion to Animal Behaviour* (pp. 460–462). New York: Oxford Press.

Appendix A

Effect of Walking Speed on Flight Distance

Flight Distance (Meters)

Trial	Walking Slowly	Walking Quickly
1.		
2.		
3.		
4.		
5.		
6.		
7.		
8.		
9.		
10.		
Mean		

Appendix B

Walking Toward the Bird's Flight Circle at a Tangent

Trial	Flight? (Yes/No)
1.	
2.	
3.	
4.	
5.	
6.	
7.	
8.	
9.	
10.	

Number of trials with flight: _____

28 PETSCOPE: PET STORES AND THE STUDY OF ANIMAL BEHAVIOR

Charles I. Abramson, Jeanine M. Huss, Kristy Wallisch, and Delissa Payne

Oklahoma State University

This activity uses pet stores to provide training in the study of animal behavior. Pet stores have a number of advantages for student research. First, pet stores carry a range of species suitable for comparative investigations. Second, pet stores are ideal for ethological studies of various species including humans. Third, pet stores do not drain departmental resources. The use of pet stores to provide animal behavior experiences for students is illustrated with two projects.

CONCEPT

The use of animals to demonstrate principles of psychology has been steadily declining over the past 20 years. Our program, called Petscope, builds on the fascination that pets hold for many students and transforms community pet stores into comparative psychology resource centers. Students work in groups or individually and can perform many noninvasive studies of animal behavior. Students can directly observe the similarities and differences among species, develop comparative research skills, and receive practical experience in the study of animal behavior. Petscope projects are ideal for classes in general psychology, comparative psychology, research methods, and experimental psychology. Petscope projects can be readily incorporated into course curriculums as laboratory experiences or independent student projects.

MATERIALS NEEDED

The materials needed are access to a pet store, a working relationship between the pet store manager/owner and instructor, a list of the animals maintained in the pet store, a project plan or worksheet distributed to students (see sample handouts in Figures 28-1 and 28-2), and apparatuses required to complete the project such as a data sheet and timer. For projects requiring size measurements, it is helpful to photocopy a ruler onto a worksheet so that students will have a ruler readily available.

INSTRUCTIONS

For the Petscope program to be effective a good working relationship between the instructor and pet store manager/owner is crucial, and permission must be sought before students begin class projects. Moreover, pet store personnel and the instructor must address issues such as the possibility of students handling some of the animals (i.e., snakes, birds, lizards, rodents, cats, dogs), creating observation stations in front of animal enclosures, establishing a time for student groups to carry out projects that do not interfere with normal business operations, the availability of first aid, the extent to which pet store staff can assist students with their projects, and the possibility of students manipulating the animals' environment either by feeding or adding toys and other stimuli. In addition to the discussion of these issues, pet store personnel should provide the instructor with a list of animals available for study. With this list the instructor is in a better position to direct and plan student research projects, and the student has an opportunity to acquire background information about an animal prior to working with it. We would also recommend that the instructor accompany the students on their first visit so they can be introduced to store personnel.

In addition to developing a good relationship with the pet store, the instructor may want to review behavioral and comparative study methods. Abramson (1994) and Bornstein (1980) provide good introductions. Describing basic research methods to the class will provide helpful guidelines for students as they design projects and analyze data.

Many projects are suitable for a Petscope program. Two are described. The first is a comparative investigation of habitat, physiology, and behavior of pet store animals; the second is a set of unobtrusive investigations of fish behavior. For instructors not familiar with the type of projects possible, Abramson (1986, 1990), Abramson, Onstott, Edwards, and Bowe (1996), Brown and Downhower (1988), Cain (1995), and Kneidel (1993) provide many useful examples for both invertebrate and vertebrate student projects.

Project 1: Creating Petscope Worksheets

The project was inspired by the old *Time-Life* animal cards. In the *Time-Life* version, each card contained interesting facts about animals such as alligators and jaguars. Our version contains both a library component and an observational–research component. To create Petscope worksheets, students visit the pet store and select animals in which they have an interest. Alternatively, the instructor may decide to focus the students' attention on a few related species such as goldfish, angel fish, and fighting fish. Once the animals are selected, you must decide whether to have the students work as part of a research team or individually. Once this decision has been made, students are assigned to the pet store and begin to create Petscope worksheets.

The library component requires the student to gather information on classification (class, order, family, genus, species), behavior, related species, range, physiology, and anatomy of the animals they select. Students with access to scanners may wish to incorporate visual images into their cards. A useful addition is to include information describing scientists who conduct research with that species. This information would include selected references, a summary of research findings, and the scientist's address. A benefit of this addition is that students learn about the work of, and perhaps network with, professors in their home institution. Moreover, the library component encourages library use, Internet searches, and discussions with experts such as pet store personnel. We have found that students enjoy helping to decide what information to include in the Petscope worksheets.

The observation–research component of the Petscope worksheet relies on information gathered directly by students at the pet store and can include information such as descriptive anatomy (e.g., color, length, weight), feeding and mating strategies, growth rate, diet, habitat, size, and popularity.

Once completed, comparisons among the cards can be made on any of the dimensions previously listed. Subsequent class discussion topics include the importance and difficulty of classification; the role of evolution and ecology in shaping biological, anatomical, and behavioral processes; the influence of pollution

Scientific Name _____

Common Name(s) _____

_____ **Picture**

Description (Size, Coloration, etc.) _____

_____

_____

Notes on Observed Behavior

_____

_____

_____

_____

Notes on Library Research (References, Latest Findings, Current Projects, and Researchers)

_____

_____

_____

_____

Figure 28-1.   Sample Petscope worksheet for Project 1.

and human encroachment on the development of species; and the importance of pets in mental health. When the assignment is completed the worksheets can be donated to the pet store and displayed or donated to local Head Start programs and other educational institutions. Figure 28-1 provides an example of a Petscope worksheet.

Project 2: The Study of Fish

Various species of fish are available in pet stores. Students can be divided in small groups and assigned a tank. Suggested areas of investigation are listed; see Figure 28-2 for an example of a project.

- *Ethological investigations:* Students can observe, describe, and compare environments, coloration of animals, ratio of male to female, food-gathering strategies, defensive strategies, and time allocated to various activities.
- *Learning investigations:* Many people have noted that their pet fish swim to the top of the tank when the aquarium lid is lifted or the aquarium light is turned on. Students can use this response to study whether fish respond to stimuli paired with feeding and to see whether time of day or the introduction of novel stimuli inhibit feeding. Students can also observe responses to new situations or novel stimuli.

Student Worksheet: Comparative Anatomy of Fish

Species Studied (Scientific and Common Names)

_____

In the space below, draw your species. Note important characteristics such as size, color, any range of colors within species, differences between male and female fish, and so forth.

Observe and describe visible fin and tail differences and similarities between your species and two other species. Are fins and tails the same size and shape? Do all three species seem to use fins and tails in the same way?

Species 1 (Name):

Species 2 (Name):

Species 3 (Name):

Figure 28-2. Sample Petscope worksheet for Project 2.

- *Comparative anatomy:* Students can compare development, shape, size, and function of anatomical features such as fins and tails.
- *Social behavior:* Students can observe and describe mating behavior, courtship behavior, group interaction, and species recognition. How do the fish react when new fish are placed into the tank? Do they behave differently if the new fish are of a different species?
- *Comparative physiology:* Basic observations could include variations in breathing rates based on species, size of fish, or male versus female fish.
- *Research methods:* Depending on the research question asked and the abilities of the students, research methods can range from recording numbers of animals to the creation of behavioral profiles for various species.

DISCUSSION
After conducting a project, students should have a general understanding of the comparative approach and the importance of animal research. Moreover, students will have learned observational and data-recording techniques. If Petscope worksheets are created, students will have exposure to CD-ROM-based databases and other library resources. Moreover, they will have developed writing skills and graphic design skills. In sharing information with the class, a student's communication and public speaking skills will also be used.

It has been our experience that pet store owners are happy to participate in the Petscope program because of the program's educational value. They also believe that the program increases business and expands the customer base. A limitation, however, is that some pet stores have a narrow range of species. In such cases the instructor can restrict the number of species or solicit participation from two pet stores that display different types of animals.

WRITING COMPONENT
In addition to creating Petscope worksheets, other writing assignments could include further research and description of animals from the perspective of home

pets. Students can also use their observational skills to chronicle the behavior of family pets and friends' pets.

REFERENCES   Abramson, C. I. (1986). Invertebrates in the classroom. *Teaching of Psychology, 13*, 24–29.

Abramson, C. I. (1990). *Invertebrate learning: A laboratory manual and source book.* Washington, DC: American Psychological Association.

Abramson, C. I. (1994). *A primer of invertebrate learning: The behavioral perspective.* Washington, DC: American Psychological Association.

Abramson, C. I., Onstott, T., Edwards, S., & Bowe, K. (1996). Classical-conditioning demonstrations for elementary and advanced courses. *Teaching of Psychology, 23*, 26–30.

Bornstein, M. (1980). (Ed.). *Comparative methods in psychology.* Hillsdale, NJ: Erlbaum.

Brown, L., & Downhower, J. F. (1988). *Analyses in behavioral ecology: A manual for lab and field.* Sunderland, MA: Sinauer.

Cain, N. W. (1995). *Animal behavior science projects.* New York: John Wiley & Sons.

Kneidel, S. S. (1993). *Creepy crawlies and the scientific method.* Golden, CO: Fulcrum.

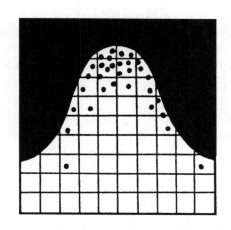

CHAPTER IV
SENSATION AND
PERCEPTION

The eight activities in this chapter offer exercises to explore several sensory systems including vision, taste, and smell, as well as higher-order perceptual processes. Activity 29 uses a simple procedure to demonstrate the distribution of rods and cones across the retina and the meaning of that distribution in terms of a person's ability to identify colors. Activity 30 demonstrates depth perception using hand-drawn anaglyphs (slightly disparate images, one drawn in red ink, the other in green).

Issues of threshold are examined in a signal detection game described in Activity 31, in which students use hit rates and false alarms to plot a receiver–operating characteristic (ROC) curve. In Activity 32, students learn how visual perception is substantially impaired during eye movements, a finding that is particularly relevant for reading. The fact that we logically arrive at a false conclusion if we begin with an erroneous premise is demonstrated in the three-dimensional illusion described in Activity 33.

Activity 34 demonstrates genetic differences in taste based on the work of Yale psychologist Linda Bartoshuk. The exercise categorizes students into nontasters, tasters, and super-tasters, and shows how those taste differences are correlated with the density of fungiform papillae on the tongue. The interaction of taste and smell is the subject of Activity 35, which makes use of jelly beans to demonstrate the importance of smell to taste. Finally, Activity 36 uses scratch-and-sniff perfume advertisements to demonstrate issues in smell perception, including gender identification from odors of body sweat and breath.

$^{\square}29$ Distribution of Rods, Cones, and Color Vision in the Retina

Charles T. Blair-Broeker
Cedar Falls High School, Iowa

Douglas A. Bernstein
University of Illinois

This simple activity illustrates the distribution of rods and cones in the retina, as well as the differing ability of these photoreceptors to detect color.

CONCEPT
The demonstration shows that stimuli in the center of the visual field are detected mainly by color-sensitive cones concentrated in the fovea, while stimuli at the edges of the visual field are detected mainly by non–color-sensitive rods in the periphery of the retina.

MATERIALS NEEDED
You will need a few pens, magic markers, or other objects of various colors (red, blue, green, yellow, and black, for example) and a student volunteer with normal color vision.

INSTRUCTIONS
Ask your volunteer to sit or stand at the front of the room, facing the class and, at your signal, to stare fixedly ahead at a spot or object at the back of the room. If the participant's eyes stray from the fixation point, the demonstration will probably not work very well, so emphasize the need for concentrated fixation. Now stand at the volunteer's left or right side. Hold one of the colored objects three or four feet away from the volunteer's left ear, at about eye level. (Keep the object concealed prior to this time.)

Ask the volunteer to identify the object in your hand and to name its color. It is very unlikely that either can be done. Now move a step toward the class and slightly more in front of the volunteer (imagine you are moving on an arcing track that would eventually place you directly in front of the volunteer), and ask the same questions. Continue to move, one small step at a time, along the arc, asking the same questions each time until the participant can correctly identify the object and its color.

DISCUSSION
You will find that most participants have excellent peripheral vision, as reflected in their ability to recognize that the object is present even when it is far off to the side. However, for most people, it will take another step or two before they can recognize what the object is, and one or two more before they can name its color (most will first say it is black, because they are seeing it only with rods). The students will be surprised at how close to the center of the visual field the object must be before its color is clearly apparent.

If the expected sequence of results does not occur, it is probably because the participant lost fixation or made a lucky guess about color. To confirm the distribution of rods and cones, and their color sensitivity, run several trials using different colors, and start from different sides of the volunteer.

You can make this demonstration an active learning experience by asking students to predict the results of the procedure and to justify their predictions based on material presented in class or in the textbook. Another option is to divide the class into teams of three and have them conduct the procedure, perhaps using objects of different sizes and colors, held at differing distances. Team members can take turns acting as volunteer, experimenter, and data recorder (whose job is to note the point on each trial where the object is first detected, correctly named, and its color identified). Afterward, teams can be asked to report their results to the class, including the effect of object size and distance and to suggest plausible explanations for discrepant data (e.g., individual differences in retinal anatomy, restricted peripheral vision, or loss of fixation during a trial).

WRITING COMPONENT Each team or small group could be asked to write their predictions, a report on their data, an explanation of the results, and a summary of the meaning of these results. If small groups are not formed, one student could record the data from one or more participants on the chalkboard, after which each class member could write a in-class essay (a 5-min paper) explaining the results based on the student's readings and class discussion.

30 STEREOPSIS: LEARNING BY DOODLING

Paul H. Schulman
SUNY Institute of Technology

Stereoscopic vision, or stereopsis, is an aspect of depth perception that fascinates students. Usually textbooks cover stereopsis in an abstract way, making it difficult for students to grasp. In this activity stereopsis is described and students are taught a method for the freehand drawing of red–green anaglyphs (three-dimensional pictures). This activity simplifies learning by enabling students to easily draw and manipulate three-dimensional pictures.

CONCEPT

Stereoscopic vision is based on two complex cues: crossed and uncrossed retinal disparities. This activity helps students understand these cues by having them draw stereoscopic pictures freehand. The type of stereoscopic pictures described are called *anaglyphs*, which are composed of nearly identical red and green pictures and viewed through spectacles with lenses of the corresponding colors.

MATERIALS NEEDED

Simply because they are the cheapest, for use in class I get lorgnette-style anaglyph lenses from Reel 3-D Enterprises, Inc., Culver City, California 90231 (phone: [310] 837-2368). Lorgnette-style lenses were not listed in the last catalog that I consulted—somewhat more expensive ones with templates were; if you want the lorgnette-style lenses, you have to ask for them. Many other companies sell anaglyph lenses also.

For drawing, I've had the best results with Crayola® red and green markers from the Crayola Color Overs® box of markers. Two kinds of markers come in these boxes: over colors and under colors. The red and green over colors work excellently. The critical thing is that the red and green marks must be virtually invisible through the corresponding lenses. (The same caveat applies if you happen to have red–blue lenses.)

INSTRUCTIONS

Background

We rarely think a floor lamp is in front of the couch when it is behind. When we reach for a nearby object we rarely reach beyond it or short of it. Our depth perception is so accurate, reliable, effortless, and immediate that it is difficult to realize that it is, in fact, mediated by the use of depth information, or cues, in the environment. Psychologists usually distinguish between monocular, or

---

I would like to thank the Binney and Smith Company for generously providing me with their entire line of markers to test for this chapter.

painter's cues, and binocular cues. The monocular cues are the cues that artists use to create the impression of depth in a picture. They are described in all perception textbooks and in nearly all introductory textbooks. Monocular cues give a powerful impression of depth. Nonetheless, no matter how vivid a painting or photograph, the depth conveyed in the actual scene is much more compelling; binocular cues account for much of this difference. Because our eyes are separated, each views the world from a slightly different direction. Thus the image on each retina is slightly different. This difference is called a *retinal*, or *binocular*, disparity and it accounts for stereoscopic vision. (See Kaufman, 1974, for an extended and excellent discussion of this topic; the other suggested reading listed at the end of this activity are briefer.)

Binocular disparities fall into two categories: crossed and uncrossed. An object farther than the fixation point produces an uncrossed disparity. In Figure 30-1 assume you are looking at the filled circle; the lines of regard are represented by the thick lines projecting to the circle. The spatial position of the *distant* filled square is determined with respect to these lines of regard. For the left eye the spatial position of the filled square—as indicated by the open square—is to the left of the left eye's line of regard; for the right eye the spatial position of the square is to the right of its line of regard.

Whereas an object farther than the point of fixation produces an uncrossed disparity, one nearer produces a crossed disparity. In Figure 30-2 assume you are looking at the filled square. Once again the lines of regard are represented by the thicker lines, and the spatial position of the *near* filled circle is determined with respect to these lines of regard. For the left eye the spatial position of the filled

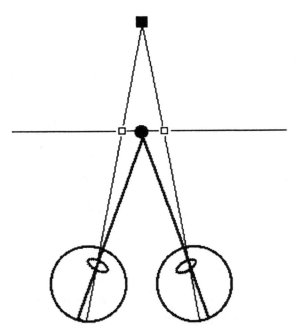

Figure 30-1. Uncrossed disparity. The observer is fixating the near, filled circle. The thick lines represent the lines of regard. Note that there is a plane drawn through the circle; the small open squares represent the image of the distant, filled square in the plane of the fixated circle. For the left eye the image of the distant square is to the left of its line of regard and for the right eye it is to the right of its line of regard. This represents an uncrossed disparity and it indicates that the square is more distant than the circle.

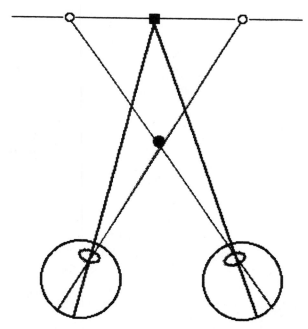

Figure 30-2. Crossed disparity. The observer is fixating the distant, filled square. The thick lines represent the lines of regard. Note that there is a plane drawn through the square; the small, unfilled circles represent the image of the near, filled circle in the plane of the fixated square. For the left eye the image of the circle is to the right of the line of regard and for the right eye it is to the left. This is a crossed disparity and it indicates that the circle is nearer than the square.

circle—as indicated by the open circle—is to the right of the left eye's line of regard. The disparity is crossed in the sense that the spatial position of the near circle viewed by each eye crosses the line of regard.

To produce stereoscopic depth in pictures, a disparity must be created. Stereograms and anaglyphs are the most common artificial ways to create this sort of disparity. A stereogram is a pair of pictures that show two views of the same scene, one from the vantage point of each eye. One view is seen only by the left eye, the other only by the right eye. An anaglyph also presents disparate views of the same scene, one drawn in red ink, the other in green ink. Anaglyphs are viewed with glasses that have red and green lenses. If one looks through a lens of one color, one sees only the other-color pattern, and it looks black; the same-color pattern is not seen through the lens. Green, but not red, is seen through the red lens.

Drawing Anaglyphs

Have students draw anaglyphs using red and green paired images. Drawing anaglyphs that contain lines can be painstaking work because the visual system does not tolerate even small differences between the two pictures. A wiggle in one line not matched by a wiggle in the other line will destroy the effect. Stereoscopic depth is easily achieved, however, by drawing with small dots, not lines. Just touch the tip of the marker to the paper to make these dots—the smaller the mark, the better. The result will look like a bunch of random red and green dots. (See Julesz [1971] for many examples of similar, though far more complicated, anaglyphs.)

Figure 30-3.   The direction rule. The top row depicts an uncrossed disparity (farther than the point of fixation) and the bottom row depicts a crossed disparity (nearer than the point of fixation). The filled dots are red; the open dots are green. The red lens is assumed to be over the left eye.

Follow two simple rules for drawing dot anaglyphs, one for direction (for distinguishing near from far) and one for magnitude (for telling how near or how far). In describing these rules I will assume that the left lens of the three-dimensional glasses is red and the right lens is green. Make the appropriate corrections if your lenses differ.

Direction Rule. A crossed disparity indicates that an object is near; an uncrossed disparity indicates that the object is far. To draw a crossed disparity, place the green dot to the *right* of the red dot. To draw an uncrossed disparity, place the green dot to the *left* of the red dot (Figure 30-3). For example, to draw a simple triangle, place pairs of dots at the vertices. If you want it to appear near, place the green dots to the right of the red. The effect is more obvious if you add a distant object for comparison. You could draw a distant square by drawing the corners and reversing the placement of the dots to create an uncrossed disparity.

Magnitude Rule. The magnitude rule is equally simple: The greater the separation between the dots, within limits, the greater the disparity and thus the greater the depth. If the separation between paired dots is too great, the effect will not work. This rule holds regardless of the direction of the disparity. That is, increased separation will make objects with crossed disparity look closer and objects with uncrossed disparity look farther away (Figure 30-4). Try a few drawings that vary the amount of depth.

Other Drawing Tips. The dots must be of the same height; if one is higher than the other, the anaglyph will not work. They should also be close to the same size; just touch the marker tip to the paper to make the dots close enough in size. Great precision is unnecessary. If you want to create anaglyphs with straight lines, use a straightedge to connect the red dots with red lines and the green dots with green lines (Figure 30-5). If the red and green lines have to cross, blot the ink with tissue paper so that one pen does not pick up the other's ink, which will destroy the effect. For curved lines draw your picture on paper (heavy brown paper bags work nicely), cut the picture out to create a stencil, and connect the dots with the same-color lines using the stencil.

DISCUSSION   I have found that students will rarely draw these anaglyphs correctly from the instructions. I have to make corrections on virtually every student's paper, so I circulate when they are drawing. Students have a tendency to draw one dot of the pair above the other, which completely destroys the effect. They also usually want

Figure 30-4.   The magnitude rule. The greater the separation between the dots, the greater the perceived depth, regardless of the direction of disparity. The filled dots are red; the open dots are green. The red lens is assumed to be over the left eye. The left side of the figure depicts a crossed disparity; the right side depicts an uncrossed disparity.

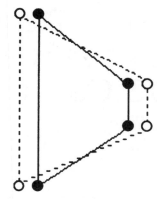

Figure 30-5. *Line anaglyphs. Connect the dots with the same-color line to create anaglyphs with lines. The filled dots are red; the open dots are green. The red lens is assumed to be over the left eye.*

to create very ambitious pictures immediately so they make lots of mistakes. The simplest pictures teach the principles best. This is the only way I have found I can get a large class to pay close enough attention to learn this topic.

REFERENCES

Julesz, B. (1971). *Foundations of cyclopean perception.* Chicago: University of Chicago Press.

Kaufman, L. (1974). *Sight and mind.* New York: Oxford University Press.

SUGGESTED READING

Coren, S., & Ward, L. (1989). *Sensation and perception.* New York: Academic Press.

Goldstein, E. B. (1989). *Sensation and perception.* Belmont, CA: Wadsworth.

Levine, M. W., & Shefner, J. M. (1991). *Fundamentals of sensation and perception.* Pacific Grove, CA: Brooks/Cole.

McBurney, D., & Collings, V. (1984). *Introduction to sensation/perception.* Englewood Cliffs, NJ: Prentice Hall.

Matlin, M., & Foley, H. (1994). *Perception.* Boston: Allyn & Bacon.

Sekuler, R., & Blake, R. (1990). *Perception.* New York: Knopf.

31 THE SIGNAL DETECTION GAME: AN EXERCISE FOR GENERATING AN ROC CURVE

Thomas W. Pierce
Radford University

■──■

This activity provides students with hands-on experience in interpreting data from a signal detection perspective. The exercise illustrates basic concepts of signal detection theory by having students analyze data collected during the course of a game in which they are asked to decide whether scores have been drawn from a population labeled noise *or from a population labeled* signal plus noise. *False alarm and hit rates are generated for various benefit–cost conditions. Students then generate a receiver operating characteristic (ROC) curve by plotting hit rates against false alarm rates.*

■──■

CONCEPT   Signal detection theory (SDT) has become an important tool in a number of fields, including psychophysics, human factors, and medical decision making. Because instructors often describe SDT in purely theoretical terms, it is difficult for students to think of it as a method for analyzing and interpreting real data. This activity provides students with an opportunity to apply basic principals of SDT to data they have collected.

MATERIALS NEEDED   You will need envelopes containing 60 slips of paper with scores from a noise population and 60 slips of paper with scores from a signal-plus-noise population, randomly mixed. These scores may be cut from photocopies of appendixes A and B. You will need one such envelope for every two students in your class.

  For every two students you will also need a handout containing (a) a graph of the frequency distributions for scores from both the signal-plus-noise and the noise populations, (b) a scoring sheet for recording results, (c) a sample receiver operating characteristic (ROC) curve, and (d) a blank ROC graph for students to generate an ROC curve using their hit and false alarm rates. These materials can be photocopied from appendixes C, D, E, and F. Finally, you will need one calculator for every two students.

INSTRUCTIONS   The exercise is designed to illustrate basic concepts of SDT. You should introduce the theory to your students and cover the topics of a decision criterion, sensitivity, an ROC curve, *d'*, and beta before conducting the exercise. These concepts are described here, and additional information is provided in the Suggested Reading section. Taking students through a situation in which SDT can be applied is especially helpful. For example, you can use the example of a physician making a diagnosis of an illness or that of an air traffic controller who must decide whether a snowstorm is severe enough to prevent an airplane from landing.

  Just prior to beginning the exercise, remind students that SDT was developed to describe decision making under conditions where it is difficult to discriminate between target events, called *signals,* and a competing set of stimuli, known collectively as *noise.* Four possible outcomes can result when an observer makes a decision. First, a *hit* occurs when the observer decides that the event in question is a signal when in reality a signal is present. Second, a *false alarm* occurs when the observer decides that the event in question is a signal when in fact the event is noise. Third, a *miss* occurs when the observer decides there is no signal when a signal was really present. Fourth, a *correct rejection* occurs when the observer correctly decides that no signal is present.

Explain to students that the game will help them understand how different benefit–cost conditions influence the rates of hits and false alarms. For example, decision makers are much more likely to respond "signal" when the benefits for a hit are high and the costs for a false alarm are low. However, decision makers are much less likely to respond "signal" when the benefits from a hit are low and the costs for a false alarm are high. The decision-making behavior of an individual in different benefit–cost conditions can be represented by generating a receiver operating characteristic (or ROC curve).

Begin the exercise by dividing the class into pairs. One student in each pair should be designated the observer and the other should be designated the data collector. Explain that the purpose of the game is to earn as many points as possible. To do this, the observer makes decisions about whether a slip of paper drawn from the envelope by the data collector is from a population labeled "noise" or from a population labeled "signal plus noise." The observer is asked to make decisions under three conditions. In Condition 1, three points are awarded for every correct detection of a signal (i.e., for every hit) and one point is deducted for saying the signal was present when it was not (i.e., for every false alarm). In Condition 2, three points are awarded for every hit and three points deducted for every false alarm. In Condition 3, one point is awarded for every hit and three points are deducted for every false alarm. The observer makes decisions regarding 20 scores in each of the three conditions.

Before any decisions are made, the observer should study the graph in the handout of the frequency distributions for the noise and signal-plus-noise populations (appendix C) and select a value to use as a decision criterion (i.e., a cutoff score to use in deciding when to respond "signal") for each of the three conditions. Because the object of the game is to gain the most points for correct decisions and to lose the fewest points for incorrect decisions, it is to the observer's advantage to make it easy to respond "signal" (i.e., use a low value for the decision criterion) when the rewards for correctly responding "signal" are high and the penalty for incorrectly responding "signal" are low. A criterion that leads to many "signal" responses is referred to as a *liberal* criterion. Similarly, it is to the observer's advantage to make it difficult to respond "signal" (i.e., use a high value for the decision criterion) when the rewards for correctly responding "signal" are low and the penalty for incorrectly responding "signal" is high. The decision criterion in this situation would be referred to as *conservative.* The criterion values should be entered on the data collection sheet in the handout and the observer should make all decisions based on the selected values.

Now have the data collector begin to draw slips from the envelope. The data collector should read the number on the slip to the observer, but not announce which population the score is from. On the basis of the number only, the observer uses the preselected decision criterion value for that condition to decide from which population the score came. The data collector records the outcome of every trial by keeping a running total of the number of hits, false alarms, misses, and correct rejections on the data collection form. After recording the result for each trial, the data collector replaces the previously drawn slip in the envelope, shuffles the slips of paper, and then draws another slip of paper to begin the next trial. This process continues until 20 trials have been completed for each of the three conditions.

When all 60 trials are complete students should calculate the points earned in each condition using the format on the data collection sheet. Identify the team or teams with the highest point total and ask which criterion value they used in each of the three conditions.

Finally, instruct each pair of students to construct an ROC curve from the data they have collected. To do this, the hit rate (the number of hits divided by the number of slips drawn from the signal-plus-noise population) and the false alarm rate (the number of false alarms divided by the number of slips drawn from the noise population) must be calculated for each of the three conditions. The three pairs of hit and false alarm rates should be plotted on the blank ROC graph provided in the handout (appendix F). The ROC curve is created by running a smooth curve starting from the lower-left corner of the graph, through the three data points, and ending at the upper-right corner of the graph.

DISCUSSION   The overall purpose of the discussion following the exercise is to clarify students' understanding of SDT concepts and to identify how these concepts are illustrated in the data. The following are important points the instructor may want to emphasize:

1. The diagonal connecting the lower-left- and the upper-right-hand corners of the graph represents the line that would be obtained if the observer guessed "signal" or "noise" at random. The distance between the ROC curve and the diagonal reflects the sensitivity of the observer, or d'. The further the ROC curve falls from the diagonal, the larger the value for d', and the more sensitive the observer is said to be. Graphically, d' is represented by the distance the ROC curve falls from the diagonal between the midpoint on the diagonal and the upper-left corner of the graph (see appendix E). ROC curves that run closer to the upper-left corner are obtained in situations in which an observer is able to generate very high hit rates while incurring low false alarm rates. This pattern reflects a high degree of sensitivity. On the other hand, if the observer were trying to make incorrect responses, the ROC curve would fall below the diagonal.

2. For each point on the ROC curve, the distance on the curve from the conservative corner (0% hit rate and 0% false alarm rate) to the liberal corner (100% hit rate and 100% false alarm rate) of the graph represents the decision criterion the observer has selected for a particular benefit–cost condition (see appendix E). This value for the decision criterion is also known in the signal detection literature as *beta*.

As they are examining their own and other ROCs from the class, ask students to decide whether particular data points reflect a liberal or a conservative decision criterion. You can also ask them to provide an intuitive estimate of whether the ROC curve they generated reflects a high or a low value for d' on the basis of how far the curve they obtained fell from the diagonal.

This activity was conducted in an undergraduate research methods class and can be completed comfortably in less than 50 minutes. Instructors in an upper-level sensation and perception class may vary the conditions of data collection in a number of ways. First, the means of the noise and signal-plus-noise distributions may be brought closer together to produce a smaller value for d' or drawn further apart to produce a larger value for d'. Second, the payoffs and costs associated with decisions may be altered to produce values for beta at any desired location on the ROC curve.

WRITING COMPONENT

Each of these three writing assignments can be used to help students think about the basic concepts of signal detection theory:

Ask students to explain in writing how SDT can be used to describe some aspect of decision making in their everyday lives.

As another option, ask students to explain how the concepts of d' and beta can be used to describe the decision faced by a jury in a famous court case (e.g., the Oklahoma City bombing trial).

Finally, ask students to write the dialogue of a conversation in which the student explains the concepts of beta, d', and an ROC curve to another student who is unfamiliar with them.

SUGGESTED READING

Coombs, C. C., Dawes, R. M., & Tversky, A. (1970). *Mathematical psychology: An elementary introduction.* Englewood Cliffs, NJ: Prentice-Hall.

Swets, J. A. (1973). The relative operating characteristic in psychology. *Science, 182*(4116), 990–1000.

Swets, J. A., Tanner, W. P., & Birdsall, T. G. (1961). Decision processes in perception. *Psychological Review, 68,* 301–340.

Appendix A

Scores from the Signal-Plus-Noise Distribution

6 S+N	8 S+N	10 S+N	10 S+N	12 S+N	12 S+N
12 S+N	14 S+N	14 S+N	14 S+N	14 S+N	14 S+N
16 S+N	16 S+N	16 S+N	16 S+N	16 S+N	16 S+N
16 S+N	16 S+N	16 S+N	16 S+N	16 S+N	18 S+N
18 S+N	18 S+N	18 S+N	18 S+N	18 S+N	18 S+N
18 S+N	18 S+N	18 S+N	18 S+N	18 S+N	18 S+N
18 S+N	20 S+N	20 S+N	20 S+N	20 S+N	20 S+N
20 S+N	20 S+N	20 S+N	20 S+N	20 S+N	20 S+N
22 S+N	22 S+N	22 S+N	22 S+N	22 S+N	24 S+N
22 S+N	24 S+N	26 S+N	26 S+N	28 S+N	30 S+N

Appendix B

Scores from the Noise Distribution

0 N	2 N	4 N	4 N	6 N	6 N
6 N	8 N	8 N	8 N	8 N	8 N
10 N	10 N	10 N	10 N	10 N	10 N
10 N	10 N	10 N	10 N	10 N	12 N
12 N	12 N	12 N	12 N	12 N	12 N
12 N	12 N	12 N	12 N	12 N	12 N
12 N	14 N	14 N	14 N	14 N	14 N
14 N	14 N	14 N	14 N	14 N	14 N
16 N	16 N	16 N	16 N	16 N	18 N
18 N	18 N	20 N	20 N	22 N	24 N

Appendix C

Frequency Distributions for Both the Noise and Signal-Plus-Noise Distributions

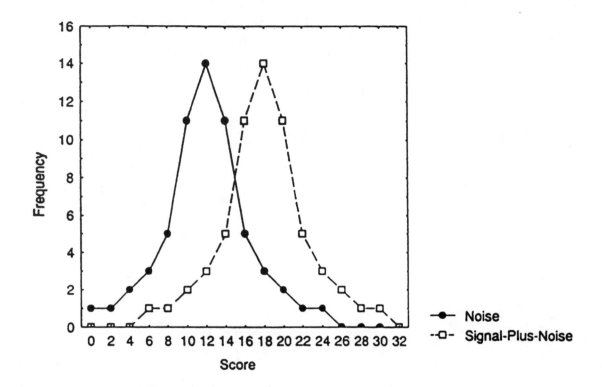

Appendix D

Scoring Sheet

Condition 1

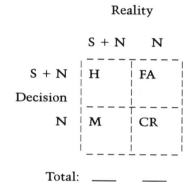

_____ Hits × 3 points = _____

minus _____ False alarms × 1 point = _____

Total condition 1 = _____

Hit rate =

Number of hits/number of signals = ___/___ × 100 = ____%

False alarm rate =

Number of false alarms/amount of noise = ___/___ × 100 = ____%

Condition 2

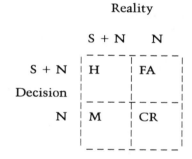

_____ Hits × 3 points = _____

minus _____ False alarms × 3 points = _____

Total condition 2 = _____

Hit rate =

Number of hits/number of signals = ___/___ × 100 = ____%

False alarm rate =

Number of false alarms/amount of noise = ___/___ × 100 = ____%

Condition 3

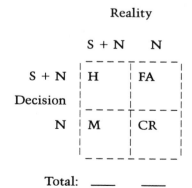

_____ Hits × 1 point = _____

minus _____ False alarms × 3 points = _____

Total condition 3 = _____

Hit rate =

Number of hits/number of signals = ___/___ × 100 = ____%

False alarm rate =

Number of false alarms/amount of noise = ___/___ × 100 = ____%

Appendix E

A Sample ROC Curve

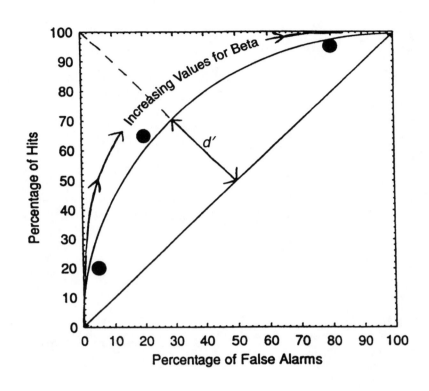

Appendix F

A Blank ROC Graph

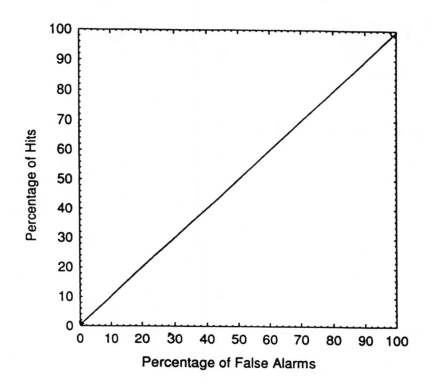

32 DECREASED VISUAL PERCEPTION DURING SACCADIC EYE MOVEMENTS

James W. Kalat

North Carolina State University

One person can see another person's eyes move, even over short distances, but cannot see his or her own eyes move in a mirror. During eye movements, visual perception is substantially impaired. This activity allows students to explore why this impairment is relevant to reading and to principles of perception in general.

CONCEPT

People have two kinds of eye movements: pursuit eye movements, in which the eyes follow a moving object, and saccadic (suh-KAH-dik) eye movements, in which the eyes alternate between *fixations* (periods of stationary focus) and *saccades* (ballistic jumps from one fixation point to another). Visual perception is greatly, though not entirely, suppressed during saccades. This suppression serves a useful function, as vision during a saccade would be blurry. People are not ordinarily aware of this suppression, any more than they are aware of the blind spot in each eye. Nevertheless, a simple procedure can demonstrate the great decrease in visual sensitivity that occurs during saccades.

MATERIALS NEEDED

Each student will need access to a small handheld mirror. Ask students to bring mirrors to class. The instructor should bring additional mirrors for students who did not bring their own. Students can share mirrors, although a ratio of more than four to six students per mirror would delay the demonstration considerably.

INSTRUCTIONS

First instruct students, "Look at yourself in a mirror and focus on your left eye. Then shift your focus to your right eye. Did you see your eyes move?" They will agree that they did not. For many, the first reaction is that the eye movement was too slight or too fast to be visible. You can discredit that hypothesis easily: "Look at your neighbor's eyes. Focus on his or her left eye, then move your focus to the right eye. Have your neighbor focus on your left eye and then move the focus to your right eye. Did each of you see the other person's eyes move?" Students consistently report that they did see the other person's eyes move. Therefore, the inability to see one's eye movement in the mirror is not simply a consequence of the high speed or short distance of the movement; rather, it demonstrates decreased vision during the movement itself.

DISCUSSION

Visual perception is largely suppressed during saccades by at least two mechanisms. First, certain areas in the parietal cortex monitor impending eye movements and send a message to the primary visual cortex to inhibit their activity during saccades. Even if someone is in total darkness, the moment of a saccadic eye movement is associated with decreased neural activity and blood flow, especially in the magnocellular pathway, which is the primary pathway for movement detection (Burr, Morrone, & Ross, 1994; Paus, Marrett, Worsley, & Evans, 1995). Second, what one perceives at the end of a saccade produces backward masking that interferes with what one saw during the saccade. If a stimulus, such as an illuminated slit, is flashed so that it both starts and stops during a horizontal saccade, a viewer does perceive a blurry light, with its width proportional to the distance the eyes moved while the stimulus was present. If, however, the stimulus persists at the end of the saccade, the viewer perceives the stimulus at the fixation and perceives the preceding blur either weakly or not at all (Matin, Clymer, & Matin, 1972). The longer the stimulus remains on during the fixation, the weaker the perception of the blur during the preceding saccade.

One consequence of the decreased vision during saccades is that we can read only during fixations, not during the saccades between them. (Thresholds for detailed pattern vision are even higher than those for movement detection.) Because we are limited to seeing about 11 characters during each fixation (Just & Carpenter, 1987), the maximum number of words one can read (not counting those that one skips over and infers) is limited by the number of fixations per second. An average college student with a text of average difficulty averages about four fixations per second, with occasional backtracks and pauses, yielding an overall reading speed of about 200 words per minute. Very skilled readers decrease the duration of their fixations, thereby doubling or tripling their reading speed while maintaining good comprehension, at least for reading material with simple vocabulary (Just & Carpenter, 1987). (Speed-reading a chemistry textbook is not a good idea.) However, saccades themselves last 25 to 50 ms, setting a theoretical limit to reading speed. Even with the unrealistic assumptions that someone keeps all saccades to the minimum of 25 ms, has fixation durations of zero (!), and reads material limited to short words (fitting two into each 11-character fixation), the maximum reading speed would be 4800 words per minute. When graduates of speed-reading courses claim to read 5000 to 10,000 words per minute, we may safely infer that they are skipping over a fair percentage of the words.

In addition to its relevance for reading, this demonstration of detecting eye movements illustrates a basic point about perception and consciousness: There are moments in time when stimuli strike our sense organs but never reach awareness.

REFERENCES

Burr, D. C., Morrone, M. C., & Ross, J. (1994). Selective suppression of the magnocellular visual pathway during saccadic eye movements. *Nature, 371,* 511–513.

Just, M. A., & Carpenter, P. A. (1987). *The psychology of reading and language comprehension.* Boston: Allyn & Bacon.

Matin, E., Clymer, A. B., & Matin, L. (1972). Metacontrast and saccadic suppression. *Science, 178,* 179–182.

Paus, T., Marrett, S., Worsley, K. J., & Evans, A. C. (1995). Extraretinal modulation of cerebral blood flow in the human visual cortex: Implications for saccadic suppression. *Journal of Neurophysiology, 74,* 2179–2183.

SUGGESTED READING

Adams, M. J. (1990). *Beginning to read.* Cambridge: MIT Press.

$\square$33 TRUNCATED-PYRAMID ILLUSION: THE LOGIC OF PERCEPTION

Clifford L. Fawl
Nebraska Wesleyan University

Despite the fact that an illusion is a nonveridical perception, the illusion demonstrated in this activity is logically derived from the information provided to the perceiver, namely the size of the retinal image created by the object and the apparent distance of the object. The participant perceives an object as changing in size, shape, and direction of movement when he or she knows it cannot in reality be doing so. The illusion is another illustration of what we know from other walks of life: We logically arrive at a false conclusion if we commence with an erroneous premise. In the case of the illusion being presented, the erroneous premise is a misjudgment of the distance of the object. Cross-cultural implications are discussed.

CONCEPT

Perception is a logical, creative activity. This applies to perceptual illusions as well as to veridical perceptions. The activity presented is an adaptation of an illusion first described by Krech and Crutchfield (1960).

MATERIALS AND CONSTRUCTION

Construct a wire frame in the shape of a truncated pyramid, as shown in Figure 33-1. Use light-gauge metal rods except for the handle, which should be heavier. The corners will need to be soldered (or better, welded). The dimensions are not crucial, but the dimensions shown in Figure 33-1 work quite well for a classroom demonstration. Note that *ABCD* forms a larger square, with 12 in. per side, than *WXYZ*, with 3 in. per side. The connecting wires are 13 in. in length. The heavier-gauged handle, by which the frame is held and turned, is placed at the midpoint of *CD*.

INSTRUCTIONS

Hold the frame by the handle so that *ABCD* (the larger square) is closer to the class than the smaller square. The smaller square does not have to be seen in the middle of the larger square by the viewers, but it will help if the smaller square is seen as entirely enclosed within the field of the larger square. Because your classroom may be spread too far from left to right to satisfy this requirement, you may need to break the class down into two groups, in which case you would present the demonstration first to one group then the other. This works well because the nonparticipant group can observe how the participant group misperceives the direction in which the truncated pyramid is turned. The distance of the viewer from the apparatus in a typical classroom of 25 to 30 students should not be a problem.

The illusions to be illustrated only work when the viewer misperceives the position of the small square, which is facilitated by eliminating binocular depth cues. Therefore, instruct the students to put a hand over one eye while they fixate with the other eye on the smaller and more distant square. Most participants will

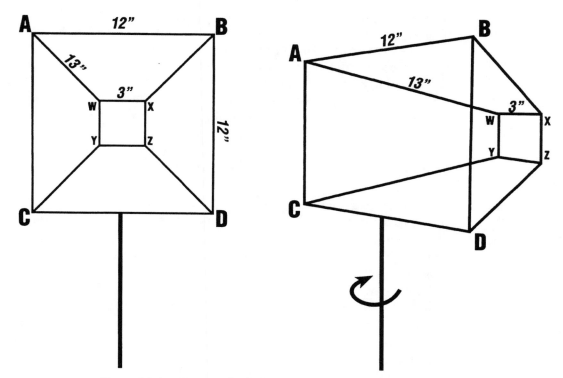

Figure 33-1. Front and off-center view of the truncated pyramid.

get a depth reversal within 15 to 30 s, thus the smaller square will now appear to be in front of the larger square. (This is the same effect found in the well-known Necker Cube.) Request that each student raise his or her free hand when the depth reversal has taken place. When a majority have done so, slowly rotate the truncated pyramid so that the smaller square moves from back to front. (The apparatus is now moving in a circular motion through the horizontal plane.) The direction in which you turn the frame is not crucial, but in the discussion to follow I will assume that the direction is clockwise. Stop when the small square reaches the front. Request that each student who now sees the small square as being in back (contrary to where it really is) keep his or her hand raised.

For these students continue to rotate the apparatus in the same direction. Interesting (even fascinating!) effects occur to the viewers. (a) The smaller square will appear to grow alternately larger (as the smaller square physically is moved closer to the viewer) and smaller (as the smaller square is moved farther), quite contrary to normal size constancy. (b) The shape of both squares will appear to change as the apparatus is rotated: It will appear to alternate between a square and a trapezoid. (c) The direction of the rotation will appear to be opposite to the true direction—that is, if the frame is rotated in a clockwise direction it will appear to the viewer that it is rotated counterclockwise. One way to demonstrate this is to have the students open both eyes while they are experiencing the changing size and shape of the square. When they do, the frame will appear suddenly to change directions.

Only those students who experience the depth reversal, and are able to maintain it as the apparatus is rotated, will get any of the three illusions described. You will find that some students initially get the depth reversal but then lose it as you start to move the frame. A slow, constant rotation without jerking motions helps the students to maintain the depth reversal. For these students who continue to have trouble maintaining the reversal, however, I normally move the frame in short segments until they get to the point that they can maintain the depth reversal. In general you will find that approximately one-half of the participants will get all of the illusions on the first try and that the majority of the remainder will obtain the effects after two or three trials. A minority will not get it at all because they cannot get the depth reversal to hold.

DISCUSSION   Even without an explanation, this is a fascinating illusion to those students who are able to maintain the depth reversal. But if they can understand the logic of the illusion, it will enhance its meaning for them. The illusion demonstrates *not* the illogic of perception but just the opposite: how strikingly logical (even though mistaken) our perceptions can be.

Size perception is based on (a) the size of the retinal image produced by the object being viewed (which in turn is based on the real distance of the square) and (b) the *apparent*, or judged, distance of the object. In the procedure outlined, the retinal image formed by the small square necessarily increases in size as the small square is moved from back to front because the physical distance from the viewer is decreasing. Because we rotate the apparatus when the viewer has depth reversal, it *appears* to the viewer that the small square is moving farther away when in reality it is getting closer. Given the conditions with which the viewer is confronted—that the small square is increasing in retinal size at the same time that the square apparently is moving away—the only logical conclusion is that the small square must be increasing in size, and this is exactly what the viewer perceives. Figure 33-2 illustrates how an object of a given retinal displacement will be perceived as larger if it appears to be at a farther distance than at a closer distance. Perception is an act of creation. The viewer creates a perception that makes logical sense even when the perception is strange, which is what an illusion is. Knowing that the small square does not change in size does not weaken the illusion. In effect, the viewer logically comes to an erroneous conclusion (that the square is changing in size) because one of the premises is wrong: The square is *not* moving away even though it appears to be. The explanation for the perception of change in shape of the square is a variation on the explanation for the

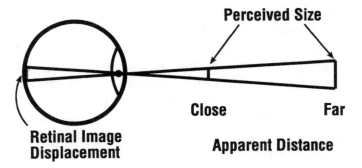

Figure 33-2.   Relationship of perceived size to apparent distance and retinal image. If two objects produce the same amount of retinal displacement, the one appearing farther away will be perceived as larger.

change in size. One side of the square is perceived as getting larger as the other side appears to be getting smaller, the result being a perceived trapezoid.

The explanation for misperceiving the direction of movement is different, but it is again a clear demonstration that perception is a creative act. It goes this way: As you move the small square clockwise from back to front it moves from the middle to the right of the viewer's visual field. That results in a shift on the retina from center to nasal side, assuming that the viewer is using his or her right eye (from center to temporal side if he or she is using the left eye). Keep in mind that the illusion is taking place at the time when the viewer has depth reversal and, accordingly, the small square appears to be closer than the large square. If indeed the small square were in front when the movement commenced, then the only way one could get a shift from center to nasal side of the retina of the right eye would be if the movement were *counterclockwise*, and this is precisely what the viewer perceives. Again, the viewer perceives what logically makes sense given his or her erroneous assumption as to the initial position of the small square.

It would appear that the perceptual apparatus is hard wired in such a way that a person makes logical sense of the information that is provided even when the person knows that the perception cannot be true and even though the person does not go through any conscious reasoning process. Perception is typically logical even when it is factually wrong! This illusion illustrates what we already know from other walks of life: We logically arrive at a false conclusion if we start with an incorrect premise.

Is this illusion culturally bound? Whether or not depth reversal occurs for the viewer may in fact be culturally influenced. Matsumoto (1994) reviewed research that strongly suggests that major culture differtences are correlated with differences in distance perception. If this is true then there may be cultural differences in depth reversal, as in the Necker Cube, for example, although to the best of my knowledge this has not been tested. If indeed it is true that there are cultures in which depth reversal could not be obtained when using the truncated pyramid, then we would not expect representatives from these cultures to experience the size, shape, or direction illusions that we report in the present demonstration. However, if depth reversal in the truncated pyramid is obtained by members of other cultures, then we would expect the other illusions (size, shape, direction) to be found, for these are based on the logic of perception. Thus I am speculating that depth perception and depth reversal may be culture bound but not the logical processing of retinal information in relation to apparent distance. But is this right? Maybe only people from verbally oriented Western cultures exhibit logical processing of perception. It would be fascinating to find out. That's what makes psychological research so exciting.

REFERENCES

Krech, D., & Crutchfield, R. S. (1960). *Elements of psychology.* New York: Alfred A. Knopf.

Matsumoto, D. (1994). *People: Psychology from a cultural perspective.* Pacific Grove, CA: Brooks/Cole.

34 How Blue Are You?: The World of Taste Variations

Margaret Davidson

L. V. Berkner High School, Richardson, Texas

The two parts of this activity are based on the work of Linda M. Bartoshuk and her colleagues. The purpose of these demonstrations is to identify individuals as supertasters, tasters, and nontasters and to illustrate an anatomical correlate of these genetic taste variations. The first part of the activity is a simple yet effective demonstration to visually identify and count the fungiform papillae on the tongue. Multiple participants provide the opportunity to view the variations in the distribution of these specialized structures. The second part of the activity is a dramatic follow-up demonstration to identify variations in taste experience through the presentation of a taste sample and the relation of those taste experiences to the density of the fungiform papillae. Discussion leads students to an understanding of the differing worlds of taste.

PART 1: CONCEPT

The purpose of this demonstration is to view the fungiform papillae, where taste buds are located, by painting the anterior tongue and observing the distribution of these papillae on individuals in the demonstration group. By using many volunteers in this demonstration, students can detect the variations in the density of taste receptors, which correlates with genetic differences in taste.

PART 1: MATERIALS NEEDED

Materials needed for this demonstration include a magnifying glass, flashlight, cotton swabs, blue food coloring, and wax paper (cut in a 1-in. square with a standard hole punch in the center of the paper) to be used as a viewing template. An alternate template for viewing would be a standard reinforcement (adhesive ring) used for notebook paper.

PART 1: INSTRUCTIONS

Initial observation will reveal varying bumps on the tongue. The most numerous of these are filiform papillae, which have no taste function. This demonstration is intended to make apparent the fungiform papillae that (under a microscope) look like tiny button mushrooms. These fungiform papillae contain the taste pores that are conduits to the taste buds that are themselves too small to be seen without a microscope. (Dr. Bartoshuk's analogy of size is that if the fungiform papillae are the size of a hamburger bun, the taste pore would be the size of a sesame seed.) To view the fungiform papillae, swab the tip of the tongue with a cotton swab dipped in a small quantity of blue food coloring. Inform participants that food coloring is not harmful to consume. The painting of the tongue should include the tip and about ³/₄-in. back in the direction of the throat. Participants should close their mouths, then move their tongues around and swallow to distribute the blue dye. When the protruding tongue is inspected with a flashlight, magnifying glass, and viewing template, pink circles (small dots) will emerge from the blue background. These are the fungiform papillae, which appear pink because they do not stain as well as the more numerous filiform papillae (Bartoshuk,

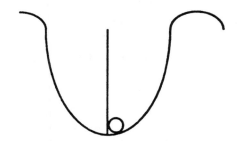

Figure 34–1.   Template placement sketch.

Duffy, & Miller, 1994). Students can view the painted tongue through the wax paper template placed at the tip of the tongue and directly to the right of the midline (see Figure 34-1). Using the standard size viewing template to ensure that comparisons can be made, students can count and record the number of bumps on the tongue. The cotton swab and the wax paper template should be discarded after each participant has finished using them.

PART 2:
CONCEPT

This part of the activity is designed as a companion classroom demonstration to tongue painting as a means of classifying participants as supertasters, tasters, and nontasters. This demonstration is also modeled after the work of Linda M. Bartoshuk (Bartoshuk et al., 1994). Volunteer students will be asked to taste a piece of paper soaked in a solution of 6-n-propylthiouracil (PROP). Scaling of 6-n-propylthiouracil (bitterness) perception will lead to the identification of subsets of tasters who rate the taste from intensely bitter (supertasters), very strong to moderately bitter (tasters), to weak or barely detectable (nontasters).

PART 2:
MATERIALS
NEEDED

For this activity you will need 6-n-propylthiouracil (PROP) papers (see the following production directions) and copies of the modified Green scale for participant response notation and for classification of the taster (see Figures 34-2 and 34-3 in appendix A).

To produce PROP taste papers, use a pan to heat 500 ml water to near boiling. Dissolve 5 g PROP in heated water to make a saturated solution. Dip pieces of filter paper, such as coffee filters, in the PROP solution until they are completely soaked. The PROP crystallizes into the filter paper and allows a method of sanitary delivery of PROP crystals to the participant. Allow the sheets to dry on sheets of aluminum foil or by hanging sheets on a line in a previously prepared sanitary location. When dry, cut filter papers into 1-in. squares. Papers should be stored in a sanitary manner. (These instructions for PROP paper preparation were provided by Linda M. Bartoshuk, personal communication, October 1997.)

PROP is a medication used to treat Grave's disease (hyperthyroidism). An individual taking this medication for Grave's disease would be prescribed 3 to 4 tablets daily of 50 mg each. Those participating in this demonstration receive approximately 1.2 mg PROP (Linda M. Bartoshuk, personal communication, October 1997). A source of pharmaceutical grade PROP is Pfaltz-Bauer, 172 E. Aurora Street, Waterbury, Connecticut 06708, telephone 203-574-0075.

PART 2:
INSTRUCTIONS

Each participant should place a piece of PROP paper on her or his tongue. Participants may chew the paper if they wish. They should keep the paper in their mouths until the taste reaches maximum bitterness (for those who experience the bitter taste). After self-evaluation, participants should dispose of the PROP paper in an available receptacle. PROP papers should not be consumed (there is nothing harmful about the PROP papers; the concentration is so low that it is pharmacologically inactive). Using the modified Green scale identified for participant use, participants should rank their judgment of bitterness response on the vertical line at a defining point (Green, Shaffer, & Gilmore, 1993). The ratings can be converted to magnitude estimation on the scale identified for conversion to ratio properties. Individuals can be identified as nontasters, tasters, and supertasters in terms of the ability to taste the PROP paper. This ability correlates with the number of fungiform papillae on the tongue as previously identified by tongue painting. Participants rating the PROP paper as less bitter (What taste?) than moderate (This is bitter.) are probably nontasters. Tasters indicate the bitterness perception as moderate to very strong (This is bitter to very bitter.). Supertasters rate PROP paper as *extremely* bitter (The worst possible taste!) (Bartoshuk et al., 1994). Note that this activity is for demonstration purposes only; scientifically accurate classification of nontaster, taster, and supertaster must take place in a laboratory setting.

DISCUSSION   "The number of taste buds on the human tongue correlates directly with tasting ability, and both vary according to a standard bell curve" (Levenson, 1995). Sample area results for the right anterior tongue anatomy fungiform papillae density include a mean of 44 for the supertaster, 32 for the taster, and 24 for the nontaster.

Approximately 25% of the general population falls into the category of supertaster. Those in this category perceive stronger tastes from a variety of bitter and sweet substances, and they perceive more burn from oral irritants (alcohol and capsaicin; the latter is the ingredient in chili peppers that produces the burning sensation). It is interesting to note that a higher percentage of women fall into the category of supertaster (Bartoshuk et al., 1994). The world is built for regular tasters that experience food as not too sweet, bitter, salty, or sour. Fifty percent of the general population falls into the category of taster. The so-called nontaster has on average only half of the fungiform papillae of the supertaster. Approximately 25% of the general population falls into this classification. Nontasters simply do not experience the intensity of foods that others do. Nontasters tend to like very spicy foods, perhaps because they may be trying to experience some strong tastes. Nontasters do not taste the bitterness in heavily alcoholic drinks, for example (Cartiere, 1997).

Research on the use of taste papers for identification of subsets of tasters began with Arthur L. Fox of DuPont Company who synthesized a chemical called phylthiocarbamide (PTC). Dr. Bartoshuk relates that after a PTC explosion in the laboratory, a colleague of Fox commented on the bitterness of the chemical. Fox was unable to taste the substance and was interested in researching taste differences. To test informally the notion of taster and nontaster, Fox handed out samples of PTC at the 1932 meeting of the American Association for the Advancement of Science. Passersby were asked to report on the taste (bitterness) of the substance. Approximately one fourth of the reports suggested that the individuals were nontasters. This established the notion of tasters and nontasters (Cartiere, 1997). Since this time, geneticists have discovered the presence of genes for the inherited quality of taste. Bartoshuk and her colleagues have extended the identification of tasters into a further subset of supertasters. Because of the health concerns with the use of PTC, research today uses the substance 6-n-propylthiouracil (PROP) in an infinitesimal amount. It has an intensely bitter taste to the supertaster and thus can discriminate between the types of tasters in the general population.

WRITING COMPONENT Following the demonstration of tongue painting, the students should analyze and categorize the individual variations of fungiform papillae among the demonstration sample. Following the taste test with the PROP taste papers, students' self-report perception of the sensation and semantic rankings can be transposed to magnitude estimations with ratio properties via the Green scale, a scaling system developed to rank bitterness of PROP paper, which has been adapted for demonstration purposes (Green, 1993). The general classification of tasters into the categories of supertaster, taster, and nontaster may encourage a discussion regarding the taste variations in the general population.

Students might interview the sample group in the nontaster and supertaster categories to determine individual food preferences. Following the interview, students can hypothesize the implications of these variations. You might ask, "Is it better to be a supertaster or nontaster? Are supertasters better informed about their environment?" Students should hypothesize about the possible effects of genetic taste perception on general health. Does one type of taster tend to prefer a particular type of food that becomes a health advantage? Is there perhaps a particular type of food that is conducive to general health that is lacking in the supertasters' diet because of the perceived unpleasant taste? Does the taster have a more balanced diet because prepared foods are produced for the taster's palate? Is it possible that the nontaster will eat possibly harmful, spoiled food as a result of her or his taste abilities? If one classification of taste is inherently better than another, why has natural selection created a population of equally represented supertasters and nontasters? Is there a cultural connection with the classification of taste? What might that be?

REFERENCES Bartoshuk, L. M., Duffy, V. B., & Miller, I. J. (1994). PTC/PROP taste: Anatomy, psychophysics, and sex effects. *Physiology & Behavior, 56*, 1165–1171.

Cartiere, R. (1997, April). Genetic clues to wine tasting? *Wine Business Monthly, 4*, 1–7.

Green, B. G., Shaffer, G. S., & Gilmore, M. M. (1993). Derivation and evaluation of a semantic scale of oral sensation magnitude with apparent ratio properties. *Chemical Sense, 18*, 683–702.

Levenson, T. (1995, January/February). Accounting for taste. *The Sciences, 35*, 13–15.

SUGGESTED READING Bartoshuk, L. M. (1995, June). Hey, Bud! *3 2 1 Contact, 158*, 8–11.

Blakeslee, S. (1997, February 18). Chocolate lover or broccoli hater? Answer's on the tip of your tongue (symposium on genetics of taste). *New York Times*, p. C2.

Getchell, T. V., Doty, R. L., Bartoshuk, L. M., & Snow, J. B. (Eds.). (1991). *Smell and taste in health and disease.* New York: Raven Press.

Appendix A

Green Scale Adaptation

For Participant Use

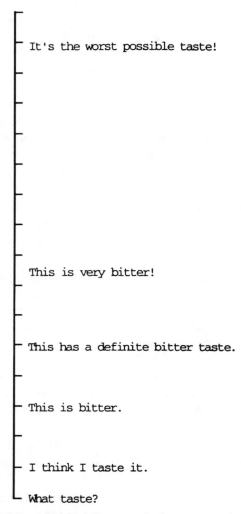

Figure 34-2. *Modified Green scale for participant use.*

For Conversion to Ratio Properties

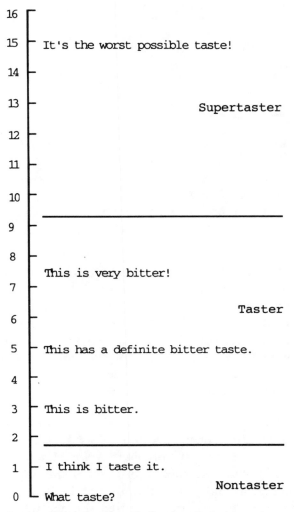

Figure 34-3. Modified Green scale for conversion to ratio properties.

35 THE INTERACTION OF TASTE AND SMELL TO CREATE FLAVOR

Bernard C. Beins
Ithaca College

When we eat, the flavor of food arises from more than gustatory sensation. Vision and smell are also critical components. This activity explores the use of jelly beans to convey the importance of smell. When olfactory cues are present as students eat the jelly beans, the flavor is apparent. Without olfactory cues, the students will not be able to differentiate jelly beans that normally have very different flavors. Students will learn the importance of the senses working in combination to generate flavor.

CONCEPT

This demonstration shows students how important smell is to the sense of taste. Textbooks often say that taste and smell interact to generate flavor, but such a simple statement does not do justice to the role of smell when we eat. In this activity, students learn that if they cannot use olfactory cues to identify flavors, their sense of taste is quite impoverished. On the other hand, olfactory cues provide a rich experience that they normally associate only with taste. This activity allows students to experience and understand the profound relationship between smell, taste, and flavor.

MATERIALS NEEDED

Quite a few different foods will illustrate the point. Jelly beans work well because they come in a variety of flavors and colors. It is helpful to use some jelly beans whose color signals their flavor obviously and some that do not. Beyond jelly beans, flavored potato chips (e.g., sour cream and onion), and foods flavored with vanilla also serve as good smell stimuli for the demonstration.

Caution: It is important to note that some jelly beans are made with gelatin, which comes from animals. Strict vegetarians might not want to participate. Similarly, students who eat only kosher foods may abstain. Finally, some students may simply not like jelly beans. It is prudent to know whether the jelly beans used in a particular demonstration are animal based and to advise students.

INSTRUCTIONS

Before class, place a few jelly beans in small bags, one bag for each student. The students work in pairs; as one eats a jelly bean, the other records the reaction. They then reverse roles.

VERSION 1

In this exercise, students take one jelly bean each from the bag, hold their noses, then put the jelly beans in their mouths. In one case, they keep their eyes closed; in the second, they keep them open. The task is to identify the flavor of the jelly bean while the student's nose is plugged. After the recording student writes the guess about the jelly bean's flavor, the student eating the jelly bean unplugs his or her nose and tries to identify the flavor. When students' noses are plugged, they will guess incorrectly most of the time; when their noses are unplugged, full flavor emerges immediately and identification is easy.

Another sensory component of flavor involves vision. In this demonstration, students often use the color of the jelly bean as a guide to its flavor. For instance, in some cases, apple-flavored jelly beans are green; students who see the green color are sometimes inclined to label the jelly bean as lime when they initially taste it. If students close their eyes and plug their noses, they will have difficulty generating any meaningful guess. This fact shows that our response to food depends not only on taste and smell, but also on visual factors.

VERSION 2 First ask the eaters to close their eyes as the recording student takes two jelly beans out of the bag. The recording student notes whether they are the same or different. Then the appropriate student plugs his or her nose and eats both jelly beans. The task is to determine whether the two jelly beans are the same or different flavors. The student guesses and then unplugs his or her nose. In most cases, students cannot distinguish different types of jelly beans by taste alone, whereas differentiation is easy with olfactory cues. Depending on the instructor's desires, systematic trials involving same- and different-flavored pairs of jelly beans can expand the scope of the demonstration.

DISCUSSION Typically, when their noses are plugged, students cannot identify the flavor of jelly beans unless they can see the jelly bean and guess the flavor from the color; nor can they distinguish different flavors until after they unplug their noses, when they experience an immediate burst of flavor. At this point, the students can distinguish the different flavors of jelly beans easily.

Most introductory psychology texts provide a basic description of taste and smell and their development across the life span (e.g., Sternberg, 1998, pp. 149–152). Greater discussion of taste and smell appears in books on sensation and perception (e.g., Goldstein, 1996, chapter 12).

After this demonstration, it is easy to make the point that flavor results from more than just the tongue. Students experience the fact that judgments of taste are influenced by smell and even by vision. Further, sometimes students can correctly identify cinnamon-flavored jelly beans because of the bite of the cinnamon on the tongue; such experience reveals that tactile stimulation also plays a role in flavor. Finally, one's expectations also affect flavor. The strong popcorn-flavored jelly beans may be perceived as disgusting until an individual knows what to expect.

WRITING COMPONENT Given what they have learned about the importance of smell in the perception of flavor, students can develop hypotheses about what components of the experience contributed to the overall experience. For instance, can a person identify the flavor of jelly beans simply by holding them under the nose and squeezing them to release the aroma? Students can easily test this hypothesis, writing about their predictions and their findings.

Another activity might involve having a student place a jelly bean on the tongue and then squeezing another jelly bean under the nose to see whether the additional olfactory cues affect the sensation. In such a demonstration, students would taste and smell the jelly bean in their mouths, but smell something else as well. Students can generate hypotheses and explain whether the results are consistent with that hypothesis.

A final hypothesis could address the purported decrease in olfactory capabilities of smokers and ex-smokers. Perkins et al. (1990) have shown that the sense of taste of smokers is equal to that of nonsmokers, although smokers experience less pleasure in the taste sensation. The sense of smell, however, differs in smokers and nonsmokers (Hepper, 1992). Students can generate hypotheses about the apparently equivalent taste responses but reduced overall flavor. One obvious speculation is that, although gustation may be normal in ex-smokers, olfaction may have deteriorated.

Two possible writing exercises that extend beyond the demonstration itself require students to comment on the experience of flavor more generally. First, students can identify different aspects of food that affect their enjoyment of different foods. For instance, soggy potato chips are not as enjoyable as those that crunch, suggesting the relevance of tactile and auditory cues. Also, students often react negatively to the notion of clam and tomato juice marketed as Clamato juice or head cheese (made from boiling the head of a pig or a calf and then pressing it into a cheeselike form) without ever having tasted it, reflecting the importance of culture on what is considered "good food."

Second, in another writing exercise, ask students to plan a meal for elderly individuals, who may have lost significant amounts of their olfactory capability while retaining the ability to taste (Bartoshuk, Rifkin, Marks, & Bars, 1986). The atmosphere of the meal and the texture, color, and arrangement of the food may become more important elements. Further, students can suggest ways to adulterate food to make it seem tastier.

REFERENCES

Bartoshuk, L. M., Rifkin, B., Marks, L. E., & Bars, P. (1986). Taste and aging. *Journal of Gerontology, 41,* 51–57.

Goldstein, E. B. (1996). *Sensation and perception* (4th ed.). Pacific Grove, CA: Wadsworth.

Hepper, P. (1992). Smoking, passive smoking, and smell. *Medical Science Research, 30,* 205–206.

Perkins, K. A., Epstein, L. H., Stiller, R. L., Fernstrom, M. H., Sexton, J. E., & Jacob, R. G. (1990). Perception and hedonics of sweet and fat taste in smokers and nonsmokers following nicotine intake. *Pharmacology, Biochemistry, and Behavior, 35,* 671–676.

Sternberg, R. J. (1998). *In search of the human mind* (2nd ed.). Forth Worth, TX: Harcourt Brace.

SELECTED READING

Ackerman, D. (1990). *A natural history of the senses.* New York: Random House.

Bartoshuk, L. M. (1991). Sensory factors in eating behavior. Presented at the 31st annual meeting of the Psychonomic Society: Symposium on experimental approaches to eating and its disorders (New Orleans, Louisiana). *Bulletin of the Psychonomic Society, 29,* 350–355.

Bartoshuk, L. M., & Beauchamp, G. K. (1994). Chemical senses. *Annual Review of Psychology, 45,* 419–449.

Forsyth, A. (1985, November). Good scents and bad. *Natural History,* 25–30.

Labows, J. N., Jr. (1980, November). What the nose knows: Investigating the significance of human odors. *The Sciences, 20,* 10–13.

Murphy, C., & Cain, W. S. (1986). Odor identification: The blind are better. *Physiology and Behavior, 37,* 177–180.

Sokolov, R. (1989, September). Insects, worms, and other tidbits. *Natural History,* 84–88.

36 TESTING SENSE OF SMELL WITH SCRATCH AND SNIFF

Steve Charlton
Kwantlen University-College

This activity uses scratch-and-sniff perfume and cologne ads to assess the student's olfactory ability and to examine issues such as sensitivity versus identification and gender differences. The exercise can be used in an introductory psychology course or a course in perception or biopsychology.

CONCEPT

Each year, approximately 3.5 billion dollars is spent on perfume for women. This activity allows students to test their ability to identify many of the more popular brands and question whether people are getting their money's worth. In addition, it allows students to examine gender differences. The competition between males and females creates an entertaining and competitive atmosphere. Also, the exercise encourages discussion of many of the key concepts in olfactory research.

MATERIALS NEEDED

The only materials needed for this lab exercise are scratch-and-sniff perfume or cologne ads from magazines. These ads are readily available from magazines such as *Vanity Fair* and *Vogue*. For this demonstration you will need to cut the scratch-and-sniff section from the surrounding ad so that no one can visually identify the brand. Then code the back of the scratch-and-sniff section with a number. Masking tape on the back of the section often provides a good background for the number. Make up an instructor's score sheet containing the different scents and their corresponding number codes. I usually use from 16 to 20 different fragrances. Half of the fragrances are fragrances made for men and the other half are fragrances made for women.

INSTRUCTIONS

Before the class starts, caution students with allergies that they may not want to participate. The students line up with their answer sheets and try the series of scents that are on the tables. Have the students write down the name of the perfume or cologne, the gender the fragrance is targeted for, and the gender of the student. Then collect and tabulate data during class or for shorter classes bring the results to the next class.

DISCUSSION

This exercise provides a good introduction to the area of smell. Most students perform very poorly on this identification task. These findings are consistent with past research (Desor & Beauchamp, 1974; Schab, 1991) showing that people typically can only identify common odors about 50% of the time. One might expect this deficit to be even greater for less common odors such as perfumes or colognes. I have also found that the students often have problems discriminating between fragrances made for males and those made for females. Initially, this result may seem somewhat surprising given past research showing people are capable of discriminating the gender of sweaty shirts and even breath odor (Goldstein, 1996). However, the ability to discriminate gender odor may have an adaptive evolutionary base that does not necessarily include the ability to discriminate commercial fragrances. These findings often provide for a lively discussion about the merits of buying expensive perfumes or colognes and whether people are capable of appreciating the variety of fragrances on the market.

Another common finding is gender differences with females outperforming males on the identification task. These results are consistent with research showing that females outperform males on both olfactory sensitivity and identification tasks (Matlin & Foley, 1997; Sekuler & Blake, 1994). Alternatively, it is also possible that the gender differences arise from females having more previous exposure to and greater interest in perfumes and colognes than males.

One very important issue for discussion is the difference between sensitivity (also referred to as detection) and identification. *Sensitivity* refers to an individual's ability to detect low concentrations of an odor. *Identification*, on the other hand, refers to an individual's ability to give a name to a specific odor. This latter task is more of a memory issue, somewhat akin to an individual giving names to objects they see. If a person were to forget temporarily the name of an object such as a chair, would this be considered a visual problem? Therefore, does this identification task necessarily measure our ability to smell? An interesting variation that the instructor can easily incorporate into this exercise is to have the students try to identify each scent. However, after attempting to identify each scent the student is allowed to see its product name. After trying all the scents, the student is given a second identification task. Consistent with past research (Desor & Beauchamp, 1974), practice will dramatically improve the identification performance. This, as noted earlier, underscores the importance of past experience with perfumes and colognes. This method offers a more reliable test of gender differences because individual differences in exposure to the perfumes and colognes are at least partially reduced. This exercise may also help the students better understand the difference between sensitivity and identification given it is unlikely that the students have suddenly developed an increased ability to detect odors.

Discrimination, another method of examining smell, also merits consideration. One possible variation of the present exercise is to examine individual differences in discrimination. To prepare for this demonstration, first choose pairs of very similar fragrances. Then present students with a series of pairs of stimuli. On half the trials the pairs should be the same stimuli and on the other half they should be different stimuli. Have the students respond "same" or "different" for each pair. A simple measure of the student's ability will be the total number of correct choices.

Other exercises may also be incorporated into this class. For example, the instructor may want to use very inexpensive perfumes or colognes. In this case, the students are tested to see if they can discriminate between more expensive and cheaper fragrances. Unfortunately, inexpensive scents do not typically show up as a scratch-and-sniff sample, making this demonstration more difficult to arrange. You may want to blindfold the students and individually present the scents to them or have a paired partner do this with them.

Another variation that the instructor may wish to try is dividing the class into smokers and nonsmokers. Smokers are worse than nonsmokers on both sensitivity and identification (Matlin & Foley, 1997; Sekuler & Blake, 1994). Similar findings have also been reported for individuals who are exposed to heavy concentrations of second-hand smoke.

A variation that uses scratch-and-sniff stimuli other than perfumes is also possible. Scratch-and-sniff scents of flowers, fruit, and so forth are available from many school teaching supply outlets. This type of demonstration, of course, is considerably more costly, but it allows students to examine the "tip of the nose" phenomenon (Lawless & Engen, 1977), which occurs when people say they are certain they know a scent but they just cannot put a name to it. However, when the person is given the name of the scent, immediate recognition occurs and the individual often cannot believe he or she did not recall it.

WRITING COMPONENT

This small writing assignment (three to five typed pages) can be given out and completed in time for the class exercise. It will give students a better understanding of some of the problems of measurement that they will encounter in the class exercise. Ask students to compare and contrast three different aspects of smell: identification, discrimination, and detection. One of the issues that students could address is how olfactory ability is measured. Psychophysical methods of assessment such as the method of limits and signal detection theory could be described (see Matlin & Foley, 1997, or Sekuler & Blake, 1994, for a review).

Another issue that students could examine is the practical significance of these different aspects of smell. What purpose do these abilities serve? There are countless real-life examples of the significance of smell. For example, students may consider our ability to smell sour milk or rancid butter, the need to add an odor to natural gas so that we can smell it, the possible role of pheromones, or our preferences for some smells (such as perfume). The ability to detect the smell of a fire is important for our survival. The ability to identify the smell as that of a fire rather than the smell of a flower is also important if we are to react appropriately. This example highlights the need to possess more than just one of these abilities and how interdependent they are. As Sekuler and Blake (1994) have pointed out, to be able to identify we must first be able to discriminate, and to discriminate we must first be able to detect.

A third area of discussion may be a comparison of these three abilities in olfaction to vision and audition. Coming up with examples of discrimination, identification, and detection in these other senses may lead to a more complete understanding of them.

REFERENCES

Desor, J. A., & Beauchamp, G. K. (1974). The human capacity to transmit olfactory information. *Perception & Psychophysics, 16,* 551–556.

Goldstein, B. E. (1996). *Sensation and perception* (4th ed.). Pacific Grove, CA: Brooks/Cole.

Lawless, H. T., & Engen, T. (1977). Association to odors: Interference, memories, and verbal labeling. *Journal of Experimental Psychology, 3,* 52–59.

Matlin, M. W., & Foley, H. J. (1997). *Sensation and perception* (4th ed.). Boston: Allyn & Bacon.

Schab, F. R. (1991). Odor memory: Taking stock. *Psychological Bulletin, 109,* 242–251.

Sekuler, R., & Blake, R. (1994). *Perception* (3rd ed.). New York: McGraw-Hill.

Gethcell, T. V., Doty, R. L., Bartoshuk, L. M., & Snow, J. B., Jr. (1991). *Smell and taste in health and disease.* New York: Raven Press.

Herz, R. S., & Engen, T. (1996). Odor memory: Review and analysis. *Psychonomic Bulletin and Review, 3,* 300–313.

Newman, C. (1998, Oct.). Perfume: The essence of illusion. *National Geographic,* 94–119.

Richardson, J. T. E., & Zucco, G. M. (1989). Cognition and olfaction: A review. *Psychological Bulletin, 105,* 352–360.

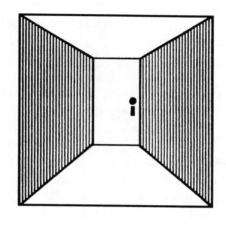

CHAPTER V
LEARNING

The six activities in this chapter cover several learning phenomena, with an emphasis on operant conditioning. Activity 37 uses a classical conditioning demonstration in humans to illustrate such principles as stimulus discrimination and generalization, extinction, and spontaneous recovery. Habituation and operant conditioning in planarians are illustrated in two exercises that are described in Activity 38.

Activity 39 describes the plans for building a Skinner box from easily acquired materials for about $20. The apparatus is intended for rats but similar-sized animals could alternatively be used. Activity 40 uses humans to illustrate six factors important in operant conditioning, including response probability and response–reinforcement interval.

Cognitive, behavioral, biological, and sociocultural perspectives are examined in Activity 41, which asks students to identify one of their bad habits, explain their behavior in terms of one of the aforementioned perspectives, and try to change that habit for the better. Finally, Activity 42 also emphasizes application by asking students to use what they know about the psychology of learning and memory to evaluate a set of claims about how to study effectively.

37 Classical Conditioning: An All-Purpose Demonstration Using a Toy Watergun

Joel I. Shenker

University of Illinois at Urbana-Champaign

This is an easy, reliable, and dramatic demonstration of classical conditioning. The teacher reads a word list, occasionally squirting a water gun at a blindfolded volunteer so that a specific word comes to predict water gun blasts. Students in class can observe examples of conditioned and unconditioned stimuli and responses, stimulus discrimination and generalization, extinction, savings during reconditioning, and spontaneous recovery.

CONCEPT
The demonstration serves as a vehicle for discussion by giving concrete, readily understood, and easily identifiable examples of classical conditioning phenomena. It is best used after students have studied classical conditioning.

MATERIALS NEEDED
You will need a large plastic garbage bag with a hole cut in the bottom large enough for a person's head to fit through, a large capacity water gun or spray bottle, and a towel.

INSTRUCTIONS
Explain to the class that classical conditioning occurs in humans as well as non-humans and is produced by a variety of different stimulus–response relationships. Ask for a volunteer and explain that participation will involve wearing a protective smock and being squirted in the face with water. It may take some coaxing to get a volunteer!

Place the garbage bag so it exposes the volunteer's head but covers the upper body. Ask the volunteer to sit in a chair facing the class. It is important that the volunteer's eyes remain closed throughout the demonstration for safety reasons. As you proceed with the demonstration, tell the students to observe silently and be ready to discuss what they have seen.

Begin by reading each word in the word list below, loudly enough that the entire class can hear and at a rate of about one word every 2 sec. Note that the word *can* appears often, sometimes in uppercase letters and sometimes in lowercase letters. Squirt the volunteer in the face only after you read the uppercase *CAN*, using a delay of about 1/2 second. Responses to the lowercase *can* test the volunteer's conditioned responses (CRs) to the target word.

Here is the stimulus word list to be used for this demonstration:

cup, can, lime, CAN, dish, girl, chalk, can, dish, CAN, key, screen, ran, CAN, desk, CAN, knob, bag, tape, CAN, dish, clip, CAN, air, ban, cheese, CAN, door, can, box, dish, hair, CAN, ring, nail, CAN, boat, cap, dish, CAN, crane, wheel, fire, CAN, dish, king, cape, apple, CAN, dog, blue, can, dish, CAN, take, call, brick, pair, CAN, spin, chair, CAN, camp,

CAN, dish, CAN, bridge, scale, can, fan, board, CAN, cool, three, horn, disk, CAN, can, cast, test, pen, dime, CAN, dish, van, can, card, stand, meat, pad, can, dish, set, can, tree, ice, plum, can, cost, bird, glass, can, light, can, sword, juice, can, dish, rock, smoke, grease, dish, keep, kid, tan, dice, hole, set, dish, eye, friend, wax, bill, bulb, dish, class, mine, mark, work, can, dish, can, bus, dish, phone, can, smart, first, can, crack, feet, can, tub, bowl, can, van, day, can, rake, dish, CAN, bluff, risk, CAN, salt, dish, CAN, ball, stack, CAN, rain, hat, food, can, van, disk, tree, can

After the demonstration, be sure to give the participant–volunteer a towel and a generous thank you. Ask your students to describe and discuss what they saw. On their own, they will probably bring up many of the important phenomena related to classical conditioning. You can identify and expand on these as they arise in the discussion.

DISCUSSION   A number of topics that relate to classical conditioning can be tied to the demonstration:

1. Acquisition is demonstrated. At first, the word *can* by itself causes no special response. After repeated pairings of the word and the water, the word by itself gradually becomes more likely to cause a CR.
2. The unconditioned stimulus (UCS) is the water squirted at the volunteer's face.
3. An unconditioned response (UCR) is usually a flinch, squint, or distinct facial expression. Often there are multiple UCRs.
4. The conditioned stimulus (CS) is the sound of the word *can*.
5. A CR is a flinch, squint, or facial expression emitted when a word is read without an accompanying squirt.
6. Stimulus generalization occurs when words that sound like *can* (e.g., *ban, ran, cap, cast*) lead to a CR.
7. Stimulus discrimination occurs when different stimulus words produce differences in the CRs. In the demonstration, CRs are strongest and most likely to occur after the word *can*. They are weakest and least likely to occur after stimulus words that do not sound at all like *can* (e.g., *dish, board, smoke*).
8. Extinction occurs when the CRs disappear or become less pronounced when the word *can* is uttered several times unaccompanied by a squirt.
9. Spontaneous recovery occurs if the word *can* again causes a CR after extinction and a long string of words where *can* is not included. Such a string occurs near the end of the demonstration.
10. Reconditioning savings is demonstrated at the end of the list where the word *can* and a squirt are again paired. At this point, fewer trials are needed to achieve strong, reliable CRs compared to the original acquisition at the beginning of the list.

This demonstration serves several useful purposes. First, it provides vivid and concrete instances of many classical conditioning phenomena. When confronted with new material relevant to classical conditioning, students can draw from their memory of the specifics of this demonstration to again piece together the components of classical conditioning. Having such vivid and concrete examples of classical conditioning phenomena are particularly useful to students who have a hard time grasping this material in an abstract form.

Second, this demonstration shows classical conditioning affects humans as well as nonhumans, a principle that students often fail to glean from the classical conditioning examples they are otherwise likely to read or discuss.

Third, the volunteer probably developed more than one CR to the CS; he or she may have developed a flinch, an eye squint, a facial expression, an upper body movement, a particular breathing pattern, and so forth. Such observations are important because they highlight the extent to which classical conditioning in the real world (i.e., outside the controlled laboratory) allows for CSs to elicit a multitude of relevant CRs, not just some specific target response that an experimenter intended to create.

Fourth, the demonstration illustrates the adaptive nature of classical conditioning. This viewpoint is especially useful to students who otherwise regard classical conditioning as trivial and unimportant in comparison to operant conditioning. Thus, students discussing the demonstration may point to the utility of squinting just *before* water hits one's eyes, as opposed to waiting until after the moment of impact. It is easy to discuss why it makes sense for organisms to learn CRs to environmental events when such stimuli come to predict significant UCSs. Or students may observe the usefulness of extinction—why bother to continue to produce a squint response when the CS no longer predicts the water in the face? Students may see similar utility in spontaneous recovery or reconditioning savings.

WRITING COMPONENT

You may want to have students write down their observations from the demonstration before you begin a class discussion. Ask students to identify the UCS, UCR, CS, and CR and to briefly describe phenomena associated with the learning they observed. This brief writing task requires all students to do their own thinking about the demonstration and might increase the number of students ready with relevant observations during discussion. As such, more students will engage in class discussion because they will have their own written comments to which they can refer.

SUGGESTED READING

Hill, W. F. (1989). *Learning: A survey of psychological interpretations* (5th ed.). New York: Harper & Row.

Kohn, A., & Kalat, J. W. (1992). Preparing for an important event: Demonstrating the modern view of classical conditioning. *Teaching of Psychology, 19*(2), 100–102.

Lieberman, D. A. (1990). *Learning: Behavior and cognition.* Belmont, CA: Wadsworth.

Sparrow, J., & Fernald, P. (1989). Teaching and demonstrating classical conditioning. *Teaching of Psychology, 16*(4), 204–206.

38 Planarians in the Classroom: Habituation and Instrumental Conditioning

Charles I. Abramson, Deborah E. Kirkpatrick,
Nathan Bollinger, Rihaneh Odde, and Shannon Lambert
Oklahoma State University

This low-cost activity uses planarians, along with a plastic cheese cutting board and an air puff from a 20-cc syringe, to demonstrate principles of habituation (and sensitization), including spontaneous recovery and influence of interstimulus interval. The same apparatus can be used to demonstrate principles of instrumental conditioning. In addition to the demonstrations, a suggested reading list is provided to enable an instructor to acquire background information on planarians and formulate ideas to modify the demonstrations.

CONCEPT

In this activity, students use planarians to learn about principles of habituation and instrumental conditioning. Planarians as subjects for psychological demonstrations offer many advantages over more traditional vertebrate animals for laboratory course work and independent study. First they are inexpensive to procure and maintain. Second, planarians can be trained in a variety of mazes, runways, and conditioning troughs that cost dollars rather than hundreds of dollars.

MATERIALS NEEDED

Each research team should have one planarian, one 20-cc plastic syringe (without needle), one stopwatch, one data sheet, one conditioning tray, one small paintbrush, and enough spring or pond water to fill the conditioning tray(s). The instructor should also have two containers: one to hold the stock colony and the other to hold the conditioned planarians. In addition, the instructor should have extra planarians to replace any that fail to respond.

Conditioning Tray

A plastic bar and cheese cutting board (manufactured by Arrow Plastics, Elk Grove, Illinois, part number 00711) makes an excellent low-cost conditioning tray. The tray costs about $2 and is available from most supermarkets. A 8-cm deep by 1.4-cm wide trough lies along the perimeter of the cutting board and serves as the conditioning trough. To prepare the trough, use the syringe to fill the trough with 15 cc of spring water. Planarian pond water can also be used (available from Ward's Biology, Rochester, New York, part number 88 W 7010). This produces a depth of approximately 5 mm, which is deep enough for the animal to swim yet still react to the air puff. If the bar and cheese cutting board is not available, a plastic butter dish or petri dish will substitute. To administer the habituating stimulus or punishment (e.g., the air puff), use a plastic 20-cc syringe, available at any drugstore or biological supply house.

Planarians

Planarians are easy to obtain and care for and are available from any number of biological supply houses such as Ward's (Web address: http://www.wardsci.com). For the more adventurous, planarians can be captured in ponds, streams, lakes and rivers throughout the United States. When planarians are ordered commercially, instructions for feeding and maintenance are included. Planarians can be housed in any container that can hold water. The most important factor in maintaining a good planarian culture is clean water. The water should be changed once a week and be chlorine free. A good time to change the water is after a feeding. Planarians are primarily carnivorous and show a preference for fresh liver, although they will eat frozen liver that has been defrosted. A weekly feeding is quite sufficient to maintain healthy planarians. When the experiment is completed, the instructor can decide to keep a stock colony for future demonstrations. If this is not desirable, the stock colony and conditioned colony can be donated to a biology/zoology department, high school, or preschool program.

Data Sheet

A data sheet suitable for both demonstrations is available in appendix A. The data sheet contains room for student information, observations, and data.

INSTRUCTIONS *Conducting the Experiment: Habituation*

In our demonstration the time between air puff presentations (i.e., the inter-stimulus interval) is 60 sec, the intensity of the air puff is 20 cc of air, the duration is approximately 1 sec (the time to depress the syringe), and the number of trials is 50. After the experimental parameters have been selected, the student will fill the conditioning trough with water and remove a planarian from the colony with a paintbrush and gently place it in the conditioning trough. Following a 5-min adaptation period, the student administers the air puff by pulling back on the plunger of the syringe until the plunger reaches the 20-cc mark. Next the student will direct the tip of the syringe to the head of the planarian and depress the plunger. On contact with the air puff, a planarian will typically contract to about one-half of its length. After the syringe is depressed the student experimenter must do two things. First, the students must start the timer to begin the inter-stimulus interval (e.g., the time between air puffs); second, the student needs to record on a data sheet the presence or absence of a contraction response. It is often convenient to record a 1 if the animal contracted and a 0 if it did not. If graph paper is placed underneath the conditioning trough the contraction response may be quantified and expressed as the number of boxes exposed. If the planarian does not contract, for example, no boxes will be exposed and the student can enter a 0 on the data sheet. With repeated applications of the air puff the number of contractions decreases. When the experiment is completed, the student should return the planarian to a home tank reserved for conditioned animals.

The experimental procedure for demonstrating habituation does not contain control procedures. It may be desirable for some members of the class to perform baseline experiments to determine the base rate of contraction in the absence of an air puff. Students also find it informative to modify the procedure to include sensitization trials to rule out sensory adaptation and motor fatigue as alternative explanations for the decrease in contraction they will observe. One way to provide such stimulation is to gently touch the animal with one of the bristles from the paintbrush. Alternatively, a small drop of water can be splashed near the animal using an eyedropper. The animal should contract to the introduction of the new stimulus and contract again when the air puff is reintroduced. If class time permits, students will find it interesting to vary the intensity of the air puff by increasing or decreasing the volume of air in the syringe. The duration of the air puff can also be easily altered by varying the speed in which the plunger of the syringe is depressed.

Conducting the Experiment: Instrumental Conditioning

In a second demonstration, students can explore the principles of instrumental conditioning by using the same air puff and cutting board used in the habituation demonstration. When filled with water, the trough in the cutting board makes an excellent rectangular planarian runway. To demonstrate the influence of response–reinforcer relationships, have the student experimenters give the planarians a series of air puffs until they turn in the opposite direction. As the training session continues the number of air puffs required to elicit turning behavior decreases.

The turning response consists of a contraction followed by an extension of the animal. Following several contractions and extensions the animal begins to turn away from the direction of the air puff and swims in the opposite direction. For example, if the animal is swimming in a clockwise direction repeated presentations of an air puff elicits a number of contractions and extensions. These behaviors are followed by the animal turning and swimming in a counterclockwise direction. In our demonstration the dependent variable of interest is the number of air puffs required to make the animal swim in the opposite direction. As training progresses the number of air puffs required to produce a turning response steadily declines.

In our demonstration the intensity of the air puff is 20 cc of air, the duration of the air puff is as short as possible (1 sec or less), the intertrial interval is fixed at 1 min, and the number of trials needed to conclude the experiment is 60. When the parameters of the experiment are decided, the student experimenter gently removes the planarian from its home container (with the paintbrush) and gives it a 5-min adaptation period.

When the animal is placed in the trough it will begin to move in one direction (e.g., clockwise or counterclockwise). Following the 5-min adaptation period the student experimenter will try and reverse this movement by giving the planarian a series of air puffs directed to its head. When the planarian changes direction, the student depresses the stopwatch to time the next intertrial interval, and the number of air puffs is recorded on the data sheet provided in appendix A. Typically it will take 12 to 20 air puffs before the animal changes direction. This will soon decrease to about 4 to 5. When the experiment is completed the subject is returned to a home container reserved for conditioned animals.

As in the habituation experiment, students enjoy creating their own experimental designs. Some of the more common variations include manipulating the intensity of the air puff, presenting the air puff on a partial schedule of reward, delaying the time between the response and presentation of the air puff, no longer presenting the air puff following a turn (extinction), varying the intertrial interval, pretreating the animal with stimulants such as caffeine, and investigating whether instrumental behavior survives regeneration.

Unresponsive Animals

Occasionally a student may encounter an unresponsive planarian. Therefore, whenever possible extra planarians should be brought to the class to replace those not contracting to the air puff or, once contracted, do not reextend. Such behavior is likely if the animals are dropping their tails, are overstimulated, or come from a polluted environment. If such behavior is observed the animals should be immediately removed from the conditioning chamber and gently returned to their home container.

DISCUSSION

The advantage of these demonstrations are their extremely low cost and versatility. Moreover, students enjoy the hands-on approach. In a small class each student can condition his or her own planarian. If the demonstration is presented to a large lecture class, the instructor can divided students into research teams where one member of the team, for example, presents the stimuli and the other member records data. An effective alternative to creating research teams is to place the apparatus on top of an overhead projector so the entire class can view the performance of a single animal.

Although not required, our students tend to enjoy the planarian demonstrations more if they are integrated into a component on learning and memory. We also recommend that the component include information on the natural history and biology of these interesting organisms. Students also enjoy hearing about the unique place planarian learning holds in the history of psychology (Rilling, 1996).

The use of planarians to demonstrate principles of nonassociative and associative learning is also useful in generating classroom discussion about the importance of learning. Points for discussion include the usefulness of cognitive explanations of behavior, what are suitable control groups, what is a suitable statistical analysis, and what is the biological significance of conditioning.

WRITING COMPONENT

One of the strengths of this exercise is that it can be easily incorporated into a research report assignment. Students will formulate a hypothesis, conduct the literature review, design and carry out the experiment, analyze, graph, and discuss the results. An alternative writing assignment is to have students conduct a literature review with the goal of comparing their planarian results with those obtained with other species (Abramson, 1986, 1990, 1994; Abramson, Onstott, Edwards, & Bowe, 1996; Sheiman & Tiras, 1996). Students can also be asked to provide written answers to the discussion questions mentioned earlier, to create a poster presentation based on their library and classroom research, or to describe how their observations of planaria fit the principles described in their textbook.

REFERENCES

Abramson, C. I. (1986). Invertebrates in the classroom. *Teaching of Psychology*, 13, 24–29.

Abramson, C. I. (1990). *Invertebrate learning: A laboratory manual and source book*. Washington, DC: American Psychological Association.

Abramson, C. I. (1994). *A primer of invertebrate learning: The behavioral perspective.* Washington, DC: American Psychological Association.

Abramson, C. I., Onstott, T., Edwards, S., & Bowe, K. (1996). Classical-conditioning demonstrations for elementary and advanced courses. *Teaching of Psychology, 23,* 26–30.

Rilling, M. (1996). James McConnell's forgotten 1960s quest for planarian learning: A biochemical engram, and celebrity. *American Psychologist, 51,* 589–598.

Sheiman, I. M, & Tiras, K. L. (1996). Memory and morphogenesis in planaria and beetle. In C. I. Abramson, Z. P. Shuranova, & Y. M. Burmistrov (Eds.), *Russian contributions to invertebrate behavior* (pp. 43–76). Westport, CT: Praeger.

SUGGESTED READING

The material in this reading list was carefully selected to provide an instructor or interested student with information on various aspects of using planarians in the classroom. The material can be used to create a reading list on a specific topic or range of topics, offer tips and insights into various aspects of planarian behavior, stimulate classroom discussion and provide ideas for future student projects and instructor demonstrations.

Bonner, J. C., & Wells, M. R. (1987). Comparative acute toxicity of DDT metabolites among American and European species of planarians. *Comparative Biochemistry and Physiology (C): Comparative Pharmacology and Toxicology, 87,* 437–438.

Katz, A. N. (1978). Inexpensive animal learning exercises for huge introductory laboratory classes. *Teaching of Psychology, 5,* 91–93.

Kessler, C. C. (1973). The effect of magnesium pemoline on learning in the planarian. *Journal of Biological Psychology, 15,* 31–33.

McConnell, J. V., & Shelby, J. M. (1970). Memory transfer experiments in invertebrates. In G. Unger (Ed.), *Molecular mechanisms in memory and learning* (pp. 71–101). New York: Plenum Press.

Owren, M. J., & Scheuneman, D. L. (1993). An inexpensive habituation and sensitization learning laboratory exercise using planarians. *Teaching of Psychology, 20,* 226–228.

Reynierse, J. H., & Gleason, K. (1974). Determinants of planarian aggregation behavior. *Animal Learning and Behavior, 3,* 343–346.

Rivera, V. R., & Perich, M. J. (1994). Effects of water quality on survival and reproduction of four species of planaria (turbellaria: tricladida). *Invertebrate Reproduction and Development, 25,* 1–7.

Sarnat, H. B., & Netsky, M. G. (1985). The brain of the planarian as the ancestor of the human brain. *Canadian Journal of Neurological Sciences, 12,* 296–302.

Note: A more complete bibliography of research with planarians is available from the author at the OSU Psychology Museum Website at http://www.cas.okstate.edu/psych/museum/index.html

Appendix A

A Sample Data Sheet

Name:_____   Experiment: Habituation, Instrumental, Other

Date:_____   Time: _____

Subject #: _____

Number of trials: _____   ISI/ITI: _____

Subject Size: _____

Stimulus intensity: _____   Stimulus duration: _____ Other: _____

Trial/Response

1	21	41
2	22	42
3	23	43
4	24	44
5	25	45
6	26	46
7	27	47
8	28	48
9	29	49
10	30	50
11	31	51
12	32	52
13	33	53
14	34	54
15	35	55
16	36	56
17	37	57
18	38	58
19	39	59
20	40	60

Notes and Observations:

_____

_____

_____

_____

_____

_____

39 Operant Conditioning in the Classroom: An Inexpensive Home-Built Skinner Box

Kenneth D. Keith
Nebraska Wesleyan University

Maintenance of animal laboratory facilities is financially and logistically prohibitive for many psychology programs. However, much can be gained from direct experience with animal activities and demonstrations. This activity shows how an inexpensive home-built Skinner box can provide opportunity for observation and shaping of rat behavior and can lead to meaningful exercises in writing and critical thinking.

CONCEPT

Psychology teachers have developed a variety of ingenious ways to demonstrate behavior principles in the absence of animal facilities (Abramson, 1990; Crisler, 1988; Owen & Scheuneman, 1993). However, alternatives may not be totally satisfying for the student and teacher who want to do more than simply imagine how animal behavior might have been shaped in Skinner's laboratory.

This activity involves construction and use of an inexpensive *Skinner box*— a term not favored by Skinner (1983) (who preferred the term *operant conditioning chamber*) but universally understood in reference to the standard operant conditioning apparatus. The apparatus itself is easily built, and its use offers many possibilities for demonstrations, behavioral observation, critical thinking, and writing.

MATERIALS NEEDED

To assemble the Skinner box you will need a rat, a small plastic or plexiglass animal cage (readily available in pet stores), a few feet of lightweight electrical wire, and the following standard Radio Shack items: plastic battery holder 2-C, #270-0385; 1.5 v DC Minibuzzer, #273-0053; E10 lamp base, #272-0357; PK16 wire nuts, #640-3057; PK2 alkaline C batteries, #230-0551; SMini SPDT lever, #275-0016; and SQ NO push switch, #275-0618.

In addition to these parts, the builder will require sufficient aluminum foil and duct tape to fashion a food hopper on the outside surface of the box and (on the inside) a small plastic receptacle to serve as a feeder. It will also be helpful to lengthen the lever by gluing a short length of wood (e.g., a piece of tongue depressor) to it. These items are assembled on a simple plywood base as shown in Fig. 39-1.

The resulting apparatus is a chamber equipped with a lever that can be easily depressed by a laboratory rat, a receptacle into which food pellets can be dropped via the hopper, and visual and auditory stimulus sources that are activated by the lever and a handheld switch. The total cost is approximately $20.

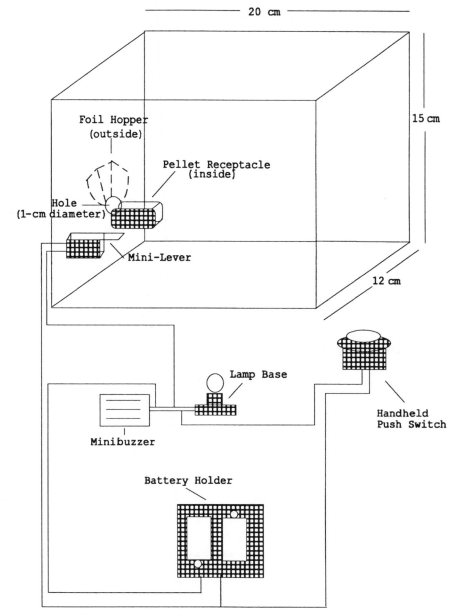

Figure 39-1. Diagram of the home-built Skinner box showing wiring connections to light, buzzer, lever, hand switch, and battery holder. The design of this apparatus is provided compliments of Sean Heard who, with the assistance of his father and with consultation from our laboratory, built the prototype for a public school science fair in Lincoln, Nebraska.

INSTRUCTIONS The home-built Skinner box can be used for nearly all the standard exercises and demonstrations that have long distinguished laboratory work in operant conditioning. These include magazine training, behavior shaping, discrimination, and extinction, among others (Michael, 1963).

A hungry rat can be readily magazine-trained through repeated presentation of the light and buzzer along with food pellets dropped into the feeder. (Precision food pellets (45 mg) are available from P. J. Noyes, Inc., of Lancaster, New Hampshire. Small bits of ordinary rat chow will also work, and Skinner [1956] reported using uncooked pearl barley.) After a few trials the rat will go to the feeder when the light and buzzer are presented.

The rat can then be shaped to press the lever by reinforcing successive approximations in the manner commonly described in standard introductory psychology textbooks (e.g., Davis & Palladino, 1997; Myers, 1998), and additional exercises (extinction, discrimination, intermittent schedules of reinforcement) can be easily added.

DISCUSSION

Animal research has a long and significant history in American psychology. Our field would clearly not be the same without such names as E. L. Thorndike, Margaret Washburn, John Watson, E. C. Tolman, B. F. Skinner, Martin Seligman, and John Garcia. As Davis (1993) argued, if our students are to understand the science of our discipline, they must be exposed to animal research and to methods and facilities appropriate to that research.

Although the majority of the top undergraduate colleges maintain animal facilities in psychology (e.g., Benedict & Stoloff, 1991), the fact remains that laboratory equipment can be extremely expensive and that maintenance of an animal colony is impossible for many (perhaps most) colleges and high schools. In my own department, animal laboratory costs are the single largest item in the operating budget.

The apparatus described allows a low-cost, hands-on activity that can provide students with a meaningful animal laboratory experience. The fact that its components require manual operation is an advantage for introductory teaching purposes, to the extent this ensures that students will be forced to examine the importance of immediacy of reinforcement, the role of discriminative stimuli, the significance of careful observation, and so forth. In addition, activities using the Skinner box provide for meaningful discussion of animal rights, research ethics, and humane standards of animal care (e.g., Herzog, 1990).

A number of computer-based programs are available to simulate animal behavior laboratory exercises. Nevertheless, I am not convinced that these "virtual" experiences engender the same enthusiasm that Skinner (1956) felt when he realized, while tinkering with his own apparatus, his kinship with Pavlov. That excitement *is* possible however, when students are offered direct experience observing and shaping animal behavior.

WRITING COMPONENT

Activities using the Skinner box lend themselves well to a variety of critical thinking and writing opportunities. One useful strategy is to ask students to prepare and discuss written answers to questions that might arise during observation of the behavior of the rat in the apparatus. Some examples would include the following:

1. Suppose that, instead of delivering a food pellet after each lever press, you simply dropped in a pellet every 30 sec. What form might the rat's behavior take? Why?
2. When the rat presses the lever you can control how quickly a pellet is delivered. What would happen if you waited 20 sec before dropping a pellet?
3. In natural environments many behaviors are maintained on intermittent reinforcement schedules. Identify and discuss some examples.

4. The light and buzzer have been paired with food as you have shaped the rat's lever pressing. What role might they play in controlling the rat's behavior? How could you determine this?

REFERENCES

Abramson, C. I. (1990) *Invertebrate learning: A laboratory manual and source book*. Washington, DC: American Psychological Association.

Benedict, J., & Stoloff, M. (1991). Animal laboratory facilities at "America's best" undergraduate colleges. *American Psychologist, 46*, 535–536.

Crisler, J. C. (1988). Conditioning the instructor's behavior: A class project in psychology of learning. *Teaching of Psychology, 15*, 135–137.

Davis, S. F. (1993). Animals in the classroom. *Psychological Science Agenda, 6*(5), 8.

Davis, S. F., & Palladino, J. J. (1997). *Psychology* (2nd ed.). Upper Saddle River, NJ: Prentice-Hall.

Herzog, H. A. (1990). Discussing animal rights and animal research in the classroom. *Teaching of Psychology, 17*, 90–94.

Michael, J. (1963). *Laboratory studies in operant behavior*. New York: McGraw-Hill.

Myers, D. G. (1998). *Psychology* (5th ed.). New York: Worth.

Owen, M. J., & Scheuneman, D. L. (1993). An inexpensive habituation and sensitization learning laboratory exercise using planarians. *Teaching of Psychology, 20*, 226–228.

Skinner, B. F. (1956). A case history in scientific method. *American Psychologist, 11*, 221–233.

Skinner, B. F. (1983). *A matter of consequences*. New York: Knopf.

SUGGESTED READING

Bare, J. K. (1987). Human operant conditioning. In V. P. Makosky, L. G. Whittemore, & A. M. Rogers (Eds.), *Activities handbook for the teaching of psychology: Volume 2* (pp. 67–68). Washington, DC: American Psychological Association.

Corey, J. R. (1990). The use of goldfish in operant conditioning. In V. P. Makosky, C. C. Sileo, L. G. Whittemore, C. P. Landry, & M. L. Skutley (Eds.), *Activities handbook for the teaching of psychology: Volume 3* (pp. 106–108). Washington, DC: American Psychological Association.

Domjan, M. (1998). *The principles of learning and behavior* (4th ed.). Pacific Grove, CA: Brooks/Cole.

National Research Council. (1996). *Guide for the care and use of laboratory animals*. Washington, DC: National Academy Press.

Sharp, P. E., & LaRegina, M. C. (1998). *The laboratory rat*. Boca Raton, FL: CRC Press.

40 SHAPING BEHAVIOR THROUGH OPERANT CONDITIONING

Peter S. Fernald
University of New Hampshire

L. Dodge Fernald
Harvard University

Through this in-class activity, the instructor conditions and shapes two responses: a high-probability response (touching one's own shoe) in one student volunteer and a much lower probability response (touching the instructor's shoe) in a second volunteer.

CONCEPTS
Six factors important in operant conditioning, especially shaping, are illustrated: activity of the participant, response probability, reinforcement, response– reinforcement interval, skill of the experimenter, and chance factors.

MATERIALS NEEDED
You will need a pencil, pen, or other small hard object that will make a clear distinct sound when tapped on the top of a lectern, table, or desk.

INSTRUCTIONS
Explain that shaping through operant conditioning procedures is similar to the children's game Hot–Cold and that you want two students to play a modified version of the game in front of the class. Ask for volunteers, and then explain to the two volunteers that you want them to leave the room while you explain certain details of the shaping procedure to the class. Once the two volunteers have left the room, explain to the class that one volunteer will be shaped to touch his or her own shoe, the other volunteer to touch your (the instructor's) shoe. Also, impress on the students that throughout the shaping process they are to remain still and quiet, offering no verbal or nonverbal signals of encouragement or disapproval to the volunteers. *This warning is essential.* Students should not, for example, snicker, giggle, or move restlessly in the chair.

Select three students to serve as recorders. They are to record both the amount of time and number of reinforcements (taps) required to shape the responses in question. Ask the remaining students to observe carefully and take notes on the shaping process, noting especially those factors that facilitate or compromise the process.

Invite one of the volunteers back into the room, and then explain the follow- ing shaping procedure—that is, the modified version of the Hot–Cold game. In- dicate that the reinforcement will be the sound of your tapping some hard object, possibly a piece of chalk or a pen, on a table or desk, and the volunteer's task is to earn as many reinforcements (taps, or points) as possible. Tell the volunteer that the shaping procedure has begun and then observe the volunteer closely for about 20 s, during which time you should note what kinds of responses the vol- unteer emits and which of them most closely approximate touching his or her own shoe. Once you have completed the 20-s (or longer) observation period, tap the table *immediately* after the volunteer emits a response indicating some sort of downward movement that might represent the beginning components of the desired (shoe-touching) response. Continue to reinforce (tap) each time this response occurs so that the frequency (probability) of occurrence of the response is enhanced. Next, discontinue reinforcement (taps) until a still closer approximation to the desired (shoe-touching) response occurs. Such a response might actually be some combination of responses, for example, bending a little at the knees or waist while reaching slightly downward with a hand. Reinforce this response, again by tapping *immediately* after the response occurs. Continue to reinforce each successive response that more closely approximates the desired response until the target (shoe-touching) response occurs.

Note that failures to tap (reinforce) immediately often result in inadvertently reinforcing a response that is further from, rather than closer to, the target response. These errors of reinforcement typically prolong the shaping (conditioning) process. On the other hand, such reinforcement errors often prove most instructive for the class, as is pointed out in the discussion presented later in this activity.

Depending on the amount of class time remaining, the ease with which the first volunteer's behavior is shaped, students' interest and background in operant conditioning, and other factors, you may or may not wish to discuss the shaping that occurred with the first volunteer before you invite the second volunteer back into the room. The advantage of discussing what occurred with the first volunteer is that the students observe the second shaping demonstration with much greater sophistication, which later is reflected by their very perceptive questions and comments. The disadvantage is that this arrangement typically requires more time and excludes the second volunteer.

Invite the second volunteer into the classroom, again explain the guidelines for the modified Hot–Cold game, and proceed to shape the desired response, in this case the volunteer's touching your shoe. Shaping behavior in the first volunteer typically takes less time than shaping the second volunteer, for reasons indicated in the discussion section that follows.

Be sure to thank the volunteers, whose contribution to the class is substantial. It is no easy task and sometimes a bit embarrassing to play the modified Hot–Cold game in front of a large group that already knows the answer.

Ask the three recorders to report the data they collected. Write the data on the chalkboard. It may be appropriate here to discuss individual differences in observation and the presence or absence of consensus. Once the issue of reliability of observation has been addressed, proceed to a discussion of the shaping process, noting particularly what the data suggest in regard to the ease or difficulty in shaping the two responses in question. Lastly, ask various members of the class to present their observations. These observations typically elicit a full account of the several concepts and principles detailed in the discussion that follows.

For a less difficult shaping task, one volunteer might be shaped to erase a certain portion of the chalkboard and another volunteer to pull the window shade down. Both are high-probability responses, higher in this particular context (i.e., the classroom) than touching shoes. Thus, they should be easier to demonstrate. However, the greater ease of shaping may also mean there is less grist for the discussion mill. Still another possibility is to let the class decide what responses will be conditioned, an arrangement that enhances students' involvement in the activity. However, precautions must be taken to ensure that the selected responses do justice to the purposes of the activity.

Another option, time permitting, is to divide the class into groups of three to five students each. After the shaping procedure has been demonstrated once, the groups are told to conduct their own demonstrations of conditioning, an arrangement that elicits in students substantial interest and excitement. In each group one student agrees to be the volunteer who is conditioned. Another student does the conditioning. And the remaining two or three students are observers, who also select the response to be shaped.

Class discussion is readily organized around one general question: Why are some participants (or responses) more quickly shaped than others? Efforts to answer the question lead to considering several factors important in conditioning, some of which may be the following.

Activity of the Volunteer

Animal trainers and operant experimenters testify to the difficulty of conditioning and shaping passive animals. This difficulty occurs with human beings as well. Some activity on the part of the volunteer must occur before reinforcement can be presented. Both amount and variability of the activity are important. Volunteers emitting a large number of different responses are easiest to shape.

Response Probability

Prior to shaping, different responses have different probabilities—that is, different frequencies of occurrence. Touching one's own shoe is more probable than touching someone else's shoe. Therefore, the former response is more readily shaped.

Reinforcement

Reinforcement is any event that increases the probability of a response. The shaping situation was a bit contrived, as the volunteers were instructed to earn as many taps (points) as possible. The instructions made a previously neutral event (tapping) into a reinforcement (or reinforcer). Make sure that students do not misconstrue reinforcement to be an event that satisfies some internal state, such as the desire to earn points. The proper definition of reinforcement makes reference only to response probability. This is a most important point. Failure to make it clear does not do justice to the behavioristic approach.

Response–Reinforcement Interval

Shaping occurs most rapidly when the interval is very brief, when reinforcement *immediately* follows the desired response. This interval is determined by skill of the experimenter.

Skill of the Experimenter

Because of their experience, both animal trainers and experimenters working in operant conditioning laboratories shape their participants to emit complex responses with relative ease. As may have been apparent in this demonstration, however, often it is difficult to shape even simple responses. For example, perhaps one or more taps were a moment too late, thus reinforcing a further, rather than closer, approximation of the desired response. Ask the students if they noted any such instances. Discussion of the details of these instances can be most instructive. Skilled experimenters and animal trainers are quick to reinforce closer approximations of the desired response. Only rarely do they mistakenly reinforce responses that are further from or incompatible with the desired response.

Chance Factors

One volunteer may emit a response similar to the desired response very early in the conditioning (shaping) session, whereas another volunteer, though very active, may emit no responses that even remotely resemble the desired response. Such differences occur for unknown reasons, which is the scientist's definition of chance or luck. For the behaviorist, however, luck in this instance refers to the volunteer's past history, which always includes reinforcement of numerous responses, some more and some less related to the desired response.

WRITING COMPONENT | Ask students to write a brief reaction to this statement: "Conditioning practices are used to control behavior. Therefore, they should be banned." After having approximately 5 min to respond to this statement, students may be given the opportunity to share their responses with one another in small groups or perhaps with the entire class. The discussion should include three points: that conditioning is a fact of life, that it is neither good nor bad, and that it is a reciprocal process.

- Whether one likes it or not, conditioning is both inevitable and ubiquitous. It occurs in every human interaction, even casual conversations. It is a reality of life.

  Conditioning per se is neither good nor bad. Rather, it is a process, a procedure, and a tool. Like any tool, it can be used for good or ill, or some combination of both. It is important to know about conditioning principles, for then we can use them to produce constructive, life-enhancing responses in ourselves and others. The alternative is to allow conditioning principles to operate apart from awareness and capriciously, in which case life-defeating or disruptive responses are reinforced. Much of the discussion surrounding policies of welfare reform focuses on this issue—that is, whether governmental assistance (reinforcement) promotes functional or dysfunctional behavior.

  Conditioning is reciprocal, meaning that in any two-person interaction each person simultaneously conditions, and is conditioned by, the other person. Although it may be possible for someone more competent to take advantage of someone less competent (e.g., a child or elderly person), the less competent often can exert some countercontrol. Consider, for example, the statement said by one rat to another: "I have the experimenter conditioned. Each time I press the bar she gives me another food pellet." Behavioral control through operant conditioning is reciprocal. Babies control their parents; parents control their babies. Teachers condition students, and vice versa. The reciprocal nature of conditioning is evident in this question: "Dad, what do I have to do to get you to loan me the car?"

SUGGESTED READING

Breland, K., & Breland, M. (1966). *Animal behavior.* New York: Macmillan.

Domjan, M. (1993). *The principles of learning and behavior* (3rd ed.). Pacific Grove, CA: Brooks/Cole.

Epstein R. (1991). Skinner, creativity, and the problem of spontaneous behavior. *Psychological Science, 2,* 362–370.

Lattal, K. A. (1992). B. F. Skinner and psychology [Introduction to the special issue]. *American Psychologist, 27,* 1269–1272.

41 USING PSYCHOLOGICAL PERSPECTIVES TO CHANGE HABITS

Rob McEntarffer

Lincoln Southeast High School, Lincoln, Nebraska

Introducing the primary psychological perspectives or theoretical orientations (e.g., cognitive, behavioral) found in every introductory psychology textbook can be tedious and confusing to students. This activity provides students with a personal context for understanding the commonly taught psychological perspectives by asking them to analyze the origins and maintenance of a personal bad habit. Students are also provided a means of modifying the undesired behavior.

CONCEPT
: This activity demonstrates the relevance and applicability of the commonly taught psychological perspectives (theoretical orientations) to the understanding of behavior. Students select an unwanted habit and use their understanding of behavioral, cognitive, biological, and social–cultural perspectives to assess the acquisition and possible extinction of the habit.

MATERIALS NEEDED
: Aside from lecture notes on psychological perspectives (or student knowledge of the perspectives prior to the day of the activity), no special materials are needed. The perspectives that have worked best are behavioral, cognitive, biological, and social–cultural. The activity can be modified to include additional perspectives.

INSTRUCTIONS
: After communicating information about the behavioral, cognitive, biological, and social–cultural psychological perspectives to the students, ask students to select a habit they wish they did not have but are willing to discuss. Provide examples such as nail biting, being late for class, smoking, and any others you wish them to consider.

After selecting the bad habit, ask students to assess the acquisition and maintenance of the habit using the four psychological perspectives. Also, have students select the perspective that best explains the habit. This assessment can be completed in class or given as homework.

Group students in pairs, instructing one student in each dyad to relate the acquisition–maintenance analysis of the bad habit to the partner. Partners should take turns identifying the proper psychological perspective being used to analyze the acquisition–maintenance of the bad habit.

The second half of the activity involves implementing an intervention (based on one of the psychological perspectives) designed to change the bad habit. Explain to the students that you would like them to change their bad habits over the next 2 weeks. Students are to keep track of the behavior in a habit journal, where they can record the habit and changes in the habit. As a means of explaining the habit journal, I read the following to my students:

For the next 2 weeks, we will attempt to alter one of the bad habits you have discussed in class, and as part of this exercise you will keep track of your progress in a habit journal. Begin your journal by explaining the intervention techniques each psychological perspective would have you employ to extinguish the habit. For instance, the technique of using rewards and punishments to eliminate the habit would come from the behavioral perspective. Choose the intervention technique or a combination of techniques you believe will be the most helpful in getting rid of your bad habit, and use them at your discretion. You will need a journal entry for each day during the next 2 weeks. Each journal entry should include a progress report on your bad habit. For example, is the intervention working? How many times have you engaged in this bad habit in the previous 24 hr? Include any additional information that might shed light on your attempt to eliminate your bad habit.

After the 2 weeks have passed, discuss with your students the progress of the habit-changing attempts. Discuss which perspectives and interventions were most effective for certain types of habits. Encourage your students to continue their habit-changing behaviors for the rest of the semester if they were helpful.

DISCUSSION   This activity demonstrates the value of psychological explanations for behavior by getting students to examine their own bad habits using psychological terms and concepts. I have noticed students are often skeptical about psychological explanations for behavior (e.g., accused criminals pleading insanity as a means of removing responsibility for criminal actions). By applying the perspectives to themselves and seeing firsthand how intractable and resistant to change some behavior is, students gain a clearer understanding of human behavior. The activity also helps the student understand psychological perspectives by applying them to a real-world example relevant to the student.

WRITING COMPONENT   Writing in the habit journal allows students to directly relate personal experiences to the understanding of psychological perspectives. It also helps remind students of their intervention and assignment.

SUGGESTED READING   Bolles, R. C. (1993). *The story of psychology: A thematic history*. Belmont, CA: Wadsworth.
Hunt, M. (1993). *The story of psychology*. New York: Doubleday.
Myers, D. G. (1992). *Psychology* (3rd ed.). New York: Worth.
Nairne, J. S. (1997). *Psychology: The adaptive mind*. Pacific Grove, CA: Brooks/ Cole.

42 APPLYING THE PRINCIPLES OF LEARNING AND MEMORY TO STUDENTS' LIVES

Allyson J. Weseley

Roslyn High School, Roslyn, New York

In studying learning and memory, students are confronted with a vast number of theories and effects. Often, even as we teach them about levels-of-processing theory, they cling stubbornly to study techniques that are based solely on more superficial strategies. This activity requires students to apply their knowledge of learning and memory by evaluating a set of claims about how to study effectively.

CONCEPT   Students will deepen their understanding of various aspects of learning and memory research by critiquing advice about how to be a more successful student.

MATERIALS NEEDED   Each student will need one group worksheet (see appendix A).

INSTRUCTIONS   After completing the unit on learning and memory, divide the class into small groups of three to five students. Give each student a copy of the group worksheet, and instruct the groups that they have 15 min to evaluate the claims presented. The amount of time required by the groups to complete the worksheet will depend on how thoroughly they have mastered the memory chapter.

After the groups have completed the task, go over the answers by asking each group to explain its analysis of a particular claim. Encourage the students to debate the answer they have deemed to be correct, thereby putting the emphasis on the reasoning behind responses rather than simple statements of agreement or disagreement.

You may want to select one member from each group randomly (by rolling a die, for instance) to come to the front of the room as a representative of the group. This encourages all group members to focus on the assigned task. Each representative can be randomly assigned to critique one of the statements. All members of the class should have the opportunity to respond to each critique.

DISCUSSION   Allow the course of the discussion to be dictated by the presenters' analyses and the response of the rest of the class. You will want to make certain that the following points surface as part of the class discussion. The first and fifth statements on the worksheet both are based on the levels-of-processing theory of memory. The advice in Suggestion 1 is good for the same reason the advice in Suggestion 5 is bad: The deeper the level of processing, the better the chance that one will remember the information at a later time (Anderson, 1990). Suggestion 2 reflects the impact of context. Research has demonstrated that the place where a person studies can serve as a cue that aids the person in retrieval (Smith, 1979).

The advice in Suggestion 3 has been found to produce retrograde interference and thus diminish accurate memory (Jenkins & Dallenbach, 1924). Suggestion 4 gets at the idea of mood congruence. Researchers have found when participants' moods during encoding match their moods during recall, their performance is superior to when the moods do not match (Bowers, 1981). Suggestion 6 addresses the self-reference effect. Kuiper and Rogers (1979) demonstrated that recall was improved when participants elaborated the material in a way that was personally meaningful. Finally, Suggestion 7 also provides useful advice according to the spacing effect (Dempster, 1988), which holds that the amount of time between successive presentations of the same material is directly related to the amount of recall.

WRITING COMPONENT

Have students write a short essay describing the extent to which they study effectively. If they employ techniques that research has shown to be less than optimally effective, why have they chosen these techniques and will they change them?

REFERENCES

Anderson, J. R. (1990). *Cognitive psychology and its implications* (3rd ed.). New York: W. H. Freeman.

Bowers, G. H. (1981). Mood and memory. *American Psychologist, 36,* 129–148.

Dempster, F. N. (1988). The spacing effect: A case study in the failure to apply the results of psychological research. *American Psychologist, 43,* 627–634.

Jenkins, J. G., & Dallenbach, K. M. (1924). Obliviscence during sleep and waking. *American Journal of Psychology, 35,* 605–612.

Kuiper, N. A., & Rogers, R. B. (1979). Encoding of personal information: Self–other differences. *Journal of Personality and Social Psychology, 37,* 499–514.

Smith, S. M. (1979). Remembering in and out of context. *Journal of Experimental Psychology: Human Learning and Memory, 5,* 460–471.

SUGGESTED READING

Baddeley, A. (1990). *Human memory.* Boston: Allyn & Bacon.

Higbee, K. L. (1988). *Your memory: How it works and how to improve it* (2nd ed.). Englewood Cliffs, NJ: Prentice-Hall.

Kantrowitz, B., & Wingert, P. (1989, April 17). How kids learn. *Newsweek.*

Loftus, E. F. (1984, February). Eyewitness: Essential but unreliable. *Psychology Today,* 22–27.

Williams, R. L., & Long, J. D. (1991). *Manage your life* (4th ed.). Boston: Houghton-Mifflin.

Appendix A

Applying the Principles of Learning and Memory to Students' Lives: Group Worksheet

You are a member of a panel of psychological experts that has been asked to review and critique a new book about how to improve study habits. Use your knowledge of psychological research on learning and memory to evaluate the author's advice. It is not enough simply to agree or disagree. You must also explain the psychological theory or research that underlies your position.

The new book *How to Succeed in School* contains the following suggestions:

1. When asked to define terms or answer questions at the end of a chapter, avoid copying the answers directly out of the textbook.
2. Study in the same place consistently, and when trying to recall the material you studied, think about the place where you studied.
3. In between studying for an exam and taking that exam, it is best to engage in another activity (read, watch television, study another subject) to minimize test anxiety.
4. Avoid studying when depressed. People learn more when they are happy.
5. The best way to learn the meaning of different terms is by repetition (for example, use flash cards).
6. It is worth it to spend time trying to relate the information you are studying to your own experience. No matter what the subject, slow down and look for connections between the topic and your personal life.
7. In preparing for a cumulative examination on a large body of information, it is better to divide your studying over several weeks preceding the exam rather than studying for an entire day or two immediately before the test.

CHAPTER VI
MEMORY

The exercises in this chapter demonstrate some of the concepts key to the psychology of memory. Activity 43 uses visual stimuli to test the storage capacity of short-term memory. Activity 44 examines the reliability of eyewitness accounts by describing a procedure to develop an eyewitness tape from television programs and the types of questions used to generate discussion. For Monopoly fans, Activity 45 describes how memory principles, such as serial position effect, chunking, and the effect of exposure on recall, can be demonstrated in an exercise that tests how well one recalls Monopoly properties.

Unconscious memory, which is also known as implicit memory, is the subject of Activity 46. This anagram-solving exercise shows how unconscious influences from prior experience can affect subjective experience that is later used as a basis for making judgments. The last activity of the chapter, Activity 47, uses a childhood game—the rumor chain—to illustrate the constructive nature of memory.

43 INFORMATION PROCESSING CAPACITY: A VISUAL DEMONSTRATION OF THE MAGICAL NUMBER SEVEN

Fairfid M. Caudle

The College of Staten Island, City University of New York

■ ─── ■

This activity provides a visual demonstration of the well-known limitation on information processing capacity represented by the G. A. Miller's phrase "the magical number seven, plus or minus two." Students are presented with an arrays of dots, arranged either randomly or in patterns. A graph of students' judgments of the number of dots in each array demonstrates the limits of information processing capacity and the facilitative effect of chunking. The demonstration also provides opportunities to explore aspects of experimental design and descriptive statistics.

■ ─── ■

CONCEPT

The phrase "magical number seven, plus or minus two" refers to the limited capacity of short-term memory (Miller, 1956). This activity, unlike the auditory demonstrations typically included in introductory texts, uses visual stimuli to demonstrate this capacity and the value of chunking. It easily can be extended to cover experimental design and descriptive statistics.

MATERIALS NEEDED

In addition to chalk and a chalkboard, you will need 17 stimulus items, each constructed from a sheet of 8½-by-11 in. white paper and black or blue colored adhesive dots approximately ¾ in. in diameter. These dots are available in office supply stores. A total of 136 dots are needed.

Prepare the 17 stimulus items as indicated in appendix A. Each must consist of one sheet of paper with the number of dots indicated distributed either randomly or in a pattern. On the back of each sheet note lightly, for your own reference, the stimulus item number as well as the number and distribution of the dots. This will enable you to check that the sheets are in the proper sequence before beginning the demonstration.

The construction of stimulus items as described here has proved adequate for classes of up to 90 students. For larger classes, you may want to construct the stimulus items by placing adhesive dots directly on overhead transparency sheets. These, however, are more difficult to handle. If you use this method, check in advance to make sure all the dots on each transparency actually project on the screen.

You may also want to prepare a summary sheet that indicates the random stimulus item numbers in order of increasing number of dots (stimulus items 6, 3, 12, 1, 16, 14, 9, 11, 5, 4, 17, 2, 8, and 13) and the patterned item numbers in the same order (stimulus items 15, 7, and 10). This will facilitate the construction of the results graph.

Preparation

On a table in front of you, arrange the stimulus items face down from Item 1 (on top) through Item 17 (on the bottom). Ask the class to turn to a blank page in their notebooks and number from line 1 through line 17.

Say to the class: "I am going to show you some sheets of paper with dots on them. For each sheet, I will give you three beats to get ready, one beat to watch, and one beat to write down the number of dots you see on that sheet. Write your answer for each sheet on a different line, going from Line 1 through Line 17. I will not be calling out line numbers, so just keep going until we finish. For each sheet, I will say, 'dah, dah, dah, look, write.'" Demonstrate with hand motions how you will hold up a stimulus item on "look."

Stimulus Presentation

Show each sheet by counting, at approximately 1 sec per beat, "dah, dah, dah, look, write." As you say "look," hold up a stimulus item. As you say "write," put the sheet face down. Repeat for each stimulus item.

RECORDING RESULTS

Draw a graph on the chalkboard. Label the vertical axis "Number of Persons Correct" and mark it in units of 10. Label the horizontal axis "Number of Dots" and number it from 1 to 14 (the maximum number of dots).

Referring to your summary sheet listing all the stimulus items, go through each item in the order of increasing dots and ask for a show of hands as to the number of students who wrote down the correct number. For example, say, "Sheet 6 had one dot. How many of you were correct?" Follow this with, "Sheet 12, two dots," and so on. It is helpful to know in advance how many are actually present so you can subtract the number of people wrong when almost everyone is correct. With a large class, divide the class into sections and have someone count each section.

Using this procedure, record the number of persons correctly responding to random arrangements of 1 through 14 dots. For each stimulus item, count the number of correct persons and plot a solid dot at the appropriate place on the graph. Connect the solid dots with solid lines to complete the graph. Then record the number of persons correctly responding to the three items with dots arranged in patterns. Indicate the number correct with small hollow circles and connect these with broken lines. Complete your graph with a key indicating that solid circles connected by a solid line correspond to random arrangements, whereas hollow circles connected with a broken line indicate pattern arrangements.

DISCUSSION

Typically, for random arrangements of dots, virtually the entire class is correct for 1 through 5 dots. Thereafter, the number of persons correct begins to decline, and does so precipitously for 10 through 14 dots. Your graph will not be perfect, but the trend should be clearly apparent.

Once you have constructed the graph for random arrangements, ask the class to interpret the graph. Identify the point where lots of people begin to make mistakes and relate this to the "magical number seven," which represents our information-processing capacity.

When dots are arranged in patterns, the number correct is always higher. Ask the class to compare the number correct for 9, 10, and 12 dots arranged in patterns with the number correct for 9, 10, and 12 dots distributed randomly. Ask for suggestions as to why the results are as they are. Introduce the concept of chunking to explain the dramatic increase in capacity when information is organized into patterns.

After discussing the main findings of the demonstration, you can extend the activity by having students analyze it in terms of experimental design. Have them identify the independent variables (there are two: the total number of dots and the type of arrangement, random or pattern) and the dependent variable (number of persons correct) for the demonstration. Ask for someone to state a relationship between the independent and dependent variables that was illustrated by this activity. (As the number of dots increased, the number of persons correct decreased. However, the number of persons correct was higher when the dots were in a pattern.)

Continuing your discussion of variables, ask the class to identify possible uncontrolled variables that might have affected the outcome. These might include such things as distance from the stimulus items, viewing angle, movement of stimulus items as you held them up, inadvertent variations in viewing time, and so forth. Ask for suggestions as to how to adequately control for these variables, and describe laboratory instruments, such as the tachistoscope, that have been designed to enable increased control over such variables.

Finally, it is good to point out how a very large number of individual responses (roughly 17 times the number of people who participated) can be summarized by means of a single graph. This illustrates the value of graphs and other forms of statistics for making data manageable and understandable.

WRITING COMPONENT

Several writing exercises can be assigned to assess students' understanding of information-processing capacity as illustrated by this activity. For example, ask the students to write a paragraph summarizing the purpose of the demonstration and describing the independent variable, the dependent variable, and the relationship between them.

As a follow-up to the classroom discussion of uncontrolled variables, you can also have students choose one of these variables and design an experiment in which it becomes an independent variable while other variables are controlled. Have students explain in writing how results could be summarized in a graph.

Finally, have students write descriptions of situations in which chunking of visual information into patterns is important. These might include occupations (e.g., air traffic controller or musician), sports (e.g., football or basketball), board games (e.g., chess), and activities of daily life (e.g., finding one's car in a large parking lot or finding items during a trip to a supermarket). In each instance, have students indicate why they believe chunking is of value. Some examples of studies reporting visual chunking are noted in the Reference and Suggested Reading sections.

REFERENCE

Miller, G. A. (1956). The magical number seven, plus or minus two: Some limits on our capacity for processing information. *Psychological Review, 63,* 81–97.

SUGGESTED READING

Allard, F., & Burnett, N. (1985). Skill in sport. *Canadian Journal of Psychology, 39,* 294–312.

Chase, W. G., & Simon, H. A. (1973). Perception in chess. *Cognitive Psychology, 4,* 55–81.

Cohen, G. (1989). *Memory in the real world.* Hillsdale, NJ: Erlbaum.

Squire, L. R. (1992). *Encyclopedia of learning and memory.* New York: Macmillan.

Appendix A

Stimulus Items

Item Number	Number of Dots	Distribution
1	4	Random
2	12	Random
3	2	Random
4	10	Random
5	9	Random
6	1	Random
7	10	Pattern (2 rows of 5)
8	13	Random
9	7	Random
10	12	Pattern (4 rows of 3)
11	8	Random
12	3	Random
13	14	Random
14	6	Random
15	9	Pattern (3 rows of 3)
16	5	Random
17	11	Random

44 Do You See What I See?: Examining Eyewitness Testimony

Steve Charlton
Kwantlen University-College

This activity describes how to create an eyewitness tape from television programs or movies and the type of questions used to generate discussion. This activity could be incorporated into an introductory psychology course or a course in cognition or memory.

CONCEPT

One of the more interesting applied areas in memory research is eyewitness testimony. I find students more eager to learn about the key concepts in memory when they are given an applied classroom demonstration. Past research (Brehm & Kassin, 1996; Loftus, 1979) has consistently demonstrated the fallibility of eyewitness memory. This activity offers students a chance to experience and perhaps better understand this type of memory failure. Some of the factors that the activity typically addresses are incidental versus intentional memory, time and sequence estimation, interference, stereotypes and expectation, stress and violence, face recognition, and recall versus recognition (for a review of some of these areas see Christianson, 1992; Searleman & Herrmann, 1994; Shapiro & Penrod, 1986; and Yarmey, 1979).

MATERIALS NEEDED

For this demonstration you will need to create an eyewitness tape. One way to create test tapes is by copying old television programs or movies that contain interesting eyewitness excerpts, usually a car accident or a robbery. The search for the perfect excerpt involves some initial effort. However, you can reduce your workload by copying numerous programs and then fast forwarding through the copies to find pertinent scenes. Crime dramas and action programs often have an abundance of such scenes. Also it is usually better to stay away from popular programs or actors that students can readily recognize. This familiarity may bias the results depending on the type of questions you want to ask (I once used a famous police show and when I asked the students who was driving in the correct direction, the police or the other car, they chose their favorite actor). Foreign films or very old programs may help avoid this problem. Another consideration is how violent or gruesome you want your episode to be. On the one hand, it is tempting to examine the effect of variables, such as violence, weapons, or victim injury on eyewitness testimony (e.g., Loftus & Burns, 1982; Steblay, 1992), but on the other hand, this may be offensive or disturbing to some students. Also, it is best to copy the short excerpt to the beginning of a tape to make it more accessible.

One last issue that needs to be addressed before you create an eyewitness tape is copyright regulations. These will vary depending on the country you live in and many change with time. Therefore your safest approach is to contact the librarian at your school who is most familiar with these issues. In the United States an instructor may repeatedly show a video in a face-to-face classroom situation if the instructor or the institution own the video. In the event the instructor copies from a television broadcast, use may be much more limited. For example, you will likely be limited to a fair use agreement of a single demonstration within 10 days of making the copy. These rules will vary, however, depending on whether the copy is from cable, satellite, or regular broadcasts. After this, you would have to apply to the copyright holder for an extension. Ultimately, it is probably more practical and less complicated to purchase the video (which is usually very inexpensive) if the segment you want to use is from a feature film.

INSTRUCTION   This demonstration usually takes about 30 min. Ask the students to watch the episode quietly and give them the following instructions: "I am about to show you a video depicting an eyewitness event. It is important that you pay full attention to the television screen. Do not talk to other students or say anything out loud. This could ruin the demonstration for everyone." Avoid saying it is a short episode because this may influence time estimates. Then give the students a question sheet and ask them to answer all the questions as truthfully as possible. Have the students write their answers on an appropriately numbered answer sheet or in the case of a recognition test, to write the correct letter. Again, remind them not to talk or say anything out loud and not to look at each others answers while answering the questions. Give the students about 5 min to write their answers. After this, collect the responses and do a tally for each question or have the students raise their hands to indicate their answers. In either case, do not perform a statistical analysis. The primary purpose of this exercise is to demonstrate the diversity of student responses and, as such, how inaccurate eyewitness memory is.

DISCUSSION   The questions may be either multiple choice or recall. In either case, this allows for a discussion about the pros and cons of the two formats. The specific questions you ask will of course depend on the type of eyewitness episode. For example, for robberies, you might ask questions along the following themes:

1. Describe the physical appearance of the assailant or assailants.
2. Describe the physical appearance of any other people in the scene (e.g., bank tellers).
3. Did the robber have a weapon? If so, describe it.
4. Describe the exact sequence of events that took place.
5. Describe in as much detail as possible the dialogue that took place.
6. Was the situation fairly violent and was there any swearing?
7. Describe the environment in detail.
8. How long did the whole episode take?

The questions the students receive are usually the same unless the excerpt is a car accident. In this case, half the students receive the question "How fast were the cars going when they smashed into each other" and the other half receive the question "How fast were the cars going when they hit each other." This allows for a discussion of the classic Loftus and Palmer (1974) experiment on the influence of a question's phrasing. Loftus and Palmer (1974) found that research participants gave higher speed estimates if the question contained the word "*smashed*" rather than "*hit*." The exercise I do in class does not always support their theory. I typically find considerable individual differences and occasionally find no group differences or group differences opposite to the direction their theory predicts. These differences in results may be a result of methodological differences between their more carefully controlled experiment and our classroom exercise (for a discussion about the robustness of their findings and subsequent failures to replicate, see McAllister, Bregman, & Lipscomb, 1988). In the event the Loftus and Palmer experiment is not replicated, the instructor may generate a class discussion about what variables may account for these differences (for example, how fast the cars really are going, the force of the collision, or the distance from the screen and size of the screen). Over the past 2 decades, numerous studies have been published demonstrating the misinformation effect (the finding that post-event information may cause inaccurate recollection). Although the effect is well documented, the explanations for the effect are far more controversial and highly debated (Lindsay, 1990; Zaragoza & McCloskey, 1989).

Other car accident questions that you may ask include the following:

1. Who was at fault?
2. Who was going in the proper direction?
3. What did the vehicles look like?
4. What did the occupants look like?
5. How long did the episode take?

Overall, the students usually perform marginally, at best, on the questions. They show a wide variety of responses to each question, highlighting the fallibility of memory and the fact that people often do not perceive or remember eyewitness episodes in the same manner. Also, some questions will yield more divergent responses than others, depending on the particular set of events the students are shown. For example, if students are asked to describe the driver of a car and the driver is very difficult to see, they will often give varying descriptions rather than admit they could not clearly see. On a multiple-choice question, I have found one student will say he or she saw a young man and another will say it was an elderly woman.

Another common finding is that the students are usually quite poor at estimating time. On a 25-second episode (the total tape they view) the responses will range from 5 seconds to 3 minutes. Point out to them that knowing when and how long events took place is often crucial to some types of criminal investigations.

One other point worth discussing is the artificial setting in which the students are viewing the eyewitness episode. For example, eyewitness situations are more likely to involve incidental memory, whereas in our demonstration the students were told to pay attention. Past research has clearly shown that attention during the encoding stage results in superior explicit recall and recognition (Searleman & Herrmann, 1994). Furthermore, the class setting is less stressful than many real-life eyewitness situations. Differences between real-life situations and the classroom environment make the class exercise even more compelling. Students realize that the memory failures they observed in the classroom setting may be even more pronounced in a real-life situation.

One variation on this exercise that also may be tried is the presentation of a series of photos of faces on the overhead. Remind students that photo identification and lineups are a form of recognition testing that one may encounter in criminal investigations (for a discussion of some of the issues involved in photo identification and lineups, see Lindsay, Nosworthy, Martin, & Martynuck, 1994; Wells & Seelau, 1995; and Yarmey, Yarmey, & Yarmey, 1996). The students are shown a series of still photos of faces of approximately the same size mixed in with a photo of the actor in the film. It can take a bit more work trying to find a photo of the actor but it provides a good demonstration given the face may show the actor smiling or with a different physical appearance such as a mustache. Still photos of actors can be found in magazines such as *People* or in film books. I also usually include a 25-year-old photo of myself with long hair and a mustache. They often laugh when they see the "rough-looking" suspect but never recognize me and sometimes choose my picture as the robber. Near the end of the class, after having discussed the problems of recognizing faces years later (such as when concentration camp survivors were asked to identify Nazi prison guards), I point out that no one recognized me. This also allows for a discussion about the role of context and stereotypes on memory (see Chen & Geiselman, 1993, and Saladin, Saper, & Breen, 1988).

WRITING COMPONENT	A possible writing assignment that you may want to add to this exercise is to have each student devise the perfect bank robbery. The students would be required to design a robbery in which eyewitness memory is at its worst (I was once asked this question by a student–inmate at a maximum security prison. A bit late however!). This would involve the students using the information they have acquired from the class exercise and discussion. For a more in-depth assignment you could also have them do a literature search to support and generate some of their ideas. This short paper (approximately two or three pages) would describe all the variables that may be manipulated to hamper eyewitnesses from identifying the robber. Examples of some of the issues that students may come up with are as follows:

1. What would be the best time of day or night for a robbery? For example, at night both color perception and visual acuity are poor.
2. How many witnesses do the students want? Is it better to have many witnesses (more varied responses) or only one?
3. Is it better for the robber to have a weapon and if so what type?
4. Is it better for the robber to swear or yell?
5. Should the robber say as little as possible (see Bull & Clifford, 1984, for a discussion on earwitness testimony)?
6. What race should the eyewitness be and what race should the robber be? This could possibly be tied to both cross-race identification and stereotypes.
7. Can you identify any ways to increase proactive or retroactive interference?
8. Are there any advantages or disadvantages to having the robber and/or the eyewitness be male or female? This may tie to either stereotypes or possible gender differences in eyewitness ability.
9. What type of clothes should the robber wear?

Do not give the students these questions but rather let them generate their own ideas. The only conditions you might impose before the students begin is that they only focus on the eyewitness issue (i.e., avoid dealing with tangential issues such as how to deal with video cameras in the bank), that the robber is not allowed to wear a mask, and that they provide a rationale for each idea.

To some extent, this is a fairly creative and subjective assignment and therefore you have to expect students to present some ideas for which there may not be clear answers. Also, it may not be easy to devise a fair and objective grading system (particularly if you are not completely aware of the literature). On this basis, it may be better to avoid treating this as a graded assignment.

REFERENCES

Brehm, S. S., & Kassin, S. M. (1996). *Social psychology* (3rd ed.). Boston: Houghton-Mifflin.

Bull, R., & Clifford, B. R. (1984). Earwitness voice recognition accuracy. In G. L. Wells & E. F. Loftus (Eds.), *Eyewitness testimony: Psychological perspectives* (pp. 92–123). New York: Cambridge University Press.

Chen, Y. Y., & Geiselman, R. E. (1993). Effects of ethnic stereotyping and ethnically-related cognitive biases on eyewitness recollections of height. *American Journal of Forensic Psychology, 11,* 13–19.

Christianson, S. (1992). Emotional stress and eyewitness memory: A critical review. *Psychological Bulletin, 112,* 284–309.

Lindsay, D. S. (1990). Misleading suggestions can impair eyewitnesses' ability to remember event details. *Journal of Experimental Psychology: Learning, Memory & Cognition, 16,* 1077–1083.

Lindsay, R. C. L., Nosworthy, G. L., Martin, R., & Martynuck, C. (1994). Using mug shots to find suspects. *Journal of Applied Psychology, 79,* 121–130.

Loftus, E. F. (1979). *Eyewitness testimony.* Cambridge, MA: Harvard University Press.

Loftus, E. F., & Burns, T. E. (1982). Mental shock can produce retrograde amnesia. *Memory & Cognition, 1,* 318–323.

Loftus, E. F., & Palmer, J. C. (1974). Reconstruction of automobile destruction: An example of the interaction between language and memory. *Journal of Verbal Learning and Verbal Behavior, 13,* 585–589.

McAllister, H. A., Bregman, N. J., & Lipscomb, T. J. (1988). Speed estimates by eyewitnesses and earwitnesses: How vulnerable to postevent information? *Journal of General Psychology, 115,* 25–35.

Saladin, M., Saper, Z., & Breen, L. (1988). Perceived-attractiveness and attributions of criminality: What is beautiful is not criminal. *Canadian Journal of Criminology, 30,* 251–259.

Searleman, A., & Herrmann, D. (1994). *Memory from a broader perspective.* New York: McGraw-Hill.

Shapiro, P. N., & Penrod, S. (1986). Meta-analysis of facial identification studies. *Psychological Bulletin, 100,* 139–156.

Steblay, N. M. (1992). A meta-analytic review of the weapon-focus effect. *Law and Human Behavior, 16,* 41–424.

Wells, G. L., & Seelau, E. P. (1995). Eyewitness identification: Psychological research and legal policy on lineups. *Psychology, Public Policy, & Law, 1,* 765–791.

Yarmey, A. D. (1979). *The psychology of eyewitness testimony.* New York: The Free Press.

Yarmey, A. D., Yarmey, M. J., & Yarmey, A. L. (1996). Accuracy of eyewitness identification in showups and lineups. *Law and Human Behavior, 20,* 459–477.

Zaragoza, M. S., & McCloskey, M. (1989). Misleading postevent information and the memory impairment hypothesis: Comment on Belli and reply to Tversky and Tuchin. *Journal of Experimental Psychology: General, 118,* 92–99.

SUGGESTED READING

Crombag, H. F. M., Wagenaar, W. A., & Van Koppen, P. J. (1996). Crashing memories and the problem of source monitoring. *Applied Cognitive Psychology, 10,* 95–104.

Memon, A., & Vartoukian, R. (1996). The effects of repeated questioning on young children's eyewitness testimony. *British Journal of Psychology, 87,* 403–415.

Wells, G. L. (1993). What do we know about eyewitness identification? *American Psychologist, 48,* 553–571.

45 MEMORY FOR MONOPOLY PROPERTIES

Dina M. Wieczynski and Kenneth A. Blick
University of Richmond

This activity illustrates various aspects of memory. Students recall the properties from the game Monopoly and rate their amount of experience and success in playing the game on a 7-point scale. The demonstration requires little preparation and gives students a concrete example of basic memory principles. Its simplicity makes it practical for classes of all sizes.

CONCEPT

Memory principles such as serial position effect, chunking, and the effect of exposure on recall are easily illustrated using the popular board game Monopoly. Students show a positive relationship between experience and success in playing the game and recalling the Monopoly properties. Instructors need to be able to conduct correlational analysis.

MATERIALS NEEDED

The only materials needed are paper and pencil. The Monopoly properties in their serial order on the game board along with respective monetary values are listed in Table 45-1.

INSTRUCTIONS

Give students 10 min to write down, in any order, the complete name of as many properties from the game of Monopoly as they can remember. Explain that complete names include *Ave., St.,* and so forth and that properties need to be spelled correctly.

Next, instruct students to indicate their level of playing experience from *very little* (1) to *very much* (7), and their level of success from *won very few times* (1) to *won many times* (7). Write the rating scale on the chalkboard or show it on an overhead projector. Have students turn in their responses so that you can compute the statistical information (e.g., correlation between correct recall of properties and experience) before the next class period.

DISCUSSION

During the next class period, focus initial discussion on the findings of the correlational analysis between the rating scales and recall of properties. The strongest correlation tends to appear between experience and recall. Finding that playing time and therefore exposure to the property names is positively associated with level of recall supports a basic premise of memory: As experience with a task increases so does the ability to remember that task. Include in your presentation a frequency distribution with accompanying descriptive statistics, a list of properties remembered most and least often, and a list of incorrect properties constructed from memory (e.g., Melvin Gardens). Discussion on how the value of the property and its position on the board contribute to serial position phenomena is often meaningful, and a graph depicting recall by position of each property helps illustrate the serial position effect.

Table 45-1. *Monopoly Properties in Order and Respective Monetary Values*

Property	Value
Mediterranean Ave.	$60
Baltic Ave.	$60
Reading RR	$200
Oriental Ave.	$100
Vermont Ave.	$100
Connecticut Ave.	$120
St. Charles Place	$140
Electric Company	$150
States Ave.	$140
Virginia Ave.	$160
Pennsylvania RR	$200
St. James Place	$180
Tennessee Ave.	$180
New York Ave.	$200
Kentucky Ave.	$220
Indiana Ave.	$220
Illinois Ave.	$240
B & O RR	$200
Atlantic Ave.	$260
Ventnor Ave.	$260
Water Works	$150
Marvin Gardens	$280
Pacific Ave.	$300
North Carolina Ave.	$300
Pennsylvania Ave.	$320
Short Line RR	$200
Park Place	$350
Boardwalk	$400

Although correct spelling is important for accuracy and assessing constructed memories, students regularly point this out as a confound in figuring correlations. The spelling of some properties (e.g., Mediterranean Ave.) is more difficult than others (e.g., States Ave.).

SUGGESTED READING

Bousfield, W. A., & Wicklund, D. A. (1969). Rhyme as a determinant of clustering. *Psychonomic Science, 16,* 183–184.

Meyer, G. E., & Hilterbrand, K. (1984). Does it pay to be "Bashful"?: The seven dwarfs and long-term memory. *American Journal of Psychology, 97,* 47–55.

Miserandino, M. (1991). Memory and the seven dwarfs. *Teaching of Psychology, 18,* 169–171.

Roediger, H. L., & Crowder, R. G. (1976). A serial position effect in recall of United States presidents. *Bulletin of the Psychonomic Society, 8,* 275–278.

46 Effects of Unconscious Memory on Subjective Judgments: A Classroom Demonstration

Benton H. Pierce

Texas A&M University

This activity describes a procedure that demonstrates the effects of unconscious or implicit memory on subjective judgments. Students learn a short list of words and later solve anagrams of the same words and judge how difficult it would be for others to solve them. The demonstration supports the claim that unconscious influences from prior experience can affect subjective experience, which is later used as a basis for making judgments.

CONCEPT
Unconscious memory can serve not only as a perceptual and interpretative device for later events or tasks, but can also influence subjective experience when one performs the task. This subjective experience, in turn, is often used as a basis for making judgments, and people sometimes misattribute the effects of memory on subjective experience to other sources.

MATERIALS NEEDED
You will need two separate lists of words, containing eight words each, for the intentional learning task, although each student will see only one list. Each list should be typed on a separate piece of paper and should contain four critical prime words and four filler words. *Prime words* are words that tend to facilitate the processing of a later target word. This facilitation can take the form of either faster or more accurate recognition of the target word. List 1 should contain the following critical primes: *chair, white, water,* and *house.* List 2 should contain the primes *tiger, light, rough,* and *short.* The four filler words—*number, appear, square,* and *jump*—are to be included on both lists. For the problem-solving and judgment task, prepare a list of eight anagrams to be shown on an overhead transparency. This list of anagrams consists of *tehwi, gteri, hriac, stroh, ehous, tilhg, tarew,* and *orguh.* The odd-numbered anagrams (i.e., *tehwi, hriac, ehous,* and *tarew*) are for the critical primes on List 1, whereas the even-numbered anagrams (i.e., *gteri, stroh, tilhg,* and *orguh*) correspond to the word primes on List 2. In addition to the stimulus materials listed, you will need an overhead projector for showing the anagrams.

INSTRUCTIONS
Intentional Learning Task

Tell students that they will be participating in a memory and problem-solving task. To begin the demonstration, mentally divide the class into two groups based on seating arrangement (e.g., students on the left side of the class versus those on the right side) and then distribute the word lists so that the left side of the class gets List 1 and the right side gets List 2. It is important, though, that the students not be aware that they are being divided and that the groups are getting separate word lists. After passing out the lists, tell the students that they are to study the words for 30 sec. After this time period is over, tell the students to turn the page over and to use this blank sheet for the ensuing problem-solving task.

Problem-Solving and Judgment Tasks

Put up an overhead for the entire class that shows the list of eight anagrams. Tell students to solve the anagrams by writing each one down on the blank sheet of paper and providing the solution word right next to it. Also tell the students that immediately after solving each anagram, they are to make a judgment concerning how difficult they think the anagrams would be for others to solve. These judgments will be made according to a 7-point scale, with 7 representing maximum difficulty and 1 representing minimum difficulty. Give the class 5 to 10 min to complete this task.

Scoring and Demonstration of Effects

After the 5-to-10-min period is over, ask for a show of hands to see who has not finished. If a significant number of people have not completed the task, allow a few more minutes. After you are satisfied that all or nearly all of the class has finished, demonstrate the effects of the exercise. First, point to the odd-numbered anagrams on the overhead and ask the students to examine their difficulty judgments on these items and to raise their hands if they judged these anagrams to be easier for others to solve than the even-numbered ones. The results should show that the side of the class that was originally given the word list containing the primes for the odd-numbered anagrams will judge them to be easier for others to solve than the even-numbered anagrams. Conversely, the other half of the class, which received the list containing the primes for the even-numbered anagrams, should judge those anagrams to be easier than the odd-numbered ones. This effect will be demonstrated by a likewise show of hands for the even anagrams relative to the odd ones. Of course, the anagrams that were primed should be easier for the students themselves to solve than the nonprimed ones because of prior exposure to the solution words, but it is not critical that you elicit this judgment from the students. What is important is their judgments about relatively difficulty for *others*.

After each set of anagrams is judged by the show of hands, comment (not seriously) that each side of the class appears to be relatively smarter on certain anagrams. At this point, ask the class for possible explanations for this phenomenon. Some students, perhaps a significant number, may say that some of the solutions to the anagrams were on the original word lists. Point out to the students that the prior learning of the solution words facilitated their performance on the anagram task. But this discovery or knowledge is perhaps the main point of the demonstration, for even if the students were aware that some of the anagrams were primed by the word list, they may not have used this information to discount their subjective experience in judging how difficult the problems would be for others. In other words, if students judge the primed anagrams as easier for others to solve, the students are behaving as though others had also had prior exposure to the solution words.

Then explain to the students that their difficulty judgments were likely to have been affected by unconscious influences. Furthermore, these influences are fairly common and the subjective experience that is influenced is extremely difficult to ignore when making judgments. For example, you may use the phenomenon known as hindsight bias, in which people with knowledge of a certain outcome overestimate what they would have known had they not had this knowledge (see Hawkins & Hastie, 1990, for a review of hindsight bias). This bias is particularly interesting because people are unaware of the effects that this outcome knowledge has on their judgments. The effect is extremely robust and is very difficult to eliminate even if participants are given instructions or practice.

The concept underlying this activity may be explained more clearly by the following procedure:

Step 1: Students study short word lists.
Step 2: Students are given anagrams to solve and either implicitly (i.e., without awareness) or explicitly (i.e., with awareness) retrieve the solution words to four of the anagrams and solve those anagrams more easily.
Step 3: Students judge difficulty of anagrams for others. If retrieval of solution words was explicit, then students should take that into consideration when rating the anagrams. That is, they should objectively rate the anagrams as if they had not seen the solution word beforehand.

Several suggestions can be made concerning this demonstration. As previously mentioned, it is critical that the two halves of the class are unaware that they are receiving different word lists in the initial learning task. In addition, you may want to experiment with adding more words to the learning task if you are concerned that the solutions are too obvious. Again, hiding the solution words is not essential to the task, but adding more words to the word list may produce somewhat stronger effects. In addition, you may want to attempt variations of this exercise involving different types of problems. For example, you could present an insight problem (e.g., the nine-dot problem), and give one half of the class a hint on how to solve it but give no hint to the other half. Then the class could be asked to rate the difficulty of the problem for others. Effects similar to those obtained in the anagram task would be found if students cannot discount the effects of receiving the hint.

DISCUSSION   This classroom exercise demonstrates fairly quickly and in a dramatic fashion how unconscious memory for a previous event can affect one's subjective experience during a future task and how this subjective experience can provide the basis for making judgments. The activity focuses on a role of the unconscious in influencing behavior that is very different from that discussed in psychoanalytic theory.

According to Freud, the unconscious influences of a previous traumatic episode can have a significant impact on one's current behavior, even though this memory is normally unavailable to consciousness. Indeed, the role of the unconscious is usually thought of in this manner. However, this activity demonstrates an alternative view of the unconscious. This view (Jacoby & Kelley, 1987; Jacoby,

Kelley, Brown, & Jasechko, 1989) holds that unconscious influences can affect behavior even when they originate from common or mundane events. As this activity shows, a particular prior experience, even an ordinary one, often has an influence on the perception and interpretation of later events, although a person is unable to recognize or recall the prior experience. This unconscious influence from a prior event has been termed *implicit memory* and is characterized as being highly automatic (Jacoby, 1991; see also Schacter, 1987). *Automatic*, in this sense, refers to a cognitive process that requires little if any mental effort. *Explicit memory*, on the other hand, refers to memory with conscious awareness and is characterized as being reflective of a person's intentions (i.e., intentional) or requiring significant mental effort. Explicit memory is that aspect of memory that is associated with conscious recollection of a prior event or episode.

It should be pointed out that when discussing unconscious or implicit memory, it is difficult to be certain that this memory is totally unconscious or without awareness—that is, it is difficult to rule out that some degree of conscious recollection is being used to influence the later event. It is likely that unconscious memory and memory with awareness (i.e., explicit) exist along a continuum, and that completely pure instances of these different aspects of memory are rare. However, this is not the main point to be made in this demonstration. This activity does not show unconscious (i.e., implicit) memory effects on the problem-solving task, as students are likely to consciously remember some of the solution words from the intentional learning task. Rather, the activity demonstrates implicit memory for the subjective anagram-rating task. If students are consciously aware of the effects of the solution words that they had learned earlier, then they should discount their subjective experience when rating the anagrams for others who had not seen the solution words. By not doing so, the unconscious influences from the prior experience of reading the solution words are revealed. Subjective experience was unconsciously influenced by the prior experience and this subjective experience was then used as a basis for making judgments.

In summary, this classroom demonstration looks at the effects of unconscious memory that are perhaps less known than those discussed by psychoanalytic theory. In an introductory psychology class, this exercise may be used in the lesson on cognitive psychology to illustrate the difference between memory with and without awareness (i.e., explicit versus implicit), to demonstrate how common unconscious influences can be, and to demonstrate the effects of memory without awareness on our judgments.

REFERENCES

Hawkins, S. A., & Hastie, R. (1990). Hindsight: Biased judgments of past events after the outcomes are known. *Psychological Bulletin, 107,* 311–327.

Jacoby, L. L. (1991). A process dissociation framework: Separating automatic from intentional uses of memory. *Journal of Memory and Language, 30,* 513–541.

Jacoby, L. L., & Kelley, C. M. (1987). Unconscious influences of memory for a prior event. *Personality and Social Psychology Bulletin, 13,* 314–336.

Jacoby, L. L., Kelley, C. M., Brown, J., & Jasechko, J. (1989). Becoming famous overnight: Limits on the ability to avoid unconscious influences of the past. *Journal of Personality and Social Psychology, 56,* 326–338.

Schacter, D. L. (1987). Implicit memory: History and current status. *Journal of Experimental Psychology: Learning, Memory, and Cognition, 13,* 501–518.

Fischhoff, B. (1975). Hindsight is not equal to foresight: The effects of outcome knowledge on judgment under certainty. *Journal of Experimental Psychology: Human Perception and Performance, 1,* 288–299.

Jacoby, L. L., Toth, J. P., Lindsay, D. S., & Debner, J. A. (1992). Lectures for a layperson: Methods for revealing unconsciousness processes. In R. F. Bornstein & T. S. Pittman (Eds.), *Perception without awareness.* New York: Guilford Press.

Nisbett, R. E., & Wilson, T. D. (1977). Telling more than we can know: Verbal reports on mental processes. *Psychological Review, 84,* 231–259.

Polanyi, M. (1958). *Personal knowledge: Towards a post-critical philosophy.* Chicago: University of Chicago Press.

Roediger, H. L., III. (1990). Implicit memory: Retention without remembering. *American Psychologist, 45,* 1043–1056.

47 CONSTRUCTIVE MEMORY/SCHEMAS: THE RUMOR CHAIN

Douglas A. Bernstein and Sandra S. Goss
University of Illinois

This demonstration uses a childhood game, the rumor chain, to illustrate the constructive nature of memory. It can be presented before or after discussing constructive memory because the power of the phenomenon is great, even when students are sensitized to it.

CONCEPT
: The rumor chain game provides a simple, enjoyable, and dramatic illustration that the encoding and retrieval of information in long-term memory can be distorted by prior knowledge, especially by our schemas about the world. These schemas include gender-role expectations and other prejudices.

MATERIALS NEEDED
: You will need a story that is short enough to allow retelling several times in class, but detailed enough that students are unlikely to remember all aspects of it. A sample is included in the following section.

INSTRUCTIONS
: Send three to five students out of the classroom (and out of earshot). Now read aloud a paragraph-length story to a student whose task it is to repeat the story as completely as possible to one of the students who is brought back into the classroom. The newcomer's task is to repeat the story to the next student who is readmitted and so on until the last student who hears the story repeats it to the class. Each rendition of the story should be loud enough so that everyone in the class can hear.

Be sure to give instructions to the class not to laugh when errors are made because this may cause the storyteller to notice and attempt to correct mistakes. To facilitate discussion, instruct the class to take notes as each student tells the story, thus tracking the errors made.

Here is a sample story that works well for us:

> A TWA Boeing 747 had just taken off from Miami International Airport for Los Angeles when a passenger near the rear of the aircraft announced that the plane was being taken over by the People's Revolutionary Army for the Liberation of the Oppressed. The hijacker held a .357 magnum to the head of Jack Swanson, a flight attendant, and forced him to open the cockpit door. There, the hijacker confronted the pilot, Jane Randall, and ordered her to change course for Cuba. The pilot radioed the Miami air traffic control center to report the situation but then suddenly hurled the microphone at the hijacker. The hijacker fell backward through the open cockpit door and onto the floor, where angry passengers took over from there. The plane landed in Miami a few minutes later and the hijacker was arrested.

DISCUSSION
: The errors made in each successive telling of the story are usually predictable and follow some basic principles of constructive memory.

First, the story gets progressively shorter as some details, such as the name of the revolutionary group and sometimes the flight's origin and destination, are left out. This is referred to as *leveling*.

Second, some details—perhaps the caliber of the gun or, especially for women students, the gender of the pilot—are often retained; this is referred to as *sharpening*. Because individuals retain different details, this leads to a discussion of the schemas already in long-term memory that help us retain information in a meaningful fashion and how these schemas differ for different people based on personal experience.

Third, because many elements of the story are encoded semantically (i.e., as the meaning or gist of the story rather than as exact words), they are likely to be altered in line with each teller's schemas. For example, because for many students, even today, pilots are men and flight attendants are women, Jane Randall may end up as the flight attendant and Jack Swanson may become the pilot. Further, the hijacker is almost always referred to as a man, often as an Arab, even though no gender or ethnic information is in the story. You can relate this phenomenon to false assumptions made about the identity of those who blew up the federal building in Oklahoma City in 1995. "The open cockpit door" may evoke an image of an outside door, such that the hijacker is described as falling out of the plane. Finally, the schema of "angry passengers" may cause expansion of the story to include their beating, or even killing, the hijacker.

By asking the class to describe how the story changed with the retelling, you should be able to illustrate a number of the principles listed here. You can then go on to discuss the role of schemas and constructive memory in other phenomena, such as racial prejudice and errors in eyewitness testimony.

WRITING COMPONENT

Two different writing assignments can follow from this demonstration. For the first one, have students write a paper in the form of a letter to a friend or family member describing how memory works. The letter should address the common view of memory as a sort of video recorder, why that view is incorrect, and the importance of constructive memory. Shared examples of constructive memory between the student and the recipient of the letter could be supplied to illustrate constructive memory. For example, siblings often have different memories of the same incident in their childhoods.

Another assignment would be to have students write a paper in the form of a newspaper column on the role of memory in eyewitness testimony or repressed memory cases. The paper should incorporate the rumor chain demonstration in a discussion of the issues surrounding these controversial topics. Remind students that their audience would be educated, but not necessarily knowledgeable about psychological principles.

SUGGESTED READINGS

Bartlett, F. C. (1932). *Remembering: A study in experimental and social psychology.* Cambridge: Cambridge University Press.

Loftus, E. F. (1992). *Eyewitness testimony: Civil and criminal.* New York: Kluwer Law.

Loftus, E. F. (1994). *The myth of repressed memory.* New York: St. Martin's Press.

Loftus, E. F., & Hoffman, H. G. (1989). Misinformation and memory: The creation of new memories. *Journal of Experimental Psychology: General, 118,* 100–104.

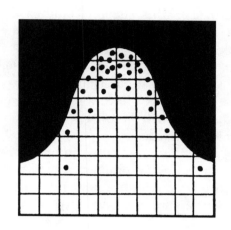

CHAPTER VII
COGNITION AND
EMOTION

Several of the activities described in this chapter could easily fit in the previous chapter on memory. They have been placed here, however, because we believe that they deal with cognitive processes broader than just memory.

Activity 48 is a demonstration of schema—in this case, place schema—and how they work in information processing. In Activity 49, students are asked to play a 33$\frac{1}{3}$ rpm record (remember records?). The problem is that they do not have a record player. Instead they are to make one from a series of items supplied by the instructor. The exercise illustrates several issues in problem solving, particularly functional fixedness.

Activity 50 demonstrates the differences between productive and reproductive thinking by emphasizing the latter, in which successful problem solvers need to develop new ways of thinking. Several of the exercises in this activity are typically associated with what is called insight learning. Selective attention is the subject of Activity 51, which shows how set affects information processing.

The final activity in this chapter, Activity 52, focuses on emotion by testing the question, "Do facial expressions help determine perceived emotional response?"

48 An Experimental Demonstration of Place Schema

Mark G. Hartlaub
SUNY-Albany

This is an interesting and concrete illustration of the influence schema have on our everyday processing of information. A minimum of preparation is needed. Any instructor can use his or her office for the demonstration.

CONCEPT

This demonstration illustrates the concept of place schema, which can be thought of as the way our cognitive structures and frameworks influence how we experience and process information concerning places we encounter.

MATERIALS NEEDED

This short classroom demonstration is quite easy to set up and virtually guarantees successful and meaningful results. Because of time constraints, however, it may not be feasible for classes with more than about 40 students.

The only materials you will need are handouts of the scale to give to the students and common office supplies (pens, clock, telephone, stapler, etc.).

INSTRUCTIONS

You will need to make some preparations in the classroom before you begin this activity. Conduct a brief inventory of a standard academic office. Create an experimental form that includes some items present in the office and some items not present in the office. Remove or hide several (usually just two or three is enough) items very commonly found in an office (I usually choose the stapler and the telephone). Any items can be chosen, just as long as they are commonly thought of as belonging in an office yet are easily removed or hidden.

To begin the exercise, lead students from their regular classroom to a currently unoccupied departmental office (the office you have already prepared). Obviously, the closer this office is to the classroom, the better. The room should hold items typically found in an academic/departmental office such as a computer terminal, a printer, several chairs, a large desk, a large bookcase, and so on. As you stand at the door, monitor the timely entrance and exit of all the students. Allow each student approximately 15 sec to enter the office and look around. Allow only one student at a time in the room. For example, Student 1 enters the office and briefly looks around the room. After 15 sec, call time and Student 1 exits the office while student 2 enters. This procedure continues until all students have participated. It takes approximately 10 to 12 min to run 30 students through the experimental procedure.

As students leave the office, they pick up an experimental form and either fill it out in the hallway or they can go to a nearby vacant room if one is available.

The experimental form lists approximately 15 objects (see appendix A). Ask students to try to remember whether they had seen each of the listed objects in the room and to indicate how confident they are about their judgments. Each object is rated on a 6-point scale ranging from −3 (*very sure it was not in the room*) to +3 (*very sure it was in the room*). As students fill out the experimental forms, they should return them to you. (I find this typically works best at the end of a class period so students can be dismissed once they complete and turn in the forms.)

Before the next class period, compute the means, standard deviations, and valid *N* for each of the items listed on the experimental form so that you are prepared to share these results with the students during the next class meeting. Entering the data for a class of 30 takes approximately 45 min.

<table>
<tr><td>**DISCUSSION**</td><td>

Schema have been defined as "mental frameworks containing information relevant to specific situations or events, which, once established, help us interpret these situations and what's happening in them" (Baron & Byrne, 1997, p. 611). Schema influence how we organize, store, and retrieve information. Many of the cognitive processes in which we engage can be thought of in terms of schema. These include cognitive expectations, priming, leading words, and stereotyping.

Psychology textbooks typically define several different types of schema. For example, Sternberg stated that self-schema "are the individual's cognitive frameworks for knowledge about her- or himself" (1995, p. 619). Event schema, or scripts, "indicate what is expected to happen in a given setting" (Baron & Byrne, 1997, p. 79). Role schema are "organized sets of expectations about how people in certain roles are supposed to act" (Baron, Byrne, & Suls, 1989, p. 69). A motor schema can be defined as "a mental organization of information providing instructions for acting" (Carver & Scheier, 1996, p. 527). There are many more types of schema than those listed here; suffice it to say, the applications of schema theory span a wide range within a variety of fields. Each type of schema is capable of influencing how we process information.

In an experimental demonstration of what they termed *place schema*, Brewer and Treyens (1981) left participants in what was believed to be a graduate student office while the experimenter purportedly checked on the possibility of giving experimental credit to another student. After approximately 35 sec the experimenter returned and led the participants to another room where the participants were told that the true nature of the experiment involved memory of places. The participants were then asked to recall the objects they thought were present in the office. In both recall and recognition tests, participants had a tendency to report seeing objects present in the office that in fact were not present (e.g., books). This is explained by the presence of a place (or, more specifically, an office) schema that leads participants to recall seeing books in a graduate student office because of previous experience and general cognitive expectations. The present demonstration is similar to the experiment conducted by Brewer and Treyens (1981).

Table 48-1 presents means, standard deviations, and valid *N* (some participants' forms were incomplete) for a class of 25 students. Of the 15 items listed on the experimental sheet, 7 of the items were actually present in the office and 8 of the items were not. The list included common office items, such as a pen and a trash can, and not common office items, such as a fish tank and a movie

</td></tr>
</table>

Table 48-1. *Identification Ratings of Office Items, Ranging from −3* (very sure it was not present) *to +3* (very sure it was present)

	M	SD	Valid N
File cabinet	+2.71	(1.23)	24
Trash can	+2.54	(1.10)	24
*Telephone	+2.00	(2.06)	25
Wall calendar	+1.76	(1.99)	25
Wall clock	+1.64	(2.01)	25
*Stapler	+1.32	(1.99)	24
Pen	+1.32	(2.23)	25
Typewriter	+1.20	(2.18)	25
Box of Kleenex	+0.72	(2.19)	25
*Paper shredder	−0.58	(2.13)	24
*Cassette tapes	−0.63	(1.91)	24
*Videotape	−0.83	(1.97)	24
*TOP GUN poster	−2.08	(1.12)	25
*Fish tank	−2.60	(0.71)	25
*Dead rat	−2.71	(0.61)	25

*Items not present in the office.

poster. The items ranged from a high positive confidence rating of +2.71 for the file cabinet to a low of −2.71 for the dead rat. These results are very typical and should be expected by anyone who conducts the experiment.

It is clear that participants expected to see certain items, such as a telephone and a stapler, in the office. These items both had positive mean scores indicating most participants reported having seen them even though they were not present. Obviously, this shows that our prior expectations can influence what we think we see and experience. This phenomenon can lead to a discussion of racial stereotypes and the classic Allport and Postman (1947) study of verbal recall of a violent incident between a White man and a Black man on a subway car. It can also be discussed in terms of eyewitness testimony and leading questions. For example, it has been determined that when people are asked a question, their answer can depend, at least partly, on how the question is asked (e.g., Loftus, 1975; Loftus & Palmer, 1974).

Likewise, items that are not typically found in an office are not likely to be identified as present. Items such as a movie poster ($M = -2.08$), a fish tank ($M = -2.60$), and a dead rat ($M = -2.71$) were all rated as very unlikely to have been present in the office. These judgments are, of course, correct, yet still influenced by the presence of schema because of their atypicality. In a variation on this procedure, a very atypical item could be added to the office. It is likely this item would be noticed quite easily and readily. For example, Brewer and Treyens (1981) used a skull and a toy top in their experiment.

You can also discuss the means and standard deviations with the class. The standard deviations of the most confident items (whether positive or negative) generally tend to be smaller than for those items in the middle of the list, as would be expected.

WRITING COMPONENT

A writing assignment would be to ask students to write one page describing what they expected to occur on the first day of class and why. For example, did they expect the instructor to hand out a syllabus and to present class policies? Briefly, how did these expectations develop?

Students could be asked to write about a time in their lives when expectations have influenced the way they viewed some event. For example, students could be asked to write a script that includes all of the typical steps that one goes through when eating at a restaurant or going to the dentist. Several of these papers could then be shared with the class. It is likely the scripts will be remarkably similar.

Although a schema can trick us into seeing something that is not there, we can also be aided by our schema because we are able to process information so quickly and efficiently. Students can be asked to list ways in which the presence of schema help and assist us in organizing and experiencing the world. (For example, it is difficult to imagine making our way through an unfamiliar airport without the presence of an airport schema.)

REFERENCES

Allport, G., & Postman, L. (1947). *The psychology of rumor*. New York: Holt, Rinehart, & Winston.

Baron, R. A., & Byrne, D. (1997). *Social psychology* (8th ed.). Boston: Allyn & Bacon.

Baron, R. A., Byrne, D., & Suls, J. (1989). *Exploring social psychology* (3rd ed.). Boston: Allyn & Bacon.

Brewer, W. F., & Treyens, J. C. (1981). Role of schemata in memory for places. *Cognitive Psychology, 13,* 207–230.

Carver. C. S., & Scheier, M. F. (1996). *Perspectives on personality* (3rd ed.). Boston: Allyn & Bacon.

Loftus, E. F. (1975). Leading questions and the eyewitness report. *Cognitive Psychology, 7,* 560–572.

Loftus, E. F., & Palmer, J. C. (1974). Reconstruction of automobile destruction: An example of the interaction between language and memory. *Journal of Verbal Learning and Verbal Behavior, 13,* 585–589.

Sternberg, R. J. (1995). *In search of the human mind*. Fort Worth, TX: Harcourt Brace.

SUGGESTED READING

Bransford, J. D., & Johnson, M. K. (1972). Contextual prerequisites for understanding: Some investigations of comprehension and recall. *Journal of Verbal Learning and Verbal Behavior, 11,* 717–726.

Cantor, N., & Mischel, W. (1977). Traits as prototypes: Effects on recognition memory. *Journal of Personality and Social Psychology, 35,* 38–48.

Fiske, S. T., & Taylor, S. E. (1991). *Social cognition* (2nd ed.). New York: McGraw-Hill.

Jussim, L. (1991). Social perception and social reality: A reflection–construction model. *Psychology Review, 98,* 54–73.

Appendix A

Office Quiz

Please indicate whether or not you observed the following items in the office and your level of confidence for each item by circling the appropriate number.

Very sure it *was not* in the office				Very sure it *was* in the office

	−3	−2	−1	+1	+2	+3

Videotape	−3	−2	−1	+1	+2	+3
Stapler	−3	−2	−1	+1	+2	+3
Cassette tapes	−3	−2	−1	+1	+2	+3
File cabinet	−3	−2	−1	+1	+2	+3
Typewriter	−3	−2	−1	+1	+2	+3
Dead rat	−3	−2	−1	+1	+2	+3
Box of Kleenex	−3	−2	−1	+1	+2	+3
Telephone	−3	−2	−1	+1	+2	+3
Pen	−3	−2	−1	+1	+2	+3
Wall calendar	−3	−2	−1	+1	+2	+3
Fish tank	−3	−2	−1	+1	+2	+3
Poster from the movie *Top Gun*	−3	−2	−1	+1	+2	+3
Paper shredder	−3	−2	−1	+1	+2	+3
Trash can	−3	−2	−1	+1	+2	+3
Wall clock	−3	−2	−1	+1	+2	+3

49 FUNCTIONAL FIXEDNESS IN PROBLEM SOLVING

Douglas A. Bernstein and Sandra S. Goss
University of Illinois

One of the most interesting obstacles to problem solving is functional fixedness, the failure to think of using familiar objects in novel or unfamiliar ways to solve a problem. The most common textbook example of this phenomenon uses the two-string problem (in which a pair of scissors must be used as a pendulum to tie together the ends of two strings that are hanging too far apart to be reached simultaneously). This activity offers another problem that appeared years ago on the Mr. Wizard television show.

CONCEPT
This demonstration helps students recognize how easily functional fixedness and other cognitive habits can form obstacles to problem solving. The demonstration also helps reveal the effects of stress, group processes, and gender stereotypes on problem solving.

MATERIALS NEEDED
Assemble an array of items including a sewing kit, a pad of 8½-by-11-in. paper, a roll of transparent tape, a marker pen, and a phonograph record. Add a number of diverse and interesting—but, for this task, useless—items such as a tennis ball, a tool kit, an apple, paper clips, and rubber bands to make the problem more difficult. If your students will be asked to solve this problem in small groups, you will need one set of materials for each group.

INSTRUCTIONS
To allow all class members to work on the problem together, show them the item array by using the pad of paper as a tray to hold and display the other objects. Tell the students that the problem to be solved is to play the phonograph record so the class can hear it, using only the materials displayed. You can appoint one student to handle the materials according to student suggestions or you can do this yourself.

If you want to make this a small-group project, the instructions remain the same. Your role is to stroll around the room observing progress while each group works on the problem with its own materials. You should note problem-solving obstacles and other phenomena for later discussion.

To demonstrate the effect of stress on problem solving, set a short time limit for playing the record or, better yet, divide the class into several competing groups with a reward for the group that solves the problem first.

DISCUSSION
Because none of the items in the materials array except the record is normally associated with record playing, it may take a while for the students to think of the following solution: Take a sheet of paper from the pad, roll it from one corner to form a cone, and tape the edge to hold that shape. Then tape a needle from the sewing kit to the outside of the narrow end of the paper cone so that its point

extends an inch or so beyond the cone. Now take the cap off the marker pen and push the point of the pen firmly into the hole in the record (be sure to choose a pen that will fit snugly). By resting the back end of the pen vertically on a flat surface and turning its barrel, the record can be turned clockwise in a horizontal plane. While turning the record in this way, grasp the edge of the large end of the paper cone between thumb and forefinger and let the needle rest on the turning record. (It often helps to have two people working together: one to spin the record and the other to hold the cone.) It will not be high fidelity or stereo, but the sound will be amplified enough for everyone to hear. If the sound is too faint, exert a little more downward pressure on the needle.

Most students have a difficult time solving this problem because they show functional fixedness about the items provided. For example, they may use the sewing kit case itself rather than opening it and using the needle. They may ignore the pad of paper, viewing it as simply something to hold the objects.

We have noticed that males often try to take over the problem-solving process. If a male says something like "I'm in engineering," the rest of the class will defer to his implied expertise. Sometimes a male will become the self-appointed leader of the group and ignore suggestions made by females. The instructor's observations of such group processes and other aspects of the problem-solving session often prompt discussions about how groups function, the role of expertise, the need for domain-relevant knowledge (students are becoming increasingly unfamiliar with the principles of the phonograph record and its amplification), and the persistence of incorrect problem solutions.

WRITING COMPONENT

Ask one person in the class, or one in each group, to record the sequence of all suggestions made to solve the problem. Students can use copies of this record as the basis of a short paper comparing their problem-solving strategy and obstacles with those discussed in class or in the textbook. Students can also be encouraged to include comments or observations about their particular group's problem-solving attempts that especially intrigued them. It is often in this section that issues like gender stereotypes and narrowed attention will be discussed.

SUGGESTED READING

Halpern, D. F. (Ed.). (1994). *Changing college classrooms: New teaching and learning strategies for an increasingly complex world*. San Francisco: Jossey-Bass.

Stice, J. E. (Ed.). (1987). *Developing critical thinking and problem-solving abilities*. San Francisco: Jossey-Bass.

$\boxed{50}$ REORGANIZATION AND PRODUCTIVE THINKING

Michael Wertheimer
University of Colorado at Boulder

Real-life problems are often solved automatically with "reproductive" problem solving, which uses habitual memorized procedures. "Productive thinking" involves using insight to solve problems for which memorized solutions do not work. This activity constitutes brain teasers intended to generate the "Aha!" experience of achieving insight or understanding about a previously confusing issue or situation.

CONCEPT

Appropriate reorganization or restructuring results in an insightful revision of one's representation of a particular problem domain. Productive thought results in changing a vague, incomplete representation that is blind to essential structural features of the problem to one that is clear, makes sense, and has no gaps in it and that views each part of the problem in terms of its place, role, and function within the problem as a whole. Such transformations are hampered by rote memorization, blind drill, and aimless search, and are facilitated by open-minded exploration of the problem, searching for its essential, crucial features.

MATERIALS NEEDED

You will need a chalkboard, chalk, pencil, and paper. In addition, many different puzzles and other examples that require reorganization can be used to convey this concept. Resourceful instructors can try out a variety of these aids to see which ones appear to work best in their courses with their students. One strategy is to begin with perceptual instances that vividly demonstrate reorganization, to help get the general idea across early, and then to proceed to progressively more cognitive, abstract, and difficult ones. At the perceptual extreme are figures such as the "droodles" that were popular some years ago. For instance, the line drawing in Figure 50-1, which first may be viewed as a side view of a squinting face, can be reorganized into a soldier and a dog passing an archway; the mouth becomes the dog's tail and the squinting eye a rifle with a bayonet. The diagram in Figure 50-2, which might first appear to be a ghoul looking over a fence and a couple of ears sticking up over the fence, can be restructured into a custodian cleaning a

Figure 50-1. A squinting cartoon face seen in profile.

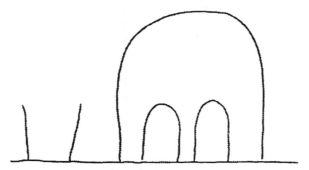

Figure 50-2.   A ghoul and a dog seen over a fence.

spot on the floor (the ghoul's eyes become the soles of the janitor's shoes, and the ears become the sides of a bucket).

Still somewhat perceptual is writing the following on the board, and asking the class what it means: Pas de l'y a Rhône que nous. At first it appears to be (nonsensical) French; but reading it out loud can result in it becoming, phonetically, "Paddle your own canoe." Rebuses by their very nature require reorganization. Here is one:

   you just me

Describing the relative positions of the words can generate *just* between *you* and *me*, or the phrase "just between you and me." Here's another:

   stood
   well
   view

Notice that *stood* is over *well* and *view* is under *well*. But one could also say "*well* under *stood* over *view*," or what one achieves with proper reorganization: "a well-understood overview."

Partly perceptual but conceptual as well is the classic puzzle that asks for the smallest number of links that needs to be opened and resoldered to make a single continuous chain of 15 links out of a broken chain that consists of five sets of 3 links each (see Figure 50-3). At first it appears that at least four links need to be cut and closed again (for instance, the right-most link in each of the first four sets of three). But the problem can also be solved by opening only three links. How? The solution requires the recognition or reorganization that the five perceptually comparable sets of three links each need not be *functionally* identical. If all three links in one set are opened and used to close the gaps between each of the remaining four sets, then that set in effect disappears and becomes what is used to close the three gaps among the other four sets.

Another somewhat comparable puzzle is the famous unicursal nine-dot problem. The task is to draw four continuous straight lines (that is, without lifting the pencil from the paper or the chalk from the board), such that each dot has at

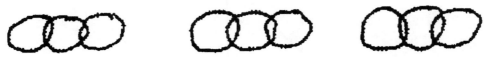

Figure 50-3.   Make these links into a continuous chain.

Figure 50-4. The nine-dot problem.

least one line going through it (see Figure 50-4). Because the implicit assumption is that the lines should not go outside the square composed of the nine dots, most participants find this puzzle hard when they first encounter it. Each of the four structurally identical solutions (one starting from each corner) requires reorganizing the conception of the pattern in a particular (nonsquare) way, such as the solution depicted in Figure 50-5.

More abstract yet is the problem of proving that any sequence of three repeated digits (*abc,abc* or *efg,efg;* 493,493 or 576,576 or 801,801; etc.) is divisible without remainder by 13. Most participants start out by having not the slightest idea of how to go about doing this. Maybe this set of examples will help a bit: 276,276; 277,277; 278,278. The solution requires recognizing that the factors of any number of the form *abc,abc* are *abc*—and 1001 (1001 times *abc* equals *abc,abc*)—and then checking whether 1001 is in fact divisible without remainder by 13. Do this, and you'll discover that it is; and other factors of *abc,abc* (that is, of 1001) turn out to exist as well: 77, 7, 11.

For students who prefer purely conceptual to mathematical puzzles, there is the classic story of the wealthy desert dweller whose caravan is finally approaching an oasis after a long, hot trek across the sand (a story that some students may have heard before; for this puzzle, and all the rest of them for that matter, it is a good idea to ask that any students who know the puzzle not give it away too soon, so as not to spoil the exercise for their colleagues). The leader says to two lieutenants, "To that one of you whose horse gets to the oasis last, I'll give this camel laden with gold." The caravan proceeds on; the lieutenants slow down, each waiting for the other to get ahead. By the time the rear guard of the caravan gets to the two lieutenants, they have dismounted their horses and are sitting on the sand, each waiting for the other to become so hot and thirsty that getting to the oasis can no longer be resisted. They tell the guard the wealthy leader's offer, and ask for help. The guard says two words to them, whereupon the lieutenants jump onto the horses and race toward the oasis. What did the guard tell them? At first most people are stumped; why should the lieutenants race toward the oasis if that one whose horse gets to the oasis *last* will win the prize? The guard's recommendation is "Trade horses."

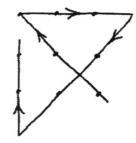

Figure 50-5. Solution to the nine-dot problem.

A striking example of reorganization is this extension of a popular story. A hunter sees a bear 1 mi due south. The hunter shoots and misses, and the bear ambles off. The hunter walks the 1 mi due south to where the bear had been, then 1 mi due east, then 1 mi due north—at which point the hunter is standing again at exactly the same spot from which the gun had been fired. Question: What color was the bear? Those who have not heard the story before are stumped; the information provided appears to have nothing to do with the bear's color. A restructuring of the problem leads to the question, *where* on the earth's surface can one go, successively, 1 mi due south, then 1 mi due east, then 1 mi due north, and end up standing at the same place one started from? It turns out that the north pole satisfies this requirement. Although the triangle traversed by the hunter looks somewhat odd (the sum of the interior angles is 270° rather than 180°, and all three sides are slightly curved), it is easy to conclude that the bear must therefore be a polar bear and hence white. The extension of the problem asks where else, other than from the north pole, one can go successively 1 mi due south, then 1 mi due east, then 1 mi due north and end up standing at the same place one started from. This problem is quite difficult, because the solution involves a pattern that does not look at all like a plane triangle—but it is a most elegant solution. The crux of it is that the north and south legs coincide perfectly, and that the east leg is a circle that is exactly 1 mi (or a perfect fraction of a mile) long, with the circle centered on the south pole (the dot in Figure 50-6). Technically, the solution sounds more complex than it is once one has understood it: any point on a circle that is exactly 1 mi north of the circumference of a circle just north of and surrounding the south pole, that is precisely 1 mi (or a fraction of one mi) in circumference.

INSTRUCTIONS   Select a series of puzzles for the exercise—preferably beginning with fairly easy and obvious ones and progressing to more challenging ones—to demonstrate the transition from confusion or bewilderment to the achievement of a well-understood overview. The sequence from perceptual to conceptual problems works well; make an effort to engage the interest and cognitive processes of every member of the class. Achieving insight into a previously fuzzy issue or problem can yield much pleasure, and every student in the class should be encouraged to have that satisfying experience with several (preferably all) of the puzzles selected. In presenting each problem, try to elaborate on it in ways that enhance the initial

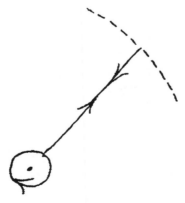

Figure 50-6.   Solution to the extension of the polar bear problem.

impasse, and then use a succession of hints to help the students discover the solution themselves. Allow sufficient time for each problem so that the students can get thoroughly engaged in it; the more involved they become in the problem, the greater their pleasure when they finally catch on to the solution.

For the rebus mentioned under the Materials Needed section, for instance, you might begin with descriptions that do not solve it, such as saying, "*stood* is above *well,* and both words are above *view*" or "*well* is between *stood* and *view*" or "*view* is below *well,* and both are below *stood.*" Hints can include such suggestions as "try using the words *over* and *under* in your description."

For the broken chain exercise, the puzzle is best presented on the chalkboard with all five segments lined up as in Figure 50-3. A powerful hint is to erase the segment at either end and redraw it underneath the other four. If that does not do it, draw the fifth segment under the other four as three circles that are not linked.

In the nine-dot problem, drawing several attempts that do not go outside the square can help reinforce the unstated assumption that the lines must remain inside the square. It turns out that the hint, "You need to go outside the square," does not help very much on its own; but adding two dots to the pattern helps most people see the solution (Burnham & Davis, 1969):

```
. . . .
  . . .
  . . .
  .
```

The two added dots show just how far the second line needs to go outside the corner of the square and thus help even the most puzzled participant catch on.

On the problem about divisibility by 13 without remainder, it is worth it to let the students try a variety of six-digit numbers that they generate themselves, dividing 13 into them, to convince them that for every number of that form, 13 is indeed a factor. The solution process can be facilitated by asking by what numbers every six-digit sequence of the form abc,abc is divisible without remainder. You can even suggest, "Is it divisible by abc?" Although a letter form of long division may not be familiar to many students, they can try it out, and discover that indeed it is. Successive versions that satisfy the algebraic conditions, such as 312,312, 313,313, 314,314, can help students realize that one quotient will always be 1001; abc times 1001 equals abc,abc. The next step is asking whether 13 goes into 1001 an even number of times, and when the students try that, they can recognize that any factor (13, and also 77, 7, and 11) of 1001 must therefore also be a factor of abc,abc.

For the polar bear problem, possible hints include exploring very near the south pole, and also pointing out that the solution is not a trick. Some students are helped by being encouraged to imagine themselves underneath the south pole and looking up at the globe from there. To ensure that every student *does* understand the solution, the instructor may need to draw it on the board, emphasizing that the southward and northward paths coincide perfectly, and that by going around a circle that is exactly 1 mi in circumference one ends up standing at the same place on the circle from which one started (a goal that can also be achieved by going twice around a circle that is $1/2$ mi in circumference or five times around one whose circumference is $1/5$ mi, etc.).

For every exercise, the point is to help the students go from a state in which they are stumped to one in which they attain insight, so that after they have caught on the entire problem appears clear, straightforward, and fully meaningful to them.

DISCUSSION It is important to give the students enough time for each puzzle so that they can thoroughly get into it and have enough time to think about, and fully understand, the solution. Again, be sure to remind those who already know a particular puzzle not to give away the answer too soon. The students will, of course, differ in how fast they catch on to any exercise. But encourage those who catch on early (and the signs of who has and who has not caught on are typically unmistakable in the students' demeanor) to help the rest of the class achieve insight. To repeat, the crucial transition is from a confused, unsatisfying conception of the puzzle to a restructuring or reorganization of the information provided in which the various components of the puzzle are fully understood, make sense, and fit together. Students who have favorite similar brain teasers can be encouraged to share them with the class, always with the same aim: The initial puzzle should be truly puzzling, and the solution should, ideally, be really elegant. Trick problems or puzzles, though, should be discouraged; they do not contribute to the exercise.

Class discussion of how the kind of learning exemplified in the exercises differs from rote memorization, conditioning, and drill can be highly productive; among the topics that you can fruitfully pursue in this context are retention, transfer, and motivation. Which kind of information tends to be better retained —memorized material or material that has been thoroughly understood? Which kind of material is more likely to be transferred to similar problems—that is, used productively and generalized to new situations? Which kind of learning is inherently more rewarding to the student—memorizing or gaining insight? And what are the implications of the psychology of productive thinking, of reorganizing and restructuring, for how one should go about studying anything one wishes to learn, including school subjects? What are the implications for how subjects should be taught? Are there subjects for which an insight approach cannot be used, and if so, what are they? What is discovery learning, and what are its advantages and disadvantages? The potential applications and implications of these exercises are enormous, and they can form the basis for extensive discussions of a wide variety of topics in education and training.

WRITING COMPONENT Many interesting brief writing assignments can be based on this demonstration. Among the topics that students can be asked to write about are any of the questions raised in the preceding paragraph, such as contrasting conditioning with insightful learning or drawing out the implications of a discovery or understanding approach for everyday classroom learning. You can also have students write a short account of an example of catching on, which can be based on their own recent experience; the example need not, of course, have to concern a school subject. Inviting students to read out loud what they have written can generate a lively discussion that shows how widespread insight, understanding, and restructuring can be in many facets of everyday life—both in school and outside of school—and what an exhilarating experience it can be to gain insight into something that was not well understood before.

REFERENCE   Burnham, C. A., & Davis, K. G. (1969). The nine-dot problem: Beyond perceptual reorganization. *Psychonomic Science, 17,* 321–323.

SUGGESTED READING   Adams, J. L. (1990). *Conceptual blockbusting: A guide to better ideas* (3rd ed.). Reading, MA: Addison-Wesley.

Holyoak, K. J., & Spellman, A. (1993). Thinking. In L. W. Porter & M. R. Rosenzweig (Eds.), *Annual review of psychology* (Vol. 44, pp. 265–315). Palo Alto, CA: Annual Reviews.

Katona, G. (1940). *Organizing and memorizing.* New York: Columbia University Press.

Sternberg, R. J., & Davidson, J. E. (Eds.). (1995). *The nature of insight.* Cambridge: Bradford and MIT Press.

Wertheimer, M. (1980). Gestalt theory of learning. In G. M. Gazda & R. J. Corsini (Eds.), *Theories of learning: A comparative approach* (pp. 208–251). Itasca, IL: F. E. Peacock.

Wertheimer, M. (1982). *Productive thinking.* Chicago: University of Chicago Press. (Original work published 1945)

Wertheimer, M. (1997, January/February). A contemporary perspective on the psychology of productive thinking. *Psychology Teacher Network* 7(1), 2–3, 6, 8, 13.

51 SET AND INFORMATION PROCESSING

Michael Wertheimer
University of Colorado at Boulder

Human beings live in an environment that supplies enormous amounts of information. Cognitive processes are normally set to select some portion of this input and ignore other parts. This simple activity can demonstrate such "set" or selective attention dramatically. The demonstration requires little time and no apparatus, and can generate lively discussion.

CONCEPT

"Set," or choosing to pay attention to some selected portion of incoming information, characterizes most cognition. Normally only those aspects of information input to which we are attuned are processed; other aspects are ignored and remain inaccessible to further processing.

MATERIALS NEEDED

All that you will need for this exercise besides a piece of paper and a pencil for each participant is a narrative, including a set of numbers, that is read aloud to the class. The particular numbers used are at your discretion (although the numbers should be fairly small and easy to process in the interest both of making the exercise realistic and of keeping the mental arithmetic that the students will engage in reasonably easy). The narrative that you read to the class might be as follows:

> Assume that you're the engineer of a passenger train. At the first station, 20 passengers get on. At the next station, 5 passengers get off and 15 get on. At the next station, 10 passengers get off and 12 get on. At the next station, 7 get off and 10 get on. At the next station, 20 passengers get off and 5 get on. At the next station, 8 passengers get off and 3 get on.

INSTRUCTIONS

Slowly read the narrative to the class, pausing between sentences and after each number phrase. (The pause after each number phrase not only permits the students to perform the mental arithmetic, but also helps imply that the students should perform the mental calculations.) After you have completed the narrative, ask the students to write down, on successive lines of a piece of paper, the numbers 1 through 5. Then ask the students to write the numbers that answer the following five questions after the numbers 1 through 5. First question: "How old is the engineer of the train?" Second question: "How many stations were there?" Third question: "How many passengers are left on the train?" Fourth question: "Altogether, how many passengers have gotten off the train since the first station?" Fifth question: "Altogether, how many passengers have gotten onto the train anywhere along its route?"

DISCUSSION

Most participants, if they have not encountered this demonstration (and probably it *will* be familiar to at least a few of them—that is one of the reasons for including the last two questions, which they are less likely to have run across before), will be startled by the first question and will react helplessly, wondering how in the world the information provided could give them any clue about the age of the engineer. When you remind the class of the first sentence of the narrative, "Assume that *you're* the engineer of a passenger train," many will groan or show other signs of insight: if *the listener* is the engineer of the train, then of course the answer is the listener's own age. In their initial processing of the information provided, the fact that *the listener* was to be considered the engineer of the train was regarded as inconsequential and hence did not make it into some students' memories. As for the answer to the second question, most participants who go through the exercise the first time are so busy keeping track of the number of passengers on the train that they fail to register how many stations there are. The third question may be answered correctly by the students who were taken in by the set to keep track of the number of passengers on the train, but it is apt to be missed by the participants who were in the know and who therefore kept track of the number of stations but not of the number of passengers. The fourth and fifth questions are there to make the point that whether or not the students were aware of the trick nature of the exercise, they still were highly unlikely to engage in the cognitive processing that would have been necessary to answer them correctly, given their understanding of the task—even though they too are perfectly reasonable questions that could easily have been answered by anyone who was set to keep track of the relevant quantities. You may wish to read the entire narrative again after all this, so that the students can try to keep track of all the information needed to answer all the questions—but none of the students will be able to do so, even with the best of intentions, without using paper and pencil; it is just about impossible to retain all four numbers mentally after each station. Modern cognitive models of attention make clear that we have a limited capacity to store and process incoming information; keeping track of more than one or two of these quantities results in information overload: The human cognitive system cannot do it without help. The point of the entire demonstration, of course, is that we attend selectively to all input and process it in only one or a few of the many ways in which it could be processed.

WRITING COMPONENT

Ask the students to write down, in no more than three or four sentences, an example of the operation of "set" or "attending selectively" or "selective cognitive processing" from everyday life. Preferably the example should describe an event from each student's own experience during the past week or two. If the students are then invited to share their examples by reading them aloud to the class, the ensuing discussion can help convince the class about how common and widespread the phenomenon of set is in everyday cognition.

SUGGESTED READING

Coren, S., Ward, L. M., & Enns, J. T. (1996). *Sensation and perception* (4th ed.). Orlando, FL: Harcourt Brace.

Corsini, R. J. (1987). *Concise encyclopedia of psychology* (pp. 1011, 1021–1022). New York: Wiley.

Gleitman, H. (1987). *Basic psychology* (2nd ed., pp. 155–158). New York: Norton.

Kramer, A. F., Logan, G. D., & Coles, M. G. H. (Eds.). (1995). *Converging opera-*

tions in the study of visual selective attention (monograph). Washington, DC: American Psychological Association.

Levine, M. W., & Shefner, J. M. (1991). *Fundamentals of sensation and perception* (2nd ed.). Pacific Grove, CA: Brooks/Cole.

Reisberg, D. (1997). *Cognition: Exploring the science of the mind.* New York: Norton.

52 THE FACIAL FEEDBACK HYPOTHESIS: ARE EMOTIONS REALLY RELATED TO THE FACES WE MAKE?

Charles Schallhorn
Munster High School, Munster, Indiana

Jeff Lunde
Mayo High School, Rochester, Minnesota

This activity demonstrates the facial feedback hypothesis. Students are instructed to hold a pencil or pen in a particular way with their teeth or lips so as to produce either a smile or a frown. Then they are asked to relate how funny a set of cartoons are. Students who are smiling usually find the cartoons funnier than students who are frowning. Several discussion topics are also suggested.

CONCEPT   The James–Lange theory of emotion (Wade & Travis, 1996) states that emotions are created by the perception of one's physical reactions. An extension of this theory is the facial feedback hypothesis that predicts that our emotions should change to match our facial expression.

INSTRUCTIONS   This demonstration should be done just before discussing theories of emotion and the facial feedback hypothesis, so students do not know what to expect from the activity before the data are collected.

Begin by distributing a cartoon packet and rating scale sheet to everyone in the class. Pass out the cartoons upside down and tell students to leave them upside down until asked to begin their ratings. Then divide the class into two groups (the left half and right half works well). Teach one group to "smile" by having each student hold a pencil or pen horizontally in the mouth just behind the front teeth. Tell them not to touch the pencil or pen with the lips. Teach the other half of the class to "frown" by instructing these students to hold a pencil or pen horizontally between the upper lip and the nose. Do not inform students they are learning how to smile or frown. Once both groups have mastered the assigned task, have everyone continue to hold the pencils while they read the cartoons and evaluate how funny each is on the rating scale sheet.

When all students have completed the cartoons, each should add the ratings for the 10 cartoons. Have students report their totals orally while you list them, by group, on the chalkboard. To compute the mean rating for each group, add the rating totals from the chalkboard and divide by 10 times the number of students in the group.

Now you can explain the James–Lange theory of emotion and the facial feedback hypothesis, which predicts that the students induced to smile will rate cartoons as funnier than the students induced to frown.

DISCUSSION Do we frown because we are angry or do we get angry because we frown? Do we smile as we become happy or do we get happier because we smile? The facial feedback hypothesis is that facial expressions help determine emotional response. This is consistent with the James–Lange theory of emotion, which argues that an emotion is determined by its associated physiological responses. Therefore, if we create facial expressions that mimic those associated with happiness or sadness, our emotion will change to match that expression.

There is research that supports the facial feedback hypothesis. When undergraduates were required to "smile" and "frown" without awareness of the nature of their expressions, they reported feeling more angry when frowning and more happy when smiling. Research participants have also reported that cartoons viewed while they were smiling were more humorous than cartoons viewed while they were frowning. These results are interpreted as indicating that an individual's expressive behavior mediates the quality of emotional experience (McCanne & Anderson, 1987; Strack, Martin, & Stepper, 1988).

In a review of studies, McCanne and Anderson concluded that the vast majority of studies have "yielded data that are consistent with the hypothesis that facial muscle activity contributes to the experience of emotions" (1987, p. 775). The authors have argued that facial expressions (and postures) are emotional behaviors that produce matching changes in feelings.

Discussion about this activity or the related research can be used to examine the role of facial expressions in many situations. For example, what function do facial expressions play during grieving? Do stoic people really feel less pain? Is it effective to "take it like a man?"

This activity can also be used as a way to introduce a variety of discussion topics, including the origins of emotions; related variables (such as language, nonverbal communication, and cross-cultural issues) that may influence emotion; the role of the facial feedback hypothesis within the James–Lange theory; interaction among physiology, cognition, and emotions; the validity of the pencil tasks as a means of manipulating facial expressions; and the usefulness of competing theories of emotion for explaining the results of this demonstration.

Most classes will experience higher ratings for the "smiling" group than for the "frowning" group. Because this is not always the case, be prepared to discuss methodological considerations such as operational definitions, potential confounding variables, the importance of replication, and so forth.

WRITING COMPONENT An easy way to incorporate writing into a unit on emotions is to have students keep an "emotional journal" for a day or more. Students could report their level of emotional happiness at intervals throughout the day. They could then write about efforts to change their emotions by "acting happy" to see if individual experience can provide anecdotal evidence to the facial feedback hypothesis and the James–Lange theory.

REFERENCES McCanne, T., & Anderson, J. (1987). Emotional responding following experimental manipulation of facial electromyographic activity. *Journal of Personality and Social Psychology, 52,* 759–768.

Strack, F., Martin, L. L., & Stepper, S. (1988). Inhibiting and facilitating conditions of the human smile: A nonobtrusive test of the facial feedback hypothesis. *Journal of Personality and Social Psychology, 54,* 768–777.

Wade, C., & Travis, C. (1996). *Psychology.* 4th ed., New York: Harper-Collins.

SUGGESTED READING

Bolt, M. (1994). *Instructor's resources for use with David G. Myers psychology* (4th ed.). New York: Worth.

Boyatzis, C. J., Chazan, E., & Ting, C. (1993). Preschool children's decoding of facial emotions. *Journal of Genetic Psychology, 514,* 375–382.

Ekman, P., & Freisen, W. (1975). *Unmasking the face.* Englewood Cliffs, NJ: Prentice-Hall.

Laird, J. D. (1984). The real role of facial response in the experience of emotion: A reply to Tourangeau and Ellsworth, and others. *Journal of Personality and Social Psychology, 42,* 909–917.

Matsumoto, D. (1987). The role of facial response in the experience of emotion: More methodological problems and a meta-analysis. *Journal of Personality and Social Psychology, 52,* 769–771.

Tomkins, S. S. (1962). *Affect, imagery, and consciousness: Vol. 2. The negative effects.* New York: Springer.

Appendix A

Data Collection Sheet

Which group are you in?   _____Lip   _____Teeth

Directions: Rate all 10 cartoons in your packet while you are holding your pencil or pen according to the instructions for your group. In each case, how funny do you think the cartoon is?

	Not funny at all					Extremely funny	
Cartoon 1	1	2	3	4	5	6	7
Cartoon 2	1	2	3	4	5	6	7
Cartoon 3	1	2	3	4	5	6	7
Cartoon 4	1	2	3	4	5	6	7
Cartoon 5	1	2	3	4	5	6	7
Cartoon 6	1	2	3	4	5	6	7
Cartoon 7	1	2	3	4	5	6	7
Cartoon 8	1	2	3	4	5	6	7
Cartoon 9	1	2	3	4	5	6	7
Cartoon 10	1	2	3	4	5	6	7

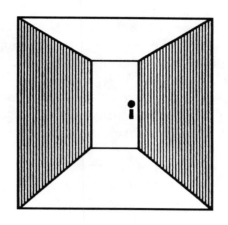

CHAPTER VIII
DEVELOPMENTAL
PSYCHOLOGY

The three activities on developmental psychology deal with pregnancy, child rearing, and the controversial subject of genetic screening. Activity 53 is a simulation exercise that allows students to experience what it would be like to be given information about their unborn baby based on genetic screening, and it allows them to explore the implications of that knowledge.

Activity 54 gives students a hypothetical pregnancy via vignettes drawn from a virtual baby basket. Some will be pregnant with a girl, some with a boy, and 3 out of every 100 with twins. Some of the virtual parents will be in their teens, others in their 40s, some are married, some are not. This project requires students to examine the economic, physical, and psychological aspects of pregnancy.

In Activity 55, students gather data on parenting from a series of interviews with parents about what they want their children to grow into as well as how they raise their children. Data are aggregated across all interviews for purposes of class discussion and can be compared to data from previous years.

$^{\square}53$ Bringing Genetic Screening Home

Richard Ely

Boston University

■———■

This simple classroom demonstration has proven to be an effective way of making the implications of genetic screening feel very real. It should follow a presentation that addresses the influence of genes on behavior, as well as a background description of prenatal screening, including mention of screening for entities like Down's syndrome. We have used this demonstration in our general psychology course. It is also suitable for courses in developmental psychology, health psychology, and biopsychology.

■———■

CONCEPT   This simulation activity allows students to experience what it would be like to be given information about their unborn baby based on genetic screening. The activity allows them to explore the implications of such knowledge.

MATERIALS NEEDED   You will need 10 3-by-5-in. cards, containing information about the cardholder's virtual baby, and envelopes.

INSTRUCTIONS   Begin by asking how many students would like to know in advance the sex of their unborn baby. Then ask them why they answered the way they did. Students who do not want to know in advance often say that it will reduce the joy, excitement, and surprise. Those who do want to know often say they would like to be able to be better prepared. You can build on this response by asking students what they mean by being prepared. This introductory discussion serves as a warm up for what is to follow.

After the introductory discussion, distribute the envelopes randomly to students in the class. Each envelope contains a prenatal diagnosis, a statement about the genetic disposition of the developing fetus. They are numbered 1 though 10 to allow you to orchestrate the type of effect desired. The effect is generally a product of both the nature of the content of each diagnosis, as well as its placement relative to the diagnoses that precede or follow it (explained later).

Students who receive an envelope are asked to stand up and read out loud the diagnosis. Be as creative as you would like in the selection of diagnoses, as well as in their wording. We have chosen to word the diagnoses in the second person (e.g., "Your baby is likely to grow up to be . . ."). However, wording the diagnoses in the first person is also effective (e.g., "My baby is likely to grow up to be . . ."). The following is the list of 10 items that we have used regularly:

1. Your baby is likely to grow up to be very neurotic.
2. Your baby is likely to grow up to be very extroverted.
3. Your baby is likely to grow up to be autistic.
4. Your baby is likely to grow up to be a genius.
5. Your baby is likely to grow up to be a genius and be very neurotic.

6. Your baby is likely to grow up to be musically very talented but also be poor at verbal tasks.
7. Your baby is likely to grow up to be a homosexual.
8. Your baby is likely to grow up to be just average.
9. Your baby is likely to grow up to be dyslexic.
10. Your baby is likely to grow up to be just like you.

Specific diagnoses with which students are unfamiliar should be explained. For some diagnoses (e.g., dyslexia, autism), it may be beneficial to provide an initial explanation that mimics the highly specialized language that physicians and clinicians sometimes use. By using this professional jargon, students are able to experience the difficulties expectant parents sometimes encounter in trying to understand what they are being told. Later you can provide follow-up explanations that use more straightforward language. After students understand all the diagnoses, ask them to consider and discuss how they would feel if they were to receive each diagnosis. Would their child-rearing practices change, knowing what they know in advance? Would they try to alter some outcomes more than others?

DISCUSSION   The diagnoses used in this exercise tap four distinct areas. First, some diagnoses (e.g., tendencies toward neuroticism and extroversion) focus on personality attributes and are based on data that suggest that some personality traits are more influenced by genes than others (Loehlin, 1992). Given this information, explore the degree to which students believe that it would be possible or advisable to modify the expression of certain personality traits. Many students will agree that parents should try to reduce or temper a genetic disposition toward neuroticism. In contrast, there is likely to be little support for the notion that parents should try to modify a genetic disposition toward extroversion. Making these views explicit can also lead to a discussion of how various cultures differentially value assorted personality traits.

Second, some diagnoses identify the tendency to excel or falter in a number of cognitive domains that have been shown to be influenced to a greater degree than others by genes. These domains include intelligence, verbal ability, and musical ability (Heller, 1993; Plomin, DeFries, & McClearn, 1990). Students should be asked to consider the degree to which they would try to alter or foster genetic dispositions in these domains. For example, would students be more willing to pay for music lessons for a child who had a genetic predisposition to be musically talented than for one who did not have such a predisposition? Would they push a child who had a genetic disposition toward being a genius to excel at academics? Would they do this even if the child not only showed little interest in academics, but actively pursued sports to the detriment of academics?

A third category is represented by only one diagnosis, the genetic tendency to become a homosexual. This is a complex topic about which many students are likely to have strong feelings. The instructor should review the evidence that sexual orientation appears to be mediated in part by genes (Bailey, Pillard, Neale, & Agyei, 1993; Hamer, Hu, Magnuson, & Hu, 1993). Students should then be encouraged to discuss, in as frank a manner as possible, how they would respond to a prenatal diagnosis indicating that there was a strong tendency for their son or daughter to become a homosexual. By asking specific questions, like those that follow, the discussion is likely to become more focused: How much would they read into the cross-gender play (i.e., girls pretending to be boys and boys pretending to be girls) that is relatively common in early childhood (Linday, 1994)? Would they try to prevent such play? How would they discuss sexuality with their child as he or she approached puberty?

The fourth area represented by the two diagnoses *just average* and *just like you*. The *just like you* diagnosis is particularly relevant following the recent data regarding sheep cloning (Wilmut, Schnieke, McWhir, Kind, & Campbell, 1997). Both the *just like you* and the *just average* diagnoses raise interesting questions about identity, self-concept, and parenting. To what degree do we seek to be unique? In what ways do we want to replicate ourselves? These two diagnoses can be tied to the other diagnoses to help bring closure to the overall discussion. For example, would a student be more likely to want her child to be *just like her* if she were a genius? Or would a student want his child to be *just average* if he were highly neurotic or a homosexual?

Throughout the exercise, the instructor should stress what is meant by genetic disposition, particularly as it is captured in the wording of the diagnoses (e.g., "Your baby is *likely* to grow up to be . . ."). The instructor should emphasize the importance of understanding that most behaviors, particularly complex behaviors, are the product of the interaction of genes and environment (Plomin, 1994). Likewise, in any offspring, the total effect of the genotype is likely to generate dispositions toward what many would consider to be both positive as well as negative attributes. Diagnoses 5 and 6 are designed to demonstrate this notion.

Finally, the social, political, and ethical implications of genetic screening should be raised (Hubbard & Wald, 1993; Kitcher, 1997; Lewontin, Rose, & Kamin, 1984; Suzuki & Knudtson, 1990). By making the implications of genetic screening personal and specific, this exercise makes such a discussion more meaningful. Again, asking students specific questions can promote a more focused discussion. Some sample questions include the following: Should prenatal screening for certain behaviors (e.g., "disorders" like autism) be mandatory? Alternatively, should prenatal screening for other behaviors (e.g., personality traits, sexual orientation) be prohibited? To what degree would the wide-scale availability and use of comprehensive prenatal screening create a de facto eugenic society?

In general, students are quite moved by this exercise and, in our experience, the discussion has always been thoughtful and reflective. They are also likely to come away from this experience with a better understanding of how genes and environment interact. Stress to the students that in their role as (future) parents, they will be providing much of the social environment that their children will encounter. Lastly, be sensitive to the cultural and religious implications that such an exercise is likely to generate. Discussing these issues in a straightforward and balanced manner is in itself often enriching.

WRITING COMPONENT   Several writing assignments can be used to enhance student's understanding of the implications of genetic screening. For smaller classes, as an alternative to an open classroom discussion, assign students to specific diagnoses and have them respond in writing to the following questions (presented earlier): Would their child rearing-practices change, knowing what they know in advance? Would they try to alter some outcomes more than others?

Another exercise would be to provide the students with the list of diagnoses, and ask them to rank-order the diagnoses in terms of how much or how little they would try to alter the identified outcomes. Ask that they justify their rank ordering.

If the groupings identified in the Discussion section were not explicitly explained in the classroom discussion, ask students if they can generate a way in which they would group the diagnoses. Then ask them to rank-order their groupings and to justify both their groupings and their ranking. We would anticipate that students would either group diagnoses as we grouped them, or they would group them in clusters that shared comparable levels of social and cultural desirability (e.g., genius status and extroversion grouped together and ranked as less likely to be modified than dyslexia and neuroticism).

As a final exercise, provide the students with the list of diagnoses. Ask them to use the diagnoses to formulate a policy statement that would be directed toward their state or federal legislators. They should address the following two questions: (a) What are the risks and benefits of wide-scale availability and use of comprehensive prenatal screening? (b) To what degree should the government fund such screening, or mandate the funding of such screening?

REFERENCES

Bailey, J. M., Pillard, R. C., Neale, M. C., & Agyei, Y. (1993). Heritable factors influence sexual orientation in women. *Archives of General Psychiatry, 50,* 217–223.

Hamer, D. H., Hu, S., Magnuson, V. L., & Hu, N. (1993). A linkage between DNA markers on the X chromosome and male sexual orientation. *Science, 261,* 321–327.

Heller, K. A. (Ed.). (1993). *International handbook of research and development of giftedness and talent.* Tarrytown, NY: Pergamon Press.

Hubbard, R., & Wald, E. (1993). *Exploding the gene myth.* Boston: Beacon Press.

Kitcher, P. (1997). *The lives to come: The genetic revolution and human possibilities.* New York: Touchstone.

Lewontin, R. C., Rose, S., & Kamin, L. J. (1984). *Not in our genes.* New York: Pantheon Books.

Linday, L. A. (1994). Maternal reports of pregnancy, genital, and related fantasies in preschool and kindergarten children. *Journal of the American Academy of Child and Adolescent Psychiatry, 33,* 416–423.

Loehlin, J. C. (1992). *Genes and environment in personality development.* Newbury Park, CA: Sage.

Plomin, R. (1994). *Genetics and experience: The interplay between nature and nurture.* Thousand Oaks, CA: Sage.

Plomin, R., DeFries, J. C., & McClearn, G. E. (1990). *Behavioral genetics: A primer* (2nd ed.). New York: W. H. Freeman.

Suzuki, D., & Knudtson, P. (1990). *Genethics: The clash between new genetics and human values.* Cambridge, MA. Harvard University Press.

Wilmut, I., Schnieke, A. E., McWhir, J., Kind, A. J., & Campbell, H. S. (1997). Viable offspring derived from fetal and adult mammalian cells. *Nature, 385,* 810–813.

SUGGESTED READING

Dunn, J., & Plomin, R. (1990). *Separate lives: Why siblings are so different.* New York: Basic Books.

Plomin, R. (1990). *Nature and nurture: An introduction to human behavioral genetics.* Pacific Grove, CA: Brooks/Cole.

Plomin, R., & Rutter, M. (1998). Child development, molecular genetics, and what to do with genes once they are found. *Child Development, 69,* 1223–1242.

Saudino, K. J. (1997). Moving beyond the heritability question: New directions in behavioral genetic studies of personality. *Current Direction in Psychological Science, 6*(4) 86–90.

Wright, L. (1997). *Twins and what they tell us about who we are.* New York: Wiley.

54 VIRTUAL PREGNANCY: THE PROJECT THAT DELIVERS

Shalynn Ford
Normandy, Tennessee

Active learning projects such as virtual pregnancy make the child psychology course a memorable learning experience. This activity examines the economic, psychological, and physical aspects of pregnancy. Students examine the practical aspects of pregnancy, keeping a journal of their feelings, observations, and experiences as they progress through their pregnancy.

CONCEPT

The purpose of this activity is to provide students the unique opportunity of experiencing a hypothetical pregnancy and its attendant costs (primarily financial, but including emotional, psychological, and lifestyle costs as well). The idea behind this exercise is to give students practical experience, information, and insight into the daunting task of seeing a pregnancy through from conception to delivery. This activity should last the entire semester; papers are handed in approximately 2 weeks before the end of the semester to allow for instructor response.

MATERIALS NEEDED

You will need five vignettes, which students will choose randomly from the baby basket. The baby basket in this activity is just a small wicker basket containing strips of paper that are number coded to match the vignettes contained on a standard-sized sheet of paper (passed out separately). Note that the hypothetical parent is almost always a mother; from time to time it is beneficial to have a father in the nontraditional role of caretaker. The circumstances, ages, and details of each vignette differ enough so that as a group, students will have the opportunity to sample a variety of hypothetical situations. (See appendix A for sample vignettes.) Mark each strip of paper with a pink or blue dot to indicate whether the pregnancy will result in a girl or boy. Place two dots on three out of every 100 strips, indicating twins.

INSTRUCTIONS

Have each student randomly select a hypothetical pregnancy vignette from a basket passed around the room. Each vignette will be number coded, so you should record the student's selection in the grade book to ensure that students keep the pregnancies they select rather than swapping. Explain to students that they are to calculate the costs of hospital charges, layette items, maternity clothing, and other miscellaneous items they think they will need for their pregnancy and delivery. After they have made a list of these things, tell students to begin making the necessary contacts via telephone calls and community visits to pregnancy-related agencies. Students should keep a log (organized in a narrative fashion and handed in at the end of the semester) of each contact person by name, title, agency, and telephone number. In addition, students will need to record the exact dollar amount or cost range of items and services. For the purpose of this exercise, students are to assume that no friends or family members would "bail them out" and that neither adoption nor abortion are options. Students should be encouraged to seek the help of the instructor in answering general questions or providing feedback as they go along. Keeping a journal is useful for students to record their thoughts and feelings as their virtual pregnancy progresses. It could also be used to apply the concepts learned in class to their situation.

DISCUSSION   Virtual pregnancy is an experiential learning project that provides many students (some students are already parents) their first opportunity to make a psychological journey into an as yet uncharted developmental stage. Even students who are themselves parents can find benefits in rediscovery and subsequent role-playing. Students can gain sensitivity to the complex issues involved with pregnancy and better insight into their own individual feelings about pregnancy (students who kept a journal while conducting their research seemed particularly adept at expressing the feelings and emotions of their character). Students have reported that this activity taught them a lot about the myriad of responsibilities that accompany pregnancy, how it felt (at least vicariously) to experience a difficult life situation, what their own view of pregnancy was (i.e., idealistic, cynical, traditional, flexible), and how those insights would ultimately shape present and future relationships and behavior. Indirect benefits of the virtual pregnancy project that inspired this activity included the improved public relations between the university's departments of psychology, nursing, and education; education in locating and accessing community resources; experience in interviewing and record keeping; and a better understanding of real-world economics. If comments made by my students at the end of the semester are accurate, the virtual pregnancy project also may have served as a deterrent of sexual behavior during the semester. There was possibly a contraceptive effect resulting from students reexamining their own sexual behavior and its possible consequences.

SUGGESTED
READING

Barnett, M., Knust, J., McMillan, T., Kaufman, J., & Sinisi, C. (1988). Research findings in developmental psychology: Common sense revisited. *Teaching of Psychology, 15,* 195–197.

Beers, S. (1985). Use of a portfolio writing assignment in a course on developmental psychology. *Teaching of Psychology, 12,* 94–96.

Byran, A. (1988). Discussion topics for developmental psychology. *Teaching of Psychology, 15,* 42–44.

Junn, E. (1989). "Dear mom and dad": Using personal letters to enhance students' understanding of developmental issues. *Teaching of Psychology, 16,* 135–138.

McCluskey-Fawcett, K., & Green, P. (1992). Using community service to teach developmental psychology. *Teaching of Psychology, 19,* 150–152.

Sugar, J., & Livosky, M. (1988). Enriching child psychology courses with a preschool journal option. *Teaching of Psychology, 15,* 93–95.

Walton, M. (1987). Science and values: Addressing practical issues in developmental psychology. *Teaching of Psychology, 14,* 50–53.

Appendix A

Sample Vignettes

1. Forget Me Not

You are 15 years old and forgetful, especially when it comes to contraception. Unfortunately, your forgetfulness, combined with a healthy dose of hormones, has led to an unplanned, unexpected, and unwanted pregnancy. However, you were raised to take responsibility for your actions, so you will do your best to see this pregnancy through to the end. What will you do now?

Thoughts to Keep in Mind

- You are a minor (find out the legalities involved).
- Your education may be interrupted. Is continuing or going back to school a consideration?
- You may be eligible for special help, given your age.
- Unless this was a divine act, there is a father involved. What's his story? What are his legal rights/responsibilities?

2. I'll Be Missing' You

You are 27 years old, single, and employed full time (without health insurance coverage). Your annual salary is $18,000. Your long-time boyfriend has made it perfectly clear he does not like kids. You do—and that's good, because as luck (and lack of planning) would have it, you will be getting the opportunity to satisfy your maternal urge in about 8½ months. What is your course of action?

Thoughts to Keep in Mind

- You are employed, but without insurance.
- You are too old to be eligible for much in social services.
- The father says he will not help.

3. Oh, What A Tangled Web We Weave

You are 36, the mother of two schoolage children, and stuck in a dead-end marriage. You've considered leaving and recently did so for 3 months. During your sabbatical from marital monotony, you met a wonderful man, also unhappily married. One thing led to another, and suddenly you find out there will soon be a 7-lb addition to your problem marriage. You are in love with someone else, have no marketable skills, seem unwilling to make it without a man, and are afraid of losing the two children you already have. You've got a lot on your mind. One thing that's not an issue—you will have this baby. Now what?

Thoughts to Keep in Mind

- Your age will probably make certain expensive prenatal tests mandatory.
- Several thorny legal questions need to be resolved.
- You need to establish your priorities.

4. Just When You Thought It Was Safe

You are 44 and free. Your children are safely in college. Your husband is at the top of the corporate heap. Life is good. Your consulting work provides you a real sense of accomplishment. You never regretted that tubal ligation you had 18 years ago. In fact, you never gave it a second thought. Recently, at your annual checkup, you received the shock of your life—the clips had slipped and you have involuntarily been drafted back into the baby stroller brigade. How will you handle this?

Thoughts to Keep in Mind

- Your age may have an impact on your pregnancy.
- You and your family will face lifestyle changes.
- The pregnancy may cause you to have special health concerns.

5. Just Say No

You are a college student (any age) who is the first and only member of your family to have the opportunity to attend a prestigious university on scholarship. The heat is on. Pressure from parents, peers, and professors keep life simmering on miserable. Then you meet him. He is every wonderful thing you ever dreamed of. He has the potential to make you happy. He is forever. And all he asks of you is to "prove" your love. You do. Then unexpectedly you are forced to learn a painful lesson about mistaking kisses for contracts. He is gone. But he's left a part of himself behind with you. You are confused, hurt, angry, and to top it all off you're also 2 months pregnant.

Thoughts to Keep in Mind

- The age you select will somewhat frame your options.
- The father may or may not be legally accountable for financial assistance with this pregnancy.
- Your goals as a college student and the level of investment your family has in your success may need to be reassessed.

55 THE ENDS AND MEANS OF RAISING CHILDREN: A PARENT INTERVIEW ACTIVITY

Frank M. Bernt
St. Joseph's University

In this activity, students interview parents concerning what they want their children to grow into as well as how they raise their children. Data are collected and tabulated, then results are compared to those of earlier studies of the issue. Similarities and differences in results generate lively discussions concerning how definitions of "successful adult" change and how those definitions influence the ways in which parents raise their children.

CONCEPT

Following a period in the history of psychology during which experts and "cookbooks" on parenting were in vogue, discussions of effective parenting have turned away from the unspoken assumptions that (a) there is a "best way" to raise children, and (b) children raised in this way will inevitably grow into ideal adults (Goodnow & Collins, 1990; Kagan, 1976). Recently, emphasis has been placed on commonsense rules of thumb to be followed and on the principle that the requirements of effective child rearing are not universal but ecological—that is, the question of how to parent cannot be addressed without considering the context in which the child is developing (compared, e.g., with the demands of the community for which the child is being socialized). Although students of child development readily adjust to this shift in thinking about parenting, their acceptance is generally more intellectual than experiential. The following activity provides students with rich opportunities to collect, analyze, and interpret data related to two issues in parenting: (a) assumptions about the most effective methods of parenting (the "how to") and (b) parents' hopes about what traits their children will possess as adults (the goal of raising children).

This activity draws on two strands of research on parenting. The first asks parents the following question (Schaefer, 1978): "Based on your personal experiences with your own children, what is the best advice you could give new parents about raising children?" The second asks parents to list the three character traits they emphasize most when rearing their children (Alwin, 1988; Lynd & Lynd, 1929). Although I generally collect data for both issues in my human development and learning course, the activity is easily scaled down for introductory courses, either by addressing only one of the two issues (goals versus means) or by choosing one of the two collections techniques (Phase I or Phase II, described later).

MATERIALS NEEDED

Interview questions and checklists are provided in the appendixes.

Parent Interview

Students interview parents from two different families (one parent from each family is sufficient). Prior to interviews, brief students on the importance of following the ethical principles of conducting research with human participants (American Psychological Association, 1992); specifically, explain the issues of informed consent and participant confidentiality as they are relevant to the activity. The interviewees may be family friends, siblings, or acquaintances (using one's own parents is discouraged). For more advanced classes, specify that each student interview two parents who differ on some particular variable (e.g., age, marital status, social class, or religious affiliation) to permit comparative analyses later.

Although the format of the interview requires only about 15 min, some parents carry the discussion much further (they enjoy talking about this subject). Provide the students with work sheets, which allow them to record parents' responses as well as to jot down information such as parents' ages, occupations, number and ages of children, and so forth. Depending on your goal as the instructor, students can collect data from one or both of the phases:

Phase I: Open-Ended Questions. Parents are asked the following (see appendix A): (a) Based on your personal experiences with your own children, what is the best advice (in the form of three commandments) that you could give new parents about raising children? (b) What three traits or characteristics do you emphasize most when raising your children—that is, what three traits or characteristics do you consider most important for them to possess as successful, happy adults?

Phase II: Checklists. Once interviewees have responded to these open-ended questions, they are given two checklists (see appendixes B and C). Checklist 1 includes 10 recommendations for effective parenting based on the comments of 50 parent couples whose children have become "successful adults" in that they were productive and apparently adjusting to society (Schaefer, 1978). Checklist 2 presents 16 items adapted from an instrument developed by Lynd and Lynd (1929). Instructors can ask students to use one or both lists (past experience indicates that Checklist 2 can be used very effectively by itself).

The following class usually begins with a review of key concepts related to socialization (agents, goals, methods, models of parenting, etc.). The focus then turns to students' reactions to their interviews. What problems, interesting comments, surprises, or insights struck them during the interviews? With written materials in hand (see the Writing Component section), students are broken into groups of four or five to share their findings (small-group work can be structured according to the particular phases and type of writing component that is assigned). After small-group work, a large group discussion provides a forum for summarizing insights gained.

Phase 1

Invite students to share their interviewees' responses to the two open-ended questions (this may be done in small groups first or simply in a large group). As responses are shared, other students can contribute by indicating whether their respondents gave similar or related answers, by evaluating the wisdom of shared responses, and by considering the parents' motives for giving such answers. Most students have strong opinions about such issues as permissiveness, punishment, and superbabies, for example.

Jot down strategies and issues on the chalkboard in a wordsplash or brainstorm format; when the sharing of ideas subsides, ask students to identify common themes or issues underlying individual instances. With a little guidance, major themes related to goals of socialization (independence, obedience, social responsibility) and to parenting strategies (control and warmth dimensions, inductive techniques, etc.) can be distilled from the larger lists of desired traits and parenting commandments produced by the interviews.

Phase 2

Totals for checklists are tallied in class (in the interest of time, this might be done in small groups or outside class time). The totals from Checklist 1 (see Table 55-1) generally create constructive debates about the relative importance of warmth versus control dimensions (Baumrind, 1989). This provides an opportunity to discuss how parents might emphasize different strategies according to where they are in the family life cycle (e.g., how young the children are). In addition, the generally low percentages given to the strategy *tend to personal/partner's needs* provides an excellent opportunity to challenge students regarding the importance of resources and support for parents in child rearing.

The totals from Checklist 2 can be compared to results from previous studies to determine whether parental values have changed over the years (see Table 55-2). A number of issues can be addressed at this point. One of the most salient is an apparent shift of emphasis from *heteronomy values* (obedience, good manners, loyalty to one's church) to *autonomy values* (independence, thinking for one's self). Alwin (1988) has reviewed 60 years of studies that indicate such a trend. Other recent trends involve increased emphasis on interdependence, service to others, and acceptance of diversity. Finding an increase in parents' selection of such traits naturally leads to a discussion of a movement away from self-interest and competition toward cooperation and altruism (Bellah, Madsen, Sullivan,

Table 55-1. *Percentage of Respondents Choosing Each Parenting Strategy as Most Important*[a]

Strategy	Survey Year[a]	
	1989	1997
Love abundantly	84	63
Discipline constructively	54	41
Teach right from wrong	46	64
Spend time with children	32	54
Really listen	23	24
Develop mutual respect	21	15
Foster independence	19	20
Be realistic	13	7
Offer guidance	5	4
Tend to person/partner needs	3	8

Note. Because each respondent identified three strategies, each column adds up to 300%.
[a]Data were collected from students in human development and learning courses during the years indicated.

Table 55-2. *Percentage of Parents Choosing Each Trait as One of Three Most Desirable Traits*

Trait	Survey and Year[a]			
	Lynds (1929)	Alwin (1978)	Bernt (1989)	Bernt (1997)
Frankness/honesty	27	26	56	38
Desire to make a name for oneself	5	1	3	4
Concentration	9	7	0	0
Social mindedness	13	26	48	30
Strict obedience	45	17	8	0
Appreciation of art, music	9	5	12	8
Economy in money matters	25	17	11	30
Loyalty to the church	50	22	12	11
Knowledge of sexual hygiene	15	8	3	4
Tolerance of others	6	47	15	11
Curiosity	1	10	17	4
Patriotism	21	4	5	4
Good manners	30	23	8	30
Independence	25	76	40	34
Academic achievement	19	6	17	30
Willingness to work hard	—	—	45[b]	64[b]

Note. Because each respondent identified three essential traits, each column adds up to 300%. Alwin's numbers, even when rounded, add up to 295%.
[a] The last column of data was collected and analyzed during my spring semester classes.
[b] Percentages are not directly comparable, given the addition of a 16th alternative that was not used in the two earlier surveys.

Swidler, & Tipton, 1985; Kagan, 1976; Peck, 1987). As other peculiarities arise from a comparison of various sets of data, encourage students to generate possible explanations for differences.

WRITING COMPONENT Preparatory readings and reaction papers may be added to the assignment to prepare students for presenting their reactions to the class. I usually assign articles by Alwin (1988), Baumrind (1989), and Kagan (1976) (all are listed in the references). Depending on how familiar students are with writing empirical research papers, this exercise might either introduce or provide an opportunity to further develop such skills. For introductory classes in which students lack the ability to write such an involved report (or in which time constraints preclude extended writing assignments), instructors may provide students with a list of focus questions to answer in preparation for small- and large-group discussions (see appendix D).

For more advanced classes, students could be instructed to write a miniarticle, which should include method, results, and discussion sections. Such a report would describe briefly how parents were chosen and contacted to interview, how interviews were conducted, how checklists were administered, and tabulation of results. How results are presented will depend on the number of parents each student interviews and how the instructor decides to group students to take into account different variables. As mentioned in the Discussion section, students will be able to use the information in this report when they share with the class their impressions about how the interviews went, as well as their own careful interpretations of what the obtained findings might mean.

REFERENCES

Alwin, D. F. (1988). From obedience to autonomy: Changes in traits desired in children, 1924–1978. *Public Opinion Quarterly, 52,* 33–52.

Baumrind, D. (1989). Rearing competent children. In W. Damon (Ed.), *Child development today and tomorrow.* San Francisco: Jossey-Bass.

Goodnow, J. J., & Collins, W. A. (1990). *Development according to parents: The nature, sources, and consequences of parents' ideas.* Hillsdale, NJ: Erlbaum.

Kagan, J. (1976). The psychological requirements for human development. In N. B. Talbot (Ed.), *Raising children in modern America: Problems and prospective solutions.* Boston: Little, Brown & Company.

Lynd, R. S., & Lynd, H. M. (1929). *Middletown: A study in American culture.* New York: Harcourt, Brace & Company.

Peck, S. (1987). *The different drum: Community making and peace.* New York: Touchstone Books.

Schaefer, C. E. (1978). Raising children by old-fashioned parent sense. *Children Today, 7,* 7–9, 36.

SUGGESTED READING

Applegate, J. L., Burleson, B. R., & Delia, J. G. (1992). Reflection-enhancing parenting as an antecedent to children's social-cognitive and communicative development. In I. E. Sigel, A. V. McGillicuddy-DeLisi, & J. J. Goodnow (Eds.), *Parental belief systems: The psychological consequences for children.* Hillsdale, NJ: Erlbaum.

Bellah, R. N., Madsen, R., Sullivan, W. M., Swidler, A., & Tipton, S. M. (1986). *Habits of the heart: Individualism and commitment in American life.* New York: Harper & Row.

Bernt, F. (1988). *The means and ends of raising children: A parent interview activity.* Paper presented at the Third Annual Conference on Undergraduate Teaching of Psychology, Philadelphia, PA.

Caplow, T., Bahr, H. M., Chadwick, B. A., Hill, R., & Williamson, M. H. (1982). *Middletown families: Fifty years of change and continuity.* Minneapolis: University of Minnesota Press.

Kohn, M. L. (1959). Social class and parental values. *American Journal of Sociology, 64,* 337–366.

Maccoby, E. E., & Martin, J. A. (1983). Socialization in the context of the family: Parent–child interaction. In P. H. Mussen & E. M. Hetherington (Eds.), *Handbook of child psychology: Vol. 4. Socialization, personality and social development* (4th ed., pp. 1–101). New York: John Wiley & Sons.

Remley, A. (1988, October). From obedience to independence: The great parental value shift. *Psychology Today,* 56–59.

Appendix A

Parent Data Sheet and Initial Interview Questions

Parent interviewed (circle one):   mother   father   both

Mother's age: 20–29   30–39   40–49   50–59   60 plus

Father's age: 20–29   30–39   40–49   50–59   60 plus

Mother's occupation: _____

Father's occupation: _____

Children (names and ages):

_____   _____

_____   _____

_____   _____

_____   _____

Additional information:

_____

_____

_____

Phase 1 Interview Questions

1. Based on our personal experiences with your own children, what is the *best advice* (three specific suggestions or strategies) that you would give new parents about raising their children?
2. What *three personality traits* or characteristics do you emphasize most when raising your children—that is, what three traits do you consider most important for them to possess as adults?

Appendix B

Checklist 1: Basic Strategies for Rearing Children
(to be completed by parent)

All of the principles below are considered important in parenting. After reading through the entire list, please place *pluses* alongside those three that *you* consider to be *most important*; place *minuses* alongside those three that *you* consider to be *least important*.

_____ *Love abundantly.* Provide a sense of security, belonging, and support; express your love and affection.

_____ *Discipline constructively.* Give clear directions; set limits and be firm and consistent (yet flexible) in enforcing them.

_____ *Spend time with your children.* Every day spend time playing, talking together, and teaching.

_____ *Tend to personal/marital needs.* Give your marriage first priority; keep your spouse happy.

_____ *Teach right from wrong.* Actively teach your children values and manners, such as kindness, respect for others, honesty, and responsibility.

_____ *Develop mutual respect.* Insist that all family members treat one another with respect (being polite, thankful, apologizing, etc.).

_____ *Really listen.* Put aside your own thoughts and try to understand your child's point of view; listen to the child as a person.

_____ *Offer guidance.* Don't force opinions as laws, but offer your solutions when your children discuss their difficulties with you.

_____ *Foster independence.* Gradually allow children more and more freedom or control over their own lives.

_____ *Be realistic.* Develop realistic expectations; don't expect things to go well all the time. Expect to make mistakes; realize that other influences will increase as your children grow.

Appendix C

Checklist 2: Traits of Greatest Importance to Parents
(to be completed by parent)

Below is a list of traits that parents might consider to be important when raising their children. After reading through the list, please place *pluses* alongside the three that you consider to be *most* important; place *minuses* alongside the three that you consider to be *least* important.

_____ Frankness/honesty in dealing with others
_____ Desire to make a name for one's self
_____ Concentration
_____ Social mindedness (concern for others)
_____ Strict obedience to authority
_____ Appreciation of art, music, and literature
_____ Economy in money matters (financial good sense)
_____ Loyalty to the church
_____ Knowledge of sexual hygiene
_____ Tolerance of others
_____ Curiosity
_____ Patriotism
_____ Good manners
_____ Independence
_____ Academic achievement
_____ Willingness to work hard

Appendix D

Possible Focus Questions for Written Component

Directions: Carefully record parent responses on a separate sheet of paper. After reflecting on the answers they gave, address each of the following topics in a two-page essay:

1. Briefly describe how your interviewees responded to the questions. Did they enjoy the interview? Were they more than willing to answer questions and offer their viewpoints, or were they anxious to get it over with?
2. If you personally know the parents, to what extent do you think their answers correspond to how they are raising their children? Does it seem that what they say (or write) matches how they behave as parents?
3. What similarities or differences were there in how the two parents responded? If the answers were different, what about the two parents might explain this? Consider social class, age, gender, number of children, personality, and so forth.
4. Imagine yourself as a parent and consider how your answers to these questions might differ from those you collected. Do you think your responses would match those of your parents? Or do you think your own parenting philosophy would be very different from theirs?
5. Imagine a survey researcher collecting this data 20 years from now. Predict how parental values might change by then. What trend might appear that would reflect the changing social context in which families develop?

CHAPTER IX
HUMAN DIVERSITY AND
PSYCHOLOGY

In the past 10 years authors of psychology textbooks have recognized that their books lacked information on human diversity and have begun to present a psychology that is broader in context and richer in understanding. The 11 articles in this chapter span the scope of diversity with exercises on ethnicity, gender, culture, and sexual orientation.

Activity 56 offers many discussion topics and writing exercises designed to integrate psychological research on prejudice and discrimination into virtually every unit in the introductory psychology course. Although it treats prejudice and discrimination in many forms, its focus is on racial and ethnic issues.

The next three activities explore cultural diversity. In Activity 57, students study the concept of the social clock in a classroom that is culturally diverse. Thus this activity would work well in a developmental psychology course and—like many of the activities in this chapter—in a social psychology class as well. Activity 58 is a role-playing exercise that illustrates the impact of cultural rules, mores, and traditions on general communication and personal relationships. It is intended to show students the difficulties of being culturally sensitive and the importance of making the effort. Activity 59 examines how research results can have dramatically different interpretations based on different cultures. It is appropriate for a research methods course, but also for courses in developmental psychology, health psychology, and biopsychology.

Activities 60 and 61 explore the topic of sexual orientation. Activity 60 lets students experience some of the prejudice often directed at gay men and lesbians. Students can experience the loss of individuality associated with categorization in an out-group. Activity 61 uses small-group discussions and large class discussions to demonstrate the difficulty in defining sexual orientation.

The last five activities in this chapter deal with the subject of gender, with most of those focusing on the psychology of women. Because it is important that students do not know one another during the activity, Activity 62 is intended to be performed on the first day of class. It uses a leadership selection task to show the prejudice against women as leaders and the fact that prejudice is stronger in some kinds of tasks. Activity 63 demonstrates the persistence of gender-role stereotypes among students today and shows students how the methods by which data on stereotyping are collected can seriously bias the results. This exercise is also quite appropriate for a research methods unit or course.

Activity 64 describes an exercise that uses classical paintings to explore issues on the psychology of women. Rather than analyzing paintings from the point of view of artistic type or history, students examine the paintings for their subject matter. In Activity 65, students view television commercials to record the number of males and females serving as product representatives used inside and outside the home as a means to illustrate gender stereotyping on television. Finally, Activity 66 involves the class in the creation of a time line for women's accomplishments in the past 100 years of psychology. The culmination of the activity is a class discussion of the time line in the broader context of psychology's history so that students can examine how gender, race, and class were factors in that history.

56 Teaching About Prejudice and Discrimination in the Introductory Psychology Course

Joseph I. Lamas
Miami Dade County Public Schools

This activity offers a variety of teaching suggestions to help students learn about the causes and effects of prejudice (attitudes and beliefs) and discrimination (behavior) based on those attitudes and beliefs at different points of the introductory psychology course. This material is of key importance in the course, and it can be taught with a minimum of class time or extra preparation, using topics that are included in most introductory psychology textbooks.

CONCEPT

Prejudice and discrimination are at the core of innumerable issues, problems, and interactions in everyday human behavior and as such should be an intrinsic part of the introductory psychology course. The desired pedagogical objective is the student's own analysis and internalization of what scientific psychology has to say about prejudice and discrimination. This understanding is a basic need in a multicultural, multiethnic society, and in an increasingly global community.

MATERIALS NEEDED

No special materials are needed to implement any of the following teaching suggestions. Although more elaborate activities and demonstrations could be developed from the ideas provided, I have attempted to make the coverage about prejudice and discrimination as smooth and instructor friendly as possible.

INSTRUCTIONS

There are many ways to apply the diverse suggestions offered that will give your students a greater understanding of the causes and effects of prejudice and discrimination. It is up to you to determine how you may wish to proceed at different points of the course. The most commonly used technique employed is simply to raise questions about the material being covered, in terms of its relevance to an understanding of prejudice and discrimination. Whereas you may wish to devote 10 to 15 min to some questions, you may be content with 1 to 2 min for others. It is also possible, even desirable, to raise a question in the context of a lecture without providing an immediate answer. Discussion of possible answers may be assigned for a future class meeting or it may become part of the writing component of the course. A written discussion of a question raised in lecture may be a most effective manner to proceed in many cases; such assignments may be short, but powerful, learning experiences for most students.

In some cases, ideas are presented just for the use of the instructor, possibly to be included in a lecture. Often the points to be made are so simple and self-evident that they do no merit discussion or further analysis.

For most of the suggestions included, the core of the learning experience is asking the student to engage in critical thinking about the relationship between the topic under study and prejudice–discrimination. Your role as the instructor is to present the student with the relevance or implications of the topic under study and provide minimal assistance to the student as he or she attempts to develop the necessary relationships or implications.

Prejudice and discrimination are obviously sensitive and value-laden topics. When you want your class to discuss an issue, create an environment in which respect and acceptance prevail. Instruction devoid of values is a mirage. We do hold significant scientific, pedagogical, and human values that are part of our teaching persona. However, students should be made to understand that almost nobody willingly chooses to become prejudiced. Most of our attitudes and their consequent behaviors are given to us by influences prior to our ability to analyze, decline, or protest particular information or learning experiences. Therefore, acceptance and understanding are necessary, particularly toward those students who may appear to be prejudiced.

As indicated, any question raised in class may become the subject of a brief essay assigned to the students. Once you have acquired a familiarity with the potential benefits of this question-and-essay approach, it should be relatively easy to identify in the course syllabus 5 to 10 short, critical-thinking writing assignments.

One major, and quite valid, concern is the obvious time limitation in the introductory course. No matter what and how we may try, we are slaves to the approaching semester's end, and there are more topics than can ever be covered in our courses. Choices must be made. Painfully, important research and cherished demonstrations must be held in reserve, until we have more time (usually, never). How, then, dare we increase the relative importance of these two related topics? Can we justify taking time away from Piaget? Freud? One of the wonderful things about an increased emphasis on prejudice and discrimination is that it takes very little class time to infuse these topics effectively into the curriculum. Most often, we need a mere 2 to 5 min; a question or a brief comment may be all that is needed.

Following are a list of topics roughly corresponding to chapter headings that will easily allow you to infuse the discussion of prejudice and discrimination. Some prompts, such as guiding questions, suggestions, or data, are supplied under each topic to assist you. The selection of topics is certainly not complete. You may be able to find other, and better, opportunities. The prompts under each topic are of a minimalist nature so that you can easily branch out beyond the scope of the prompts provided. Finally, you will probably choose *not* to infuse content on prejudice and discrimination at every possible point in the curriculum. Start with a modest agenda and then add more in subsequent classes. Your individual judgment regarding the importance of the topic and your perception of the students' needs will determine how much infusion should take place.

Introductory Chapter

Education and training of a psychologist: Psychology as a profession is not keeping pace with the changing demographics of American society. The introductory psychology course may be key in motivating students of all ethnic backgrounds to pursue psychology as a career.

Research methods in psychology: Most theory building and research have focused on male nonminorities. To what extent are the results of this theory building and research applicable to other segments of the population? Note the Freud–Horney and Kohlberg–Gilligan controversies.

Biological Bases of Behavior

Dendritic branching: Laboratory research with rats has shown that dendrites develop more complex and intricate branching when subjects are exposed to enriched and variable external stimulation. What could this mean for many infants and children reared in deprived or limited socioeconomic environments?

Perception

Effect of organismic variables on perception: Human perceptions are not an accurate representation of stimulus variables. Rather, they represent the interplay of stimulus variables with such organismic variables as motivation, set, attitudes, interests, and memories. Learning plays a key role in this process. To what extent are perceptions of minority individuals and groups realistic?

Selective attention: How could selective attention affect the social perceptions of a Klan member? Of a misogynist?

Perceptual processes: How can perceptual processes such as constancy and organization affect prejudice?

Top-down processing: Explain the following in terms of prejudice both in terms of its acquisition and maintenance. (a) Perceptual set: The perceiver has some kind of perceptual readiness, or expectancy—that is, the observer is *set* to perceive something. (b) Schemas: All information is processed and fit into the individual's schema, distorting the input when necessary to make it fit. (c) A Chinese proverb states, "We see what is behind our eyes" (i.e., what is already in our minds); today, we call it the effect of expectation on perception.

Learning

Classical conditioning: How can prejudice be learned through the contiguity or contingency models of classical conditioning? Can anyone in class remember an applicable personal experience?

Instrumental learning: How can prejudice be learned through instrumental or operant conditioning? Can anyone remember a personal experience?

Schedules of reinforcement: Variable ratio (VR) and variable interval (VI) schedules of reinforcement are particularly resistant to extinction. What does this mean when applied to the attitudes or behavior of a prejudiced individual?

Learned helplessness: Can society at large better understand the behavior of certain individuals who are members of oppressed groups by applying the concept of learned helplessness?

Reinforcement-induced stereotypy: Can society at large better understand (not necessarily accept) the aggressive behavior of minority gang members by applying the concept of reinforcement-induced stereotypy (the tendency to follow a previous pattern of responses that has produced consistent rewards)?

Observational learning: In what settings are we most likely to learn prejudice and discrimination through the process of observational learning? Can any students in class think of an example?

Memory

Episodic memory: Would a negative personal experience have a disproportionate effect on the creation of prejudice?

Reconstructive memory: As nonminority members remember past events regarding minority individuals or groups, are they likely to retrieve only the factual details from long-term memory or are they likely to combine the factual memories with items that seem to fit the occasion?

Thought and Language

Defining attribute: In a prejudiced individual, what could be the defining attributes for *Black, Hispanic, Asian, Native American,* or *woman*? Once these defining attributes are developed, what effect will they have on our perception of reality.

Basic-level categories: Is *Black* or *African American,* as applied to race, a basic level or a subordinate category? As Benjamin, Hopkins, and Nation (1994) noted, "Categories at the basic level are easy to differentiate from other categories, and the members of a basic level category are easy to classify, even with only visual perceptual information" (p. 300). Basic-level categories appear to be the first categories learned in life. If *Blackness* is a basic-level category, what impact does this have on the possible formation of prejudice?

Misuse of availability heuristics: Are more crimes committed by Blacks or Whites? Do Blacks commit more crimes of aggression than crimes that involve no aggression? Do Whites commit more or fewer white-collar crimes? The mere availability of partial information and not of other, complementary information could lead us to wrong answers.

Language development: Universal adaptability refers to the capacity of all human babies to make the same sounds and acquire the phonemes of any language. They begin to lose this plasticity after 1 year of age. What does this mean regarding the nature versus nurture controversy as it relates to language behavior of different national, cultural, or social groups? What does this mean regarding the oneness of the human species?

Sexism and language: What effects does male-oriented, gender-biased language have on the development of the self-concept of females? Could gender-biased language contribute to perpetuating stereotypical expectations of behavior for both sexes?

Human Development

Piaget's cognitive theory: According to Piaget, prior to the formal-operations stage (adolescence and adulthood), humans are not able to engage in abstract, hypothetical, or deductive thinking. Does this mean that up to that point we are more at the mercy of family and societal conditioning with respect to the development of prejudicial attitudes?

Peer interactions: What situations affecting prejudice and discrimination may develop as a result of the increased importance of peer pressure during adolescence?

Kohlberg's stages of moral judgment: What racial, ethnic, or sexist attitudes are individuals likely to internalize as part of their moral schemas prior to the development of Level III (postconventional, or principled, level)? If Kohlberg is correct in indicating that not many people reach Level III, what does this mean in terms of dealing with the problems of prejudice and discrimination in our society?

Sex differences in moral judgment: Did Kohlberg (or Freud, Erikson, or Piaget) persistently misrepresent women by using male filters to interpret information and build theory? Carol Gilligan, Karen Horney, and others would say yes.

Erikson's psychosocial theory: What special problems would members of oppressed minority groups have when reaching the industry versus inferiority stage (Age 6 to puberty) and the identity versus role-confusion stage (adolescence).

Motivation and Emotion

Cognitive dissonance theory: When an individual experiences thoughts, attitudes, or beliefs that are dissonant (inconsistent) with the individual's behavior, a stressful, psychologically uncomfortable state predominates. This motivates the individual to try to reconcile the existing discrepancies, achieve consonance, and diminish stress. How can this phenomenon facilitate or hinder the development and maintenance of prejudicial attitudes or discriminatory behavior?

Achievement motivation: What effect could perceived prejudice against yourself have on the interplay between the tendencies to achieve success and avoid failure?

Affiliation motivation: In a school in which 90% of the students are White, what effect could the environment have on the affiliation motive of minority students?

Universality of emotional facial expression: What does this mean regarding the sameness or differentiation of human beings around the world?

Development of fear and anxiety: What effect could lack of familiarity with someone from a different ethnic group have on the development of fear or anxiety toward that group?

PERSONALITY

Freud's psychosexual theory: To what extent are Freudian stages of development applicable to women? What criticism does Karen Horney have of Freudian theory?

Personality differences: Are some personality types more likely to become prejudiced than others? How can we help students who possess a so-called authoritarian or prejudiced personality deal with the extra risks they bear? (See Allport, 1954.)

Psychological Assessment

Test construction and standardization: Most psychological tests are normed on a White, middle-class standardization sample. To what extent can those tests be applied validly to members of a population that was not included in the standardization sample?

Examiner effects: What does the research show about the effects of male versus female examiners on test performance of males and females. Ask the same question for examiners who are White versus those from various ethnic minorities.

Race and IQ testing: Can we fully separate nature from nurture factors as we try to compare Black and White IQ scores? "To attribute racial differences to genetic factors granted the overwhelming cultural–environmental differences between races is to compound folly with malice" (Kamin, 1974, quoted in Benjamin et al., 1994, p. 457).

Health, Stress, and Coping

Addictive behaviors and health: To what extent does the socioeconomic environment of the inner city affect substance abuse and substance dependence?

Sources of stress: If we compare the average upper-class suburbanite with the average inner-city resident on Holmes and Rahe's (1967) table of life change events, what differences would we be likely to find? How valid would that table be in assessing the sources of stress for high school or college students?

Coping with stress: To what extent are the usual avenues to cope with stress (support groups, relaxation training, meditation, biofeedback, etc.) available to low socioeconomic-level minorities?

Abnormal Psychology and Treatment

The sociological model of abnormality: Some conditions, such as depression, are "more common among people in lower socio-economic groups and among women, perhaps because they have fewer options for dealing with the stress of daily living" (Benjamin et al., 1994, p. 639).

Availability of treatment: Given that approximately one third of all persons in the United States will suffer some type of acute mental illness in their lifetime, what is the likelihood of a poor male or female finding adequate mental health treatment if he or she cannot pay for it and has no health insurance?

Deinstitutionalization: What is the relationship between deinstitutionalization and homelessness in America? Does racial prejudice play a role in our society's ability to deal effectively with this problem?

Therapist variables in treatment: Is the field of psychology recruiting and maintaining sufficient numbers of Blacks, Hispanics, Asians, and other minorities to supply much needed services to these groups and to their expected growth in America in the twenty-first century? According to the APA, psychology as a profession is not doing well in recruiting minorities into the discipline (APA, 1997).

Social Psychology

Attitude formation: People are not born with a set of attitudes; those attitudes are learned via the principles of learning. It is important that this be discussed in the appropriate chapter.

Attitude change and persuasion: Attitude change is possible when the communicator is perceived as a credible expert who is likable, and the message is "not very different from the listener's own position . . . offers a two-sided argument for the listener who disagrees . . . Contains messages that are not excessively emotional and that provide information on how to reduce emotion" (Benjamin et al., 1994, p. 544).

> The teaching of psychology implies a special social responsibility. The understanding of human learning, cognitive and moral development, attitude formation, etc. . . . can have a profound effect on the creation of a world where understanding replaces prejudice, acceptance takes the place of discrimination, and social justice prevails over oppression. Because knowledge of psychology has an especially powerful potential to bring about a better future, teachers must embrace this special responsibility and commit to the reaching of these critically important goals (from the mission statement of the Committee on Ethnic and Minority Affairs of Teachers of Psychology in Secondary School, an APA affiliate).

Fundamental attribution error: People are more likely to make personal attributions than situational attributions when evaluating other people's unacceptable behavior. (If he's poor and has no job, it's because he's lazy.) Does the society at large often think in this manner about members of minority groups?

The self-fulfilling prophecy in education: Teacher's expectations for their students' performance can have a very strong effect on what students do in the classroom, as well as on the ways teachers evaluate student performance. Do we relate in the same manner and expect as much from Blacks, Hispanics, and other ethnic groups as we do from Whites? Elementary students tend to perform better when they are expected to. This Pygmalion effect is reached by teachers creating a warmer verbal and nonverbal climate, teaching more material, interacting more, giving more differentiated feedback, and not accepting low-quality responses (see the movie *Stand and Deliver*, based on the true story of a high school math teacher, Jaime Escalante, who set high expectations for his students and helped them reach those lofty goals).

Deindividuation: "An individual in a group may become so caught up that he or she loses a sense of individual responsibility, and a kind of mob psychology takes over" (Benjamin et al., 1994, p. 564). Can this help us understand behavior during riot situations?

Conformity: How much of a student's prejudice and discrimination is an attempt to adopt the social norms or attitudes of a reference group or of the society at large?

Stereotypes: Are we aware of our own stereotypes? Why do we use stereotypes? What stereotypes do others have of us? Are they valid? Are the stereotypes we hold of others any more valid? If we allow ourselves to maintain stereotypes of others, do we in fact give permission to others to hold stereotypes of us?

Development of racial prejudice: Children appear not to be sensitive to racial differences until they reach 4 or 5 years of age. Why are children not sensitive to racial differences before that age?

How easy is it to develop prejudice? Jane Elliot's third-grade class at Ricefield Community Elementary School in Iowa made "blue eyes" smarter and superior to "brown eyes," creating differentiation and segregation. The students placed in the role of superiors changed their behavior more, and the others developed instant hate against the teacher for being assigned to an inferior group. "Those who are seen as inferior and those who are seen as superior feel and act accordingly" (Zimbardo, 1990). What do we learn from this demonstration? Discuss why it would be considered unethical to repeat this demonstration today.

Reducing prejudice and discrimination: Contact is not enough. Some necessary conditions for achieving productive integration are "1) firm endorsement of integration by those in authority, 2) absence of competition among members of the different racial groups, 3) equivalence of status of the different groups, and 4) interracial contacts that would permit learning about each other as individuals" (Benjamin et al., 1994, p. 573). Why is contact alone not enough?

Superordinate goals: The introduction of goals that are important to both groups but that could only be attained if they cooperated can lead to reduced intergroup conflict. Can we structure this into our teaching by using cooperative learning groups?

Ethnocentrism: Ethnocentrism is the belief that one's own group—especially racial, ethnic, or national groups—is superior. How does ethnocentrism affect self-esteem?

Industrial–Organizational Psychology

The following observations and comments are derived from the author's 15 years of experience in major American corporations and in different industrial sectors (transportation, heavy industry, food distribution, and financial services), prior to moving into education:

Discrimination in hiring: Stereotypical views of women's ability and corporate roles are still alive and well. "Good ol' boys" in charge of most major corporations have internalized the values and expectations of their predecessors. The perspective that "We will hire as many Blacks and minorities as it takes to stay out of trouble with the government or the media" still exists. Can students find evidence in the media of how prejudice or stereotyping affects employment?

Discrimination in promotions: Women, Blacks, Hispanics, and other minorities are often accepted in the corporate structure up to the middle-management level; beyond that, they are suspect in ability and style. Women are often expected to masculinize in the process, and yet are often criticized for being "too masculine." What is seen as competitiveness in men is seen as aggression in women. Ask students about the concept of the "glass ceiling."

Plight of ethnic minority managers: Ethnic minority managers know that it is probable that superiors as well as subordinates have racist attitudes. Hence they tend to distrust subordinates and superiors until proven trustworthy, and are extra careful and conservative in most organizational climates. This distrust interferes with everyday management functions such as delegating, motivating, and monitoring progress. The cut-throat climate of many corporations adds to the insecurity and sense of alienation. How does a concept such as self-fulfilling prophecy work in such environments?

Some Last Thoughts

If you now have a feeling that it is impossible to do justice to all the possibilities for teaching about prejudice and discrimination in the introductory course, remember that it is not necessary to hammer the message home too often. We know what our students can take before their attitudes turn negative toward the message. Pick and choose those areas that you are comfortable with, add your own, and join an increasing group of teachers who are making the teaching of psychology not only scientifically solid, but humanly and socially valuable.

REFERENCES

Allport, G. W. (1954). *The nature of prejudice.* Reading, MA: Addison Wesley.

American Psychological Association. (1997). *Visions and transformation—The final report.* Washington, DC: Author.

Benjamin, L. T., Jr., Hopkins, J. R., & Nation, J. R. (1994). *Psychology* (3rd ed.). New York: Macmillan.

Holmes, T. H., & Rahe, R. H. (1967). The social readjustment rating scale. *Journal of Psychosomatic Research, 11,* 213–218.

Zimbardo, P. (1990). *Discovering psychology.* [Video series]. Burlington, VT: The Annenberg/CPB Project.

SUGGESTED READING

Bronstein, P., & Quina, K. (Eds.). (1988). *Teaching a psychology of people: Resources for gender and sociocultural awareness.* Washington, DC: American Psychological Association.

Dovido, J. F., & Gaertner, S. L. (Eds.). (1986). *Prejudice, discrimination, and racism.* Orlando, FL: Academic Press.

Gilligan, C. (1982). *In a different voice: Psychological theory and women's development.* Cambridge, MA: Harvard University Press.

Jones, J. M. (1997). *Prejudice and racism* (2nd ed.). New York: McGraw-Hill.

Matsumoto, D. (1994). *People: Psychology from a cultural perspective.* Pacific Grove, CA: Brooks/Cole.

Zanna, M. P., & Olson, J. M. (Eds.). (1993). *The psychology of prejudice: The Ontario Symposium* (Vol. 7). Hillsdale, NJ: Erlbaum.

57 THE CONTACT HYPOTHESIS: INTERVIEWING ACROSS CULTURES

Pat A. Bradway and Sarah Atchley
Berkshire Community College

This multicultural classroom activity, based on the model of the contact hypothesis, demonstrates the concept of the social clock and promotes the exchange of information between psychology students and students of different cultural backgrounds. Students develop an understanding of the diversity of human experience through the investigation of culturally determined social clocks, a developmental concept. The activity consists of reciprocal interviews and culminates in a brief writing exercise.

CONCEPT

Western psychology is often confused with universal experience. The activity described is designed to expose students to the variety of experiences in development through cross-cultural interviews. This application bases the interviews on the concept of the social clock, a "culturally set timetable [that] establishes when various life events are appropriate and called for" (Berger, 1994, p. 486). To ensure successful interviews, the guidelines of the contact hypothesis as described by Amir (1976) and Norvell & Worchel (1981) are followed: equal status and participation, an intimate setting, and support.

MATERIALS NEEDED

You will need handouts of previously developed interview questions, a large enough classroom to accommodate many small groups, moveable furniture, a world map, and refreshments. The participation of an organized group of culturally diverse students, such as an English as a second language (ESL) class, an international students' organization, or an intercultural club is also necessary.

INSTRUCTIONS

This activity requires prior collaboration between the psychology instructor and the instructor/advisor/leader of the international students. In preparation, students in both the psychology class and the multicultural group develop a set of questions about social clocks to elicit information about the timing of life events for adults in different cultures. Typical questions developed by students include the following:

- At what age is it considered acceptable to begin dating in your country?
- Is that age the same for both men and women?
- When are young people expected to be self-supporting and to live on their own?
- At what age do people marry?

Ten questions is a manageable number. The question sets are exchanged before the groups meet, allowing preparation time for students less proficient in English or less knowledgeable about psychological concepts.

The international students and the psychology class combine for a single class meeting. After brief introductions and refreshments, assign students to small groups—ideally made up of two international students and two psychology students. Cultural background, language proficiency, and gender are other important factors in the composition of groups. Once in small groups, students interview each other using the questions they previously developed but allowing for related digressions. Encourage the students to take notes. At this stage faculty intervention is minimal, although the presence of instructors in the classroom keeps the interviews focused and ensures everyone's participation.

The classroom is typically somewhat quiet at first; however, the volume quickly increases. Although changing the makeup of groups would increase exposure to more cultural variations, it is not advisable unless the class period is especially lengthy. In our experience, students are still on task and content in their original groups after 50 min of discussion. It takes time to establish a level of comfort that allows for an exchange of information.

Four conditions based on the contact hypothesis help to ensure effective interaction among group members (Amir, 1976; Norvell & Worchel, 1981):

1. Group members must have either the same status in the contact situation or the status of the minority group must be the higher of the two. The psychology students and the international students are all students and in this sense equals. Both groups have information the other needs; members of each group spend time asking and answering questions.
2. Authority figures in the situation must promote contact. Scheduling class time for this exercise affirms the importance of the activity. Teachers circulate among the groups; however, most of the group facilitation occurs preparing for the class meeting and developing and interpreting the interview questions.
3. The contact should be pleasant and intimate. Small groups concentrating on interview questions of an often personal nature promote intimacy; sharing food helps to make the contact pleasant, easing initial awkwardness.
4. The success of the activity depends on the contributions and cooperation of both groups. Each student needs information from other students. To gather information for their papers, the psychology students are dependent on the responses of the international students. Objectives of the international students may be to gather information for a paper on multicultural experiences or to practice their English-speaking skills.

The four conditions of the contact hypothesis are equally important in establishing an effective reciprocal exchange.

The final minutes of the class period are spent in a large group discussion in which students are encouraged to share their impressions. This exposes students to the experiences of other groups and gives them the opportunity to reflect on the process while it is still fresh. A successful opening question to get discussion started is, "What did you learn today that surprised you?"

The classroom exchange can serve as a basis for a wide variety of topics in subsequent class sessions. Psychology students might be encouraged to think critically about the lack of diversity in populations commonly researched in psychology. The values and drawbacks of the interview method of gathering information could be discussed. Another focus might be the importance of the conditions established by the contact hypothesis to the success of the classroom interaction and the application of this concept to more encompassing issues such as breaking down stereotypes and overcoming prejudice.

DISCUSSION

This activity generates enthusiasm because an interview is an interactive experience. Students have control of the class; they have designed the interviews, and their participation reflects their involvement. The idea of multiculturalism is no longer an abstract concept. When students realize how difficult it is to speak for their culture as a whole, they are more reluctant to generalize about the cultures of others.

For students who have never interacted with people from another culture, the experience can expand their interpersonal comfort zones. One student who works as a police officer in a small rural town wrote: "This interview was the most interesting task I have ever experienced. . . . I have never had an opportunity to talk with international students before. I almost stayed home because of fear I guess. . . . I have never talked to anyone out of this state let alone the country." After this formal introduction to people from other cultures, informal contacts on campus become less threatening and more frequent.

International students gain confidence in their language skills and in themselves. As a result of the experience, they too feel more comfortable seeking out new friends. The fact that their cultures are of interest to others is empowering; however, in our experience, at times the psychology students overwhelm the international students with their questions, making them feel, as one student said, "like guinea pigs." This underscores the importance of keeping the interaction equal. During the class, we intervene when we sense that the exchange is becoming one-sided.

In our experience, students have been eager to meet again to continue their multicultural exploration. Although this activity limits the discussion to the social clock, other successful topics for the interviews have included cultural comparisons of dating practices, marriage and divorce, gender roles, parent–child relationships, views of abnormal behavior, and treatment of older persons. We have used this interview technique in a number of courses: introduction to psychology, developmental psychology, psychology of women, and, of course, ESL. The approach works; it can be used to explore psychological concepts in a number of courses. Most important, we believe, this activity promotes not only college community but global community.

WRITING COMPONENT

Prior to the activity students prepare interview questions. During the exchange they take notes. Finally, psychology students might write a two- or three-page paper in which they address some of the following questions: How does the information gathered in the interviews illustrate the concept of social clock as described in the textbook? What are the limitations and benefits of the interview as a research method? What problems did you encounter when conducting the cross-cultural interview? How does information about other cultures expand our knowledge of developmental psychology?

Students respond well to the writing component of this exercise: Writing about a real experience is immediate and therefore easier for some students than reacting to the research of others. Analyzing the process they themselves have designed encourages critical thinking.

REFERENCES

Amir, Y. (1976). The role of intergroup contact in change of prejudice and ethnic relations. In P. A. Katz (Ed.), *Towards the elimination of racism* (pp. 245–308). New York: Pergamon Press.

Berger, K. S. (1994). *The developing person through the lifespan* (3rd ed., pp. 441–641). New York : Worth.

Norvell, N., & Worchel, S. (1981). A reexamination of the relation between equal status contact and intergroup interaction. *Journal of Personality and Social Psychology, 41*(5), 902–908.

SUGGESTED READING

Amir, Y. (1994). The contact hypothesis in intergroup relations. In W. J. Lonner & R. Malpass (Eds.), *Psychology and culture.* Needham Heights, MA: Allyn & Bacon.

Fisher, R. J. (1994). Genetic principles for solving intergroup conflict. *Journal of Social Issues, 50,* 47–66.

Rubin, J. (1994). Models of conflict management. *Journal of Social Issues, 50,* 33–45.

Staub, E. (1996). Cultural-social roots of violence. *American Psychologist, 51,* 117–132.

Stephen, W. G., & Bringham, J. C. (1985). Intergroup contact: Introduction. *Journal of Social Issues, 41*(3), 1–8.

58 THE IMPORTANCE OF CROSS-CULTURAL SENSITIVITY IN PSYCHOLOGY

Lani C. Fujitsubo
Southern Oregon University

The impact of cross-cultural variables within psychology has far-reaching consequences. This activity is designed to demonstrate to students in introductory psychology as well as upper-division and graduate-level counseling courses the importance of understanding another person's cultural traditions, mores, rites, and communication styles. This activity uses a role-play exercise that allows students to experience how difficult and subtle cross-cultural exchanges can be and the difficulty of being culturally sensitive. The writing components allow the students to apply cross-cultural variables to their own lives.

CONCEPT

This exercise is designed to demonstrate the importance of cross-cultural sensitivity. It illustrates the impact of cultural rules, standards, mores, and traditions on general communication and interpersonal relationships. This exercise can be conducted in small groups or as a class demonstration.

MATERIALS NEEDED

You will need written vignettes for the role-play (an example appears later). The "reporters" in the role-play will need paper and a pen or pencil.

INSTRUCTIONS

Volunteers are asked to role-play either a family member or one of two newspaper reporters who will be interviewing this family for the local newspaper. The volunteers who are acting as family members are given a written vignette describing the rules of their interactions, customs, mores, and traditions. Here is an example of a vignette:

> You are a family (mother, father, and child) from outer space whose spacecraft recently landed in the United States. You are doing your best to assimilate into this society and are being interviewed because your child won the local spelling bee. On your planet of origin you show respect by laughing out loud before answering a direct question. Men are not allowed to speak directly to others, and must whisper their requests and answers to females who will then communicate directly. It is traditional to offer a gift or compliment to someone before making a request or asking for anything. If offended you use nonverbal communication to express your hurt feelings, the most common form of which is to briefly (for 2 to 3 s) turn your back to the person. Apologies are made by briefly dipping your head. No one on your planet is considered more important than anyone else, and competition is an unknown concept. Eye contact with males is considered offensive. A question is usually never answered directly because this implies that someone is an expert and causes others to lose face.

If you are doing this exercise as a classroom demonstration, ask the volunteer family to step out into the hall for about 5 min to discuss and rehearse their roles. At this time explain to the volunteers who are acting as reporters that their job is to interview this family in a way that would be of interest to the readers of the local newspaper. At the end of the interview they should have a working idea of what they would write in their article. Ask the family to come sit in front of the class. The interview should last 10 min.

You may choose from several alternatives when conducting this activity. Read the vignette to the class while the volunteer reporters are out of the room. This alternative allows the class to see the dynamics and the impact of the cross-cultural variables during the role-play. You may also choose to have the class watch the interaction without prior knowledge of the dynamics within the vignette and have them hypothesize what they believe the cross-cultural variables to be.

A second alternative is to break the class into groups of five. Three people in each group would be aliens and two would be reporters. The exercise is then run the same way. Reporters hypothesize and report to the class the cross-cultural variables demonstrated by the "family."

DISCUSSION

This activity demonstrates the important role cross-cultural variables play in everyday life. Students role-playing as the reporters often express frustration, confusion, feelings of being misunderstood, anger, or helplessness in trying to interview this family. Students role-playing as the family members might find themselves feeling offended, disrespected, minimized, angry, frustrated, sad, and misunderstood. These feelings lead to a powerful discussion focusing on cross-cultural factors that affect everyday interactions. The students usually conclude that it is important to learn how to listen, question, and respect all communications.

In introductory psychology classes this exercise could lead to meaningful discussions on discrimination, prejudice, problems and benefits of naturalistic observation, attribution theory, and communication styles. Students usually contribute their own experiences of prejudice or racism and speculate on how these experiences are rooted in misunderstanding and ignorance.

In counseling or family therapy classes this exercise can be used to demonstrate possible effects of transference and countertransference. It is also useful as an introduction to the importance of counselors knowing and understanding their own cross-cultural variables, which they bring to the therapeutic relationship.

WRITING COMPONENT

Have students write several rules, traditions, standards, and mores important for others to know about their own culture. The possibilities include various ways of celebrating or acknowledging important events, ways of interacting or communicating, rules involving sex or gender roles, or rites of passage.

Students could be asked to write a one-page reaction paper on one of several topics. One option would be to write about a time when cross-cultural variables affected them or their behavior. Students could also write on the present impact of cross-cultural variables. Finally, students could write an essay on the impact of entering into a culture in which no one else understands their values and history.

SUGGESTED READING

Atkinson, D., Morten, G., & Sue, D. (1989). *Counseling American minorities: A cross-cultural perspective* (2nd ed.). Dubuque, IA: W. C. Brown.

Baruth, L., & Manning, M. (1991). *Multicultural counseling and psychotherapy.* New York: Merrill.

Pedersen, P. (Ed.). (1985). *Handbook of cross-cultural counseling and therapy.* Westport, CT: Greenwood.

Sue, D., & Sue, D. (1990). *Counseling the culturally different* (2nd ed.). New York: Wiley.

$\square$59 MAKING RESEARCH COME ALIVE: EXPLORING THE EFFECTS OF CULTURE AND CONFOUNDS

Richard Ely and Carter Yeager
Boston University

This activity stages a discussion of the study titled "Prenatal Marijuana Exposure and Neonatal Outcome in Jamaica: An Ethnographic Study." The presentation illustrates several topics, including the importance of recognizing the role of culture and context, as well as the effects of potentially confounding variables. This activity is suitable for courses in general psychology, developmental psychology, health psychology, and biopsychology.

CONCEPT
Beyond the overall goal of making research come alive, this activity can serve a number of specific pedagogical goals: (a) It fosters discussion of the dangers of prenatal drug exposure. (b) It illustrates how culture and outcome interact. (c) It highlights a number of issues regarding research methods (e.g., sampling, confounding variables).

MATERIALS NEEDED
You will need the following props for the activity to be most effective: a baby doll, a lab coat, and a stethoscope (it need not be functional). You should also obtain a copy of "Prenatal Marijuana Exposure and Neonatal Outcome in Jamaica: An Ethnographic Study" (Dreher, Nugent, & Hudgins, 1994).

INSTRUCTIONS
Several days before actually implementing the classroom demonstration, ask for two student volunteers. Although one of the volunteers ideally should be a female, a male could play the female role. If your class includes premed or nursing students, urge them to serve as volunteers.

Explain to the student volunteers that they will be asked to dramatize a doctor–patient interaction. Assign one student the role of doctor. The other student will play the role of a pregnant mother who is being seen and evaluated for the first time. The dramatized interactions will take place in two settings: a local neighborhood health center and a neighborhood health center in Jamaica. In the first scene, the student playing the role of the pregnant mother will be from the local community; in the second scene, she will be from a local community in Jamaica.

Tell each student that the exercise focuses on the dangers that may be associated with prenatal drug exposure. Briefly review for the student volunteers the risks associated with smoking cigarettes, drinking alcohol, ingesting cocaine or heroin, and smoking marijuana while pregnant. The student playing the role of the doctor should be given a card on which the following items are listed: (a) cigarettes, (b) alcohol, (c) heroin and cocaine, and (d) marijuana.

In the actual classroom demonstration, the two student volunteers are asked to come forward. The student playing the doctor is presented with the lab coat, the stethoscope, and any other medical props that may be available. The student playing the pregnant mother is presented with the baby doll (which she may tuck under her shirt or sweater if she wishes to). This last touch usually generates a bit of humor and tends to make the volunteers feel more relaxed.

Next, set up the dramatic play for the class by saying "Maria is 5 months pregnant. She has come to Dr. Louise's neighborhood health center for the first time. One of the many things Dr. Louise will want to discuss with her involves drug use and the degree to which such drug use could harm the developing fetus."

At this point, the two students should play out their parts, with help from the class. The student playing the role of the doctor should ask the student playing the pregnant mother about the possible use of each drug in the order listed on the card.

After asking about each drug listed, Dr. Louise should then turn to the class and ask: "Why do I want to know about this drug? What effects could this drug have on Maria's developing baby?"

Encourage the students to offer what they feel might be the effects of each drug. Keep a tally on the chalkboard, identifying the potential positive and negative effects of each drug. Where students are unsure about specific effects (e.g., smoking associated with prematurity and low birth weight; alcohol with fetal alcohol syndrome), you should be prepared to supply the information.

When Dr. Louise asks Maria about the last drug on the list, marijuana, she is asking the important question. Students in the class will have a number of responses to the question posed by Dr. Louise: "What effect does marijuana have on Maria's unborn baby?" Some will claim that there will be adverse effects to prenatal exposure to marijuana. However, others are likely to be aware of some of the therapeutic effects associated with marijuana, including its antinausea and appetite stimulating properties (Lehrman, 1996; Voth & Schwartz, 1997).

Once Dr. Louise has completed her questions, she should get the class to come to a bottom-line recommendation for all the drugs discussed. Ideally, the class will agree that women who are pregnant or who are anticipating becoming pregnant should avoid all exposure to drugs (Vega, Bohdan, Hwang, & Noble, 1993).

Turning to the student playing Dr. Louise, you will now say, "Now, Dr. Louise, you have just been given an opportunity to continue your training in Jamaica. You will be working in a neighborhood clinic similar to the one you are in now, and you will be treating patients like Maria. Would you say the same thing regarding drug use to Maria if she were Jamaican?" You can ask the students for their input as well. They are likely to find the question intriguing, but their bottom-line recommendation will be the same: No drugs during pregnancy!

By changing the location from the students' current community to Jamaica, the students are asked to consider how behavior in one cultural context may be evaluated in another. This manipulation serves as a set up and challenges the students to question the tendency to generalize predictions (or therapeutic recommendations) across cultures. Describe the published study in summary form, emphasizing the following points.

Design

- In Jamaica, a convenience sample of pregnant marijuana users was matched with pregnant nonusers on age, parity, and socioeconomic status.
- The behavior of the exposed neonates was compared with the behavior of the nonexposed neonates by administering a neurobehavioral exam at 3 days and 1 month after birth. It may be useful to describe some of the ways you would assess the neurobehavioral status of an infant (using the baby doll as a prop). This would include assessing how quickly the baby habituates to stimuli such as a bell or a light; assessing how well the baby tracks, or orients to visual stimuli; assessing how robust the baby's body tonus is; assessing how irritable the baby is; assessing how cuddly the baby is (how comfortably the baby responds to being held) and how easily she or he is able to soothe herself; and, finally, assessing how easily the baby startles (Brazelton & Lester, 1983).

Results

- There were no differences between exposed and nonexposed babies at 3 days.
- There were significant differences at 1 month.
- The exposed infants showed more psychological stability than the unexposed infants.
- As compared with the unexposed infants, the heavily exposed infants (whose mothers smoked more than 21 marijuana cigarettes a week) were more alert, less irritable, better able to regulate themselves, and judged to be more rewarding for caregivers.

Ask students to come up with possible explanations for the findings. Students will generate a number of possible reasons for the findings, and the discussion is quite often lively. When all responses have been elicited, share with the class the information that mothers who were heavy users were also better educated, were less reliant on the baby's father for support, had fewer children at home, and had more adults at home. In fact, a number of these women were *Roots Daughters*, a Rastafarian term describing "women with a purpose who think, reason and smoke like a man" (Dreher, Nugent, & Hudgins, 1994, p. 255). This information is shared with students only after the fact to allow them the opportunity to think of all the possible explanations for the findings.

DISCUSSION   Although observational field studies similar to the study described here have many advantages, they are especially vulnerable to confounding. Two variables are confounded when they vary together (Kachigan, 1986). In this study, groups of mothers who differed with regard to the measured variable (marijuana use) also differed systematically with regard to other variables (e.g., maternal education, number of other children at home) that may have been relevant to their infants' neurobehavioral status. Because the demographic variables may be responsible for the observed differences between the neurobehavioral outcomes of their babies, attributing a causal connection between one variable (marijuana exposure) and the hypothesized effect is not justified. Although the mothers who smoked marijuana regularly tended to have babies who performed well neurobehaviorally, it would be a mistake to infer from this that marijuana use was causally connected to the positive outcome. In fact, the observed differences in demographic variables across the two groups are a more immediately plausible explanation for the findings.

For the purposes of discussion, emphasize to students that to infer a beneficial effect of prenatal marijuana exposure, it would be necessary to randomly assign expectant mothers to either smoke marijuana or not and to observe the subsequent effects of exposure in the babies' behavior. By randomly assigning mothers, the potential demographic confounds would be controlled. However, such a design raises serious ethical issues, another topic suitable for class discussion.

It is also important to describe alternative experimental designs. In doing this you should emphasize that if we are to make any claims for therapeutic effects of prenatal exposure to marijuana, we would need to assess the degree to which it is present in the fetus by assessing fetal blood levels of tetrahydrocannabinol (THC, the active ingredient of marijuana). In addition, it should be mentioned that the study's authors point out that marijuana constituents may be passed on to the babies through breast-feeding. This fact may explain in part why there are significant effects found at 1 month but not at 3 days. If a significant positive correlation between fetal (and perhaps later neonatal) levels of THC and the babies' behavior were present, we would be closer to asserting a causal connection between exposure and outcome. Finally, it would be wise to elicit comments regarding the need for replication and, more important, the need for follow-up studies. Students could be encouraged to consider some of the following questions: What are the long-term effects of growing up in households in which there may be high levels of passive exposure to marijuana? Would highly exposed babies be any more likely to become heavy users as adolescents or adults? Does the study justify considering the use of THC for the treatment of colic in infants? Is it appropriate to characterize high levels of marijuana use as drug abuse in Jamaica? Would students expect to find the same results if the study were conducted in their community?

These last two questions get at the essence of the cross-cultural component of this activity. Practices that may appear maladaptive in one culture may not be maladaptive in another. Thus in most North American communities drug use is seen as maladaptive and is associated with suboptimal care-giving environments. In contrast, in some communities in Jamaica, the use of a drug like marijuana is not viewed as maladaptive, and its consumption is associated with a cluster of attributes and behaviors that include greater maternal competence and a better-than-average caregiving environment.

Students may be willing to recognize and accept the notion that culture can differentially affect behavioral outcomes in softer domains such as parenting styles, self-concept, and even drug use itself. They may have a harder time accepting the notion that culture and context can also exert an effect on what might be considered to be primarily biopsychological or neurobehavioral domains. Although, as noted earlier, the study described does not demonstrate that THC is the causal factor in the findings, it does begin to assess the presumed effects of THC in the neurobehavioral domain. The study begins to address the question: Are the effects of any given biologically active substance (e.g., a drug) universal? Most students will answer this question in the affirmative.

By making this research paper come alive, this activity encourages students to take a harder look at some of the assumptions that might underlie their initial response. We have found that by dramatizing the study described here we are better able to demonstrate how different cultural contexts may have the potential to generate distinctly different (and counterintuitive) outcomes. In addition, we are able to give the students a concrete example of how research is conducted and how alternative experimental designs might lead us to a better understanding of the phenomena under study.

WRITING COMPONENT

A number of the issues raised in the demonstration could be addressed by students in writing. For example, as mentioned earlier, students could be asked to write down what they felt were the potential adverse effects of prenatal drug exposure. In addition, they could be asked to address in written form the ethical issues that random assignment would raise. Finally, students could be asked to speculate in writing about other phenomena whose prevalence and meaning may vary as a function of cultural context (e.g., eating disorders; see Hsu, 1996).

REFERENCES

Brazelton, T. B., & Lester, B. M. (Eds.). (1983). *New approaches to developmental screening of infants.* New York: Elsevier.

Dreher, M. C., Nugent, K., & Hudgins, R. (1994). Prenatal marijuana exposure and neonatal outcomes in Jamaica: An ethnographic study. *Pediatrics, 93,* 254–260.

Hsu, L. K. (1996). Epidemiology of the eating disorders. *Psychiatric Clinics of North America, 19,* 681–700.

Kachigan, S. K. (1986). *Statistical analysis: An interdisciplinary introduction to univariate and multivariate methods.* New York: Radius Press.

Lehrman, S. (1996). Acceptance of marijuana therapy prompts call for more research. *Nature, 384,* 95.

Vega, W. A., Bohdan, K., Hwang, J., & Noble, A. (1993). Prevalence and magnitude of perinatal substance exposures in California. *New England Journal of Medicine, 329,* 850–854.

Voth, E. A., & Schwartz, R. H. (1997). Medicinal applications of delta-9-tetrahydrocannabinol and marijuana. *Annals of Internal Medicine, 126,* 791–798.

SUGGESTED READING

Field, T. M., Sostek, A. M., Vietze, P., & Liederman, P. H. (Eds.). (1981). *Culture and early interactions.* Hilldale, NJ: Erlbaum.

Harwood, R. L., Miller, J. G., & Irizarry, N. L. (1995). *Culture and attachment: Perceptions of the child in context.* New York: Guilford Press.

Stigler, J. W., Shweder, R. A., & Herdt, G. (Eds.). *Cultural psychology: Essays on comparative human development.* New York: Cambridge University Press.

Super, C. M. (Ed.). (1987). *The role of culture in developmental disorder.* New York: Academic Press.

Whiting, B. B., & Edwards, C. P. (1988). *Children of different worlds.* Cambridge: Harvard University Press.

$^{\square}60$ Prejudice and the Loss of Individuality: An Experiential Exercise

George L. Moutsiakis
Seattle, Washington

This activity is designed to have students experience the loss of individuality that typically accompanies prejudice. For a 2- to 3-week period (depending on the instructor's schedule) students wear pins displaying upside-down pink triangles. If asked what the pin represents they respond, "I am wearing this pin to commemorate the gay men and lesbians killed and tortured during the Holocaust." In class, after wearing the pin, students discuss the nature of prejudice and explain their reactions to the exercise using selected lecture topics. In addition, students may be required to write a paper summarizing their experiences.

CONCEPT
Despite the wealth of theory and research in the area of prejudice, it is often difficult for nonminority students to appreciate the depersonalizing effects of this phenomenon. This activity allows students to experience the loss of individuality associated with categorization in an out-group. This is a powerful exercise because you are asking the students to allow themselves to be associated with a group (gay men and lesbians in this case) that is subject to strong prejudice from some sectors of our society, a group that some of the students themselves may hate or fear. It is therefore very important that you clearly explain the intent of the exercise, and that you fully debrief the students and discuss their reactions when the exercise is over. This is also an ideal activity for illustrating a range of topics such as cognitive dissonance theory, distinctiveness theory, the false consensus effect, social norms, and out-group perceptions.

MATERIALS NEEDED
You will need to provide students with upside-down pink triangle pins. These could either be made of construction paper or cloth and attached to garments with safety pins, or you could purchase the pins from a local store catering to the gay and lesbian community.

INSTRUCTIONS
The instructions are provided on the first handout (see appendix A) and should be reviewed with the students the day the assignment is scheduled to begin. The duration of the exercise has been left blank so that you may chose a period of time appropriate for your class. Experience has shown that 2 to 3 weeks of wearing the pin allows enough time for students who are reluctant to perform the exercise to attempt it once or twice. You are also encouraged to have the students read and discuss the second handout (appendix B) on the day the activity is set to begin.

DISCUSSION Explaining the purpose of the exercise and debriefing the students when it is over are *essential* to ensure that this is a positive learning experience for everyone involved.

This activity has been implemented since 1989 in both a large public university in Detroit and a small Catholic university in Seattle. The focus of this exercise is on how the students themselves react. This exercise is not about homosexuality per se but really about prejudice. When the project is assigned, most students will be reluctant to participate. They will fear that people will think they are homosexual. They will imagine that everyone is looking at them. They will imagine that everyone knows the symbolism of the pin. Almost all of their fears are unfounded and need to be discussed in class.

The vast majority of the general public has not seen the pink triangle before, does not know anything about it, and will not comment on it. Most students will not receive any comments or reactions. About 25% of the students will receive a single negative comment, whereas only about 10% will receive more than one comment or reaction. No student has ever been physically harassed or harmed in any way.

It is difficult to get students to participate in this assignment, and no student should be forced to do so. Despite the resistance, the vast majority of students (about 85%) have commented afterward that they found this to be a valuable learning experience. The main point that should arise in the final classroom discussion is that students felt like they were being classified based on the pin and no one was paying attention to their individual traits and abilities. This can lead to a discussion of stereotypes and the effects of social categorization.

WRITING COMPONENT This activity is well suited for an accompanying writing assignment. Some suggested questions that students might answer in such a paper are the following: Did any people make comments toward you that might be considered prejudicial? How did those comments make you feel? How did *you* feel about wearing the pin? Were you afraid? Were you tempted not to wear it? How did you feel while wearing the pin? If you didn't want to wear the pin, what do you think caused that reaction? Did any of your own reactions toward the pin and the assignment reveal prejudices of your own? What specific topics from this class have you seen in action during this exercise? Describe them in detail.

SUGGESTED READING Grau, G. (1995). *Hidden Holocaust?* London: Cassell.
Heger, H. (1972). *Die manner mit dem rosa winkel.* Hamburg: Merlin.
Plant, R. (1986). *The pink triangle.* New York: New Republic Books.

Appendix A

Instructions

The major purpose behind this assignment is to make each of you think about prejudice in a more personal manner.

For the next _____ weeks you are to wear the pink triangle pin distributed in class. When people ask about the pin you must say that you are wearing it to commemorate the gay men and lesbians tortured and murdered during the Holocaust. The background information given to you [appendix B] should help answer any general questions people might ask.

During the exercise you should keep notes. We are most interested in two things: (a) How people respond to you, and, more important, (b) how you feel while wearing the pin. If people do not make comments to you about the pin it is acceptable to show them the pin and try to get them to talk about it.

As we all know, many Jews, gypsies, Russians, and others were killed during the Holocaust. The reason you are wearing a pin commemorating the gay men and lesbians (all gay men and lesbians were affected, not just Jewish gay men and lesbians), instead of one of the other groups is that prejudice against homosexuals is still considered socially acceptable by a substantial portion of our society. Prejudice against the other groups is often (though not as often as many of us may desire) deemed inappropriate. Likewise there is a great deal of prejudice in our society against African Americans and other people of color. This exercise in no way implies that the struggles of any one group exceed those of another.

Wearing the pin does not mean that you are a homosexual. It does not mean that you are a representative of the homosexual community. It does not mean that you support homosexual activities. The pink triangle symbol originated during World War II and is currently used to represent many organizations serving both the homosexual community and the heterosexuals who support them. This symbol is worn by people of all sexual orientations and is not a symbol used by homosexuals to identify each other. We are wearing the pin to commemorate those who were tortured and murdered, and in the process we hope to learn something about prejudice.

Appendix B

The Pink Triangle

There are no memorials. There was no compensation for the survivors. There are few books. We are the forgotten ones of Hitler's concentration camps. We are the People of the Pink Triangle—the 175s according to the number of the German law under which homosexuals were to be exterminated—or, as we were referred to, "filthy queers." After the war, as others raised anguished voices to tell the world of the incredible sufferings, our story was the object of deliberate suppression. This is the history as gathered from sentences and a few paragraphs in the various books on the Nazis and from Heinz Heger (not his real name) who published his memoirs in 1972.

In October 1936, Heinrich Himmler, head of the S.S., called for the total elimination of homosexuals. He was following Hitler's views, as recorded in his book *Mein Kampf*, that gays were an integral part of the degeneracy that had resulted in the German defeat in World War I. Homosexuals, as "a Third Race," not only threatened "natural Nordic superiority" but, as Himmler told the führer, gays were organized in a secret "Order of the Third Sex," which was plotting to take over the world in the same manner as were the Jews. There was a "Homosexual Question" even as there was a "Jewish Question," and both demanded a "Final Solution."

In line with Himmler's goal, a special section of the Gestapo—Department II—was set up to deal with "the problem." It did not concern itself with women. They, the Nazis believed, had no choice but to submit to the male. What they did otherwise was not important and did not threaten the party's concepts of male superiority.

According to the law, "any form of lewdness" was sufficient to warrant arrest. This meant holding hands, a kiss, any sign of affection between two men. Also enough was a denunciation by an anonymous informer.

In the hands of the Gestapo, the machinery of the state moved with a gross inevitability. There was no appeal—no matter what one's station in life. You were taken to a holding prison, there to be forced to wear the pink triangle, the sign of your "degeneracy." It was much like the yellow star worn by the Jews except that ours was 2 to 3 cm larger. This, to show that gays were the lowest of the low, filth to filth, to be easily singled out for special brutality.

Then came transportation to the camps: Dachau, 12 mi outside Munich, and then, after they had been established, Büchenwald, Sachenhausen, and Auschwitz, among others. On arrival, as Heger described it, 175s were forced to strip and had all their hair removed. They were given a number in place of their name and required to answer "Queer 4567," for example, whenever addressed. Those who were known or were thought to be lovers had to watch as first one, then the other, was raped and after killed with a broom handle pushed up the rectum, clubbed to death as the guards jeered, or torn apart by dogs trained to go for the genitals. Often, in January's cold, homosexuals were taken out in the snow, naked, and had bowls of water poured over them. Then they were made to stand in the frigid air until they froze to death. Homosexuals were special targets for medical experiments, used as living targets to train sharpshooters, and put to work in quarries from which few, if any, emerged alive.

It was Christmas Eve 1942. At Flossenburg camp, the commandant had reported to him eight men, four pairs of lovers. On that evening he had them stand together before the entire camp. Then each pair was hung, one pair to a steel post, each one condemned not only to suffer his own death agony of slow strangulation but to watch his lover's torment as well. In front of them stood a Christmas tree before which the other homosexuals of the camp were forced to stand and sing Christmas carols. According to the account, the guards and officers stood watching the whole scene with undisguised delight as the *Arschfickers* sang to the dying faggots strangling to death on the eve of Christmas.

How many were included in the holocaust of the gays? Numbers vary, but the best estimate was that between 50,000 and 100,000 of us died.

How many survived? It is impossible to tell. After the war, German laws against us remained in force. Survivors had little choice but to try and slip back into the population. Despite our agony, we were still criminals.

Today, Dachau is preserved as a monument against Nazi evil. Visit it as I have done. Walk the grounds and think. As Heger wrote,

What infamous crime? . . . What had I done? I had loved a friend of mine.

His words echo in the air above the camp—and ring more loudly when you remember that Hitler was not only a German phenomenon but a human phenomenon. One hangs one's head. For our love, who we were, we died.

Source unknown

61 Exploring the Concept of Sexual Orientation Through Small-Group Discussion

Mark G. Hartlaub
SUNY-Albany

Using a small-group format, this activity was created to help students understand the difficulties in defining sexual orientation. Once they have completed the exercise, students will be able to list and briefly discuss several factors relevant to defining sexual orientation.

CONCEPT

Although psychologists generally realize how difficult it is to define sexual orientation, students often do not. This activity will allow you to introduce students to the concept of sexual orientation and then extend the discussion into various aspects of sexual orientation, starting with the measurement or definition of sexual orientation. Kinsey's continuum model (Kinsey, Pomeroy, & Martin, 1948), which offers essentially two categories, can be contrasted with other, more complex models such as that by Storms (1980), which offers four categories.

This activity also allows students to see and understand why psychologists cannot give unequivocal answers to some questions, such as how many people are homosexual and how many are heterosexual. One popular human sexuality textbook states that 80% of males are exclusively heterosexual and 2% are exclusively homosexual, whereas approximately 90% of females are exclusively heterosexual and 1% are exclusively homosexual; the rest fall in between, depending on the definition one uses (Hyde, 1994). It is often a surprise to students to hear that there is a gray area in defining sexual orientation.

This activity is designed to allow students to explore, via small-group and classroom discussion, factors that may be important in defining sexual orientation, such as age, forms of behavior, emotional attachment, sexual fantasy content, and present contextual situation.

MATERIALS NEEDED

You will need several copies of a group worksheet that lists brief descriptions of various individuals. An abbreviated copy of the form I have used is shown in appendix A, although any individual instructor can create brief scenarios that present a particular difficulty in defining sexual orientation.

INSTRUCTIONS

Begin the activity by informing students of the small-group work ahead. Encourage them to move the desks to create groups. Once groups of four or five students are created, either invite the groups to elect a spokesperson or select one yourself. Give a group worksheet, with spaces provided for the names of the group members, to each group leader/recorder (see appendix A).

Give the student groups approximately 15 min in which to work. The spokesperson of each group reads the short description of each hypothetical individual to the other members, and then, as a group, the members try to decide where the person should fall on a 7-point continuum ranging from *definitely homosexual* to *definitely heterosexual*, and why the person belongs there. This scale is similar to the 7-point scale used by Kinsey (Kinsey et al., 1948). Once the group members have discussed each of the individuals, they try their best to define the terms *homosexual* and *heterosexual*. I stress that although it may be difficult to do, their definitions should be consistent with the decisions they made concerning each of the individuals they have just discussed.

Once all the groups have finished or nearly finished, they should return their seats to their original positions and a class discussion can begin. Essentially, the class will discuss in turn each of the brief descriptions on the handout. Ask group leaders to share their group's response with the class. Once they give a ranking (e.g., "One to the left of *definitely heterosexual*"), always ask, "Why?" Record key comments and factors mentioned by the groups on the chalkboard or the overhead projector.

I almost always have at least one group that takes a relatively extreme stance such that if any person ever engages in homosexual behavior, they are necessarily *definitely homosexual*. I try not to be confrontational in my classes; I often respond with a question such as, "What about a person who is exclusively homosexual yet has one heterosexual encounter? Is that person, then, heterosexual?" Alternatively, I often change the descriptions to make a point. For example, when discussion centers on the young boy who wishes to marry an adult male, groups tend to answer with something like "We [the group] said you can't make a decision. He's too young." I respond, "What if he was 15 years old?" "What if he was 25 years old?"

Finally, the group shares its definitions of homosexuality and heterosexuality with the rest of the class. Have the group turn in their worksheets once the class period is finished. Although I usually only glance at these briefly, turning in the sheets helps groups feel they are being held accountable for their discussion.

DISCUSSION   This activity can be very helpful in teaching students important factors associated with defining sexual orientation. Evaluations have shown that students find this exercise both valuable and enjoyable.

The effect of the small-group discussion was assessed by asking students in two sections of a general psychology class ($N = 49$) to write down as many factors as they could think of in 4 min that could influence how sexual orientation is defined both before the small-group exercise was begun and after it was completed. A correlated-groups t-test showed that participants were able to list significantly more factors after they had participated in the exercise ($M = 6.3$) than before the exercise ($M = 3.4$), $t(48) = -6.79$, $p < .001$. This indicates that the small-group exercise was effective in exposing students to several factors that influence the definition of sexual orientation that they did not know when the exercise was begun.

Clearly, as a result of this activity students were better able to understand how it may be very difficult to offer a clear-cut answer to questions concerning sexual orientation. Because sexual orientation is such a highly charged issue for some students, this is a good exercise to help begin investigation of the topic, because it encourages discussion and critical thinking without putting students on the defensive.

WRITING COMPONENT
Several different writing exercises could be incorporated with this activity. The simplest would be a one-page summary of what students learned from the activity. Another would be to have themselves create several scenarios that present the reader with difficult decisions. In this way, students are encouraged to think of significant factors on their own. Students could be asked to write a short paper arguing for the relative importance of one factor over another in determining sexual orientation. For example, why sexual behavior is more relevant in defining sexual orientation than is the content of sexual fantasy.

A more challenging exercise might involve students responding to criticisms (either in support or in defense) of the well-known study of impersonal sex in public places (Humphreys, 1970). Specifically, as a result of this activity students will be better able to think critically about the participants in that study and make judgments concerning whether the study investigated homosexuals, heterosexuals, homosexual behavior, impersonal sexual behavior, or something else.

REFERENCES

Humphreys, L. (1970). *Tearoom trade: Impersonal sex in public places.* Chicago: Aldine.

Hyde, E. J. S. (1994). *Understanding human sexuality* (5th ed.). New York: McGraw-Hill.

Kinsey, A. C., Pomeroy, W. B., & Martin, C. E. (1948). *Sexual behavior in the human male.* Philadelphia: W. B. Saunders.

Storms, M. D. (1980). Theories of sexual orientation. *Journal of Personality and Social Psychology, 38*(5), 783–792.

SUGGESTED READING

Bell, A. P., Weinberg, M. S., & Hammersmith, S. K. (1981). *Sexual preference: Its development in men and women.* Bloomington: Indiana University Press.

Billy, J. O. G., et al. (1993). The sexual behavior of men in the United States. *Family Planning Perspectives, 25,* 52–60.

Coleman, E. (1987). Bisexuality: Challenging our understanding of human sexuality and sexual orientation: In E. E. Shelp (Ed.), *Sexuality and medicine* (Vol. 1, pp. 225–242). New York: Reidel.

Dworkin, A. (1987). *Intercourse.* New York: Free Press/McMillan.

Appendix A

Group Members

_____

_____

_____

_____

Directions: Read the brief descriptions of people. As a group, try to decide whether the person should be considered a homosexual or a heterosexual. Once you have finished, synthesize your answers and define a homosexual and a heterosexual.

A. Person A is a man who is married and has three children. Approximately once a month he engages in impersonal sex with another man in a public restroom or bathhouse.

Definitely   Definitely
Homosexual ____ ____ ____ ____ ____ ____ ____ Heterosexual

B. Person B is a 58-year-old man who lives alone. He has never been married, nor has he had any sexual contact of any kind. He occasionally buys pornographic magazines, which depict male-to-male sexual contact, although he does not enjoy these very much.

C. Person C is a 29-year-old woman. She was sexually active with men from the time she was 19 until she was raped at 24. She has had no sexual contact since that time. She is no longer interested in sex with men, but says she would consider a sexual relationship with another woman.

D. Person D is a 44-year-old woman who has been married for 20 years. Occasionally during intercourse with her husband she imagines engaging in sex with another woman. She has never had any sexual partner besides her husband.

E. Person E is a woman who shares an apartment with another woman. They have not had any sexual contact other than an occasional hug and kiss when greeting or departing.

F. Person F is a 5-year-old boy who enjoys watching basketball. When asked whom he wants to marry he answers, "Michael Jordan."

G. Person G is a 28-year-old man who has been sent to prison. From the time he was 20 until he was sent to prison he engaged in intercourse with his girlfriend approximately twice weekly. Now he engages in intercourse with other male inmates approximately twice weekly. He plans to continue his sexual relationship with his girlfriend once he is released from prison.

Definition of homosexuality:

Definition of heterosexuality:

62 GENDER BIAS IN LEADER SELECTION
Michelle R. Hebl
Rice University

In this classroom exercise, students experience how stereotypes can result in biased leader selection. Students are placed in initially leaderless mixed gender groups and asked to select leaders for a competitive or cooperative group activity. Overall, a disproportionate number of men are selected as leaders, substantiating the idea that gender stereotypes guide individuals in selecting leaders. The bias is strong in competitive groups, but weak in social cooperative groups. Provocative discussion questions that address these findings are included.

CONCEPT This activity is designed to illustrate the potential behavioral ramifications of gender stereotyping and the notion that gender stereotyping may have a differential impact on leader selection when type of leadership is manipulated. Specifically, students experience firsthand gender stereotyping when they select leaders of small mixed-gender groups for either a task-oriented competitive situation or a social cooperative situation.

MATERIALS NEEDED You will need two sets of written instructions, one describing the task-oriented competitive task and the other describing the social cooperative task.

INSTRUCTIONS Divide students into groups of four or six, each composed of an equal number of men and women. Any students left over can be grouped together and their data later discarded or analyzed separately. If possible, students should not know other members of their group because previous direct experience may override the heuristics of gender stereotyping and weaken the effects of the demonstration. (It might be desirable to use this exercise at the beginning of a course.)

The demonstration should be used before students read about gender stereotypes and group dynamics. The activity can be introduced as a "psychology game." Distribute written instructions describing the group task to each member of each group; otherwise the person receiving or reading the instructions might be chosen or accepted as the leader. Each group receives four copies of one of two sets of instructions.

Task-Oriented Competitive

Give students the following instructions:

> You will be playing a board game with your group. The board game involves competition against another group and you will focus on specific tasks. Try your hardest to win the game. To do this, focus on the game's objectives as much as possible. To start, your group should first select a

---

SOURCE: Hebl (1994). Reprinted with permission from Lawrence Erlbaum.

person who will be in charge of the group. After this leader is selected, I will give you specific instructions about the game and you will start playing.

Social-Oriented Cooperative

Give students the following instructions:

> You will be playing a board game with your group. The board game does not involve winning but instead, involves agreeing with each other, supporting one another, and setting aside differences in order to get along maximally with each other. To start, your group should first select a person who will be in charge of the group. After this leader is selected, I will give you specific instructions about the game and you will start playing.

Playing the Game

Students take 2 min to read their instructions and select group leaders. Groups are not specifically instructed about how to select leaders. Any method of nomination and selection is acceptable as long as all group members ultimately agree on the leader.

After verifying that leaders for each group have been chosen, inform the groups that they will not play a game after all. Instead, the actual purpose of the activity was to examine leader selection and processes. Compile a list that specifies the gender of those students chosen as task-oriented and social leaders. Then you or a student volunteer can record both the gender of the leader selected as well as the technique each group used in selecting its leader.

DISCUSSION   This activity was derived from past research, which shows that men are significantly more likely to be chosen as leaders than women in initially leaderless, mixed-gender groups (Eagly & Karau, 1991). Gender stereotypes about leadership likely play a large role in influencing these findings. For example, men are more likely than women to be perceived as able to "separate feelings from ideas," "act as leaders," and "make decisions" (Broverman, Vogel, Broverman, Clarkson, & Rosenkrantz, 1972). These and other stereotypically masculine items have been positively correlated with college students' perceptions of leaders (Lord, De Vader, & Alliger, 1986). Eagly and Mladinic (1989) proposed that gender stereotypes also are composed of beliefs that men occupy advantaged social positions of power and status relative to women. Such views lead us to perceive men as more in control and powerful than women, even when they are not. Indeed, research by Porter, Geis, and Jennings (1983) has revealed that given an ambiguous setting involving both men and women, independent raters perceive men to be in charge much more often than women.

Stereotypes about women may also enhance biases in leader selection (Geis, Brown, Jennings, & Corrado-Taylor, 1984; Nye & Forsyth, 1991). Geis, Brown, Jennings, and Porter (1984) suggested the most general stereotype about women is that they are not autonomous and are unqualified to assume achievement-oriented responsibilities in the world. However, women, relative to men, are believed to be more "talkative," "tactful," and "aware of others' feelings" (Broverman et al., 1972) and more expressive and communal (Eagly & Mladinic, 1989). Thus, gender stereotyping may have a differential impact on leader selection when

Table 62-1. *Number of Leaders Selected by Gender and Instructions*

| Type of instruction | Gender | | |
| | Men | Women | Total |
	Observed/expected		
Task-oriented	40/32.2	11/18.8	51
Social	25/32.8	27/19.2	52
Total	65	38	103

Source: Results from "Gender Bias in Leader Selection," by M. R. Hebl, 1994, *Teaching of Psychology, 22,* pp. 186–188. Used by permission.

type of leadership is manipulated (Eagly & Karau, 1991). Whereas task-oriented competitive leaders focus on task contributions and productivity, social cooperative leaders focus on social contributions, prosocial behavior, and social climate. Male group members make more task-oriented contributions than do females (Wood, 1987), so males may be chosen as leaders in task-oriented competitive situations more often than they are chosen as social leaders. By contrast, social leaders may focus on prosocial behaviors, and therefore females may be selected as social leaders more often than they are selected as task-oriented competitive leaders.

The results obtained from this demonstration can be compared with Hebl's (1994) results indicating that, overall, leadership positions were most likely to be filled by men, especially under task-oriented (competitive) conditions in which the ratio of male to female leaders was nearly four to one. Eagly and Karau (1991) suggested that as leadership goals change from a position that requires task-oriented behaviors to one requiring socially complex tasks or the maintenance of good interpersonal relations and group harmony, slightly more women than men emerge as leaders, a trend also visible in Hebl's study (1994; see Table 62-1).

In sum, this classroom activity produces reliable and provocative effects that should make students more cognizant of gender stereotypes and their effects on leader selection. Class discussion after the activity could be stimulated by the following questions:

1. How was the selection procedure determined? Did men or women more commonly nominate themselves? Which gender was more commonly nominated by other group members? What were the common procedures used in selecting leaders? In Hebl's (1994) study, students' descriptions of their selection process included "He was chosen because he was the tallest . . . he looked like he should be in charge," "I knew from the beginning he would be the leader—he just looked the part," and "The two women in our group asked him to be the leader."
2. What stereotypes were used in selecting leaders? When and why are stereotypes about men and women likely to influence leader selection? Are these stereotypes used when the groups meet for longer periods of time?
3. What were the possible causes for the bias against female leaders? In everyday life, we witness more men than women as leaders; how might that affect leader selection? Do women avoid leadership positions? When women become leaders, how are they typically viewed in comparison with men?

4. What gender differences result when the task becomes one in which a social leader is required? Does the gender bias disappear? If so, why?

One possible variation of the current demonstration is to assign groups to either feminine or masculine gender-typed activities. For instance, one group might be told to choose a leader for a discussion of the use of cloth versus disposable diapers for babies. The other group's discussion topic could be the choice of repairing cars at home with the guidance of manuals and friends versus taking the car to a repair shop. The visibility of stereotypes should be demonstrated as women are selected more often when the task is feminine gender-typed and men when the task is masculine gender-typed. In both cases, gender stereotypes guide individuals in their selection of leaders.

WRITING COMPONENT Ask students to submit either formal or informal written responses to some of the discussion questions previously listed. In particular, they might be asked to consider and write about other behaviors that may result from underlying stereotypes about the sexes. The pervasiveness of stereotypes and the ways in which stereotyping may affect behavior are often not evident to students and not easily illustrated through textbooks or class discussions. The combination of this in-class demonstration and a writing assignment may motivate students to begin thinking more about the prevalence of stereotypes in their daily lives and the biasing effects such stereotypes can trigger.

REFERENCES Broverman, I. K., Vogel, S. R., Broverman, D. M., Clarkson, F. E., & Rosenkrantz, P. S. (1972). Sex-role stereotypes: A current appraisal. *Journal of Social Issues, 28*(2), 59–78.

Eagly, A. H., & Karau, S. J. (1991). Gender and the emergence of leaders. *Journal of Personality and Social Psychology, 60,* 685–710.

Eagly, A. H., & Mladinic, A. (1989). Gender stereotypes and attitudes toward women and men. *Personality and Social Psychology Bulletin, 15,* 543–558.

Geis, F. L., Brown, V., Jennings, J., & Corrado-Taylor, D. (1984). Sex versus status in sex-associated stereotypes. *Sex Roles, 11,* 771–785.

Geis, F. L., Brown, V., Jennings, J., & Porter, N. (1984). TV commercials as achievement scripts for women. *Sex Roles, 10,* 513–524.

Hebl, M. R. (1994). Gender bias in leader selection. *Teaching of Psychology, 22,* 186–188.

Lord, R. G., De Vader, D. I., & Alliger, G. M. (1986). A meta-analysis of the relation between personality traits and leadership perceptions: An application of validity generalization procedures. *Journal of Applied Psychology, 71,* 402–410.

Nye, J. L., & Forsyth, D. R. (1991). The effects of prototype-based biases on leadership appraisals: A test of leadership categorization theory. *Small Group Research, 22,* 360–379.

Porter, N., Geis, F. L., & Jennings, J. W. (1983). Are women invisible as leaders? *Sex Roles, 9,* 1035–1049.

Wood, W. (1987). Meta-analytic review of sex differences in group performance. *Psychological Bulletin, 102,* 53–71.

63 GENDER STEREOTYPES AND METHODOLOGY: WHAT'S THE CONNECTION?

Eugenia M. Valentine
Texas A&M University

This activity combines the identification and examination of gender stereotypes with a look at how methodology can bias results through forced-choice measures. It is appropriate for an examination of gender or methodology and includes class discussion and writing.

CONCEPT

Stereotypes are cognitive simplifications or shortcuts in the perception and processing of interactions with others. Social stereotypes encompass gender roles, which are behaviors and expectations defined by society as being culturally appropriate for each gender (O'Neil, 1982). Gender-role stereotypes, therefore, are rigid and exaggerated expectations of how each gender should behave (Basow, 1992).

To date, the oft-cited but dated study of sex-role stereotypes by Broverman, Vogel, Broverman, Clarkson, and Rosenkrantz (1972) has not been replicated. The datedness of this study leaves questions on how current undergraduates compare with their peers on measures of gender stereotyping. Indeed, the datedness of this study leads many students to believe that such stereotyping would not occur in their generation. However, a more recent study (Bergen & Williams, 1991) indicated that gender stereotyping still exists in the undergraduate population. This activity increases students' awareness of their own gender stereotyping by prompting them with some of the same items that were found to be the most stereotypical in Broverman et al.

In addition, this activity illustrates how methodology can shape research findings in a forced-choice versus non–forced-choice format. In a meta-analytic study on gender typing in children, Signorella, Bigler, and Liber (1993) found that when faced with a forced choice of male or female, older children made more stereotypic categorizations of occupations. Conversely, when faced with a choice of male, female, or both, stereotypic categorizations of occupations by older children significantly decreased. In this activity, students may experience this bias by answering similar questionnaires on gender stereotypes.

MATERIALS NEEDED

For each student in your class you will need one sheet of paper with a copy of Questionnaire A (appendix A) on one side and a copy of Questionnaire B (appendix B) on the other side.

INSTRUCTIONS

Pass out sheets with Questionnaire A face up to half of the class, and pass out sheets with Questionnaire B face up to the other half of the class. Instruct stu-

---

dents not to turn the sheets over until directed to do so and not to write their names on them. Then ask students to read silently and follow the instructions on their sheets. While the students are writing their responses, write each trait on the chalkboard or overhead. When it appears that all have finished, instruct the students to turn over their sheets and silently follow the new instructions.

When students are finished, collect the questionnaires from them. Shuffle and redistribute them to the students to maintain confidentiality. Ask the students to turn to Questionnaire A and take a count of the "female" responses on Question 1 by asking for a show of hands, then take a count of the "male" responses for Question 1. Write an *F* or an *M* next to the trait on the board according to the majority opinion. Do the same for the rest of the traits on Questionnaire A. Next, have the students turn to Questionnaire B and ask for a show of hands for those picking each of the five numerical responses for Question 1. Do the same for the rest of the traits on Questionnaire B. After this second round of questions, write an *F,* an *N,* or an *M* next to the first letter for each of the 10 traits on the board.

When all responses have been recorded on the board, invite students to discuss what differences in responses they notice. Point out to the students that some received Questionnaire A first and some received Questionnaire B first, so the results are not just a result of order effects. It is expected from previous administrations of this activity that some traits will be rated as "neutral" for Questionnaire B that were gender typed for Questionnaire A, but also that some traits will remain gender typed. Elicit from the students which traits had the most different answers between the two questionnaires and which traits were more varied when rated in a scale. Discuss how the Likert format changed the responses on some items as compared to the forced-choice format.

After some discussion of this format difference, ask students on which traits the ratings stayed the same. Focus on this discussion, pointing out that these responses are similar to the responses students made to the same items in 1972. Traits that tend to remain gender typed are "emotional," "logical," "neat," and "tactful." Point out that there is usually a kernel of truth in stereotypes, especially when involving college students. Stereotypes are mainly only a problem when decisions such as occupation or employment are based on them.

Involve the class in a discussion on the formation, maintenance, and stability of gender stereotypes. Ask why stereotypes are so prevalent and difficult to change for most people, and discuss how social environment, past experiences, and culture are factors in gender stereotypes. What are some other gender stereotyped traits that they could add to this list? How could the list be updated from the 1972 version?

EXERCISE VARIATION

As an alternative or additional exercise, ask students to think of a person they know, then pick out five to eight traits from Questionnaire A that describe this person. Then instruct the students to turn the sheet over and rate the same person, using the Likert scale, on the same traits that they checked on Questionnaire B. You will want to delete the instructions from the tops of both questionnaires if using this exercise, leaving only the 10 traits. Write all 10 traits on the board while they are rating.

After they are done, ask the students who were thinking of a female for a show of hands of who picked Trait 1 for their female on Questionnaire A. Do this for all 10 traits, then do the same for those students who were thinking of a male.

Compare the traits most endorsed on Questionnaire A for females with the most endorsed male traits; stereotypes should be evident.

Next, ask the students to turn to Questionnaire B and discuss whether their ratings were more accurate when they were able to use the numerical differential. This comparison can lead to a discussion about how the two measurement methods differ in methodology and results.

As a further consideration for each of the activities described, the students completing the questionnaires could be asked to indicate their own gender by marking F or M on the form. Then the data could be discussed in terms of any difference in stereotyping between genders.

DISCUSSION Students' answers to Questionnaire A should be very stereotypical as a result of the forced-choice format. Signorella, Bigler, and Liben (1993) suggested that answers to forced-choice stereotype questions reflect knowledge of stereotypes, whereas non–forced-choice formats more accurately reflect attitudes toward stereotypes. This suggestion should be revealed to the class in discussions of Questionnaire B. Although differing from Questionnaire A greatly, there should still be enough stereotypical responses to Questionnaire B to help students explore their own attitudes toward gender stereotypes. Susan Basow's work (1992) is especially helpful for the discussion on the formation and maintenance of gender stereotypes.

If the students' gender stereotypes are random or nonexistent, the discussion could focus on what has changed about society since the original study. Elicit from the students ideas on how stereotypes change over time and what exactly changes stereotypes (culture change, personal experiences, etc.).

Students should also come away from the activity with the realization of how the format methodology influenced their responses. Discuss what researchers who used Questionnaire A only might have found and how accurate that finding might be.

WRITING COMPONENT As a wrap-up to this discussion, have students write a "minute paper" (Wilson, 1986) about where they believe some of their own gender stereotypes originated, either from childhood or even the present time. After a minute has gone by, instruct students to either swap these papers with a neighbor and discuss these sources briefly or hold on to them and volunteer some of their sources to the class (at the teacher's discretion).

You could also ask students to write about any time that a gender stereotype of their own changed a situation or an outcome for them or for someone else. Perhaps they voted for a male candidate for student government over a female candidate based on gender and not qualification. Because this type of revelation is likely to be more sensitive, the teacher must again use discretion on how or whether to ask students to share these experiences.

REFERENCES Basow, S. A. (1992). *Gender stereotypes and roles* (3rd ed.). Pacific Grove, CA: Brooks/Cole.

Bergen, D. J., & Williams, J. E. (1991). Sex stereotypes in the United States revisited: 1972–1988. *Sex Roles, 24,* 413–423.

Broverman, I. K., Vogel, S. R., Broverman, D. M., Clarkson, F. E., & Rosenkrantz, P. S. (1972). Sex-role stereotypes: A current appraisal. *Journal of Social Issues, 28*(2), 59–78.

O'Neil, J. M. (1982). Gender-role conflict and strain in men's lives. In K. Solomon & N. B. Levy (Eds.), *Men in transition: Theory and therapy* (pp. 5–44). New York: Plenum Press.

Signorella, M. L., Bigler, R. S., & Liben, L. S. (1993). Developmental differences in children's gender schemata about others: A meta-analytic review. *Developmental Review, 13,* 147–183.

Wilson, R. C. (1986). Improving faculty teaching: Effective use of student evaluations and consultation. *Journal of Higher Education, 57,* 196–211.

Appendix A

Questionnaire A

Decide whether each of these traits is characteristically a masculine or feminine trait, then write down *male* or *female* in the blank next to each trait.

1. Very emotional   _____

2. Very active   _____

3. Very objective   _____

4. Very religious   _____

5. Very tactful   _____

6. Very logical   _____

7. Very neat   _____

8. Very ambitious   _____

9. Very loud   _____

10. Very talkative   _____

Note to teacher: Items 1, 4, 5, 7, and 10 are "female" traits, and items 2, 3, 6, 8, and 9 are "male" traits (Broverman et al., 1972).

Appendix B

Questionnaire B

Decide the extent to which each of these traits is more characteristic of males or females, and circle the corresponding number on the scale. If you think that the trait is equally characteristic of both males and females, circle the 3 in the middle.

1. Very emotional   male   1   2   3   4   5   female
2. Very active   male   1   2   3   4   5   female
3. Very objective   male   1   2   3   4   5   female
4. Very religious   male   1   2   3   4   5   female
5. Very tactful   male   1   2   3   4   5   female
6. Very logical   male   1   2   3   4   5   female
7. Very neat   male   1   2   3   4   5   female
8. Very ambitious   male   1   2   3   4   5   female
9. Very loud   male   1   2   3   4   5   female
10. Very talkative   male   1   2   3   4   5   female

64 ISSUES IN THE PSYCHOLOGY OF WOMEN: EXPLORATIONS THROUGH ART

Fairfid M. Caudle

The College of Staten Island, City University of New York

In this activity, classical paintings are used to explore issues in the psychology of women. Examples of paintings are suggested, for presentation in slide form, that pertain to stereotyped portrayals of women as passive victims, evaluations of women based on beauty, and violence against women.

CONCEPT

This activity examines classical paintings to determine what they reveal about issues in the psychology of women. It is an abbreviated version of a more extensive segment of a six-credit study abroad program in psychology and women's studies developed for The College of Staten Island, City University of New York, in which students explore issues in the psychology of women by visiting museums, art galleries, historical sites, social institutions, and dramatic performances in London, England. Rather than analyzing paintings from the point of view of art history or style, the paintings are examined for their subject matter and thematic content. What do paintings of actual persons or events reveal about issues that women have faced in society, past and present? What do paintings that allude to literary works reveal about the issues and situations faced by women portrayed in those works? What do paintings based on some aspect of classical mythology or legend reveal about attitudes toward women embodied in myth and legend and perpetuated through their representation within works of art? And what issues do all the paintings illustrate that are still pertinent to women today?

MATERIALS NEEDED

This activity requires from 6 to 12 or more slides of paintings selected for appropriate themes and subject matter. The number of slides will depend to some extent on the amount of class time available. The paintings noted here are all in the collection of the National Gallery in London and may be purchased as slides; see appendix A for ordering information. The entire collection of the National Gallery is reproduced in its catalog (National Gallery, 1995a), although these images are small. A far better source for personal study is the CD-ROM version of the National Gallery's catalog (National Gallery, 1995b), which includes high-quality reproductions together with indexed and cross-referenced catalog information.

INSTRUCTIONS

The following examples suggest paintings that you may use as focal points to help students explore three issues that are generally considered in the psychology of women course: (a) stereotyped portrayals of women, (b) the representation of ideals of physical beauty and their consequent use as standards for the comparative evaluation of women, and (c) violence against women.

Stereotyped Portrayals of Women

Stereotypes abound in art that is based on legend and mythology. Of many possibilities, only one stereotype will be considered—that of woman as a passive victim awaiting rescue. Two examples of paintings that illustrate this portrayal are noted.

St. George and the Dragon by Paolo Uccello was painted circa 1460. According to the legend alluded to in this painting, a dragon was appeased and kept from entering a city by being periodically allowed to devour some of its inhabitants. When it came time for the king's daughter to become one of these victims, St. George is said to have arrived just in time to wound the dragon and rescue the princess. The painting depicts St. George at the moment of piercing the dragon with his lance, in front of a cave, with the princess standing passively to the side and observing the action.

Angelica Saved by Ruggiero by Jean-Auguste-Dominique Ingres was painted sometime after 1819. The painting depicts Ruggiero attacking a sea monster with his lance, while Angelica stands by passively, chained to a rock.

Such paintings reveal how the stories of myth and legend can perpetuate stereotyped portrayals of women, in this instance in the role of victim. As an antidote of sorts, ask students presented with either of these paintings to imagine that a painting might portray, and how their responses might change, if the genders of rescuer and rescuee were reversed.

Ideals of Beauty

Since the dawn of classical art and sculpture, ideals of women's beauty have been portrayed that have not been representative of the average woman. Valuing a woman of greater beauty more highly is deeply embedded within Western culture. Several paintings portraying the mythological goddess Venus provide contexts for exploring the role of physical beauty in the evaluation of women.

The Judgment of Paris, painted by Peter Paul Rubens circa 1632–1635, alludes to the mythological story in which Paris, exiled son of the Trojan king, was visited by Mercury, the messenger of the gods, and was instructed by him to judge which of three goddesses was most beautiful: Juno, Minerva, or Venus. Paris chose Venus and gave her a golden apple.

In the psychology of women, this painting and the mythological tale to which it refers illustrate the pervasive practice of judging women for their physical attributes and rewarding them accordingly. In at least one account of this legend, the three goddesses were asked to disrobe before being judged. The painting invites comparisons with contemporary evaluations of women, and students might be encouraged to imagine an updated painting in which, instead of a golden apple, a beauty contest trophy is awarded.

The Toilet of Venus, known more familiarly as *The Rokeby Venus*, was painted by Velazquez, circa 1647–1651. This is one of the most famous paintings at the National Gallery. It depicts a nude, reclining Venus, gazing at her reflection in a mirror held by Cupid. The London *Times* once described the Rokeby Venus as "perhaps the finest painting of the nude in the world. . . . She is . . . the Goddess of Youth and Health, the embodiment of elastic strength and vitality—of the perfection of Womanhood at the moment when it passes from the bud to the flower" (cited by Barnard, 1993, p. 84).

In 1914, a suffragette tried to destroy the painting with an ax as a protest against the government's treatment of a suffragette leader and also because she "didn't like the way men visitors at the gallery gaped at it all day" (cited by Barnard, 1993, p. 84). The painting, together with this historic anecdote, invites comparisons with modern-day portrayals of the ideal woman in fashion magazines, representations that usually present ideals impossible for women to attain.

A startling contrast in the way that the issue of female beauty is approached is provided by the painting titled *A Grotesque Old Woman*, attributed to Quinten Massys, circa 1525. This painting is thought to satirize the aging process by portraying a withered old woman who has tried to recreate her youth by wearing a low-cut gown and elaborate headdress. The painting suggests a number of comparisons with contemporary issues, such as the paucity of portrayals of elderly women in any medium and gender differences reflected in society's attitude toward age-appropriate dress.

Violence Against Women

The existence of violence against women is an ancient and long-standing issue, and paintings can provide a context demonstrating that women have faced violence across the centuries. The three examples that follow all suggest parallels with contemporary events.

The painting *Apollo and Daphne* depicts an episode from the Roman poet Ovid's *Metamorphoses* (Ovid, 1955). Apollo, wounded by Cupid's arrow, fell in love with the nymph Daphne. However, Cupid also wounded Daphne with a special arrow that ensured that she would never fall in love. Eventually, Apollo tried to capture Daphne and, as he chased after her, she cried out to her father, the river god, for rescue. She was saved just in time by being turned into a laurel tree, and the painting shows Daphne with her arms extended and turning into tree branches, just as Apollo is reaching for her. Thus, Daphne had to relinquish her freedom and her identity to escape her pursuer.

This painting of an ancient myth suggests a parallel with a contemporary issue for women: When a woman is faced with unwelcome pursuit by a violent predator, such as a potential rapist, a batterer, or a stalker, who must, in general, relinquish freedom, the predator or the pursued? A discussion of this question can consider, for example, the various social and legal remedies available to protect women from pursuit and the degree to which they require behavior to be altered by women rather than men. At one extreme, for example, a woman might be pressured to change to a more modest mode of dress; at the other extreme, a battered woman may have to leave her home for the sanctuary of a shelter, while the batterer remains free. In the myth of Apollo and Daphne, students might consider how the story might have changed if it had been Apollo who had been rendered powerless to pursue Daphne.

Sexual harassment is the theme of several paintings of *Susannah and the Elders*, including a version by Guido Reni, circa 1600–1642. The story of Susannah, taken from the apocryphal chapters of the Book of Daniel, is of a virtuous woman who was spied on by two elders as she was bathing. They confronted her and told her she must lie with them or they would accuse her of adultery with another man, a crime for which she could be punished with death. She chose not to give in to them and they proceeded to accuse her publically of this crime. The elders were at first believed because of their status in the community. As Susannah was about to be led off for execution, Daniel intervened and persuaded those who would judge her that the elders had been false witnesses. Reni's painting shows Susannah's startled response as she is confronted by the leering elders. A full account of the story of Susannah, together with reproductions of a number of paintings that allude to this story, can be found in Sölle, Kirchberger, & Haag (1994).

Once again the events that constitute the theme of this painting invite students' comparisons with contemporary media accounts of sexual harassment. Susannah's accusers were authority figures within the community. They used their power and status to pressure her to submit to sexual acts. When she stood up to them, they attempted to follow through on threats to have her executed.

In addition to the obvious issue of sexual harassment, the painting raises the issue of disparities in penalties for adultery committed by women as compared with penalties for male adulterers, and this can lead to a discussion of cross-cultural differences concerning this culture value. It is certainly the case that, even today, women in some cultures continue to be put to death for infractions that would be acceptable or viewed as minor within Western society. Finally, a painting of *Susannah and the Elders* once again provides yet another example in which a woman who finds herself in precarious circumstances is rescued by a man.

Whereas paintings of Susannah refer to the issue of sexual harassment through the abuse of power, the consequences for the victim of sexual violence can be approached through a consideration of a painting that alludes to the impact that rape had on a woman of Roman times. *A Lady as Lucretia* by Lorenzo Lotto, painted circa 1533, is of a sixteenth-century Venetian noblewoman named Lucretia, who holds in her hand a drawing of her namesake, the virtuous Lucretia who lived in Roman times. It is not clear whether the Lucretia of ancient times is a legendary figure or someone who actually lived (Radice, 1973). However, her story is certainly a credible one. The Roman Lucretia is known for having offered hospitality, while her husband was away, to a man who was both a colleague of her military husband and the son of the king. This man took advantage of her and raped her, which led her to commit suicide by stabbing herself. She did this because she felt sullied and could not endure the dishonor that she believed now tainted her. In the painting by Lotto, the Roman Lucretia is shown in a detail, the drawing (held by the Venetian subject of the painting) in which she is about to stab herself after having been raped. Another significant detail of the painting can be found in a piece of paper, shown on a table, which contains a quotation that can be translated as "Nor shall ever unchaste woman live through the example of Lucretia" (Langmuir, 1994, p. 128).

In the psychology of women, this painting alludes to the issue of blaming the victim, or the victim blaming herself, for what happened to her. The painting also raises the question of whether a woman who has been the innocent victim of sexual violence is consequently viewed by her culture as tarnished and less desirable as a mate. The painting provides a context for exploring the extent to which such attitudes still exist in this and other cultures.

The examples noted and the issues to which they have been related represent only the proverbial tip of the iceberg and are merely suggestive of possibilities. Paintings can also be used to explore many other issues that relate to the traditional topics examined in a psychology of women course. Among the many themes that can be explored through art are the ideal body across history and culture; women as decorative objects; relationships among fashion, freedom, and status; ceremonies and rituals; marriage, the family, and gender roles; women and achievement in history; women as leaders and heroes; symbolism; communication through body language; and some health issues, including eating disorders and alcohol abuse. Students can also use art to address the stereotypes of woman as icon of purity, woman as goddess, woman as nurturer, woman as temptress, and the fallen woman. Finally, students can consider the issues of the gender, nationality, or culture of the artist and how these might influence the portrayal of women.

Deciding when to use paintings in a psychology of women course will be determined to some extent by the availability of materials. Initially, as examples are acquired and as you become familiar with them, they may be used most effectively in a single class designed to illustrate how the same issues so pervasive in contemporary news, advertising, and other media are also central to some works of art.

Once a critical mass has been reached so that several paintings can be presented relevant to each of a number of issues, the paintings might profitably be interspersed throughout the course. Students can then grow accustomed to looking at works of art to see what they reveal about issues in the psychology of women, which can enhance both sensitivity to these issues as well as involvement in art outside the classroom.

Psychology teachers are encouraged to search local galleries and to cast their nets widely to build up a slide collection as well as to determine what slides are available for borrowing from art departments, museum slide libraries, and other sources. Slides can be made from postcards, books, and other reproductions.

WRITING COMPONENT

Have students write paragraphs in which they relate issues raised by the paintings to issues raised in course readings. Have them read their writings aloud without noting the particular painting to see if other students can recognize what painting is being described.

Another writing assignment would be to have students compare the portrayal of women in paintings with contemporary portrayals in advertising, film, or television.

You could also have students imagine an updated version of a painting and describe it as an artist might paint it today, within the context of the women's movement.

For paintings that you present at first without noting the specific content, treat the paintings as if they were Thematic Apperception Test (TAT) items. Using classical paintings that portray women in some way, have students write stories in which they discuss who the people are, what is happening, what led to the situation, and what will happen. Have the students share their stories to determine the degree to which they saw the painting as depicting similar situations or issues in the psychology of women.

A final thought to anyone who sets out to build a collection of materials to assimilate art into the psychology of women course: You are embarking on an endlessly fascinating, enriching, and compelling treasure hunt that will forever influence the way that you yourself perceive and respond to art.

REFERENCES

Barnard, J. (1993). *The woman's travel guide: London.* London: Virago Press.

Langmuir, E. (1994). *The National Gallery companion guide.* London: National Gallery Publications. Distributed by Yale University Press.

National Gallery. (1995a). *The National Gallery: Complete illustrated catalogue.* London: Author.

National Gallery. (1995b). *The National Gallery complete illustrated catalogue on CD-ROM.* London: Author.

Ovid. (1955). *The metamorphoses of Ovid.* Harmondsworth, Middlesex, England: Penguin.

Radice, B. (1973). *Who's who in the ancient world: A handbook to the survivors of the Greek and Roman classics.* London: Penguin Books.

Sölle, D., Kirchberger, K. H., & Haag, H. (1994). *Great women of the Bible in art and literature.* Grand Rapids, MI: William B. Eerdmans.

SUGGESTED READING

Thomas, A. (1994). *An illustrated dictionary of narrative painting.* London: John Murray, in association with National Gallery Publications.

Appendix A

Slide Ordering Information

The following list provides catalog numbers of slides referred to in this article. Slides are priced at 80 pence each (approximately $1.35) plus shipping and can be ordered from National Gallery Publications Limited, 5/6 Pall Mall East, London SW1Y 5BA, United Kingdom. Specify credit card details and air or sea delivery.

Theme	Catalog No.	Artist	Painting
Woman as victim	#6294	Uccello	*St. George and the Dragon*
	#3292	Ingres	*Angelica Saved by Ruggiero*
Ideals of beauty	#6379	Rubens	*The Judgment of Paris,* ca. 1632–1635
	#2057	Velazquez	*The Toilet of Venus (The Rokeby Venus)*
	#5769	Massys	*A Grotesque Old Woman*
Violence against women	#928	Pollaiulo	*Apollo and Daphne*
	#196	Reni	*Susannah and the Elders*
	#4256	Lotto	*A Lady as Lucretia*

65 GENDER STEREOTYPING IN COMMERCIALS

Margaret A. Lloyd
Georgia Southern University

In this activity, students view television commercials and record the number of males and females serving as representatives for products used inside the home and products used outside the home. Student findings are discussed in class. The instructor uses the activity to introduce the topic of the gender stereotyping on television. This activity can also be adapted to study the representation of ethnic groups in commercials.

CONCEPT

This activity increases students' awareness of gender stereotyping in television commercials and gives students practice "doing psychology" by having them record data outside of class.

MATERIALS NEEDED

Students will need access to a television and a videotape recorder. You will need to make copies of the instructions (appendix A) and the data summary sheet (appendix B) for each student.

INSTRUCTIONS

This activity is conducted in two phases: an out-of-class data-gathering phase and a subsequent in-class discussion phase.

Out-of-Class Phase

Provide each student with a copy of the instructions and the data summary sheet. If you would like to grade the data summary sheet as an assignment, you may want to provide two copies: one to be handed in and one for the student to use for discussion.

In-Class Phase

Divide the class into groups of four to six students to share and discuss their findings. The small group discussion usually lasts about 15 min. If time permits, ask a student from each group to give an informal summary of the group's findings to the class. If you employ this option, it is a good idea to forewarn students so the volunteers will be prepared.

In full-class discussion, develop the operational definition of gender stereotyping as the overrepresentation of males in commercials for products used outside the home or an overrepresentation of females in commercials for products used inside the home. Point out that although this data-gathering activity was not a controlled study, the results generally parallel researchers' findings that there is gender stereotyping in both television commercials (Bretl & Cantor, 1988; Lovdal, 1989) and television programs (Davis, 1990).

Next, ask why psychologists (and others) are interested in gender stereotyping on television. Students usually respond with something like "Because viewers may believe that stereotypes are accurate portrayals of reality." Does the media's use of stereotypes reinforce and perpetuate them? This raises the issue of whether television is merely an entertainment vehicle.

From here you can explain the importance of gathering empirical data on the prevalence and effects of gender stereotypes. You may want to review the results of relevant empirical studies (Repetti, 1984; Signorielli & Lears, 1992) that generally show a modest relationship between television viewing and gender stereotypes. Also, children who watch a lot of educational television tend to hold less traditional views about gender roles than children who do not. Of course, because these are correlational studies, it is likely that other factors (parental values, for example) also play a role.

DISCUSSION Because students select the commercials, they are typically interested in the results of the activity. Also, students enjoy exchanging their findings and views with others in the small group discussion. Many students are surprised at the prevalence of gender stereotyping in television commercials, but not all students will find such instances. For this reason, it is important to point out commercials in which the genders are equitably represented. You can also find examples of commercials for products that typically have featured one gender, but are now featuring persons of the other gender as well. This activity can easily be adapted to study the representation of ethnic groups in commercials.

Another option is for the instructor to videotape the commercials and show them in class. Then students working in pairs can calculate reliability coefficients for the coding scheme.

WRITING COMPONENT This activity can be used to help students learn to translate numerical data into meaningful verbal statements. One way to do this is to have the students bring the following written assignments to class before the in-class discussion.

First, have students write a summary statement about the representation of males and females in commercials for products used inside the home. Students should use percentage data from the data summary sheet to justify their statements.

Next, have students write a summary statement about the representation of males and females in commercials for products used outside the home. Here too students should use percentage data from the data summary sheet to justify their statements.

Finally, have students compare, in writing, the representation of males and females for inside-the-home products and outside-the-home products. Again, students should use percentage data from the data summary sheet to justify their statements.

REFERENCES Bretl, D. J., & Cantor, J. (1988). The portrayal of men and women in U.S. television commercials: A recent content analysis and trends over 15 years. *Sex Roles, 18,* 595–609.

Davis, D. M. (1990). Portrayals of women in prime-time network television: Some demographic characteristics. *Sex Roles, 23,* 325–332.

Lovdal, L. T. (1989). Sex-role messages in television commercials: An update. *Sex Roles, 21,* 715–724.

Repetti, R. L. (1984). Determinants of children's sex-stereotyping: Parental sex-role traits and television viewing. *Personality and Social Psychology Bulletin, 10*(3), 457–468.

Signorielli, N., & Lears, M. (1992). Children, television, and conceptions about chores: Attitudes and behaviors. *Sex Roles, 27,* 157–170.

Appendix A

Instructions for Gender Stereotyping Activity

1. For this activity, you will need to videotape a number of commercials. Try to view these commercials during prime time for adults (8:00–11:00 p.m. in the Eastern time zone) or prime time for children (4:00–5:30 p.m. weekdays in the Eastern time zone and Saturday mornings).

2. After you watch each commercial, classify it into one of two categories: inside-the-home product (foods prepared and consumed inside the home, cleaning products, home furnishings, personal care products, medications, and so forth) or outside-the-home product (lawn mowers, lawn fertilizers, exterior paint, deck sealants, and so forth). Do not record data for commercials for nonhome products (cars, candy, restaurants, and so forth). Record enough commercials, in sequential order, so that you have a minimum of 10 for inside-the-home products and 10 for outside-the-home products.

3. Using the video and the data summary sheet, code the first 10 inside-the-home commercials and the first 10 outside-the-home commercials for both visible product representatives (visible individuals who ask you to buy the products) and for voice-overs (unseen individuals whose voices are used to make comments about the products). Use marks to record each instance into one of the following categories: "male only," "female only," "both male and female," or "not applicable" (no human product representatives used—e.g., cartoon characters).

4. When you have finished recording the data, total your marks for each category. Then calculate the percentages as indicated.

Appendix B

Data Summary Sheet   Name: _____

Inside-the-Home Products

	Male Only	Female Only	Both	N/A*	Total
Product representatives	_____	_____	_____	_____	10
	____%	____%	____%	____%	100%
Voice-overs	_____	_____	_____	_____	10
	____%	____%	____%	____%	100%

Outside-the-Home Products

	Male Only	Female Only	Both	N/A*	Total
Product representatives	_____	_____	_____	_____	10
	____%	____%	____%	____%	100%
Voice-overs	_____	_____	_____	_____	10
	____%	____%	____%	____%	100%

*Human males or females not used (e.g., cartoon characters)

66 HISTORY OF WOMEN IN PSYCHOLOGY: A TIME LINE

Bernice S. Strauss

Sam Houston State University

In this activity students are asked to research and bring in the names and accomplishments of women who made significant contributions to the field of psychology in the past 100 years. The names and accomplishments brought in by students are then used to construct a time line. The teacher provides a historical context with significant dates in world history. Discussion focuses on issues of race and class as they interact with gender. Finally students are encouraged to add their own names and personal achievements or those of a family member and her or his accomplishments.

CONCEPT This simple, highly visual activity might serve to introduce a section on the psychology of women or gender issues. It allows the instructor to familiarize students with women in the history and to theorize with students why there have been so few. It also provides an opportunity to introduce issues of race and class as they affect gender. An important part of the time line is the historical events, beyond psychology, that have had an impact on the discipline.

MATERIALS NEEDED In addition to chalk and a chalkboard, you will need names and dates of contributions made by two to three women in the field of psychology to be brought in by students. The number assigned will vary depending on the size of the class and the time allocated for the exercise. Students will need to be able to define the psychologist's accomplishments and to list any important dates. You will also need significant historical dates to place these accomplishments in context.

INSTRUCTIONS Draw a long line on the chalkboard with some dates as reference points. Ask students, in turn, to come up and at the appropriate place enter the date, the name, and the accomplishment of the psychologist that they want to recognize. You can also add dates along the time line that illustrate the roles and status of women in America. Dates that are used can include the following:

1839 Mississippi was the first state to allow married women to own property in their own names (however, in case of divorce men kept legal control of children and property.)

1915 The American Medical Association began to admit women.

1920 Women got the right to vote. (However, not until 1984 was the first woman chosen as a candidate on a national ticket [Geraldine Ferraro]).

1925 The Scopes "monkey trial" took place.

1926 Federal Council of Churches supported prohibition.

1939 The ship the *St. Louis* left Germany carrying 930 Jewish refugees who were attempting to escape Hitler. They sailed to Cuba where they were refused admittance. The U.S. government also refused to admit them, and the ship returned to Germany.

1942   Franklin Roosevelt established the War Relocation Authority. More than 110,000 Japanese Americans were sent to internment camps.

1954   *Brown v. Board of Education* was tried.

You may also include phrases or poems that further exemplify the experiences of diverse women throughout this period; for example, you or a student volunteer might read the poem "Phenomenal Woman" by Maya Angelou (1978) or the speech "Ain't I a Woman" by Sojourner Truth (1995) to the class.

Finally encourage students to add their own birth date or accomplishment to the time line.

DISCUSSION   Discussion may include what it is like for male students to participate in an exercise that is not male oriented or gender balanced. What is this experience like for women of color? What might this experience be like if it occurs repeatedly over time? What does this activity say about how our society decides who we recognize? Depending on the level of the course, students may be able to integrate relevant learning from other psychology courses.

WRITING COMPONENT   Ask students to write a one-page paper examining their reactions to the experience. They could address one of the following topics: (a) What is it like seeing the names of so many women being honored? (b) What would it be like to have one's own name added to the list? (c) How should we decide whose contribution deserves recognition (i.e., do women have to participate in the public sector or do accomplishments in the private sector, family, and home deserve recognition also)? (d) What social issues contribute to whether a person becomes famous? (e) How do events in history affect individuals accomplishments?

REFERENCES   Angelou, M.(1978). Phenomenal woman. In *And still I rise*. New York: Random House.

Truth, S. (1995). Ain't I a woman? In L. Wagner-Martin & C. N. Davidson (Eds.), *Women's writing in the United States*. New York: Oxford University Press.

SUGGESTED READING   Cott, N. F., & Pleck, E. H. (Eds.). (1979). *A Heritage of Her Own: Toward a New Social History of American Women*. New York: Simon & Schuster.

Furumoto, L. (1985). Placing women in the history of psychology course. *Teaching of Psychology, 12*, 3–6.

Lerner, G. (1979). *The majority finds its part: Placing women in history*. New York: Oxford University Press.

Scarborough, E., & Furumoto, L. (1987). *Untold lives: The first generation of American women psychologists*. New York: Columbia University Press.

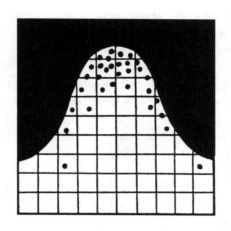

CHAPTER X
SOCIAL PSYCHOLOGY
AND PERSONALITY

The 12 articles in this chapter offer a multitude of concepts and principles in social psychology and personality, with activities on such topics as attribution, group dynamics, attitudes, personal space, aggression, and the concept of self. Activity 67 is a class discussion exercise that teaches students the four important characteristics that distinguish groups from nongroups (collections of people that are not groups). In Activity 68, students role-play opposing sides in a debate on homelessness. In the debate they use various applications of attribution theory to support their positions.

Introducing students to the field of personal relationships is the subject of Activity 69. Students are asked to create their own theories about how romantic relationships develop, and those theories are used as the basis for a class discussion about the psychological study of interpersonal relationships. Activity 70 teaches students about attitude measurement by examining attitudes toward public assistance. Included in the activity are explorations of the Likert method, response set, and the concepts of norms and scale validity.

Personal space is the subject of Activity 71, a simulation exercise in which students learn about spatial behavior as a form of nonverbal communication. This activity demonstrates cultural, social, and situational differences in the size of the personal space zone.

Activity 72 allows students to examine the psychological principles used in smoking advertisements. The exercise focuses on an analysis of the tobacco companies' attempts to portray smoking as an attractive, exciting, and positive activity and allows students to evaluate the effectiveness of the surgeon general's warnings.

In Activity 73, students read a short passage from the novel *The Adventures of Tom Sawyer* and explain how it demonstrates the relationship among behavior, cognition, and attitudes. It focuses particularly on the social–psychological concepts of cognitive dissonance, self-perception, overjustification, and reframing.

Activity 74 is an extraclassroom exercise that has students view an aggressive and a non-aggressive television program and categorize the aggressive behaviors. These data are aggregated in class and are used as the basis of a class discussion on media violence.

Conflict resolution is the subject of Activity 75, in which students use two alternative techniques—mediation and negotiation—to resolve a conflict about financial responsibility for property damage. Students learn that these techniques can bring about successful resolutions of conflicts, rather than resorting to more painful, expensive, and time-consuming strategies such as lawsuits. Activity 76 continues the legal theme by having students form jury groups to determine whether Shakespeare's Hamlet was insane when he killed Polonius. The jury deliberations follow the students' viewing of a videotape, *Insanity Trial of Hamlet*, available from C-SPAN.

Activity 77 encourages students to construct a collage that communicates aspects of their identity. This exercise addresses many concepts in social and developmental psychology, such as social role, values, gender, ethnicity, identity, attribution, prejudice, and discrimination. Activity 78 also explores the self by having students read and discuss two novels by Wallace Stegner. Central themes include stress and coping, aging, integrity, self-denigration, and meaning across the life span.

67 THE NATURE OF GROUPS: AN EXERCISE FOR CLASSROOM DISCUSSION

Robert P. Agans
University of Maryland

The purpose of this activity is to generate class discussion about the nature of groups. Participants will discover that not all human gatherings constitute groups from a psychological perspective. More important, they will understand the four essential characteristics that distinguish groups from nongroups: interdependence, structure or patterned behavior, common goals, and perceived groupness.

CONCEPT

This activity is designed to generate class discussion about various aspects of groups and to sensitize students to the perplexities that researchers face when attempting to describe group phenomena. Though social scientists do not agree on one precise group definition, four important characteristics distinguish groups from nongroups (Pavitt & Curtis, 1994). These essential characteristics are (a) interdependence (Cartwright & Zander, 1968), (b) structure or patterned behavior (Newcomb, 1951), (c) common goals (Mills, 1967), and (d) perceived groupness (Smith, 1945).

MATERIALS NEEDED

You will need to make copies of the questionnaire at the end of this activity for each of your students (see appendix A).

INSTRUCTIONS

At the beginning of the class, give each student a copy of the questionnaire. Instruct the class to read each statement carefully and check it if the statement represents what they consider to be a group. Students should leave blank statements they do not believe constitute a group. Tell them to respond to items on the basis of their personal beliefs, not what they think others would say or what they think their instructor wants. Tell them the questionnaire will be collected, but that they should not put their names on it.

Allow students 5 min to finish the questionnaire. An easy way to tabulate the data is to collect the questionnaires and redistribute them in random order, so that students get a copy other than their own. This precaution reduces the embarrassment students may feel about sharing their individual responses. Next, use a show of hands to record the data on the board. For each item, count the number of hands that signify the respondent checked the item as representing a group. By subtracting this number from the total number of students, you can quickly calculate the number of students who did not believe the item represented a group (Benjamin, 1985). Students relate to the data most easily if you take the time to quickly convert these raw scores to percentages. Tabulating the data takes only about 5 min in a small class.

In large classes, consider administering and collecting the questionnaire the class period before you discuss this topic. This gives you plenty of time to tabulate the results in advance for the appropriate class period, thus allowing the majority of the class time to be spent on discussion.

DISCUSSION

Despite the lack of a unified definition of groups in the social sciences, most of the experimental work consists of groups whose members (a) are interdependent, (b) develop structure or patterned behavior, (c) have common goals, and (d) create an atmosphere of perceived groupness. This activity allows students to discover and explore these characteristics as they identify groups and nongroups.

Start class discussion by identifying items least likely to be identified as groups. For example, Items 1, 5, 10, and 19 should yield the lowest percentage of checks because they are generally considered nongroups. On the other hand, Items 4, 7, 12, 15, and 18 should have the highest percentage of checks. These items incorporate the four essential characteristics of groups: interdependence, structure or patterned behavior, common goals, and perceived groupness.

The remaining items reflect varying degrees of these four characteristics. They should be marked by only a portion of the students and should evoke the most controversy. Items 8, 9, 16, and 20 are based on the interdependence theme. Items 2, 3, 6, and 13 are chiefly structural or patterned. Items 11, 14, and 17 could be psychological groups if the people involved perceive a sense of groupness or common goals.

It may be useful to point out characteristics that are missing for certain items. For example, it should be evident that friends standing in line to purchase concert tickets (Item 13) do not constitute a group because there is no interdependence among these people: Even though norms guide individual behavior and create expectancies, one could just as easily buy concert tickets without such a crowd. On the other hand, two strangers speaking over the telephone (Item 9), even though they are dependent on each other to hold the conversation, do not constitute a group because no patterned behavior has emerged yet. It is also unlikely that these strangers would have a sense of groupness or perceived common goals. Similarly, the argument that all the people on planet Earth (Item 5) are one big group can be laid to rest because such a mass does not include any interdependence or structured behavior. Lunch with a Mytonian (Item 20) will probably create the most confusion among students because they have no working knowledge of Mytonians. This item can be used to demonstrate how categorization (labeling) and social knowledge affect our perception of what is and is not a group.

In sum, authentic groups consist of individuals who are interdependent, have developed patterned behavior and structure, have common goals, and perceive themselves as a group. With these characteristics in mind, it becomes much easier to distinguish groups from nongroups.

REFERENCES

Benjamin, L. T. (1985). Defining aggression: An exercise for classroom discussion. *Teaching of Psychology, 12,* 40–42.

Cartwright, D., & Zander, A. (1968). *Group dynamics: Research and theory* (3rd ed.). New York: Harper & Row.

Mills, T. M. (1967). *The sociology of small groups,* Englewood Cliffs, NJ: Prentice-Hall.

Newcomb, T. M. (1951). Social psychological theory. In J. H. Rohrer & M. Sherif (Eds.), *Social psychology at the crossroads* (pp. 31–49). New York: Harper.

Pavitt, C., & Curtis, E. (1994). *Smallgroup discussion: A theoretical approach.* Scottsdale, AZ: Gorsuch Scarisbrick.

Smith, M. (1945). Social situation, social behavior, social group. *Psychological Review, 52,* 224–229.

Appendix A

What Constitutes a Group?

Check each statement you believe represents a group.

1. _____ three people sitting in separate rooms
2. _____ students in a college class
3. _____ sorority sisters attending a lecture together
4. _____ an army defending its borders
5. _____ all people on planet Earth
6. _____ a mob of angry protesters marching on Capitol Hill
7. _____ a family
8. _____ Jena and Bob out on a first date
9. _____ two strangers speaking over the telephone
10. _____ newborns in the maternity ward
11. _____ three rival gang members on a desert island
12. _____ colleagues assigned the task of writing a final report
13. _____ friends standing in line to purchase concert tickets
14. _____ members of Greenpeace
15. _____ the Dallas Cowboys
16. _____ natives entertaining a foreign visitor for the evening
17. _____ people from the Republic of China
18. _____ a construction crew building a bridge
19. _____ pedestrians on the corner of Fifth and Main Streets
20. _____ lunch with a Mytonian

68 APPLICATION OF ATTRIBUTION THEORY TO THE SOCIAL ISSUE OF HOMELESSNESS

Susan H. Franzblau
Fayetteville State University

The objective of this activity is to show students, by their own experience, the relevance of applying social psychological principles to the analysis of important social events. Students role-play opposing sides on the issue of homelessness, using various applications of attribution theory to support their positions. Their use of attribution theories, as well as emergent ethnocentrism as a result of establishing opposing groups, is addressed in both oral and written form.

CONCEPT

The objective of this activity is to show students that psychological principles can be used to analyze important social events. This exercise is designed to teach students about attribution theory in the context of learning about homelessness. It requires students to make a presentation in a hearing or courtroom form, taking one or the other side of an issue.

MATERIALS NEEDED

You will need two versions of the attribution exercise, each typed on a single sheet of paper and alternatively handed out to each student (appendixes A and B). In Version 1 the student is a member of a group of homeless people. In Version 2 the student is a representative of New York City.

INSTRUCTIONS

A class of not more than 25 students is preferable. Five to six class periods should be allowed, or students could work with their groups outside of class.

Set up the activity by requiring that students do preliminary reading on attribution theories. Then either lecture or hold a discussion on attribution theory that includes the following topics: naive tendencies to determine attributions of causality on the basis of consensus, distinctiveness, and consistency (Kelley, 1967), fundamental attribution errors (Ross, 1977), actor–observer effects (Jones & Nisbett, 1971), self-serving bias and self-defeating bias (Miller & Ross, 1975), impression formation (Asch, 1946), and creating a psychological perspective (Storms, 1973).

Have the students divide themselves into two groups, forming circles at opposite ends of the room. More than two groups representing each side may be formed, depending on the size of the class. It is best not to exceed more than five to six students per group.

Discuss the exercise with the entire class, advising them that each group's mission is to prepare themselves to testify on behalf of their group at a citywide hearing on homelessness, for which they must pull together all they have learned from attribution theory. Their job is to convince the officers at the hearing that

(a) as representatives of New York City the homeless are mentally ill, cannot be responsible for themselves, and should be evicted from the subways and placed in temporary shelters or (b) as members of a group of homeless people they have the right to sleep in the subways if they wish, they are not mentally ill, and the problem of homelessness will not be solved by building more shelters but by building more low-cost homes.

After approximately a week of group discussion the hearing/debate should take place. The judges should include the principle interrogator (the instructor) and one judge from each group, chosen by the group. Each group is to prepare a list of expert witnesses who will sit before the judges and plead their case. Each group's witnesses are presented alternatively with the other group's witnesses. The debate can be conducted formally or informally, according to the dynamics of the class and the instructor's preference. I have used a debate format in which each side was represented in alternating sequence. After flipping a coin to determine which side goes first, I ask them to consider the benefits of recency and primacy effects (Asch, 1946).

At the end of the debate you should initiate an open discussion that includes the following topics:

1. each student's feelings before, during, and after the exercise regarding the likability of the group they are in and their feelings toward the out-group;
2. what factors drew them closer to their group,
3. the techniques they used to attribute causality of the problem of homelessness to the other group and to build a psychological perspective in their favor,
4. the disequilibrium caused by the other group,
5. the general effectiveness of the exercise, and
6. what they learned about themselves as persons in social situations.

DISCUSSION   At first the groups might be disorganized and uninvolved, but interest will increase as the groups continue to meet. To inspire involvement it is critical to keep the hearing component. As the groups evolve, group leaders will emerge and people will take on different roles, depending on the dynamics of each group (Sherif, Harvey, White, Hood, & Sherif, 1961). In-group ethnocentrism (Sumner, 1906) will also develop as they create a psychological perspective favorable to their group (Storms, 1973). Each time you try this exercise you will find that group members are affected differently, depending on their perspectives on homelessness when they first enter the group. The work the groups do, including research on homelessness, will also depend on the dynamics of each group. In one situation, the city group chose to remain objective inasmuch as they entered this group with a bias toward homeless people; however, at the end of the exercise most indicated that they were unable to remain objective and were drawn into defending the arguments of their group. Some people became more involved than they initially believed they could, which surprised them. Although the activity was presented to the students as an exercise on use of attribution theories, they also came to an experiential understanding of group polarization, the role of social comparison and information, and ethnocentrism, which then enabled them to read about and discuss these processes from their own experience. During the hearing, the involvement of the students will increase as the hearing evolves.

WRITING COMPONENT

Assign students to write an analysis of their use of attribution theory to prove their case at the citywide hearing. You could also have them discuss their experience of identifying with a new group and how it affected the group process and their feelings toward the other group. Appendix C presents the directions for students to use when completing the writing assignment.

This activity is very powerful and tends to influence students' beliefs about particular issues. It is possible to explore other socially useful topics in the context of teaching about attribution theory. For example, I have done this exercise to teach students about how attribution theory can be used to defend lesbians and gay men against discrimination. I tend to tread very carefully when organizing opposing groups on issues such as lesbian/gay rights or racism, given that students can be influenced by the group process to change or enhance their initial attributions. You can do this exercise without using the opposing-groups method. However, if you choose the opposing-sides method, depending on the circumstances, I suggest having students use the writing assignment to defend the alternative perspective.

REFERENCES

Asch, S. E. (1946). Forming impressions of personality. *Journal of Personality and Social Psychology, 41*, 258–290.

Jones, E. E., & Nisbett, R. E. (1971). The actor and the observer: Divergent perceptions of the causes of behavior. In E. E. Jones, D. E. Kanouse, H. H. Kelley, R. E. Nisbett, S. Valins, & B. Weiner (Eds.), *Attribution: Perceiving the causes of behavior* (pp. 79–94). Morristown, NJ: General Learning Press.

Kelley, H. H. (1967). Attribution theory in social psychology. In D. Levine (Ed.), *Nebraska Symposium on Motivation* (Vol. 15, pp. 192–240). Lincoln: University of Nebraska Press, 192–240.

Miller, D. T., & Ross, M. (1975). Self-serving biases in the attribution of causality: Fact or fiction? *Psychological Bulletin, 86*, 93–118.

Ross, L. (1977). The intuitive psychologist and his shortcomings: Distortions in the attribution process. In L. Berkowitz (Ed.), *Advances in Experimental Social Psychology, 10* (pp. 173–220). New York: Academic Press.

Sherif, M., Harvey, O. J., White, B. J., Hood, W. R., & Sherif, C. W. (1961). *Intergroup conflict and cooperation: The Robbers Cave experiment.* Norman: University of Oklahoma Book Exchange.

Storms, M. D. (1973). Videotape and the attribution process. Reversing actors' and observers' points of view. *Journal of Personality and Social Psychology, 27*, 165–175.

Sumner, W. G. (1906). *Folkways.* Boston: Ginn.

SUGGESTED READING

Children's Defense Fund (1998). *The state of America's children—Yearbook 1998.* Washington, DC: Author.

Jones, J. M., Levine, I. S., & Rosenberg, A. A. (Eds.). (1991). Homelessness [Special issue]. *American Psychologist, 46*(11), 1188–1207.

Parker, E., & Spears, R. (Eds.). (1996). *Psychology and society: Radical theory and practice.* London: Pluto Press.

Spurlock, J., & Robinowitz, C. B. (Eds.). (1990). *Women in context: Development and stresses.* New York: Plenum Press.

Appendix A

Attribution Exercise 1: Member of a Group of Homeless People

You are a group of homeless people who have just found out that the city of New York is planning to evict more than 5000 of you from the subways during the winter, even during times of below-freezing weather. Because of the actions of other groups against this policy, a citywide hearing has been called during which both sides (the homeless people and their advocates and the city representatives and their advocates) will be called to testify. Your job is to show that the situation of homelessness needs remedy requiring building apartments and homes for homeless people, that the homeless are not just a bunch of crazy people who do not know better than to stay out of the cold, that homeless people are intelligent enough to speak for themselves and do not need others to speak for them, and that homelessness is a problem in many cities not because of a type of person called "homeless" but because of the severe economic crisis and resultant unemployment, gentrification (kicking out poor people to build high-income housing), and warehousing (keeping buildings empty when the market will not allow for high rents).

Use all that you have learned from attribution theory to make your case at this hearing, including (a) naive tendencies to look at consensus, distinctiveness, and consistency to determine attributions of causation, (b) fundamental attribution errors, (c) actor–observer effects, (d) self-serving bias and self-defeating bias, (e) impression formation for creating salience, (f) the power of creating a psychological perspective, and (g) the effects of power and status in creating attributions.

Appendix B

Attribution Exercise 2: Representative of New York City

You are representatives of New York City. Your administration has just enacted a policy of evicting the estimated 5000 homeless from the subways during the winter, including times when the weather is below freezing. Because of the actions of other groups against this policy, a citywide hearing has been called during which both sides (the homeless people and their advocates and the city representatives and their advocates) will be called to testify. Your job is to show that homeless people are mentally ill and that their occupation of the subways is creating problems for citizens of the city who want to go to work unoffended by the presence of people who beg, evade fares, and sleep in the subways. You advocate putting homeless people in shelters and have advanced a strategy of busing them systematically from the subways to the shelters during the winter months. You are to convince people at the hearing that homelessness results from a desire of people who do not want to sleep in shelters and who have voluntarily opted to sleep in the streets or subway stations, despite attempts to give them shelter. You are to advocate that the homeless create problems for businesses that want to attract customers to their stores, which is the more critical problem during this time of economic recession. Business must be picked up and the homeless are getting in the way.

Use all that you have learned from attribution theory to make your case at this hearing, including (a) naive tendencies to look at consensus, distinctiveness, and consistency to determine attributions of causation; (b) fundamental attribution errors; (c) actor–observer effects; (d) self-serving bias and self-defeating bias; (e) impression formation for creating salience; (f) the power of creating a psychological perspective; and (g) the effects of power and status in creating attributions.

Appendix C

Directions for Writing Assignment

Your assignment is to write up your in-class exercise on the application of attribution theory to the issue of homelessness. The following is a general outline you might adopt:

First state the problem; then describe how you went about solving it, beginning with an investigation of the literature on how attributions are made, including theories on our naive tendencies to determine causation on the basis of consensus, distinctiveness, and consistency. Then discuss the fundamental attribution errors we make that result in actor–observer effects and self-serving biases. Next go into the work on impression formation and other information from perception to show how salience is created, including the work showing how to create a psychological perspective. All of this research is to be put together to show how you influenced the citywide hearings to see the perspective of either homeless people or representatives of New York City regarding the evictions of homeless people from the subways.

Your essay is to be four pages in length, typed and double-spaced, and should follow APA style. Assume the naive reader, define your terms, and support your opinions and assertions with research.

69 ROMANTIC RELATIONSHIPS: STUDYING THEORIES OF PERSONAL RELATIONSHIP DEVELOPMENT

Elizabeth L. Paul
The College of New Jersey

The personal relationships field has developed over the past 3 decades into a thriving discipline. To introduce students to the subject matter, this activity requires each student to create her or his own theory of how romantic relationships develop. Students' theories are then used as the basis for a discussion about the psychological study of interpersonal relationships.

CONCEPT   This activity uses models of the development and progress of interpersonal relationships to introduce the personal relationships field. Social penetration, social exchange, attraction-based, individual developmental, and stage theory models of relationship development are demonstrated and discussed, as well as such interpersonal processes as communication, relationship cognition, conflict, relationship maintenance, and commitment. In addition, the functions of stereotypes, idealized or romanticized social scripts, and lay theories of relationship development are addressed. This activity is useful for introductory psychology, social psychology, and personal relationships courses.

To explore this activity, use the following scholarly models of relationship development:

1. *Social penetration theory* focuses on changes in communication (especially self-disclosure), starting with superficial or impersonal topics, broadening and deepening as uncertainty reduces to more intimate interactions (Altman & Taylor, 1973; Baxter, 1988).

2. *Social exchange theory* applies an economic model to relationship development in which individuals are motivated to maximize gains and minimize losses. Relationship development and satisfaction are based on rewards, costs, expectations, perceived alternatives, and investments (Levinger & Huesmann, 1980; Rusbult, 1983; Thibaut & Kelley, 1959).

3. *Attraction-based theories* focus primarily on the initial phases of interpersonal attraction, highlighting the importance of proximity, physical attractiveness, and similarity and complementarity in physical attractiveness and other personal characteristics (Berscheid, Dion, Walster, & Walster, 1971; Hatfield & Sprecher, 1986).

4. *Individual developmental models* build on such seminal developmental theories as those of Erikson (e.g., 1963) and Sullivan (1953) in which relationship development is an individual developmental milestone building on evolving psychological strengths and abilities (Franz & White, 1985; Paul & White, 1990).

5. *Stage theories* conceptualize relationship development as evolving through a specific set of stages in a particular order. These include the two-stage theory of Kerckhoff and Davis (1962), Reiss's (1960) four-stage theory, Lewis's (1972) multistage theory, and Murstein's (1976, 1987) stimulus-value-role theory.

MATERIALS
NEEDED

You will need a chalkboard or white board and, of course, creative students.

INSTRUCTIONS

This activity must take place before students have been introduced to the personal relationships field in an introductory course or at the beginning of a personal relationships course. This way students are not biased by existing scholarly work in this area. One week prior to the introduction of this field, instruct students to create a theory of how romantic relationships develop and proceed. They may list and describe stages, draw a flow diagram, or identify general processes that occur. There is no limit to the creativity with which this assignment is completed (I have received collages, cartoons, and yard-long flow diagrams). Tell students that they must not consult their textbooks or any other scholarly materials for this assignment; however, encourage them to consult with friends. Students should bring their one- or two-page presentations of the theory to the next class period. (Alternatively, students may work in groups in class to develop theories. This is less effective than the take-home assignment but is still an effective discussion tool.) Students do not receive a specific grade for their theory papers; rather, they receive credit toward their class participation grade.

In class, ask five students to volunteer to write an abbreviated version of their theories on the board (if the students have easy and quick access to a copy machine, they could put their diagrams or illustrations on overheads to show the class; this may be especially effective in a large lecture class). By walking around the classroom before class starts and identifying promising and diverse student papers, you could encourage particular students to volunteer. Ask the volunteers to give a brief explanation of their theories to the class. Then encourage the students to discuss the theories as a class.

This exercise has been found to be very effective in seminar-style classes as well as large lecture classes. The following are suggestions for facilitating this exercise in a large lecture course: (a) have student volunteers write their theory on an overhead transparency to aid in presentation ease and clarity; (b) have students hand in their theories ahead of time, which will allow you to select five examples to copy onto transparencies and present; and (c) have students cluster in small groups to begin the discussion of their theories, assigning one student per group to be the recorder of issues raised by their group that can be used to facilitate contributions to the large group discussion to follow.

After the discussion, give students 5 min in class to comment in writing about how their ideas of relationship development changed as a result of the class discussion.

Variations

The following are two additional variations of the exercise suitable for any class format (e.g., seminar, lecture):

1. Have half of the students develop models of one type of relationship while other students develop models of another type. Possible relationship type comparisons include (a) close platonic friendships with romantic relationships, (b) cross-sex friendships with cross-sex romantic relationships, (c) same-sex friendships with cross-sex friendships, (d) same-sex romantic relationships with cross-sex romantic relationships, and (e) same-sex friendships with same-sex romantic relationships. In the class discussion, examine relationship type differences and similarities. Discuss possible causes of relationship type differences.

2. As a follow-up to the relationship development theory exercise, review major scholarly theories of relationship development with students. Then divide the class into small work groups and assign a scholarly theory to each group. Select one student's relationship development theory and instruct each group to revise this personal theory, tailoring it to their specific assigned scholarly theoretical orientation (e.g., social penetration or social exchange theory). Have a member of each group record the group's revision on an overhead transparency or on the chalkboard. In the discussion that follows, compare and contrast the different theory revisions. Explore the strengths and weaknesses of each scholarly model. Looking across all the different scholarly theories, what is understood about relationship development and what questions are left unanswered?

DISCUSSION   Most students initially greet this assignment with excitement, thinking that it is easy. Once they start developing their own theories, they realize that this is quite a challenging task. They begin to recognize the many variables involved and the many variations such factors create. Use this new awareness of the complexity of interpersonal relating to expose students to the vast terrain of the personal relationships field.

The five volunteers usually present varied theories; there will be similarities, disagreements, and unique ideas. The following are suggestions for guiding the discussion:

1. Begin the discussion by asking the class to comment on the five theories. Compare and contrast the theories. What are the features with which students agree or disagree?

2. Are the theories realistic portrayals of how romantic relationships develop and proceed? Or are they idealized and romanticized? How do the idealized theories reflect societal myths or fantasies (i.e., social scripts) about romantic relating (emphasis on passionate love, "conflict phobia," living "happily ever after")? What is the function of such social scripts? How do social scripts affect interpersonal relationships?

3. What interpersonal processes or qualities are reflected in the theories (e.g., attraction, trust, honesty, commitment)? Are they described in any detail or are they simply listed as unreflective or automatic responses? What is the function of such glib responses? In what order do various interpersonal processes or qualities occur in theories? For example, when does sexual interaction (if noted) occur? When does commitment occur? Many theories reflect a very fast-paced sequence in which sexual interaction and commitment come directly after attraction and meeting the partner. Discuss

such sequences in the context of the current social and sexual climate. How does such sequencing affect the later course of a relationship?

4. What interpersonal processes or qualities are absent from students' theories? Students often to not include communication (other than superficial chatting), conflict and the negotiation of conflict resolution strategies, relationship cognition (including active decision making about the course of the relationship or, future planning), or relationship maintenance strategies (most theories end with engagement or marriage without thought to processes or qualities necessary for maintaining a long-term relationship). Many theories do not include sexual interaction. Discuss with students their hesitation about including sexual interaction, societal taboos about direct communication about sexual interaction, and how such factors affect romantic relationships. For example, could such reticence be the root of sexual conflict or unwanted sexual activities in relationships?

5. What is the function of a theory in a field such as personal relationships? For decades, scholars have tried to develop models of how relationships develop and proceed. Identify the scholarly models most closely represented by students' theories (social penetration, social exchange, attraction-based, and individual developmental). In what ways could such models be useful for research and application? Should a relationship development model be an idealized model to which we should strive or a realistic model detailing the difficulties that often arise?

6. Explore individual differences in personal relationship development theories. For example, are there sex or race differences among students' theories? Is a universal model of romantic relationship development and progress possible? Is it useful? Should theories vary by age, cohort, gender, sexual orientation, ethnicity and race, health, socioeconomic status, geographic region within the United States, or nationality? How? Have scholarly theories considered such variation? How inclusive has personal relationships theory and research been?

WRITING COMPONENT

As noted earlier, this activity includes a two-stage writing component: First, students write creatively about romantic relationship development and, second, they are given a 5-min in-class reflection period during which they note in writing how their ideas about romantic relationship development have changed as a result of the class exercise. These short reaction papers can trigger further class discussion. They may also be collected for instructor commentary.

REFERENCES

Altman, I., & Taylor, D. A. (1973). *Social penetration: The development of interpersonal relationships.* New York: Holt, Rinehart & Winston.

Baxter, L. A. (1988). A dialectical perspective on communication strategies in relationship development. In S. Duck (Ed.), *Handbook of personal relationships* (pp. 257–273). New York: Wiley.

Berscheid, E., Dion, K., Walster, E., & Walster, G. W. (1971). Physical attractiveness and dating choice: A test of the matching hypothesis. *Journal of Experimental Social Psychology, 7,* 173–189.

Erikson, E. (1963). *Childhood and society.* New York: Norton.

Franz, C., & White, K. M. (1985). Individuation and attachment in personality development: Extending Erikson's theory. In A. Stewart & B. Lykes (Eds.), *Gender and personality*. Durham, NC: Duke University Press.

Hatfield, E., & Sprecher, S. (1986). *Mirror, mirror . . . The importance of looks in everyday life*. Albany: State University of New York Press.

Kerckhoff, A. C., & Davis, K. E. (1962). Value consensus and need complementarity in mate selection. *American Sociological Review, 27*, 295–303.

Levinger, G., & Huesmann, L. R. (1980). An "incremental exchange" perspective on the pair relationship: Interpersonal reward and level of involvement. In K. K. Gergen, M. S. Greenberg, & R. H. Williw (Eds.), *Social exchange: Advances in theory and research* (pp. 165–188). New York: Plenum Press.

Lewis, R. A. (1972). A developmental framework for the analysis of premarital dyadic formation. *Family Process, 11*, 17–48.

Murstein, B. I. (1976). The stimulus-value-role theory of marital choice. In H. Grunebaum & J. Christ (Eds.), *Contemporary marriage: Structures, dynamics, and therapy* (pp. 165–168). Boston: Little, Brown.

Murstein, B. I. (1987). A clarification and extension of the SVR theory of dyadic pairing. *Journal of Marriage and the Family, 49*, 929–933.

Paul, E. L., & White, K. M. (1990). The development of intimate relationships in late adolescence. *Adolescence, 25*, 375–400.

Reiss, I. L. (1960). Toward a sociology of the heterosexual love relationship. *Marriage and Family Living, 22*, 139–145.

Rusbult, C. E. (1983). A longitudinal test of the investment model: The development (and deterioration) of satisfaction and commitment in heterosexual involvement. *Journal of Personality and Social Psychology, 45*, 101–117.

Sullivan, H. S. (1953). *The interpersonal theory of psychiatry*. New York: Norton.

Thibaut, J. W., & Kelley, H. H. (1959). *The social psychology of groups*. New York: Wiley.

SUGGESTED READING

Duck, S. (Ed.). (1997). *Handbook of personal relationships: Theory, research and interventions* (2nd Ed.). Chichester, England, UK: Wiley.

Erber, R., & Gilmour, R. (Eds.). *Theoretical frameworks for personal relationships*. Hillsdale, NJ: Erlbaum.

Fletcher, G. J. O., & Fitness, J. (Eds.). (1996). *Knowledge structures in close relationships: A social psychological approach*. Mahwah, NJ: Erlbaum.

Perlman, D., & Fehr, B. (1987). The development of intimate relationships. In D. Perlman & S. Duck (Eds.), *Intimate relationships: Development, dynamics, and deterioration*. Newbury Park, CA: Sage.

70 Measuring Attitudes Toward Public Assistance

Peter S. Fernald
University of New Hampshire

L. Dodge Fernald
Harvard University

Students are administered a 16-item scale that measures attitudes toward public dependency—or, more specifically, toward individual initiative, self-reliance, and economic independence. Each student determines his or her individual score and anonymously submits it to the instructor, who calculates and announces the mean and range of the class. Referring to both the students' scores and other data, the instructor leads a discussion that addresses several topics: the nature of an attitude, measurement, the Likert method, response set, and the concepts of norms and scale validity. The scale identifies wide variations in attitudes that are highly relevant for contemporary times. The activity can be included in a unit on social behavior (especially attitudes) or measurement.

CONCEPTS   Eight concepts are considered: attitude, measurement, Likert method, response set, validity, norms, personality, and resistance to attitude change.

MATERIALS NEEDED   You will need the attitude scale shown in appendix A.

INSTRUCTIONS   Hand out a copy of the scale to each student and allow about 5 min for students to complete the scale. Then instruct the students to score their answers (an explanation of the lettered codes is presented in appendix A). Statements numbered 1, 4, 7, 9, 10, 11, 13, and 15 are scored in the following manner:

Response	SA	A	TA	TD	D	SD
Points	0	1	2	3	4	5

The other eight statements, numbers 2, 3, 5, 6, 8, 12, 14, and 16, identified by the period following SD, are scored in the opposite fashion as follows:

Response	SA	A	TA	TD	D	SD
Points	5	4	3	2	1	0

Lastly, indicate that the total score is the sum of the ratings for the 16 statements, and have students determine their respective total scores.

DISCUSSION   The discussion can be organized around six topics: the nature of an attitude, measurement, the Likert method, response set, the importance of norms, and validity of the scale. Depending on whether the class is the introductory, social, research methods, or testing course, these topics can be expanded or omitted to meet the instructor's goal.

Attitude

Indicate to the students that knowing the title of the scale sometimes influences a participant's responses, and, for this reason, you did not include the title on the handout containing the scale items. Then ask the students to describe in just a few words the attitude measured by the scale. Another way to address the issue is to ask, "What title would you give to this scale?" Students will describe the scale with great accuracy though they probably will not indicate the exact title. Point out that some of their brief descriptions would make good titles and that the actual title is public dependency scale. According to its originator, the scale is a measure of "general value orientations concerning individual initiative, self-reliance, and economic independence" (Anderson, 1965, p. 113).

Point out that an attitude always includes an evaluation, a judgment about whether an object or person, or some aspect of either, is good or bad. Then ask the class, "Do you think the public dependency scale accurately assesses your attitude toward public assistance?" In the discussion that follows, it is often appropriate to mention that an attitude has three components (beliefs, feelings, and actions), illustrated in the following questions: Do you believe public assistance programs encourage dependency? Do you have a positive or negative feeling about such programs? If you were financially destitute, would you accept public assistance?

Measurement

Tell the students that measurement involves comparisons and the systematic identification of differences. When measuring with a ruler, for example, one makes comparisons and notes differences. Even when two objects are declared identical in length, the conclusion of identical lengths is based on a comparison and the observation, "There is no difference."

With regard to the discipline of psychology, measurement refers to the identification of individual differences relating to any aspect of human nature. In the present case, the focus is on attitudes toward public assistance. Typically, the student's scores show a wide range, suggesting substantial individual differences in their attitudes toward public assistance.

The Likert Method

Point out to the class that numerous methods are used to measure attitudes and that the other paper-and-pencil method is the true–false format. Then ask the students, "Would you have preferred the true–false procedure?" Their answers to this question will lead to a discussion of the Likert method, which consists of a 7-point scale for each item. Ask the students what advantages the 7-point scale has over the 2 point (true–false) scale. If students conclude the 7-point scale is preferable to a 2-point scale, suggest that perhaps an 11- or 15-point scale would be even better. After obtaining their reactions to these scales, indicate that research, conducted by Likert in the early 1930s, established 7 points as the maximally efficient scale. With only 2 or 3 points, participants are not allowed sufficient choice. With 5 or more points, participants have more choices, but with more than 7 choices they become confused and their ratings are less reliable. The usual Likert scale has 7 points, the mid-point indicating neither agreement or disagreement. With no midpoint, the 6-point scale used to measure attitudes toward public dependency forces participants to indicate at least some small preference in one direction or the other.

Response Set

Mention that half of the items in the scale are stated positively; these items (numbers 2, 3, 5, 6, 8, 12, 14, 16) indicate a favorable attitude toward public assistance. The remaining items are stated negatively, expressing unfavorable attitudes toward public assistance. Ask the students why it is important to include both types of statements. This question will lead directly to a discussion of response sets, especially yea-saying and nay-saying.

The Importance of Norms

Address the concept of norms by asking the students, "Do you regard your score as high, medium, or low?" "What specifically do the terms *high, medium,* and *low* mean?" Some students may indicate that their scores are high or low on the basis of the frequency of scores of 0 and 1 or 6 and 7 they received. However, further questioning will reveal that they do not know for certain whether their scores are high, low, or average without knowing how others score on the scale, and herein lies the necessity for and importance of norms. More details regarding norms are considered in regard to the known-groups validation technique, discussed next. Before proceeding to the next part of the discussion, however, have students submit their scores anonymously on an unsigned slip of paper. Total their scores, and divide by the number of students to determine the class mean. Write the mean and range on the chalkboard. With these figures on the chalkboard, point out that a group's overall performance is readily indicated by measures of central tendency and variability—in this case the mean and range. As both a continuation of the discussion of norms and bridge to the subsequent discussion of validity, ask the class, "Does the mean score for this class suggest a liberal or conservative stance toward public dependency?"

Validity

Briefly describe (or review) the concept of validity, and then ask the students, "Do you think the scale is valid?" Whatever their answers, ask them to indicate their reasons. Then inform them that the investigator who constructed the scale attempted to answer the validity question by using the known-group validation technique, which consists of administering the scale to groups having known attitudes toward issues measured by the scale. The scale was administered to five groups, the names and descriptions of which are presented in the following chart. After naming and reading about these groups (and perhaps even writing the names and descriptions on the chalkboard), give the students the following instructions: "Indicate which group you would expect to score lowest (i.e., be least favorable to welfare programs) by placing 1 in the appropriate blank at the left, which group you would expect to score next lowest by marking 2 in the appropriate blank, and so on up to the group you would expect to score highest, which should receive a rating of 5."

_____ 200 Ohio State University students.
_____ 38 members of the Wyoming Farm Bureau Federation. Generally speaking, these are self-employed individuals who reside in rural areas that are removed from the welfare problems of urban centers.
_____ 50 applicants for public assistance living in Franklin County, Ohio.
_____ 42 Mormon farmers residing in southeastern Idaho. In many respects, these individuals resemble members of the Wyoming Farm Bureau Federation. Mormon theology emphasizes welfare services, but such services are regarded as a church responsibility rather than a public one.
_____ 52 Mormons residing in Columbus, Ohio. These individuals differ from the Idaho Mormons in that they are in close contact with urban problems.

The rankings, top to bottom, should be 4, 1, 5, 2, 3, which is as the investigator predicted (Anderson, 1965). This finding supports the validity of the scale. The mean scores for the five groups were as follows:

Groups	Mean Score
Wyoming Farm Bureau Federation members	20.4
Idaho Mormons	31.1
Columbus Mormons	33.8
Ohio State University students	40.6
Franklin County welfare applicants	52.6

The question raised earlier concerning the stance of the class—liberal, moderate, or conservative—toward public dependency is readily answered when one knows how other groups have scored. By comparing scores, one can infer that the attitudes of the class regarding public dependency are similar to those of high-scoring Franklin welfare applicants or those of low-scoring Wyoming Farm Bureau Federation members, or somewhere in between, whatever the case may be. Thus, in addition to indicating the validity of a scale, known groups also provide norms that may be used in interpreting scores.

Another option is to consider the concept of reliability. The scale could be administered twice, with several weeks intervening between administrations. This arrangement would establish a context for discussing both the reliability of the scale and the stability of attitudes. Research studies indicate that the scale has a high degree of reliability and validity (Anderson, 1965).

Perspective

Point out that the scale measures a general attitude and therefore provides only general information. More specific and perhaps more useful information about people's attitudes toward public dependency could be obtained by designing scales that assess attitudes toward particular programs and specific aspects of the programs.

WRITING COMPONENT

Because they know how their individual scores compare with those of their classmates and also with the groups mentioned, you might ask students to write a brief statement indicating whether they regard themselves as holding a liberal, moderate, or conservative view of public assistance programs. They should answer this question: "Why do you categorize yourself as you do?" To illustrate the findings that attitudes generally are highly resistant to change, you might also ask the students to write out an answer to this question: "What would it take, or what would need to happen, for your attitude to become distinctly more liberal (or conservative)?" Given the data at hand, students have little difficulty writing out their answers to the first question. Their difficulty answering the second question can lead to a discussion of their resistance to attitude change.

Another possibility is to ask students to define, compare, and contrast the concepts of attitude and personality trait. Give them, at most, 5 min to write. The discussion should include the following points.

- A personality trait is a constellation of thoughts, feelings, and behavior that are consistent over time and situations. The person exemplifying the trait of introversion, for example, keeps most thoughts and feelings to him- or herself, does not interact frequently with others, and behaves in this manner in most situations and from one time to the next. Also, traits typically are neutral. Introversion is no better or worse than extroversion or ambiversion.

- The concept of attitude does not emphasize consistency over time and situations. Rather, the emphasis is on evaluation, on whether something or someone is perceived as good, bad, or indifferent. We ask someone, "What is your attitude toward X?" When we do so, we actually are asking more specific questions: Do you believe X is a good (bad) thing? Would you be disappointed (happy) if you did not have X? Would you work hard to have more (less) X in your life? Attitudes always include judgments of good (*liking*) and bad (*disliking*).

REFERENCE

Anderson, C. L. (1965). Development of an objective measure of orientation toward public dependence. *Social Forces, 44,* 107–113.

SUGGESTED READING

Eagly, A. H., & Chaiken, S. (1993). *The psychology of attitudes.* Fort Worth, TX: Harcourt Brace.

Kraus, S. J. (1995). Attitudes and the prediction of behavior: A meta-analysis of the empirical literature. *Personality and Social Psychology Bulletin, 21,* 58–75.

Likert, R. A. (1932). A technique for the measurement of attitudes. *Archives of Psychology, 20*(140).

Schuman, H., & Katlan, G. (1985). Survey methods. In G. Lindsey & E. Aronson (Eds.), *Handbook of social psychology* (3rd ed.). New York: Random House.

Appendix A

Attitude Toward Public Dependency

Below are 16 statements pertaining to an important social problem. As you read each statement, decide to what extent you agree or disagree with it, then circle the appropriate letter in the left-hand margin. The letters are defined as follows:

SA strongly agree   TD tend to disagree
A   agree   D   disagree
TA tend to agree   SD strongly disagree

SA A TA TD D SD   1. Public assistance programs have gone too far in this country.

SA A TA TD D SD   2. Public assistance to the dependent adult encourages him or her to become independent.

SA A TA TD D SD   3. Very few dependent adults are getting something for nothing.

SA A TA TD D SD   4. Public aid makes people rely less on their own efforts.

SA A TA TD D SD   5. Most people on public assistance are needy, not greedy.

SA A TA TD D SD   6. Most dependent adults desire independence.

SA A TA TD D SD   7. Public assistance kills the spark in individuals that made this country great.

SA A TA TD D SD   8. Most dependent adults really deserve public assistance.

SA A TA TD D SD   9. Dependence on public assistance becomes a habit.

SA A TA TD D SD   10. The dependent adult is too willing to receive help from others.

SA A TA TD D SD   11. Public assistance to the dependent adult kills initiative for self-support.

SA A TA TD D SD   12. If I became dependent, I would expect help from public agencies.

SA A TA TD D SD   13. Public assistance programs are serving to weaken the backbone of our nation.

SA A TA TD D SD   14. Most of those who accept assistance from a public agency do so as a last resort.

SA A TA TD D SD   15. Most dependent adults would rather receive relief than work.

SA A TA TD D SD   16. The dependent adult is usually dependent because he or she "has to be," not because he or she "wants to be."

Adapted from "Development of an Objective Measure of Orientation Toward Public Dependence," by C. L. Anderson, 1965, *Social Forces, 44,* pp. 107–113. Used by permission.

71 PERSONAL SPACE INVASION

Robert Sommer

University of California, Davis

This activity acquaints students with the form and dimensions of the personal space bubble. Working in pairs, students invade each other's space. Experimental conditions include front versus side invasions and eyes open versus eyes closed. Class discussion emphasizes spatial behavior as a form of nonverbal communication.

CONCEPT Personal space is the emotionally charged zone around the human body. Often compared to a bubble, snail shell, or body buffer zone, it does not resemble a perfect circle, but is more like an hourglass with smaller dimensions at the sides than in front. Personal space plays an important role in maintaining privacy. Cultural, social, and situational differences in the size of the personal space zone can be demonstrated through simulated invasions.

MATERIALS NEEDED You will need a classroom with open space at the sides or front or a combination of spaces that allows students to work in pairs. A hallway, corridor, or lounge can be used, or outside space if the weather is suitable. You also will need a written instruction sheet for half the students, which includes a centimeter scale (0 to 25 cm) on one side to measure distances (appendix A). Each student should have a pencil or pen.

INSTRUCTIONS Divide the class into pairs according to a random system (for example, passing out numbers containing pairs to the class) or employ a representative sampling plan intended to yield a certain percentage of female–female, male–male, and female–male pairs. Facilitate the pairings, making sure that no students are left out. You will need to become a participant if the class has an odd number of students. After pairing, students move to locations where the invasions can be staged. The instruction sheet in appendix A is self-explanatory.

DISCUSSION Following the sessions, which take about 5 to 10 min, have the class reassemble. Begin the discussion by asking open-ended questions about students' reactions to the exercise—for example, how did they feel invading another person's space and having their own space invaded? Did they notice any pattern in the distances used? These are followed by specific questions relating to variables that have been found to influence interaction distance.

Typically, distances will be longer in front than at the sides and greater when the partner has eyes open rather than eyes closed. This is the time to discuss the role of cultural, gender, friendship, height, and other variables that influence interaction distance. Previous research has shown that individuals from Latin cultures often have small interaction distances—that is, they sit and stand closer—than do people from Anglo-Saxon cultures. Interesting effects materialize when people are paired with others from different ethnic groups. In general, people stand closer to those like them and farther away from those who differ from them. Gender affects distance in complex ways. Female–female pairs tend to have smaller interaction distances than male–male pairs, and the distance between female–male pairs depends on the relationship between the pair. Tall height and bright clothing increase interaction distance, whereas sunglasses, similar to the eyes-closed condition, decrease distance (Bell, Fisher, Baum, & Greene, 1996; Gifford, 1997; Sommer, 1969). A status difference is also likely to increase interaction distance (Rosenfeld, Giacalone, & Kennedy, 1987).

This is also an opportunity to discuss the theoretical basis of personal space. Hall (1959) described interpersonal distance as a form of nonverbal communication, a means by which we indicate our interest or lack of it in other people. The concept has also been viewed developmentally according to social learning theory with children learning spacing rules from their parents, initially through nonverbal means, such as a frown or raised voice when the child stands too close or too far away, and later through explicit instructions—for example, the admonition to "stay away from strangers." Researchers have found that childrens' interpersonal distance increases with age and by puberty tends to resemble that of adults (Burgess, 1983). Others see personal space as a form of self-protection, as a way to reduce emotional or physical threats, or simply as a means to protect one's privacy (Altman, 1975).

The ethics of invading people's space in public locations can be explored with the class. Experimental invasions have been staged in elevators, libraries, parks, sports dressing rooms, and many other settings. People whose space has been invaded typically leave sooner than control participants. The ethical issues in invading the space of people who did not consent to participate in a psychological experiment should be discussed with students.

WRITING COMPONENT These writing assignments are not a necessary part of the exercise, but they can complement class discussion by focusing student attention on space use in other contexts and by training students to interpret space as a silent language in social interaction (Hall, 1959). Systematic analysis of space use can be a valuable tool in cross-cultural research where interaction distance can be recorded without knowing the language.

Have students collect and analyze the data obtained in class and write a paper in APA style comparing interaction distance in front and at the sides for both the eyes-open and eyes-closed conditions, with groups classified as female–female, male–male, female–male.

Another exercise would be to assign students to write an essay describing their responses to invading someone else's space and having their own space invaded. Tell students to imagine doing this to a stranger and having a stranger invade the student's space. Students should describe how the exercise influenced their awareness of space as a variable in social interaction.

Have students visit a park, lounge, or other public location and interpret the social relationships among the people present based on their spatial locations. Students can describe the cues that influenced their interpretations. Ask students to observe how the body language of people sitting or standing alone differs from that of people in groups.

Invite students to visit a playground and describe group structure based only on what they can observe. They should be sure to notice groupings of children according to age, gender, ethnicity, and other factors.

Ask students to draw a diagram of social relationships among people in the student union or library based on where and with whom people are sitting. Tell students to notice patterns relating to gender, activity (studying and not studying), and ethnicity.

REFERENCES

Altman, I. (1975). *Environment and social behavior.* Pacific Grove, CA: Brooks/Cole.

Bell, P. A., Fisher, J. D., Baum, A., & Greene, T. C. (1996). *Environmental psychology* (4th ed.). Fort Worth, TX: Harcourt Brace.

Burgess, J. W. (1983). Developmental trends in proxemic spacing behavior between surrounding companions and strangers in casual groups. *Journal of Nonverbal Behavior, 7,* 158–169.

Gifford, R. (1997). *Environmental psychology* (2nd ed.). Boston: Allyn & Bacon.

Hall, E. T. (1959). *The silent language.* New York: Doubleday.

Rosenfeld, P., Giacalone, R. A., & Kennedy, J. G. (1987). Of status and suits: Personal space invasions in an administrative setting. *Social Behavior and Personality, 15,* 97–99.

Sommer, R. (1969). *Personal space.* Englewood Cliffs, NJ: Prentice-Hall.

SUGGESTED READING

Aiello, J. R. (1987). Human spatial behavior. In D. Stokols & I. Altman (Eds.), *Handbook of environmental psychology* (pp. 389–504). New York: Wiley.

Bechtel, R. B. (1997). *Environment and behavior: An introduction.* Thousand Oaks, CA: Sage.

Appendix A

Measuring Personal Space

Put all belongings, notebooks, and so forth to one side. Have nothing in your hands.

1. Approach the person directly from the front until you feel that you are getting too close for comfort. Using the centimeter scale on this page, measure the distance nose to nose between you and the other person and record it here.

   _____ centimeters

2. Repeat the invasion, but approach the other person from the side. Your partner keeps looking ahead as you approach from the side. Stop when you feel you are getting too close for comfort. Measure and record the distance between your chest and his or her shoulder.

   _____ centimeters

3. Switch roles and now you remain stationary while your partner invades your space from the front. The partner should stop just before the distance becomes too close for comfort.

   _____ centimeters

4. Now your partner invades your space from the side. Measure the distance.

   _____ centimeters

5. The stationary person closes his or her eyes while the invader approaches from the front. The invader must decide where to stop for comfort's sake. Measure the distance nose to nose.

   _____ centimeters

6. Switch roles and repeat the procedure in Number 5. Record the nose-to-nose distance.

   _____ centimeters

Note to instructor: Centimeter "ruler" not to scale. Before distributing to students photocopy a ruler that is to scale and instruct students accordingly.

72 THE MARLBORO COWBOY VERSUS THE SURGEON GENERAL: WHO IS WINNING THE WAR ON SMOKING?

Tami Eggleston
McKendree College
Frederick X. Gibbons
Iowa State University

This demonstration allows students to examine the psychological principles used in smoking advertisements. By answering questions regarding the images portrayed in these advertisements, students examine the tobacco companies' attempts to portray smoking as an attractive, exciting, and positive activity. In addition, students evaluate the effectiveness of the surgeon general's warnings.

CONCEPT

This activity is used to examine the content of smoking advertisement images and the attempts of the surgeon general to counter their effects. The activity fosters the discussion of attitudes, stereotypes, and the assessment of theories such as the health belief model.

MATERIALS NEEDED

Assign reading on attitude change or health psychology from your introductory textbook prior to the demonstration. You will also need a number of smoking advertisements from old newspapers or magazines: every small group will need three to five advertisements to assess. Given the number of advertisements needed, you may want to have students collect their own. Students will also need a copy of the handout (see appendix A).

INSTRUCTIONS

Preparation

Social psychologists have found that the social images or prototypes that young people associate with certain behaviors can influence their participation in those behaviors. This is especially true for behaviors involving some health risk, such as smoking and drinking, because they are primarily social activities. Compared to adults, young people are much less likely to drink or smoke alone. Adolescents who possess a favorable image of what the advertisements portray as the typical smoker or drinker, for example, are more likely to start smoking or drinking (especially with their friends) than individuals who hold a less favorable image (Gibbons & Gerrard, 1995). Conversely, having a negative image is associated with a decline in smoking (Gibbons & Eggleston, 1996).

Several questions remain. What is the impact of advertising on the acquisition and development of these influential prototypes? The image receiving the most attention, from a marketing perspective, is that of the typical smoker. Millions of dollars are spent each year shaping and promoting the image that typical people, especially young people, smoke. This marketing strategy produced Joe Camel, the Marlboro Man, and Virginia Slims. Teens are the primary source of new smokers (*Consumer Reports*, 1995; Pierce & Gilpin, 1995).

Although smoking advertisements have been banned from television, they continue to appear in magazines and on billboards. Attempting to regulate the impact of smoking advertisements in print, the surgeon general required that a warning label be present in all cigarette advertisements and on cigarette packages. These warnings inform people of the dangers associated with smoking, offsetting the positive image the advertisers promote. Four different warning labels (see appendix A) are rotated to accompany the specific advertisement.

The Activity

After covering the preceding information in class and summarizing the attitude change or health psychology sections from the textbook, place students in small groups. Distribute the smoking advertisements and the handout. Allow students 15 min to write answers on the handout and examine and discuss the various advertisements before beginning the class discussion.

DISCUSSION   *Handout Tally*

Discuss the questions on the handout. List or tally the (a) types of people or activities portrayed in the smoking advertisements, (b) characteristics the people in the ad possess, (c) warning labels in the advertisements, (d) contradictions between the explicit (warning labels) and implicit (smoking is sexy and exciting) messages, and (e) rank order of the most effective warning labels. Students report favorable descriptions (attractive, young, exciting) of the people engaging in exciting, often risky, activities (e.g., riding horses, driving motorcycles). Students may also report that they can "see through" the ads, believing the ads will only affect others. This could lead into a discussion on the False Uniqueness Effect (Perloff & Brickman, 1982).

Warning Labels

Students may note that the warning contained in the advertisements often matches the readership of the magazine or the images contained in the advertisement. In other words, the advertisers may actually be engaging in *reverse-targeting*, a process whereby the least threatening warning is selected for the typical readership of the magazine. For example, pregnancy warnings are presented in magazines with (primarily) male readership. Carbon monoxide warnings are presented in advertisements depicting automobiles and motorcycles, suggesting that cigarettes do contain some carbon monoxide but ingesting cigarette smoke will not expose one to as much carbon monoxide as the reader's car or motorcycle emits.

Students also discover that the images portrayed in the advertisements often match the magazine's readership. Smoking race car drivers are found in magazines with a primarily male readership, whereas stylish female executives who smoke in an attempt at weight loss are found in magazines with a predominantly female readership. Many of the images associated with smoking that are shown in young women's magazines involve slim, attractive women with sayings such as "slim & sassy."

An interesting tangential discussion may result from evaluating the warning "Quitting Smoking Now Greatly Reduces Serious Risks to Your Health," which may be difficult to understand, especially for young readers. Written ambiguously, it implies that in the past it was not necessarily true that quitting smoking improved health, whereas quitting today (i.e., now) will be beneficial. It also seems likely that this warning, because of its encouraging message, does the least to diminish the impact of the positive images in the smoking advertisements.

Attitude Change

Determine the number of people who report that their attitudes changed after critically examining the advertisements. In general, people do not realize or acknowledge the impact that images have on their behavior. Prior to the demonstration, individuals will report that the warnings are quite effective. After critically examining the advertisements, students often reverse this opinion, finding the warnings less effective. Discussing the students' own attitude change provides a transition into the persuasion literature. For example, discussion could focus on persuasion techniques described in the elaboration likelihood model (ELM). These techniques include peripheral cues such as having an attractive, popular, exciting person as the source of communication (Petty & Cacioppo, 1986). Ask students the following questions:

1. How do the advertisements attempt to change opinions?
2. How effective are these efforts likely to be?
3. What psychological processes involving attitude change and persuasion can you identify?

Use this demonstration to illustrate the ELM at work. Mention that advertisements are usually viewed quickly, using a peripheral route. In class, the mere process of examining the advertisements critically will switch students from peripheral route to the central route, thereby changing their attitudes or opinions of the message.

This demonstration fits in with the health section of the textbook, especially within the context of the health belief model (Janz & Becker, 1984). Focus discussion on the following questions:

1. Which warnings are most likely to emphasize serious health threats (i.e., severity)?
2. What benefits and pleasures are emphasized in the ads?
3. What benefits of smoking are implied in the warnings?
4. Based on the health belief model, do you think adolescents who view these advertisements would see more benefits or barriers to smoking? Would adolescents view the warning labels differently? Why?

Other psychological phenomena discussed in conjunction with this demonstration include dissonance and illusions of invulnerability. Explain how dissonance can be reduced by changing the behavior (i.e., by stopping smoking) or cognitions (e.g., by reducing the risk perceptions; Gibbons, Eggleston, & Benthin, 1997). A discussion emphasizing adolescents' illusions of invulnerability to the negative consequences that accompany smoking is recommended.

Variations

The entire demonstration could be done on an individual basis. For very large classes, have students complete the handout individually and summarize some of the interesting results. Have students respond to the handout, answer the key discussion questions, and evaluate one smoking advertisement on their own time.

Students could also assess the advertising techniques used in other domains. For example, the images associated with alcohol use are quite similar to those presented in smoking advertisements. In addition, there currently is a great deal of publicity to promote meat products ("Beef: It's what's for dinner") and milk (celebrities with milk mustaches). Many of the same psychological principles are used in these advertisements as in the smoking advertisements.

WRITING COMPONENT

Add the following three questions to the demonstration to provide closure and creative writing opportunities. Students can turn in their answers or use them as journal entries (if a journal format is being used in the class).

1. If you became president of a large tobacco company, what type of ad and warning label would you recommend for your company?
2. If you became the surgeon general, what type of ad and warning label would you recommend? Would the target audience (males, adolescents, etc.) make a difference in your decision? Why?
3. What are the ethical and professional dilemmas of advertising? Given the evidence of media influence, what psychological versus capitalistic questions are raised by allowing the advertising of potentially dangerous products? What dilemma does this raise for psychologists hired by tobacco companies and other potential health-risk industries to promote their products?

REFERENCES

Consumer Reports. (1995, March). Hooked on tobacco: The teen epidemic.

Gibbons, F. X., & Eggleston, T. J. (1996). Smoker networks and the "typical smoker": A prospective analysis of smoking cessation. *Health Psychology, 15,* 469–477.

Gibbons, F. X., Eggleston, T. J., & Benthin, A. (1997). Cognitive reactions to smoking relapse: The reciprocal relation of dissonance and self-esteem. *Journal of Personality and Social Psychology, 72,* 184–195.

Gibbons, F. X., & Gerrard, M. (1995). Predicting young adults' health risk behavior. *Journal of Personality and Social Psychology, 69,* 505–517.

Janz, N. K., & Becker, M. H. (1984). The health belief model: A decade later. *Health Education Quarterly, 11,* 1–47.

Perloff, L. S., & Brickman, P. (1982). False consensus and false uniqueness: Biases in perceptions of similarity. *Academic Psychology Bulletin, 4,* 475–494.

Petty, R. E., & Cacioppo, J. T. (1986). The elaboration likelihood model of persuasion. In L. Berkowitz (Ed.), *Advances in experimental social psychology, 19,* 123–205. New York: Academic Press.

Pierce, J. P., & Gilpin, E. A. (1995). A historical analysis of tobacco marketing and the uptake of smoking by youth in the United States: 1890–1977. *Health Psychology, 14,* 500–508.

SUGGESTED READING

Consumer Reports. (1995, May). Selling to school kids, 327–329.

Fischer, M. D., Schwartz, M. P., Richards, J. W., Goldstein, A. O., & Rojas, T. H. (1991). Brand logo recognition by children aged 3 to 6 years (Mickey Mouse and Old Joe the Camel). *JAMA, 266*(22), 3145–3148.

Lane, S. M. (1993). Marketing cigarettes to kids: A consumer guide to the harmful tactics of tobacco companies. *A Special Report from the American Council on Science and Health* (April).

Steinem, G. (1990, July/August). Sex, lies, and advertising. *Ms.,* 18–28.

Appendix A

Handout

Before answering the questions about your specific smoking advertisement, please answer the following two questions individually.

1. How much impact do you think the media has on establishing positive images in people's minds (e.g., a positive image of the typical smoker)?

$$1 \quad 2 \quad 3 \quad 4 \quad 5 \quad 6 \quad 7$$

no impact   a great amount of impact

2. How effective do you think the surgeon general's warning labels have been in reminding people of the negative consequences of smoking?

$$1 \quad 2 \quad 3 \quad 4 \quad 5 \quad 6 \quad 7$$

not at all effective   very effective

Using your smoking advertisement(s), answer the following questions:

1. From what magazine did you get your smoking advertisement?
2. What type of readership does this magazine have (e.g., men, teenagers)?
3. What type of person or activity is portrayed in the smoking advertisement?
4. What types of traits (adjectives, descriptors) come to mind when you look at this advertisement?
5. Would the activity or person in the advertisement appeal to the readership of this magazine? Why or why not?
6. What warning label is in your advertisement?
7. Rank order the following four warning labels from 1 (most effective in preventing smoking) to 4 (least effective in preventing smoking):
   _____ a. Cigarette smoke contains carbon monoxide.
   _____ b. Smoking by pregnant women may result in fetal injury, premature birth, and low birth weight.
   _____ c. Smoking causes lung cancer, heart disease, emphysema, and may complicate pregnancy.
   _____ d. Quitting smoking now greatly reduces serious risks to your health.
8. Do you think the warning is appropriate or effective for the readers of the particular magazine?
9. What general impressions do you have of either the advertisement or warning label?

After you have assessed some smoking advertisements, please answer the following questions individually.

1. How much impact do you think the media has on establishing positive images in people's minds (e.g., a positive typical smoker image)?

   1   2   3   4   5   6   7

   no impact   a great amount of impact

2. How effective do you think the surgeon general's warning labels have been in reminding people of the negative consequences of smoking?

   1   2   3   4   5   6   7

   not at all effective   very effective

3. Do you think age of the reader is a factor in determining the impact of the ad?
4. Did your attitudes about advertisements and warning labels change? Explain your answer. Did your attitudes toward smoking change?
5. Do you think your classmates' attitudes about advertisements, warning labels, and smoking have changed?

73 Tom Sawyer: The Fence and Social Psychology

Alan Feldman
Perth Amboy High School, New Jersey

Rebecca Lafleur
Beaver College

In this activity, students read a short passage from the novel The Adventures of Tom Sawyer *and explain how it demonstrates the relationship between behavior and attitudes, specifically focusing on the social psychological concepts of cognitive dissonance, self-perception, overjustification, and reframing. They then write an original story that demonstrates a similar reframing motif.*

CONCEPT

Students often have difficulty understanding abstract social psychological concepts. This activity encourages them to move beyond passive text-reading by having them actively apply what they have learned in class to a piece of fiction. Students will have the opportunity to demonstrate their understanding of particular social psychological concepts by analyzing a passage from the novel *The Adventures of Tom Sawyer* by Mark Twain.

MATERIALS NEEDED

Students will need a copy of the passage from *The Adventures of Tom Sawyer* included in appendix A or all of chapter 2 of the novel. Note that the full text of this book is available on the World Wide Web. Just search the title.

INSTRUCTIONS

This activity can be used in an introduction to psychology class and in social psychology classes after students have completed the unit on attitudes and behavior. One explanation for how people's behavior guides their attitudes is the theory of cognitive dissonance, which holds that whenever a person has two conflicting thoughts, beliefs, or ideas, he or she experiences an uncomfortable state of arousal (dissonance). That individual is then motivated to reduce this dissonance by altering thinking or behavior. An alternative explanation for why behavior guides attitudes is self-perception: We infer our attitudes from our behavior, much as an observer would. Specific examples of this concept include overjustification (when people are rewarded for something that they previously performed out of intrinsic motivation, they end up liking that activity less) and the foot-in-the-door technique (people are more likely to comply with a large request if they have first complied with a small request).

Once you have presented these concepts in class, students read the brief passage from *The Adventures of Tom Sawyer* in which Tom persuades his friend Ben to help him paint a fence by reframing it as a fun activity rather than work. This passage was selected because it demonstrates the social psychological concepts described earlier. For example, Ben experiences cognitive dissonance because his beliefs that "Painting is work" and "Work is not fun" are inconsistent with his observation that Tom seems to be enjoying the task. Therefore, he is motivated to change his beliefs by reframing the activity of painting as "fun" rather than "work."

Alternatively, this scenario could be explained by self-perception and perception of motivation. As Ben begins to help Tom paint the fence, he observes his own behavior and the situations under which it is occurring: "I'm painting this fence, and I'm not getting paid to do it." Based on these observations, he then infers his attitudes toward the activity of fence-painting: "I guess I must be painting the fence because painting is fun and enjoyable."

During class, have students discuss how the passage demonstrates each of these concepts as well as the differences between the related concepts of cognitive dissonance and self-perception. Ask questions such as "What do you think would have happened if Tom offered to pay his friends to help him paint the fence? What would their attitudes toward painting be?" "At what point in the passage does Ben start to experience cognitive dissonance?" and "What techniques of persuasion and compliance does Tom use to get his friend to help him paint the fence?" Overall, the activity should take about 20 to 30 min but can easily be expanded or shortened depending on time constraints.

| DISCUSSION | This activity has worked especially well in small classes in which all students are able to participate actively in the discussion. In larger classes, it is beneficial first to divide the students into small groups of four or five and provide them with focused discussion questions pertaining to the passage from *Tom Sawyer* and the link between behavior and attitudes. After this discussion, students can report back to the rest of the class their reactions and responses to the passage. The activity is particularly useful at illuminating the distinctions between the theories of cognitive dissonance and self-perception, and it allows students to discuss amongst themselves which theory they find more convincing. |

One of the advantages of the task is that it can be modified to meet the needs of different instructors. For example, in addition to a class discussion, it can easily be used as a test question, a take-home essay, or as an introduction to a unit on attitudes and behavior.

WRITING COMPONENT

As a follow-up assignment to this activity, students can engage in one of several writing exercises. For example, have students write an original story that has a similar reframing theme. They can then indicate which social psychological principles are demonstrated in their story.

An alternative would be to have students write an essay that shows how politicians, parents, or psychotherapists often try to reframe situations to achieve a certain outcome.

SUGGESTED READING

Aronson, E. (1995). *The social animal* (6th ed.). New York: W. H. Freeman.
Myers, D. (1996). *Social psychology* (5th ed.). New York: McGraw-Hill.
Twain, M. (1987). *The adventures of Tom Sawyer*. New York: Viking Press.
Watzlawick, P. (1990). *Munchausen's pigtail*. New York: Norton.

Appendix A

Excerpt from *The Adventures of Tom Sawyer* by Mark Twain

Tom surveyed his last touch with the eye of an artist; then he gave his brush another gentle sweep and surveyed the result, as before. Ben ranged up alongside of him. Tom's mouth watered for the apple, but he stuck to his work. Ben said:

"Hello, old chap, you got to work, hey?"

Tom wheeled suddenly and said: "Why it's you Ben! I warn't noticing."

"Say—I'm going in a swimming, I am. Don't you wish you could? But of course you'd druther work—wouldn't you? Course you would!"

Tom contemplated the boy a bit, and said: "What do you call work?"

"Why ain't that work?"

Tom resumed his whitewashing, and answered carelessly: "Well, maybe it is, and maybe it ain't. All I know, is, it suits Tom Sawyer."

"Oh come, now, you don't mean to let on that you like it?"

The brush continued to move.

"Like it? Well I don't see why I oughtn't to like it. Does a boy get a chance to whitewash a fence every day?"

That put the thing in a whole new light. Ben stopped nibbling his apple. Tom swept his brush daintily back and forth—stepped back to note the effect—added a touch here and there—criticized the effect again—Ben watching every move and getting more and more interested, more and more absorbed. Presently he said:

"Say, Tom, let me whitewash a little."

Tom considered, was about to consent; but he altered his mind: "No—no—I reckon it wouldn't hardly do, Ben. You see, Aunt Polly's awful particular about this fence—right here on the street, you know—but if it was the back fence I wouldn't mind and she wouldn't. Yes, she's awful particular about this fence; it's got to be done very careful; I reckon there ain't one boy in a thousand, maybe two thousand, that can do it the way it's got to be done."

"No—is that so? Oh come, now—lemme just try. Only just a little—I'd let you, if it was me Tom."

"Ben, I'd like to, honest injun; but Aunt Polly—well Jim wanted to do it, but she wouldn't let him; Sid wanted to do it, and she wouldn't let Sid. Now don't you see how I'm fixed? If you was to tackle this fence and anything was to happen to it—"

"Oh, shucks, I'll be just as careful. Now lemme try. Say—I'll give you the core of my apple."

"Well, here—. No, Ben, now don't. I'm afeared—"

"I'll give you all of it!"

Tom gave up the brush with reluctance in his face but alacrity in his heart. And while the late steamer "Big Missouri" worked and sweated in the sun, the retired artist sat on a barrel in the shade close by, dangled his legs, munched his apple, and planned the slaughter of more innocents.

74 AGGRESSION ON TELEVISION

Margaret A. Lloyd

Georgia Southern University

In this activity, students view an aggressive and a nonaggressive television program outside of class, record the frequency of aggressive acts depicted in both programs, and compare their findings from the two programs. Students discuss their findings in small groups. In the full-class discussion, the instructor uses the activity to introduce the topic of media violence. This activity is suitable for introductory psychology, psychology of adjustment, social psychology, and developmental psychology.

CONCEPT

This activity increases student awareness of aggressive behavior on television. Students also get to "do psychology" by recording a specific social behavior outside of class. The class discusses its findings, which leads to an introduction of the topic of media violence and its effects on human behavior.

MATERIALS NEEDED

Students will need access to a television, a data summary sheet (see appendix A), and a pencil. Access to a videotape recorder is recommended, but not essential. Written instructions (see below) are advised, but oral instructions can be substituted.

INSTRUCTIONS

This activity is conducted in two phases: an out-of-class, data-gathering phase and a subsequent in-class discussion phase. To conduct the activity, prepare a handout that describes the purpose of the activity and details the instructions (presented next). Distribute two copies of the data summary sheet.

Out-of-Class Phase: Instructions to Students

Decide whether you want to watch two children's or two adult programs. Under whichever category you choose, select two programs to view. One should be a program you expect to contain a lot of aggression; the other should be one you expect to contain relatively little aggression. For example, if you decide to watch children's programs, you might compare *Sesame Street* or *Mr. Rogers' Neighborhood* (nonaggressive programs) with a *Road Runner* cartoon (aggressive program). If you want to view adult programs, you might compare a situation comedy (nonaggressive program) with a detective show (aggressive program).

Using one of the data summary sheets, review and become familiar with the various types of physical and verbal aggression. Next, practice recording the various aggressive behaviors by viewing a sample program for 5 to 15 min. Use a hash mark to note each instance of aggression, recording in pencil so you can reuse the form. This practice run will familiarize you with the different categories of physical and verbal aggression and increase the accuracy of your recording.

When you are ready, view each program for 30 min (1 hr total), recording the aggressive acts on the data summary sheet. If you can, videotape the two segments; this will make observation and recording easier. (*Note:* You will be comparing your findings with those of other students; to ensure that the data are comparable, record exactly 30 min of each program.)

When you have finished recording the data on your sheet, convert your hash marks to actual numbers. Total the numbers and calculate the percentages as indicated. Write the titles of the two programs you watched within the parentheses at the top of each column.

Complete the writing assignment on the reverse side of the data summary sheet (see the Writing Component section). Make yourself a copy of your findings to use in the classroom discussion, and bring both copies of your data recording sheet to class on the date your instructor requests.

In-Class Phase

Collect one copy of the data summary sheets on the date specified, setting them aside for grading. (How you choose to use these is, of course, optional.) Next, divide students into groups of four to six, where results (using the other copy of the data summary sheet) will be shared.

Your instructions to students for the small group activity will vary depending on your goals for the students and how much time you want to devote to the activity. A relatively simple option is to ask them share their findings with each other, look for similarities and differences among the findings, and talk about what stood out for them.

A more complex option involves distributing a blank data summary sheet to each group and asking someone in each group to record the findings of the other members for "total physical and verbal acts" for the aggressive programs, non-aggressive programs, and both programs. While students are doing this, write on the chalkboard three parallel headings (*aggressive programs, nonaggressive programs,* and *both programs*); if you do not want to take the time to calculate percentages, you do not need the last column. When the groups have finished collating their data, ask each group to call out the total physical and verbal acts while you record the data under the appropriate columns. When all groups have reported, tabulate the total frequencies under each column (and calculate the percentages if you wish) and summarize the findings for the class.

Regardless of the option you choose, bring the small group to a close after about 15 min. Point out that the data-gathering activity was not a controlled study, but that the results generally parallel those found by professional researchers—in other words, that there is a high degree of violence on television programs, including children's programs. Pose the question of why psychologists (and parents) are interested in the issue of aggression on television. Students usually respond with something like "Because it causes children to be aggressive" or "Because it contributes to the high level of aggression in the United States." This raises the question of the role of media violence in aggressive behavior. From here, talk about the importance of gathering empirical data (versus speculation) on the effects of televised aggression. Review the results of relevant empirical studies (Geen, 1991; Geen & Thomas, 1988; Huesmann & Eron, 1984; Wood, Wong, & Chacere, 1991).

DISCUSSION   Because students can select programs of interest to them, they are especially interested in the results of the activity. Students enjoy exchanging their findings and views with others in the small-group discussion. Many students are surprised at the amount of aggression on television and the frequency with which it occurs in situational comedies and in some children's programs. Of course, some programs contain relatively little violence (i.e., several educational television programs), and it is helpful to mention some of these.

WRITING COMPONENT

The activity can be used to help students learn to translate numerical data into meaningful verbal statements. Include the following statements on the reverse side of the data summary sheet:

Using complete sentences, state whether you observed any difference in aggressive behavior between the two programs with regard to (a) total physical acts, (b) total verbal acts, and (c) total physical and verbal acts. Use the percentage data in your summary sheet to support your conclusions. (*Note:* Be prepared to assist students who have difficulty remembering how to compute percentages or who have difficulty translating their numerical findings into words.)

Comment on anything noteworthy you observed that the numerical data did not reveal.

REFERENCES

Geen, R. G. (1991). Behavioral and psychological reactions to observed violence: Effects of prior exposure to aggressive stimuli. *Journal of Personality and Social Psychology, 40,* 868–875.

Geen, R. G., & Thomas, S. L. (1988). The immediate effects of media violence on behavior. In L. R. Huesmann & N. M. Malamuth (Eds.), *Journal of Social Issues, 42*(3), 7–27.

Huesmann, L. R., & Eron, L. D. (1984). Cognitive processes and the persistence of aggressive behavior. *Aggressive Behavior, 10,* 243–251.

Wood, W., Wong, F. Y., & Chacere, J. G. (1991). Effects of media violence on viewers' aggression in unconstrained social interaction. *Psychological Bulletin, 109,* 371–383.

Appendix A

Aggression on Television: Data Summary Sheet

Type of Program _____

Types of aggressive acts	Aggressive program ( )		Nonaggressive program ( )		Total incidents in both programs	
	f	%	f	%	f	%
Physical assaults with a weapon or object						
Physical assaults without a weapon or object						
Total physical acts						100%

Verbal threats of harm						
Derogatory or slanderous remarks						
Sarcastic or caustic comments						
Blaming others for own failures						
Critical verbal remarks						
Other:						
Total verbal acts						100%
Total physical and verbal acts						100%

75 Using Negotiation and Mediation to Resolve Disputes

Elizabeth V. Swenson
John Carroll University

■ —————————————————————————————— ■

This dynamic learning activity allows students to participate in the negotiation and then the mediation of a dispute between friends about a house party. The conflict involves financial responsibility for damage to property. Groups of two students negotiate settlements followed by a teacher-guided mediation between the two students who were most successful in their negotiations.

■ —————————————————————————————— ■

CONCEPT   This activity demonstrates mediation and negotiation, two alternative dispute resolution (sometimes referred to as ADR) techniques applied to resolve conflicts. With increasing frequency parties to a dispute are turning to gentler methods of conflict resolution that emphasize reasonable cooperation over the more traditional adversarial approach.

MATERIALS NEEDED   You will need to duplicate enough copies of Kelly's Perspective (appendix A) and Taylor's Perspective (appendix B) so that every student can be provided with one or the other.

INSTRUCTIONS   *Negotiation*

The first part of this activity involves negotiating the settlement of a dispute. In a preceding class session, explain the negotiation process, paying particular attention to the need for negotiating parties to identify common interests and discover creative solutions. Students will now have an opportunity to apply this process to a hypothetical case in which a house party has caused property damage.

Divide the class into pairs to negotiate this dispute. To avoid spending too much time on the physical arrangements, ask students to work with the person sitting in the next seat, as long as this person is not a close friend.

One student in each pair is given the Kelly's Perspective handout (Appendix A), which contains the basic facts of the case and some additional information regarding Kelly's point of view. The final paragraph of the handout contains Kelly's best alternative to a negotiated agreement, or BATNA (Fisher, Ury, and Patton, 1991). The other student in the pair represents Taylor and is given the other handout (Appendix B). The last paragraph contains Taylor's BATNA. Students should keep the information in these last paragraphs secret from one another.

Students now find their own space and have 20 min to negotiate an acceptable resolution. While they are negotiating, attempt to circulate among all of the dyads. Because of the limited time, your only purposes will be to answer critical questions, defuse any high levels of anger, and remind intransigent negotiators of the need to negotiate in good faith.

Mediation

At the end of the allotted time, have each pair report the success of their negotiation. The "Kelly" who has the combination of the greatest amount of money and the most apology is identified, along with the "Taylor" who has been most successful in having Kelly agree to the least money and apology. The class could vote to decide this if the winners are not readily apparent. These two students are usually fully committed to their positions and feel proud of themselves for being the class winners. Now these two students (who are furthest apart in their expectations), are placed in a new situation in front of the class with the instructor acting as a mediator. It usually is not possible to fully mediate this dispute in the time remaining in the class, but the strategies that a mediator needs to use to deal with difficult positions can be illustrated.

In mediation, the mediator is a neutral third party who facilitates the resolution of the dispute by the opposing parties themselves. Begin the mediation with an explanation of the advantages of mediation to the parties so that they feel that their time will be well spent. Mediation, a private process, can decrease costs and eliminate adverse publicity while keeping the parties in control of the outcome. In the best circumstances, the parties will feel good enough about being able to work out their differences that they will be able to carry on a peaceful relationship after the resolution and both will feel that they have been successful. Set forth the ground rules for the mediation, which should stress the importance of good faith during the process.

Give each party an opportunity to state, without interruption, his or her own perspectives on the dispute and the issue to be resolved. Then ask each person to explain the point of view of the other person. Next, ask the parties to generate possible options for resolution, no matter how outlandish they may seem. With a scrupulous neutrality, you can use active listening and move the discussion along by reframing statements, asking open-ended questions, and suggesting alternatives. When there is any agreement, no matter how small, note this for the parties. As people begin to understand the perspectives of their opponents and the options for consensus, they often begin to soften their own positions. Even if the two parties make little progress in the time allowed, students will still see the use of mediation techniques.

DISCUSSION

This activity was designed to show negotiation and mediation in a short period of time. This is why the dispute in question emphasizes a monetary issue as opposed to one that is solely interpersonal. I find that a monetary dispute is less emotional and more factual in nature. It is also easier to compromise on the solution, and it is much simpler to select the student who has won the most and the student who has lost the least for the mediation round. The same principles can be applied to more complicated and ambiguous conflicts.

It is important to emphasize that disputes can often be resolved more quickly, less expensively, and with far less residual ill will by alternative dispute resolution than by litigation. Particularly within families or among friends, the added benefits of retaining a sense of control over one's life, maintaining important relationships, avoiding negative publicity, and resolving disputes cooperatively are powerful incentives to give negotiation or mediation a try.

Student response to this activity is enthusiastic. The major criticism is that the activity is too abbreviated and that the class must quickly move on to another topic. With more time available, one could build in more realism, but this activity demonstrates how negotiation and mediation can produce alternatives for resolving disputes.

REFERENCES

Fisher, R., Ury, W. L., and Patton, B. M. (1991). *Getting to yes: Negotiating agreement without giving in* (2nd ed.). New York: Penguin.

Swenson, E. V. (1994). An ADR activity for a legal environment course. *Focus on Law Studies—American Bar Association Commission on College & University Legal Studies, 9*(2), 4.

SUGGESTED READING

Allen, E. L., & Mohr, D. D. (1997). *Affordable justice.* Encinitas, CA: West Coast Press.

Fisher, R., & Brown, S. (1988). *Getting together: Building a relationship that gets to yes.* Boston: Houghton-Mifflin.

Folberg, J., and Taylor, A. (1984). *Mediation.* San Francisco: Jossey-Bass.

Reuben, R. (1996, August). The lawyer turns peacemaker. *American Bar Association Journal, 82,* 54–55.

Wrightsman, L. S., Nietzel, M. T., and Fortune, W. H. (1998). *Psychology and the legal system* (4th ed.). Pacific Grove, CA: Brooks/Cole.

Appendix A

Kelly's Perspective

You and Taylor were acquaintances in high school. On learning that you would be attending the same university in a neighboring state last fall, you decided to become roommates. Although you each hung out with your own circle of friends, you got along well.

It is the summer after your freshman year. You are living at home and Taylor, whose parents have moved out of town since the school year began, has come for a visit to see old friends. You and Taylor plan a party for friends from high school who have also been away at college. The party is noisy and fun. Without parents at home, the music is loud and beer flows freely from two kegs in the backyard. Cars are parked on the yard, and guests fall asleep on the grass.

By the next afternoon it is apparent that a gigantic cleanup is required to return the property to its original condition before your parents return. Wallpaper and furniture in the living room have been damaged by flying beer and food. The carpet is stained. Cars have torn up the lawn, flower beds, and even the neighbor's vegetable garden. You, feeling responsible and afraid of the consequences, hire a neighbor with a landscaping business to do a quick repair on the outside property. You also hire some high school students down the street to help with the interior cleanup and repairs. The cost for all this is $847.50. You assume Taylor would split the cost, but Taylor maintains that the destructive students were only your friends and refuses.

Both you and Taylor wish to resolve this dispute. You are willing to settle for $300, a sincere apology from Taylor, and help gluing together some of the family china which has been broken and hidden away.

Appendix B

Taylor's Perspective

You and Kelly were acquaintances in high school. On learning that you would be attending the same university in a neighboring state last fall, you decided to become roommates. Although you each hung out with your own circle of friends, you got along well.

It is the summer after your freshman year. Because your parents have recently moved from your hometown, you have gone to visit Kelly, who is living at home for the summer. This is an especially good time for a visit because Kelly's parents are out of town for a week. You and Kelly plan a party for friends from high school who have also been away at college. The party is noisy and fun. Without parents at home, the music is loud and beer flows freely from two kegs in the backyard. Cars are parked on the yard, and guests fall asleep on the grass.

By the next afternoon it is apparent that a gigantic cleanup is required to return the property to its original condition before Kelly's parents return. Wallpaper and furniture in the living room have been damaged by flying beer and food. The carpet is stained. Cars have torn up the lawn, flower beds, and even the neighbor's vegetable garden. Kelly, feeling responsible and afraid of the consequences, hires a neighbor with a landscaping business to do a quick repair on the outside property. Kelly also hires some high school students down the street to help with the interior cleanup and repairs. The cost for all this is $847.50. Kelly assumes you will split the cost; but you refuse, maintaining that the destructive students were only Kelly's friends.

Both you and Kelly wish to resolve this dispute. You would consider paying half of the damage amount, if Kelly would just admit that the guests Kelly invited were rowdy, disrespectful, and drank more than their share of the beer.

76 THE INSANITY TRIAL OF HAMLET: A TEACHING ACTIVITY

Elizabeth V. Swenson

John Carroll University

This activity allows students to study the insanity defense and jury dynamics by viewing a C-SPAN videotape, "Insanity Trial of Hamlet," and then deliberating in jury groups. When a jury has completed its deliberations, students fill out a verdict form and write up their observations of the deliberation process. This activity combines substantive knowledge of the insanity defense with jury dynamics in an active learning task.

CONCEPT

This activity deals with the question of whether Hamlet was insane when he killed Polonius. It demonstrates the relevant evidence needed to determine insanity, the role of the forensic mental health expert, and the need to view the evidence from different perspectives to come to a conclusion. Students also experience the dynamics of jury deliberation. This activity is most suited to a course in psychology and law, although it could also be used in courses in applied psychology, social psychology, and psychopathology, depending on its emphasis. This activity could also be used in an interdisciplinary humanities course or in an ethics course.

MATERIALS NEEDED

You will need a videotape player, a copy of the videotape "Insanity Trial of Hamlet," produced by the Boston Bar Association (1996) and available from C-SPAN, a verdict form, pencils and paper, and space for groups of 6 to 12 students to deliberate together. The videotape runs $3^{1}/_{2}$ hr, so you may need to edit out material that is not part of the actual mock trial, such as interviews and debriefing. The following materials are available in hand-out form: The American Law Institute (ALI, 1962) Model Penal Code test for insanity, the diagnostic criteria for depressive and manic episodes from the *DSM-IV* (American Psychiatric Association, 1994), a list of the experts and the attorneys for each side with space for taking notes, and a printed copy of the jury instructions from the videotape. (Copies of the handouts for this activity are available from the author at Department of Psychology, John Carroll University, University Heights, OH 44118.)

INSTRUCTIONS

Prior to the beginning of this activity, students have studied the insanity defense in class. In addition, so that all of the students are familiar with the fact pattern of this case, they must have all read the play *Hamlet*. Ask them to try to read the play from a psychological, rather than a literary, point of view. Although it would also be acceptable for students to view one of the videos of *Hamlet* or see the play in live format, I prefer that they read the play so that they will not be biased by a particular actor's interpretation of the character.

Tell students that they should put themselves in Hamlet's place and try to understand his feelings and motivations. At the beginning of the class, give students the following instructions:

> You are serving on the jury to decide whether or not Hamlet was insane at the time he killed Polonius. The record in this case is the play *Hamlet*, which you have read. Pay attention to the arguments of the experts, but do not make up your mind until the end of the trial. Because the videotape of this trial will not be completed in one class period, you must not discuss this case with your classmates between this class and the next.

Then have students view the videotape of the mock "Insanity Trial of Hamlet." When the videotape is completed, divide students into juries of 6 to 12 people, depending on the number in the class.

Give students a printed copy of the jury instructions read by the judge in the videotape. These instructions stress several points. It is a fundamental principle of our criminal law that a person is not criminally responsible for an act if the person was insane at the time of the act. It is the job of that person's defense to prove insanity by a preponderance of the evidence (more likely than not). The ALI (1962, § 4.01) Model Penal Code test for insanity will require the student to think through several steps in coming to their decision. It states the following:

> A person is not responsible for criminal conduct if at the time of such conduct as a result of mental disease or defect he lacks substantial capacity either to appreciate the criminality [wrongfulness] of his conduct or to conform his conduct to the requirements of the law.

First the students must determine if the defendant has a mental disorder. If the answer is yes, then they must decide whether this disorder resulted in the lack of a substantial capacity to either appreciate the criminality of the conduct (a cognitive consideration) or to conform the conduct to the law (a volitional consideration). Finally, the student jurors are told not to concern themselves with Hamlet's actual guilt or innocence in the crime of killing Polonius. If he is criminally responsible, then he will be tried on criminal charges at some other time and place.

I also give the students a copy of the manic depressive diagnostic criteria from the *DSM-IV* (American Psychiatric Association, 1994) because the defendant's expert argues that Hamlet suffers from a bipolar disorder.

The juries then go to their deliberation rooms or spaces and are given about 1 hr to elect a foreperson and to come to a verdict. Those students who have been absent from class for the videotape are observers but do not participate in the deliberation. At the end of the hour the students reassemble and the verdicts are read. The verdict form asks the students whether, in the *Matter of Denmark v. Hamlet*, the members of the jury, find the defendant Hamlet criminally responsible or not criminally responsible (i.e., not guilty by reason of insanity). Then the foreperson asks if the jury verdict was unanimous or not unanimous, as well as how many jurors were in favor of and against this verdict. (The verdict does not have to be unanimous.) The foreperson then signs the form. This is followed by either a discussion or a written assignment in which students reflect on the evidence that was most persuasive and the process their jury went through to reach its decision.

DISCUSSION Every time I have this activity students have been excited, enthusiastic, and diligent in their deliberations. Juries have unanimously found Hamlet criminally responsible or have been unable to reach a unanimous verdict, but they have never been unanimous for a verdict of not guilty by reason of insanity. The deliberations are usually heated and even the quieter students seem eager to talk about the evidence that was the most persuasive for them.

What I particularly like about this videotaped mock trial is that the experts arguing for and against the criminal responsibility of Hamlet are Alan Stone, MD, and Thomas Guttheil, MD, two eminent scholars in this field. The videotape is worth showing just to see the method of analysis used and the way the behavior of an individual can be interpreted from two different perspectives. It also illustrates the use of forensic mental health experts in the courtroom. An extra bonus is that the trial is presided over by Justice Anthony Kennedy of the U.S. Supreme Court. His judicial temperment is exemplary and worthy of comment in the class.

An earlier version of "Insanity Trial of Hamlet" was produced by the Washington, DC, Bar Association (1994) with different attorneys but the same experts and presiding judge. It is somewhat shorter in length. After using both tapes, I now combine the two so that my favorite attorneys do the questioning and opening and closing statements. One potential problem with doing this is that the burden of proof is on the government in the Washington, DC, tape and on the defendant in the Massachusetts tape. I deal with this conflict by instructing the jury that the defendant must prove himself not guilty by reason of insanity by a preponderance of the evidence (more likely than not). This avoids the more difficult issue of having to prove the defendant sane, and it provides an interesting point of discussion by referring to the DC standard used in the case of John Hinckley (the man who shot Ronald Reagan). In fact, I do not think that most students consider the burden of proof at all but rather focus on the question of sanity or insanity, whether or not the defendant was criminally responsible.

From start to finish this activity takes about 4 hr and can easily take another hour if you do not edit the videotape. An activity that takes this much class time must be worthwhile. Although many courses in psychology and law use more class time for student-conducted mock trials (American Psychology–Law Society, 1993), this activity brings together more of the substantive content. It has a real courtroom atmosphere. It illustrates the role of forensic mental health experts. It allows the students to use their critical thinking skills to evaluate the evidence and then to come to a verdict on the mental state of the defendant. It gives the students an opportunity to analyze the jury process. And by using a Shakespeare play it brings a humanities focus to the course.

WRITING COMPONENT My preference is to make the writing part of this activity an in-class assignment. Ask students to think through their decision based on the evidence presented, as well as to analyze the jury deliberations. I do not grade these papers, but rather include them in a class-participation component of the semester grade.

REFERENCES American Law Institute. (1962). *Model Penal Code* (1962 Proposed Official Draft), § 4.01.

American Psychiatric Association. (1994). *Diagnostic and statistical manual of mental disorders* (4th ed.). Washington, DC: Author.

American Psychology–Law Society. (1993). *Psychology and law syllabi* (3rd ed.). Burnaby, British Columbia: Author.

Boston Bar Association. (Producer). (1996, March 11). *Insanity trial of Hamlet* [Videotape]. (Available from C-SPAN/Purdue Public Affairs Video, 400 N. Capitol Street, Suite 650, Washington, DC 20001. 1-800-423-9630.)

Shakespeare, W. (1947). *The Tragedy of Hamlet, Prince of Denmark*. New Haven, CT: Yale University Press.

Washington, DC, Bar Association. (Producer). (1994, March 17). *Trial of Hamlet* [Videotape]. (Available from C-SPAN/Purdue Public Affairs Video, 400 N. Capitol Street, Suite 650, Washington, DC 20001. 1-800-423-9630.)

SUGGESTED READING

Hermann, D. H. J. (1997). *Mental Health and Disability Law*. St. Paul, MN: West.

Reisner, R., and Slobogin, C. (1990). *Law and the mental health system* (2nd ed.). St. Paul, MN: West.

Sales, B. D., and Shuman, D. W. (1996). *Law, mental health and mental disorder*. Pacific Grove, CA: Brooks/Cole.

Wrightsman, L. S., Nietzel, M. T., and Fortune, W. H. (1998). *Psychology and the Legal System* (4th ed.). Pacific Grove, CA: Brooks/Cole.

77 EXPRESSING YOUR IDENTITY

Jane S. Halonen

James Madison University

This activity encourages students to communicate aspects of their identity through the construction of a collage. The collage communicates both a social role and the values associated with it. The classroom display of collages and students' explanation of the symbols they used provides some vivid examples of social psychological concepts and can help bring diversity issues to life in the classroom.

CONCEPT
: This activity addresses multiple concepts in social and developmental psychology, including social role, values, gender, ethnicity, and identity. Subsequent class discussion can address attribution processes, prejudice, and discrimination.

MATERIALS NEEDED
: Students make their collages out of available materials in their homes.

INSTRUCTIONS
: Explain to students that the purpose of this activity is to help them become more aware of their own social roles and the values, beliefs, attitudes, and dispositions associated with them. The activity will also help students broaden their mastery of social psychology terms and concepts.

  The activity requires each student to select one of the many social roles he or she plays and construct a collage that helps capture the experience. Emphasize that the collage needs to communicate not only the role but also the values enacted in this role. A value is (a) chosen freely, (b) chosen from among alternatives, (c) chosen thoughtfully and reflectively, (d) prized (i.e., one is satisfied with one's choice), (e) affirmed by the public when the occasion calls for it, (f) acted on, and (g) repeated and persistent (see appendix A for a list of values).

  For example, students can construct a collage about what it means to be an American, or what it means to be a Japanese American. They can explore broad gender roles or more explicit social roles (brother, student, sandwich shop attendant, etc.).

  The construction can be made from materials students have at home. The resulting image should be complex but aesthetically pleasing and should illustrate what the chosen identity means to the student. All students must also submit a one-page reflection about what they learned from the process of constructing the collage. Give students 1 week to prepare their collages and reflections so they do not feel rushed to complete the project.

  Arrange for students to display their collages during the appropriate class period. If enough time is available, all students should take a few moments to explain their creations.

  Specific criteria for evaluating performance on this activity can include whether the student (a) produces a complex visual image about personal identity, (b) adopts one vantage point to communicate about identity, (c) constructs a relatively portable collage, and (d) reflects adequately on the meaning of the process in a one-page paper.

DISCUSSION Students' collages are usually quite provocative and interesting. They enjoy talking about why they included certain images and excluded others. Instructors can draw parallels between collages that address the same role. Some of the collages will also suggest themes that can be easily exploited in class discussion devoted to topics such as prejudice and discrimination.

WRITING COMPONENT Ask students to explain in writing what they learned about themselves and their values from this project? Other writing variations are possible. Following the classroom display of the collages, students can contrast their own values with the values they see depicted in another's student's collage. Students can also be encouraged to write about aspects of the selected role that they chose not to represent in the collage or to explore disadvantages of enacting that role. If the writing assignment occurs subsequent to the class discussion on discrimination, the students' writing can focus on whether or not they have experienced discrimination in that role.

SUGGESTED READING Alverno College Faculty. (1980). *Valuing at Alverno: The valuing process in liberal education.* Milwaukee, WI: Alverno Productions.

Halonen, J. S., Reedy, M., & Smith, P. C. (1995). *Psychology: The active learner* [CD-ROM]. Madison, WI: Brown & Benchmark.

Matsumoto, D. (1994). *People: Psychology from a cultural perspective.* Pacific Grove, CA: Brooks/Cole.

McKeachie, W. J. (1994). *Teaching tips* (9th ed.). Lexington, MA: Heath.

Appendix A

A Partial Listing of Personal Values

achievement	belonging	sensory stimulation
family	self-regard	approval
altruism	patriotism	self-efficiency
loyalty	sensory pleasure	peace
preservation	environmental preservation	self-worth
independence	personal authority	physical service
health	care–nurturance	wisdom
materialism	fidelity	creativity
order–discipline	certainty	productivity
interdependence	tradition	play
thrift	responsibility	security
religion	justice	control

From J. S. Halonen, M. Reedy, & P. C. Smith, 1995, *Psychology: The active learner* [CD-ROM]. Dubuque, IA: Brown & Benchmark. Reprinted with permission of the publisher, The McGraw Hill Companies.

78 Interpreting the Self Through Literature: Psychology and the Novels of Wallace Stegner

Dana S. Dunn
Moravian College

This activity uses two novels by Wallace Stegner to examine the subjective nature of the self. Students read and discuss A Shooting Star *or* Crossing to Safety, *novels that examine stress/coping and aging/integrity, respectively, among other psychological themes. The activity allows students to explore the interpretive links between psychology and literature.*

CONCEPT

Teachers sometimes forget that psychology, like literature, is fundamentally an interpretive enterprise; one beginning and ending with the self. Whether reacting to a book or reflecting on their own experiences, students interpret these realities through subjective perceptions. This activity allows students to consider interpretation and self-perception by discussing psychological aspects of the self presented in two novels by Wallace Stegner. Students examine stress and coping, as well as self-denigration, by reading and discussing *A Shooting Star* (Stegner, 1996). In contrast, *Crossing to Safety* (Stegner, 1987) highlights issues of aging, integrity, and the meaning of self across the life-span. Your goal as the instructor is to demonstrate that the interpretive qualities of self-psychology are relevant to discussing literature, Stegner's novels in particular.

MATERIALS NEEDED

Students will need to purchase a copy of *Crossing to Safety* or *A Shooting Star*. Both novels are available in reasonably priced paperback editions.

INSTRUCTIONS

Wallace Stegner (1909–1993) was an American novelist whose work mined timeless topics of self and character, such as love, confronting adversity, friendship, sacrifice, personal integrity, and forgiveness (Benson, 1996). I use his novels in a teaching activity on the self for two of my classes: *Crossing to Safety* in a class on contemporary approaches to the study of the self and *A Shooting Star* in a course on stress, coping, and health. Both novels lend themselves to sustained discussion of the interpretive qualities of the self, as well as issues of human development and behavior more broadly defined.

To begin the activity, draw a distinction between subjective (self-psychology) and objective (personality psychology) psychological accounts of the self (Brown, 1997). Self-psychology is phenomenological in orientation; how we perceive the world, people, and events is of greater interest than the actual state of these entities. Personality psychology focuses on establishing the objective qualities of the self, as well as determining whether people can provide accurate accounts of their thought and behavior.

To forge links among self, interpretation, and literature, give students brief directions on how to approach either novel. While reading the novel, for example, students can adopt the perspective of a main character portrayed in the work. Tell students to follow a book's narrative as if it were a representation of their own experience. Short summaries of each novel and directions for discussion follow.

Summary of A Shooting Star

A Shooting Star is the story of an intelligent woman, Sabrina Castro, who is financially independent but emotionally bankrupt. Caught between a loveless marriage and a rigid family upbringing, she yearns to start her life anew, but that hoped-for beginning is an ill-fated affair with a married man followed by a retreat to her childhood home, where her aging mother and a prideful ancestry reign. A slow spiral of self-denigration ensues and, before hitting bottom, Sabrina realizes that she must rebuild her life on the remnants of the old one: The pull of one's past life is inevitable, there is no way to completely start over again.

Class discussion concerning *A Shooting Star* can focus on the frequently self-imposed nature of stress in American society; we often place ourselves in unhappy circumstances to satisfy societal expectations (e.g., overwrought materialism; marriage for wealth or prestige, not love). Lazarus and Folkman's (1984) stress and coping model is useful in discussing this work because it is transactional and phenomenological: Stress occurs as a result of the fit between the person and the perceived environment. The idiosyncratic nature of stress allows students to empathize with the main character's experience, while simultaneously considering alternatives. Self-respect and self-responsibility are key themes in the novel, and they take on new meanings when examined in stressful contexts.

Summary of Crossing to Safety

Departing from an exclusively individualistic focus, *Crossing to Safety* is about two married couples who share a very long but sometimes difficult friendship. Both wives are afflicted with human ills—one has polio, the other an unquenchable drive to control the destinies of those around her. The latter character, in fact, gathers the couples together for one last time, as cancer is ending her life. Charity Lang's death, like her life and that of her family, must be carefully orchestrated to the last. The bittersweet reunion of the two couples allows the narrator, Larry Morgan, to review the pleasures, pains, subtle rivalries, and shared successes of this 40-year friendship and what in those years lends meaning to life.

Students are frequently drawn to the opposing marital styles displayed by the two couples. Superficially, one marriage seems idyllic and mutually supportive whereas the other appears to be static, carefully scripted, and based on dependence. Closer reading and discussion of the text reveals that both marriages share many similarities beneath the surface, but that one cannot adequately summarize human relationships by pointing to a few differences. Aging, distance, and reconciliation imposed by time, experience, and acquired perspective matter a great deal to self-understanding. Students initially ask, "How could these people remain friends?" Subsequently, the question becomes, "How could they not be friends?"

I find it very useful to guide discussion of this novel by focusing on generativity, or what psychological goods one individual (or generation) leaves behind for another. Each of the husbands and wives gives something of themselves to the others in the course of the friendship. Invite students to reflect on their own lives to date, asking them to identify what theme or message in their own experiences could be worth sharing with others. To emphasize the role this generativity plays in the self and its interpretive mission, I discuss McAdam's (1993) work on personal myth and autobiography, in which the concept serves to pull together life themes. The great virtue of *Crossing to Safety* is that the reader sees generativity played out in the lives of the characters; their complex, variegated lives serving as examples to readers. The novel also delivers the poignant message that reflection on aging, long life, and existential meaning can be a grace, not merely a duty or ending.

DISCUSSION   Great fiction inspires and teaches its readers (Coles, 1989). Indeed, storytelling is an important human activity, as we come to know ourselves through the stories we tell (McAdams, 1993). It is also true that we can see and learn about ourselves through reading, discussing, and interpreting the stories of others. Literature, of course, is excellent fodder for understanding the self; any story will contain issues of human development, drama, or comedy. Ironically, perhaps, few psychology courses use novels, let along link their themes to interpretive views of the self.

This activity links psychological topics with literature by exploring the views of the self portrayed in these two Wallace Stegner novels. Why the self? Because character, author, and reader meet in the course of reading and discussing a novel: How people think about themselves becomes apparent in their interpretations of the actions of others. This occurs inevitably, as students interpret the motivations, personalities, and individual natures of characters by relating them to their *own* selves.

The discussion usually takes one or two class periods. Always begin by reminding the students that their purpose is to explore the subjective nature of the self by discussing their reactions to the story told in the novel. If you, as the instructor, have read and thought about the novels in advance, you will be able to bring a set of discussion questions that link course topics to plot, characters, and themes. How should readers feel about Sabrina, her character, and the choices she makes? What would they do in her place? Why? Do not rely on these questions unless or until free-wheeling, student-led discussion lags. The novelty of discussing books in psychology class results in a very lively discussion.

Emphasize to students that there are no right answers or correct interpretations of these novels. Doubtless, as class discussion will reveal, there are interpretations that are more tenable given a novel's plot and the intent of the psychology course where the book is being read. This lack of objectivity is also to be expected, indeed welcomed, given the subjective nature of the self.

Finally, there is something oddly refreshing about reading and teaching a novel in a psychology class. Students do not expect to encounter novels in social science courses, nor are they used to discussing them the way most authors intend: as interpretations of life. Invariably, students are often surprised when they enjoy the novels and learn that sustained discussion about literature is an agreeable, enlightening exercise. It is also a valuable exercise because it allows students to see and think beyond the arbitrary disciplinary boundaries separating the study of mind from that of prose.

WRITING COMPONENT

Two writing exercises can be used to explore themes pertaining to the self in these novels. First, ask students to write a book review of either novel, slanting the review toward a course topic. For example, if *Crossing to Safety* were read in a course on human development or life-span, the requisite themes in the novel could be reviewed in light of relevant psychological data or theory on adult friendship, aging, and even death, as well as the topic of generativity (McAdams, 1993). Encourage students to adopt a persona as they write their reviews; whether they choose to write from the perspective of a book critic or academic psychologist affects the tone of the review, as well as insights drawn therein.

A second writing assignment could be a more focused character study of one or more of the main features from either novel. Any such character study should rely heavily on a model or theory from psychology to bolster the interpretation. If one were to study Sabrina Castro's character in *A Shooting Star*, the aforementioned transactional model of stress and coping would be a useful touchstone. Students can readily write an analysis of a protagonist's character by seeing how well this model of stress explains a character's reactions in the course of the novel.

REFERENCES

Benson, J. J. (1996). *Wallace Stegner: His life and work.* New York: Viking.

Brown, J. D. (1997). *The self.* New York: McGraw-Hill.

Coles, R. (1989). *The call of stories: Teaching and the moral imagination.* Boston: Houghton-Mifflin.

Lazarus, R. S., & Folkman, S. (1984). *Stress, appraisal, and coping.* New York: Springer.

McAdams, D. P. (1993). *The stories we live by: Personal myths and the making of the self.* New York: William Morrow.

Stegner, W. (1987). *Crossing to safety.* New York: Penguin Books.

Stegner, W. (1996). *A shooting star.* New York: Penguin Books.

SUGGESTED READING

McAdams, D. P. (1985). *Power, intimacy, and the life story: Personological inquiries into identity.* New York: The Guilford Press.

McAdams, D. P., & Ochberg, R. L. (Eds.). (1988). *Psychobiography and life narratives.* Durham, NC: Duke University Press.

Stegner, W. (1996). *Remembering laughter.* New York: Penguin Books.

Stegner, W. (1997). *Recapitulation.* New York: Penguin Books.

Vaillant, G. E. (1995). *Adaptation to life.* Cambridge: Harvard University Press.

Vaillant, G. E. (1995). *The wisdom of the ego.* Cambridge: Harvard University Press.

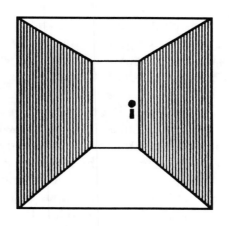

CHAPTER XI
PSYCHOLOGICAL DISORDERS AND TREATMENTS

The six articles in this chapter explore a variety of topics in clinical and counseling psychology, such as addiction and personality disorders and empathy and group therapy treatments. Activity 79 is an involving simulation exercise that allows students to experience some of the components of drug addiction in a safe and effective manner. One goal of the exercise is to teach students the interaction of the biological, psychological, and sociological processes of drug addiction.

Activity 80 allows students to interpret a common dream and then shows them how the interpretation of dream reports can be influenced by prior knowledge, expectancies, motivation, emotion, and other top-down processes. It illustrates how easily a clinician's knowledge about a client might lead to very different conclusions about the meaning of a dream.

Activity 81 is designed to help students discern the differences among personality disorders. Part of the exercise requires students to identify the kinds of jobs and the kinds of life partners that would make the most satisfying matches for individuals with various personality disorders.

The role-playing exercise in Activity 82 uses a group therapy setting to help students apply diagnostic nomenclature to an assessment situation. The class discussion that follows the role-playing illustrates the limitations of diagnostic categories and the importance of observational skills and data collection in clinical assessment.

Activity 83 explores the concept of empathy, which the author refers to as the cornerstone of counseling. Students respond to actual case material from a counseling session by selecting from a list of 10 statements, some that are empathic, others that are not. A writing component allows the students to compare projection with empathy.

In activity 84, students use brief written clinical case histories as a basis for students making decisions on diagnoses and then recommending appropriate psychological treatments. An extra dimension to this exercise is that the student judgments are made from differing psychological perspectives, such as cognitive, behavioral, and psychoanalytic.

79 ADDICTION SIMULATION EXERCISE: ICE CUBE ADDICTION

Todd C. Campbell
Marquette University

This activity presents a dynamic learning exercise aimed at exposing students—in a safe, involved, and effective manner—to the biological–psychological–social model of drug addiction. An outline of the exercise is presented and student reactions to the exercise and recommendations for teachers are discussed.

CONCEPT

Drug addiction is one of the most pressing health problems facing the United States today (Harrison & Hughes, 1997). The effects of drug addiction are studied in a wide array of disciplines including psychology, psychiatry, sociology, criminology, biology, political science, and economics. Considering the wide-ranging implications, it is important that students begin to grasp the dynamic processes that underlie drug addiction. These processes are biological, psychological, and sociological in nature (Doweiko, 1990), and collectively they form what is commonly referred to as the bio–psycho–social model of drug addiction.

Developing a safe, ethical, and effective active learning exercise on the subject of addiction carries many difficulties. The value of this simulation is that it allows students to experience and understand, through a safe, active learning exercise, the interaction of the biological, psychological, and sociological processes of drug addictions and the effects on the addicts themselves.

MATERIALS NEEDED

You will need a hospital patient identification bracelet for each participant (if you cannot obtain these bracelets, pieces of colorful yarn can be used instead; do not tell the students *where* to wear the bracelets), and the Addiction Simulation Exercise: Ice Cube Addiction handout (appendix A).

INSTRUCTIONS

Simply follow the guidelines put forth in the Addiction Simulation Exercise: Ice Cube Addiction handout. Because students tend to become very involved in this activity it is important to stress to them that it is simply a *learning exercise*. Tell students not to engage in any behaviors that they deem to be immoral or illegal. Instruct them that although they will receive the most benefit from this exercise by participating in it fully, they can terminate their participation at anytime. Be aware that there is a methamphetamine drug known by the street name "ice." Make this known to the students and stress that this exercise involves frozen water and *frozen water only*. No other substances should be substituted for the ice. Some students have suggested that food or drink should be used, but with the prevalence of eating disorders, this would not be a wise decision.

The follow-up discussion is done in the format of a self-help recovery group (*Alcoholics Anonymous*, 1976; *Narcotics Anonymous*, 1982), even having the stu-

dents introduce themselves as "Hi I'm _____ and I'm an ice cube addict."
I suggest that teachers attend an open meeting of Alcoholics Anonymous (AA) or
Narcotics Anonymous (NA) to familiarize themselves with the format. In keeping
with the spirit of an open meeting, all students are encouraged to participate in
the discussion, including those who did not begin or complete the first part of
the exercise. In my experience, students readily fell into the role and seemed to
enjoy this format for processing the exercise. During this time, students shared
and processed their experiences with each other and the teacher. Though in an
actual meeting of AA or NA, there is little cross-talk between the participants,
open discussion is encouraged in this exercise. Particular attention should be paid
to the emotional experiences, strategies used by the students, the insights gained
from the exercise, and the process of change and recovery from a drug addiction.
Students can use their logs and write-ups to aid in the discussion.

The range in level of participation of students can be a focus of discussion.
Questions can be posed that use the different levels of participation to portray
the abstinence–use–abuse–addiction continuum. Examples of such questions are
as follows:

1. Why do some people develop addictions and others do not?
2. What kept you from even wanting to try this?
3. How did you just "dabble" for a day?
4. Were you surprised at the effort you expended?

DISCUSSION   In using this exercise, I have found that students were surprised at what little
reaction their friends or family had to their bizarre behavior regarding their "addiction." Behavior that went unquestioned ranged from "knocking on dorm room
doors at 11:00 p.m. asking for ice" to "putting ice in my coffee" to "using all of
my roommate's ice and then turning the refrigerator on its side in order to fill it
up with bags of ice." This allowed students to realize how easy it is to hide an
addiction, even from those who should be aware.

Students were also surprised by some of their own actions, particularly some
of the actions that, prior to the exercise, they had adamantly said that they would
not do. These were actions such as putting ice in their coffee, carrying stashes of
ice (in an insulated mug) at work, and avoiding roommates in the community
bathroom so as not to show their "tracks." Several students stated that their
obsession with planning manifested itself in learning where all the ice machines
on campus were located.

This was a very powerful active learning exercise that allowed students to
experience some of the biological, psychological, and sociological aspects of addiction. Processing the student's feelings and reactions about participating in this
exercise is extremely important, because it may conjure up memories of significant others' true addictions, or possibly the students may even question their use
or their friends' use of alcohol or other drugs. Teachers should be aware of resources that students can access to help with any difficulties that may arise from
this exercise.

Student reaction to this exercise has been extremely positive. Most students
participated fully, some students only participated for 1 day, and a few students
chose not to do the exercise at all. Those students who did participate described
gaining insight into the tremendous amount of planning it takes to maintain an

addiction and some of the dynamics involved in maintaining an addiction. The ice cube addiction exercise brings out many psychological and sociological points and could be used effectively in a variety of classrooms to stimulate discussion, motivation, and learning.

REFERENCES

Alcoholics Anonymous. (1976). New York: Alcoholics Anonymous World Services.

Doweiko, H. E. (1990). *Concepts of chemical dependency.* Pacific Grove, CA: Brooks/Cole.

Harrison, L., & Hughes, A. (Eds.). (1997). *The validity of self-reported drug use: Improving the accuracy of survey estimates.* (National Institute on Drug Abuse Research Monograph Series 167; NIH Publication No. 97-4147.) Washington, DC: National Institutes of Health.

Narcotics Anonymous. (1982). Van Nuys, CA: Narcotics Anonymous World Service Office.

SUGGESTED READING

McNeece, C. A., & DiNitto, D. M. (1998). *Chemical dependency: A systems approach* (2nd ed.). Boston: Allyn & Bacon.

Miller, W. R., & Heather, N. (Eds.). (1998). *Treating addictive behaviors.* New York: Plenum Press.

Peele, S., & Brodsky, X. (1991). *The truth about addiction and recovery.* New York: Fireside.

Washton, A. (1989). *Cocaine addiction: Treatment, recovery, and relapse prevention.* New York: W. W. Norton.

Appendix A

Addiction Simulation Exercise: Ice Cube Addiction (Handout)

Rationale

This exercise will allow you to experience, first hand (though nowhere near to the same extent as an actual addiction), some of the physical (thirst being analogous to the cravings for drugs), social, cognitive, and emotional experiences of a person who is actually addicted to a drug. Participation in this exercise is voluntary. You may choose to end your participation at any time during the exercise, though you will achieve the full benefit of the exercise if you choose to follow through to the end.

Protocol

You are to engage in this exercise for 48 consecutive hours sometime between now and the next class. The more strictly you adhere to the guidelines, the more effective the exercise will be for you.

1. *Drug.* Your drug of choice is ice cubes. You used to be able to "get off" simply on water, but your addiction has progressed way beyond this. You now need specially processed water—ice cubes. This is analogous to progressing from powder cocaine to crack cocaine.
2. *Craving.* Thirst is your craving for the drug ice cubes. Every time you take a drink of *any* liquid, you must have an ice cube in the liquid. Yes, this will be difficult and will require much planning. *Anticipate!* This applies to all drinking situations including coffee, water from drinking fountains, cans or bottles of beverages, and even late-night drinks of water after you have awakened from a deep sleep. (Make sure your ice trays are full before going to bed.)
3. *Legality.* Ice cubes are socially unacceptable and illegal. Do not let "regular people" see you or catch you using ice cubes. This applies to friends and family. The only people with whom it is acceptable to be open about your use of ice cubes are other "addicts" who are participating in this exercise. This will take some creative thinking at home, in restaurants, and other public places.
4. *Obsession.* To simulate the obsession aspect of drug addiction you are to keep an hourly log (waking hours only). Please obtain a notebook in which you can answer the following questions hourly: 1. Are you thirsty now? 2. Where is your next ice cube coming from? 3. What is your plan to satisfy your cravings? Think ahead.
5. *Tracks.* You will be given a hospital patient identification bracelet to wear. Wear the bracelet at all times during the exercise. This bracelet is analogous to an addict's needle tracks, so it is socially unacceptable to wear the bracelet. Try your best to keep "regular people" from seeing the bracelet, because they might ask what it is about and this would put you in a difficult situation trying to explain it. Remember, you are trying to hide your addiction from "regular people." The bracelet will also serve as a reminder that you are participating in the exercise. It will be easy to forget for a few hours so you will have to be diligent in your participation. Remember, addicts cannot turn off their cravings at will.
6. *Write-up.* At the end of the 48-hr period, please write one to two pages describing

your thoughts, feelings, and reactions to the exercise. This paper is free form, so write in any manner that you feel is appropriate. Please bring your paper and log to the next class.

7. *Discussion.* This exercise will be discussed in the next class. We will use a simulation of a self-help recovery group to discuss your experiences.

$^\square$80 The Role of Prior Information in Dream Analysis

Douglas A. Bernstein
University of Illinois

In this activity, the class receives a handout describing the demographic characteristics and brief life history of a woman named Doris, along with a dream she reported having. At the bottom of the handout, there is space for the student to interpret the meaning of Doris's dream. The dream is the same on each handout, but the description of Doris is not.

CONCEPT

This activity is designed to help students understand that the interpretation of dreams, like the interpretation of other stimuli, can be influenced by prior knowledge, expectancies, motivation, emotion, and other top down processes. More specifically, it illustrates how easily a clinician's prior knowledge about a client might prompt very different conclusions about the meaning of dream content.

This activity provides an easy way to show students the link between principles that guide the perception of objects and those that operate in social perception in general and in psychotherapy in particular.

MATERIALS NEEDED

You will need copies of each of the three handouts given in appendixes A, B, and C. Collate the three items before you hand them out, so that one third of the students will receive each version.

To aid class discussion of varying dream interpretations, it is helpful to have each version of Doris's demographics and life history on overhead transparencies in print large enough to be read from the back of the room.

INSTRUCTIONS

Give each student a version of the Doris handout. After a few minutes, ask the students to write their interpretation of the dream at the bottom—and perhaps the back—of the handout. You can either collect and read aloud some of the interpretations, or just ask students to read them aloud.

DISCUSSION

As the readings proceed, it will soon become obvious to the class that something is amiss. At this point, reveal the differences in the three descriptions of Doris and point out the influence those differences had on the interpretations of Doris's dream.

You can end this demonstration by pointing out that clinicians are aware of the role of prior knowledge in dream analysis (and other aspects of therapy). This is why, for example, they tend to base conclusions about clients on a series of dreams rather than on just one and why they seek to combine assessment information from various sources, such as tests and interviews. I have found that stimulating class discussions result from pointing out that, in spite of such efforts, clinicians are as vulnerable as the rest of us to the biasing effects of expectancy in dealing with clients.

In addition to having students write their interpretation of the dream in class, you might also ask students to write a summary of the purpose of the demonstration and what they learned from it. This can be done in 5 min at the end of the exercise or at the end of class. A quick perusal of the summaries can show if students understood the point that you were trying to make. Summaries are efficient ways to check for student understanding.

REFERENCE

Ullman, M. (1986). Access to dreams. In B. B. Wolman & M. Ullman (Eds.), *Handbook of states of consciousness*. New York: Van Nostrand Reinhold.

Appendix A

Handout 1

At the time of the following dream, Doris S. was a 65-year-old woman living in a Chicago suburb. She had four grown children, two boys and two girls. Her husband of 40 years died two years before she had the dream. Though in excellent health for decades, she had just been diagnosed as having breast cancer. Her prognosis was good, but she worried about her health. She also worried about one of her grandchildren, a boy, who was born autistic and retarded. Other than these rather unfortunate problems, Doris had lived a very normal life and had never experienced serious psychological problems.

Doris's Dream

"I am at my friend Betty's house. I call Ann up to make an appointment to get my hair highlighted. I speak to the receptionist at the beauty parlor. I speak in a Russian accent. She asks when I can come. I say in a couple of days. I think that might be Wednesday. She asks 'Are you sure because we are changing things around here,' implying that it won't be good if I change my mind and cancel the appointment. After speaking to her, I realize that I don't need to have my hair highlighted yet, because my hair hasn't grown out yet. But George and I go on the 'A' train to the beauty parlor. It goes through a neighborhood that I have never seen before. The train travels outside. George gets out at a stop as if he nonchalantly is doing something. The train leaves without him. I wave to him and feel bad that he is not on the train." (Ullman, 1986, p. 539).

Jot down notes about your interpretation of the dream in the space below:

_____

_____

_____

_____

_____

Appendix B

Handout 2

At the time of the following dream, Doris S. was an 18-year-old woman living in a rural area. She was getting ready to graduate from high school and begin the long road toward a medical degree (she would have been the first child in her family to become a doctor) when she found out that she was pregnant. Her parents were not yet aware of the situation and she and her boyfriend were in the midst of deciding whether to try to arrange an abortion or to get married, though the latter option meant the end of her medical school aspirations. Beyond these rather unfortunate problems, Doris lived a very normal life and had never experienced serious psychological problems.

Doris's Dream

"I am at my friend Betty's house. I call Ann up to make an appointment to get my hair highlighted. I speak to the receptionist at the beauty parlor. I speak in a Russian accent. She asks when I can come. I say in a couple of days. I think that might be Wednesday. She asks 'Are you sure because we are changing things around here,' implying that it won't be good if I change my mind and cancel the appointment. After speaking to her, I realize that I don't need to have my hair highlighted yet, because my hair hasn't grown out yet. But George and I go on the 'A' train to the beauty parlor. It goes through a neighborhood that I have never seen before. The train travels outside. George gets out at a stop as if he nonchalantly is doing something. The train leaves without him. I wave to him and feel bad that he is not on the train." (Ullman, 1986, p. 539).

Jot down notes about your interpretation of the dream in the space below:

_____

_____

_____

_____

_____

Appendix C

Handout 3

At the time of the following dream, Doris S. was a happy and healthy 28-year-old woman living in a comfortable Chicago condominium with her husband of 5 years. Both she and her husband had high-paying jobs in advertising (they had met at work) and were generally enjoying life as yuppies. They got along well together and, beyond the usual conflicts over small things, the only problems they had were her overbearing mother (who they perceived as trying to run their lives) and a very stressful decision about whether to move to Los Angeles, where her husband, but not she, had the opportunity for an exciting new job at even higher pay. Beyond these rather routine problems, Doris lived a very normal life and had never experienced serious psychological problems.

Doris's Dream

"I am at my friend Betty's house. I call Ann up to make an appointment to get my hair highlighted. I speak to the receptionist at the beauty parlor. I speak in a Russian accent. She asks when I can come. I say in a couple of days. I think that might be Wednesday. She asks 'Are you sure because we are changing things around here,' implying that it won't be good if I change my mind and cancel the appointment. After speaking to her, I realize that I don't need to have my hair highlighted yet, because my hair hasn't grown out yet. But George and I go on the 'A' train to the beauty parlor. It goes through a neighborhood that I have never seen before. The train travels outside. George gets out at a stop as if he nonchalantly is doing something. The train leaves without him. I wave to him and feel bad that he is not on the train." (Ullman, 1986, p. 539).

Jot down notes about your interpretation of the dream in the space below:

_____

_____

_____

_____

_____

$^\Box 81$ FOR LOVE OR MONEY

Jane S. Halonen

James Madison University

This exercise is designed to help students discriminate among personality disorders through student collaboration. Following a minilecture on the nature of personality disorders and their role in abnormal and clinical psychology, students speculate about the kinds of life work and life partners that would make the most satisfying match for individuals with various personality disorders.

CONCEPT　Personality disorders can be challenging to teach. This diagnostic category describes enduring interpersonal difficulties related to personality structure. Students are most likely to grasp the meaning and significance of personality disorders when they are presented in an exaggerated form.

MATERIALS NEEDED　The handout (see appendix A) will help students focus attention on their assigned task and will encourage them to take notes from the reports of other student groups.

INSTRUCTIONS　Provide a minilecture on the nature of personality disorders. A table summarizing the disorders is included (see appendix B). This presentation should address the following points:

- Personality disorders represent clusters of traits that are interpersonally maladaptive.
- Individuals with personality disorders often do not recognize the problems they create.
- Personality disorders may not be crisp; an individual can often be diagnosed with mixed personality disorder patterns.
- Personality disorders are hard to treat.
- The category of personality disorder is a controversial one with lower diagnostic reliability and increasing challenges about insurance liability for the cost of therapy for those unlucky enough to have this diagnosis.

Freud once observed that mental health is related to love and work. Point out that a large number of individuals with personality disorders will never seek treatment if they are fortunate enough to find the right occupation and the right kind of social situation or partnership that fits with their particular challenging pattern. Distribute the handout (appendix A) and ask groups in the class to be responsible for two or three personality disorder types. They should describe the personality characteristics of the disorder assigned and then speculate about the kind of work and life partner (if any) that would give them their best chance at simulating mental health. It does not matter if groups discuss the same type; this overlap only makes the class discussion about their speculations more lively. Having each group complete all personality disorders usually takes too much time.

Convene a large class discussion in which you compare the judgments of the groups. By making a copy of the handout as an overhead transparency, you can track the best contributions to help students take complete notes.

DISCUSSION
Students enjoy the opportunity to think critically about the characteristics of personality disorders. The range of responses that you will get to this stimulus is usually quite impressive. The individual student discussions tend to be light-hearted. Large group discussion continues the spirit even though students appropriately follow their proposed choices with more serious discussions about how difficult it would be to have the patterns described or to be involved with those who do. You can use this class itself to help evaluate whether the proposed choices are on target. As long as you make the discussion have the feeling of brainstorming, participation is usually quite strong. Following are the answers your students are likely to generate:

Personality Disorder	Work	Partner Characteristics
Avoidant	Routine, no-risk jobs	None; another avoidant
Dependent	Military, homemaker	Take-charge person
Obsessive–compulsive	Librarian, accountant	Mess maker
Passive–aggressive	Self-employed	Infinitely patient
Paranoid	Spy	None
Schizoid	Lighthouse manager	None
Schizotypal	Artist	Schizotypal
Antisocial	Burglar, used car sales	Antisocial
Borderline	Commune dweller	Caretaker
Histrionic	Actor	Audience
Narcissistic	CEO	Wealthy

Warning: Be prepared for the occasional reference to teachers as narcissistic and histrionic.
(This is often quite accurate.)

For this exercise to be effective, the textbook for the course must provide a thorough discussion of the characteristics of personality disorders. Students may also consult the summary table of the disorders, shown in appendix B.

WRITING COMPONENT
This exercise can be followed up with a short, in-class writing assignment. Ask students to select one of the personality disorders and describe what life would be like if they were assigned to be roommates with that person during college. The criteria for the writing assignment should include an accurate description of the characteristics of the personality disorder, reasonable applications of the impact of those characteristics on a college lifestyle, and an explanation of the advantages and disadvantages of the partnership.

REFERENCE
American Psychiatric Association. (1994). *Diagnostic and statistic manual of mental disorders* (4th ed.). Washington, DC: Author.

SUGGESTED READING
Costa, P., & Widiger, T. (1994). *Personality disorder and the five-factor model of personality.* Washington, DC: American Psychological Association.

Kreisman, J. J., & Straus, H. (1989). *I hate you—don't leave me: Understanding the borderline personality.* New York: Avon Books.

Mallinger, A. R., & DeWyze, J. (1993). *When being in control gets out of control.* New York: Random House.

Oldham, J. M. (1994). Personality disorders: Current perspectives. *Journal of the American Medical Association, 272,* 1770–1776.

Appendix A

Worksheet

Personality Disorder Characteristics	Possible Work	Possible Partner
Avoidant		
Dependent		
Obsessive–compulsive		
Passive–aggressive		
Paranoid		
Schizoid		
Schizotypal		
Antisocial		
Borderline		
Histrionic		
Narcissistic		

Appendix B

Clusters and Characteristics of Individual Personality Disorders as Described in the *DSM-IV* (American Psychiatric Association, 1994)

Anxious, Fearful Cluster	
Avoidant	Heightened sensitivity, avoids new events
Dependent	Indecisive, overreliant on others
Obsessive–compulsive	Overconscientious, rigid, perfectionist
Passive–aggressive	Procrastinates, "forgets" commitments

Odd, Eccentric Cluster	
Paranoid	Guarded, overcautious, unforgiving
Schizoid	Isolated, emotionally inexpressive
Schizotypal	Peculiar behavior and appearance, detached

Dramatic, Emotional, Erratic Cluster	
Antisocial	Guiltless, law-breaker, exploitative
Borderline	Unstable, untrusting, fearful of being alone
Histrionic	Seductive, shallow, moody
Narcissistic	Shows entitlement, jealousy, self-absorbed

82 Diagnosis of Psychological Disorders: A Group Therapy Simulation

John R. Rudisill
Wright State University School of Medicine

This activity helps students apply an understanding of psychological disorders to a diagnostic situation. The students (in the role of the clients) and the instructor (in the role of the group therapist) role-play an initial, group therapy session. Following the brief group therapy simulation, students are asked to share their observations of each member of the group to arrive at a DSM-IV diagnosis.

CONCEPT

This teaching exercise requires the students to demonstrate or observe abnormal behavior to formulate a diagnosis based on the *Diagnostic and Statistical Manual of Mental Disorders* (4th ed.). The simulation will allow students to apply an understanding of diagnostic nomenclature to an assessment situation. Discussion will illustrate processes of diagnosis, the current limitations of diagnostic categories, and the importance of observational skills and data collection in assessment.

MATERIALS NEEDED

You will need scripts for each client experiencing a psychological disorder, *DSM-IV* descriptions for each psychological disorder, a script guide for the instructor/group therapist, and a means to display diagnostic possibilities (e.g., a chalkboard or a flip-chart).

INSTRUCTIONS

Begin by explaining that despite the light-hearted nature of this learning exercise, clinical diagnosis is a serious, complex, and considered process. Diagnosis in professional practice requires the careful collection of multiple data well beyond the data available in a brief encounter within a group therapy setting.

Ask 10 students to volunteer to act as the clients in a role-play exercise. Then assign the remaining students the role of observers. The observers are to carefully attend to the behavior of the clients in the group. Arrange the room so that the 10 students who are clients are seated in an inner circle with you and the remaining students seated in an outer circle of chairs.

Hand out one script to each student in the group (see appendix A for sample scripts or develop your own scripts from the *DSM-IV* casebook) with the relevant diagnostic section of *DSM-IV* attached. The script outlines a client role for the student in the group consistent with the attached *DSM-IV* description of the disorder. Next, give the students 5 min to study their scripts and their corresponding *DSM-IV* description, but ask them not to share their scripts or diagnoses with students around them.

Now you are ready to set the stage for the group therapy role-play by stating the following:

We are going to role play an initial group therapy session. I will act as the group therapist and you will be clients attending the group therapy. You may use your real name for the role-play. As we begin, stay in your role throughout the group therapy session, contributing and answering questions as the person with the disorder might answer them.

Following this brief introduction to the session, identify yourself as the group therapist and introduce the group session: "Welcome to the group. I'm looking forward to getting to know each of you better and to beginning our work together."

Encourage the group members to participate by answering the following questions:

"Who would like to start our group today by introducing themselves and saying a few words about why they have come to the group and what they would like to get out of coming?" (Allow the members to share their stories. If a group member does not participate, you may need to call on the "client" directly.)

"It is often initially helpful in a group experience for people to learn what other people's first impression is of them. Would anyone like feedback on how you've come across so far? Who would like to go first? Can the group members provide some information for (whomever volunteers)?"

After approximately 15 min announce, "Our time is almost gone for today. How did you feel about today's group session? Does anyone in the group want to make any final comments? Thank you for attending. I'll see you next time."

Following the role-play, process the exercise by asking the entire class to focus on each client in turn:

"How did you see (_____) behaving in the group? What did you observe? What kinds of difficulties did the client manifest? Can you list the diagnostic possibilities? (As students answer, you should list each of their responses on the board.) What features differentiate each of these disorders? What aspects of (_____) behavior suggest each diagnosis? How many of you feel that the correct diagnosis for (_____) is (ask students to vote on each diagnostic possibility)? What was your actual diagnosis, (_____)? (The student reveals his or her diagnostic identity at this point.) Tell us what symptoms you were trying to portray and how it felt to behave like this in the group?" (Perform the same process with each group member, taking time to raise and to discuss issues that are suggested by the processing and to make appropriate teaching points.)

Following the completion of the exercise, thank the students and observers and jokingly add that no one was typecast.

DISCUSSION   This activity is particularly engaging when offered at the end of a course in abnormal psychology or psychology.

You can expect student interest to be reflected by laughter and excitement. The student's critical thinking can be encouraged and challenged during the processing portion of the exercise, during which you can raise many issues. For example, by giving a male student the role of a hysterical personality, you can raise issues of sexism in diagnosis. You also might ask students about the effects of ethnic or cultural variables on specific diagnoses. When the student who played the "normal" personality is given diagnoses by the students, the students can discuss the difficulty in identifying abnormal versus normal behavior. The class can also discuss the process of making differential diagnoses and the questions needed to make such diagnostic distinctions. You also could ask students to discuss the range of behaviors that might represent a particular diagnostic characteristic. Challenge student ideas suggestive of stereotyping or assumptions that psychological diagnosis is made easily and is always clear-cut.

Often, the group therapy in this activity is not particularly productive therapeutically. This phenomenon can be discussed in terms of group composition if this issue is applicable to the class content.

WRITING COMPONENT

To emphasize writing skill, ask students to write out their diagnosis and their supporting arguments regarding the differential diagnostic issues. You can ask the students to write questions about the current state of diagnostic nomenclature arising from the exercise. Students may discuss these questions during this or the next class period. Alternatively, ask students to write down in brief their perceptions of the group dynamics and how the social force of the group influenced the expression of individual pathology (e.g., the schizoid client talked sparingly in the group). Finally, the students who played the roles of the various clients can write about the phenomenology of their individual roles.

REFERENCES

American Psychiatric Association. (1994). *Diagnostic and statistical manual of mental disorder* (4th ed.). Washington, DC: Author.

Spitzer, R. L., Gibbon, M., Skodol, A. E., Williams, J. B. W., & First, M. B. (1994). *DSM-IV casebook*. Washington, DC: American Psychiatric Association Press.

SUGGESTED READING

Hersen, M., & Turner, S. (1991). *Adult Psychopathology & Diagnosis*. New York: John Wiley.

Millon, T., & Davis, R. (in press). *Disorders of personality: DSM-IV, Axis II* (rev. ed.). New York: John Wiley.

Millon, T., & Klerman, G. (Eds.). (1986). *Contemporary directions in psychopathology: Toward the DSM-IV*. New York: Guilford Press.

Sutker, P., & Adams, H. (Eds.). (1993). *Comprehensive Handbook of Psychopathology*. New York: Plenum Press.

Appendix A

300.29
AGORAPHOBIA
(WITHOUT
HISTORY
OF PANIC
DISORDER)

Chief Complaint

You have a fear of being trapped in a public place and not being able to escape. This feeling is especially intense when you get in crowds. You become afraid that you might have a heart attack and might not be able to get through the crowd to get help. You have found that since the development of this fear two years ago, you have gradually restricted your activities so that you no longer attend concerts, movies, or plays. In fact, you are beginning to avoid even small parties.

History

You have always been a somewhat anxious person who has a tendency to be fearful. However, you have been productive, conscientious, and are liked by a small circle of friends. The only other relevant historical information is the accidental death of your father while on a remote military tour.

Reason for Attending the Group

You have noticed an increasing avoidance from ordinary life activities and believe that you need help. Your friends have also been encouraging you to come and see someone about your problem. Groups are extremely frightening for you and you would much prefer dealing with your problems on a one-to-one basis with your doctor.

301.7
ANTISOCIAL
PERSONALITY
DISORDER

Chief Complaint

You are in trouble with the law (stealing, drugs, and fighting). You have been mandated over to the group for outpatient treatment. You just want to get off probation.

History

You have had numerous minor difficulties with the law, but you have shown an amazing ability to get out of the charges. Currently, you are living with a teenager, but have had numerous other relationships with a noticeable lack of intimacy and longevity.

Reasons for Attendance at the Group

You want to appear the model group member to get off probation. If you can have some fun with the group or individual members, that would be okay too.

307.51
BULIMIA
NERVOSA,
PURGING TYPE

Chief Complaint

You complain of being concerned about your appearance, feeling sexually unattractive, and wanting others to react more positively toward you. You have periods of depression and "running yourself down" followed by eating binges. After the eating binge, you induce vomiting and then often go on a very strict diet. The pattern gets repeated over and over. You know this is not normal, but you are uncomfortable sharing this information with the group.

History

Your parents are both obese and you've struggled most of your life to guard against obesity, having been somewhat overweight as a teenager. Because of this, you usually hide your eating from others.

Reason for Attending the Group

You want help in learning to feel more attractive and coming to accept yourself as a sexually attractive person. You secretly want to trust the group enough to reveal your secret to them.

**301.4
OBSESSIVE–
COMPULSIVE
PERSONALITY
DISORDER**

Chief Complaint

You lost your job after 20 years as a clerk for a local company and have been quite anxious with compulsive symptoms. These symptoms seem beyond your control and as hard as you try to resist them, they keep reoccurring.

History

You have had a very stable career and have been viewed as a productive worker but also as being rigid and eccentric. You have been married for 18 years and your spouse is extremely worried about you lately, but admits that your communication in the marriage has always been poor.

Reason for Attending the Group

You want help for your symptoms and life directions, but you have extreme difficulty sharing your true feelings.

**300.11
CONVERSION
DISORDER
(PHYSICAL
ABUSE OF
ADULT)**

Chief Complaint

You are experiencing difficulty with your memory that is too extensive to be explained by ordinary forgetfulness. After being evaluated by your family physician and the neurological specialist, this memory disturbance does not appear to be a result of an organic mental disorder, so you have been referred to group therapy. Your family physician has noticed that your marital difficulties, stemming from your spouse paying little attention to you, have been eased as a result of your illness. You do not see the point of group therapy for you. You are concerned with getting help for your spouse, but your spouse will not come to therapy. You are unaware of any problems that you are causing in the marital relationship.

History

You've had three divorces, but you say you really love this spouse. Several incidents involving domestic quarrels have been reported. You have told the police highly dramatic stories regarding your spouse's abusive treatment toward you provoking you to throw a lamp. Although you have had various physical concerns over the years, your health has been good.

Reason for Attending the Group

You do not see much point in being in the group in terms of your memory loss. You would like to get your spouse into therapy. Your style is very dramatic and approval is important for you; if you do not get it, you can become quite demanding.

**300.4
DYSTHYMIC
DISORDER**

Chief Complaint

You have been depressed for most of your life, but especially the past 5 years. When you are strongly depressed you have a loss of interest in your hobbies and activities and are unable to enjoy your work and home duties. You are very upset with yourself and you have been irritable at home; you feel trapped and do not seem to enjoy family life the way you want to.

History

Always somewhat of a perfectionist, you have become more and more prone to guilt and depression over the past few years despite the support of your loving family. No major problems have resulted. You feel unworthy of their continuing support, however.

Reason for Attending the Group

You are tired of feeling bad and want to be a good parent and a good spouse and enjoy life. The thing that has you really scared is that you are having reoccurring thoughts of suicide by running your car into a telephone pole. Despite your need for help, you are pessimistic about whether your case can be helped.

**V65.2
MALINGERING**

Chief Complaint

You complain that the auto accident that occurred nearly 2 years ago has disabled you psychologically. You are no longer happy, you do not feel comfortable working, and you believe that you will never be the same.

History

You have been referred by your attorney to the psychiatrist for treatment as a way of documenting your psychological distress. You are currently in court to try to obtain damages for the accident and also are receiving disability from your work. Despite your symptoms, you seem to be not experiencing obvious distress.

Reason for Attending the Group

You want to convince the group, for purposes of your trial, that you deserve compensation for your injury. There appears to be a discrepancy between your claimed distress and the signs and symptoms you actually show.

**317
MILD
MENTAL
RETARDATION**

Chief Complaint

Since your recent promotion to supervisor of the janitorial crew at a local factory, you state that your boss has been on your back. You were happy doing your janitorial chores, but your boss is losing patience with your inability to do paperwork and carry out supervisory responsibilities.

History

You have no particular psychological problems, but have always had difficulties with academic skills, dropping out of school in the seventh grade. You live with your parents, but were planning to get a place on your own until the recent problems at work.

Reason for Attending the Group

You need guidance and assistance with dealing with job stress and do not know how to handle this situation.

NORMAL

Be as "normal" as you can be!

301.0 PARANOID PERSONALITY DISORDER

Chief Complaint

You have had some very bad experiences lately, which you say mainly involve someone stabbing you in the back. Even though you have always known that people are not to be trusted, you are even more upset about people now because your spouse has recently separated from you. Your spouse complains that you are difficult to live with and need professional help. Your spouse says that you are a cold fish and are hypersensitive.

History

You have held a job as a computer hardware repair person for several years. You have had some difficulties with your manager, but you acknowledge that "as long as the boss is the boss, I will follow orders." Your marital history has been stormy. Your spouse has left you twice before after you accused your spouse of having affairs behind your back.

Reason for Attending the Group

You want to complain to the group about your spouse and to get ammunition to use against your spouse.

295.30 SCHIZOPHRENIA, PARANOID TYPE

Chief Complaint

You have felt on a downhill slide for the past 6 months. Strange things have been happening to you, which make you believe that someone is tampering with your mind. The experience that bothers you most is when your dead sister speaks to you during the day. You have a hard time talking about this experience and your style of speaking is somewhat incoherent. As a result of these problems, your personal and professional life has deteriorated.

History

You are a loner whose only friend was your late sister. Your interests are in the occult, and you would never think of leaving the house without checking the daily horoscope.

Reason for Attending the Group

You can no longer deny the frightening aspects of your experience and you want to check this out with a professional person. However, you are frightened to be around people and find yourself quite withdrawn in the group. You are also somewhat suspicious of at least two people in the group and wonder if they have manipulated your presence in the group.

305.00
ALCOHOL ABUSE
305.90
OTHER (OR UNKNOWN), SUBSTANCE ABUSE

Chief Complaint

You have been reprimanded at work for absenteeism and have been getting into frequent arguments with your 13-year-old son. You would like your family and employer to get off your back. You drink excessively but are not able to see the contribution of alcohol and drugs to your problem. You have had blackouts in the past but are currently on the wagon.

History

You graduated from high school by being favored by teachers for your athletic ability. You dropped out of college because of low grades after being highly successful as social chairperson of one of the Greek houses. You returned home and married your childhood sweetheart and have continued to have difficulties with drinking, which has become quite severe the past few years.

Reason for Attending the Group

Your employer and spouse have threatened that unless you get treatment for your problem, you will lose your job and your marriage.

302.3
TRANSVESTIC FETISHISM WITH SEXUAL DYSPHORIA

Chief Complaint

You are not comfortable with who you are and you are presented to the group as having complaints about your identity. Your deeper concern is wanting to live as a member of the opposite sex and you feel uncomfortable with wearing the clothes of your own sex. Frequently, you will cross-dress. You like traditionally opposite-sex activities.

History

You have been uncomfortable with your gender since childhood. You kept this secret from your friends and family until recently, however. You have periods of depression, which are related to attempting to live in your present sex role.

Reason for Attending the Group

You want help in reducing the sense of discomfort and alienation you feel from your sex role.

V62.82
BEREAVEMENT

Chief Complaint

You are very depressed as the result of the recent death of your mother. You complain of poor appetite, weight loss, and insomnia. You think that your feelings are probably normal but cannot stand feeling the way you feel.

History

You own and manage a small restaurant that is well-regarded. You had a close relationship with both parents, but wished you could have spent more time with your mother prior to her death.

Reason for Attending the Group

You want reassurance that your reaction to the death of your mother is normal, and you would like help in feeling relief from your insomnia and anorexia.

83 EMPATHY: THE CORNERSTONE OF COUNSELING

Peter S. Fernald
University of New Hampshire

L. Dodge Fernald
Harvard University

Reading a brief passage taken from an actual counseling session, the instructor plays the role of a sad and struggling client. Students are provided with 10 statements that a counselor might think or say in reaction to what the client said. The task is to identify which statements are empathic and which are not empathic. The activity provides students with the opportunity to imagine themselves in the role of counselor and to consider what they might or might not say, assuming their primary intentions were to be empathic.

CONCEPT

This activity addresses the concept of empathy, considered by counselors to be a critical, if not the most essential, feature of any approach to counseling. In the writing component, the concept of projection is compared and contrasted with the concept of empathy. This activity is appropriate for a general counseling, advanced undergraduate, or graduate course.

MATERIALS NEEDED

A handout titled "Listening Empathically" (see appendix A). The handout includes a statement by a client and 10 therapist responses (or thoughts) that students evaluate for empathic quality. Instructions to the students, which are presented in the third paragraph of the following section, may also be included in the handout.

INSTRUCTIONS

Indicate that a major aspect of any type of counseling or psychotherapy is empathic listening. Mention too that, for some approaches, the counselor's empathy is both central and critical (e.g., Kohut, 1982; Rogers, 1951, 1961). Then tell the students that the activity that they are about to engage in will help them better understand both the nature and difficulties of listening empathically.

Define empathy as the act of adopting the client's perspective or, metaphorically speaking, the act of walking in the client's psychological shoes. The counselor's task, Rogers (1951) said, is

> to assume, in so far as he is able, the internal frame of reference of the client, to perceive the world as the client sees it, to perceive the client himself as he is seen by himself, to lay aside all perceptions of the external frame of reference while doing so, and to communicate something of this empathic understanding to the client. (p. 29)

Provide each student with a copy of the handout (appendix A). Allow the students 2 or 3 min to read the handouts. Then read the following instructions, which may also be included in the handout: "As you listen to me role-play a client, pretend you are a counselor or a therapist. Your task is to adopt my—that is, the client's—perspective. Try to see the world through the client's eyes. Assuming you are able to do this, imagine which of the 10 statements listed on the bottom half of this handout might run through your mind as I speak for the client. Place a check mark by each of these statements. Remember, you are to check only those statements that indicate you adopted the client's perspective."

Next, assuming the client role, read the statement aloud with feeling so that the students have a clear sense of your sadness and struggle. After the reading, ask the students to check those statements that indicate an empathic perspective. Allow the students about 5 min to complete this task.

Students' interest and involvement is substantially enhanced if they are organized into small groups with instructions to arrive at a consensus for each therapist statement. However, this procedure, which is not essential, requires a greater amount of time.

DISCUSSION

Ask the students (or a representative of each small group) what their reactions were to the counselor's first statement. Was it empathic? Does it indicate that the counselor adopted the client's perspective? Some students will take the position that the statement is empathic. Other students will disagree, and the latter students are correct. The first statement is not truly empathic, because the client, even though he obviously struggles to express himself, indicates no concerns about getting started talking. The discussion may become quite spirited, as some students may insist that the counselor's desire to help the client indicates empathy. It is important that these students understand the distinction between wanting to be helpful and listening empathically.

Proceed to the second statement and again ask the students whether or not it is empathic. Most students indicate this statement also is not empathic, and they are correct. The client's statement may suggest indecisiveness, but the client indicates no specific concerns about indecisiveness. Also, he makes no reference to any instances of indecisiveness. The statement, therefore, represents the counselor's concern and has little or nothing to do with anything the client expresses. It reveals the counselor's agenda, possibly his or her theoretical perspective. The statement clearly is not an instance of empathic listening.

Continue the discussion by proceeding through the remaining statements. Statements 3, 6, 7, 8, and 10 indicate empathic listening. The other five statements are not empathic. Discussion of the first few statements may be a bit lengthy. However, as the students gain a better understanding of what it means to listen empathically, discussions of subsequent items take less time.

WRITING COMPONENT

Ask students to write a statement in which they define, compare, and contrast two concepts: empathy and projection. Possible answers and discussion might focus on the ways in which the two concepts both overlap and are distinct. They overlap in the sense that both involve one person attempting to understand the motives and emotions of another person. It has been suggested that projection is the basis of empathy. In so far as a therapist's emotional reaction to a particular circumstance—for example, sadness or anger over the death of a parent—is the same as the client's reaction, projection may provide a basis for empathy.

However, the concepts actually are quite distinct. According to a psychoanalytic perspective, projection occurs when one erroneously attributes his or her own unwanted thoughts, motives, or feelings to another. The more general definition of projection is a perception influenced by one's needs, wishes, and hopes. Whether we refer to the classical or more general definition, projection differs substantially from empathy. Suppose, for example, that the therapist responding to the passage in this activity had many unhappy childhood experiences that he or she wished had never occurred. In such a case, Statement 9 would be regarded as a projection or, more specifically, as countertransference.

REFERENCES

Kohut, H. (1982). Introspection, empathy, and the semi-circle of mental health. *International Journal of Psychoanalyses, 63,* 395–407.

Kohut, H. (1984). *How does analysis cure? (Contributions to the psychology of the self.).* Chicago: University of Chicago Press.

Rogers, C. R. (1951). *Client-centered therapy.* Boston: Houghton-Mifflin.

Rogers, C. R. (1961). *On becoming a person.* Boston: Houghton-Mifflin.

Rogers, C. R. (1980). *A way of being.* Boston: Houghton-Mifflin.

SUGGESTED READING

Fernald, P. S. (1995). Teaching students to listen empathically. *Teaching of Psychology, 22,* 183–186.

Kahn, E. (1985). Heinz Kohut and Carl Rogers. *American Psychologist, 40,* 893–904.

Appendix A

Listening Empathically

Client: I don't feel very normal, but I want to feel that way. I thought I'd have something to talk about—then it all goes around in circles. I was trying to think what I was going to say. Then coming here it doesn't work out. I tell you, it seemed that it would be much easier before I came. I tell you, I just can't make a decision. I don't know what I want. I've tried to reason this thing out logically—tried to figure out which things are important to me. I thought that there may be two things a man might do. He might get married and raise a family. But if he was just a bachelor, just making a living—that isn't very good. I find myself and my thoughts getting back to the days when I was a kid and I cry very easily. The dam would break through. I've been in the army four and a half years. I had no problem then, no hopes, no wishes. My only thought was to get out when peace would come. My problems, now that I'm out, are as ever. I tell you, they go back to a long time before I was in the army. I love children. When I was in the Philippines—I tell you, when I was young I swore I'd never forget my unhappy childhood—so when I saw these children in the Philippines, I treated them very nicely. I used to give them ice cream cones and treat them to movies. It was just a period—I'd reverted back—and that awakened some emotions in me I thought I had long buried. (A pause. He seems very near tears.)

1. I wonder if I should help you get started talking.
2. Why your indecisiveness? What could be its cause?
3. It's really hard for you to get started talking.
4. What is meant by your focus on marriage and family?
5. The crying, the *dam* sound as though there must be a great deal of repression.
6. Decison making just seems impossible to you.
7. You want marriage, but it doesn't seem to you to be much of a possibility.
8. You feel yourself brimming over with feelings reminiscent of your childhood.
9. At some point you will probably need to dig into those early unhappy experiences.
10. Being very nice to children has somehow had meaning for you.

Rogers, Carl R. *Client-Centered Therapy.* Copyright © 1951 by Houghton Mifflin Company. Adapted with permission.

84 THE DOCTOR IS IN: HOW TO TREAT PSYCHOLOGICAL DISORDERS

Allyson J. Weseley

Roslyn High School, Roslyn, New York

Chuck Schira

Portage Central High School, Portage, Michigan

■————————————————————————————————■

Students find psychological disorders and treatments fascinating, but they often confuse them. This activity, written for classrooms of between 15 and 30 students, requires students to diagnose "clients" based on short case histories, and to recommend appropriate treatments. Students are challenged to apply the information they have learned in this engaging way to review information taught in the disorders and treatments units.

■————————————————————————————————■

CONCEPT

Students will learn to use their knowledge of psychological disorders to diagnose mock clients and will evaluate the effectiveness of different perspectives in treating different disorders.

MATERIALS NEEDED

You will need 21 index cards (5 of one color, 5 of a second color, and 11 of a third color). You will also need the case histories presented in appendix A.

INSTRUCTIONS

Preparation

First, write each of the following five terms on an index card of the same color: *humanistic, biomedical, cognitive, behavioral,* and *psychoanalytic.* Label these five cards "Perspective Cards."

Next, cut out the 11 case histories (appendix A) and paste each onto an index card (use different color cards for this set). Label these cards "Case History Cards." The disorders described in the case histories are as follows: Karl—fugue, Julio—disorganized schizophrenia, Brian—multiple personality disorder, Gerri—conversion disorder, Keshona—social phobia, Tuan—antisocial personality disorder, Trent—zoophilia, Ken—obsessive–compulsive disorder, Samantha—posttraumatic stress disorder, Don—bipolar disorder, and Ikimba—generalized anxiety disorder.

Finally, write each of the following five terms on an index card (use a third color for this set): *bulimia, catatonic schizophrenia, seasonal affective disorder, agoraphobia,* and *hypochondriasis.* Label this set of cards "Bonus Round."

How to Play: Round 1

Divide the class into five teams and have each team select a perspective card. Each team will represent that perspective for the entire first round. Have each team choose a representative to sit in the front of the class. These representatives will be the first players. Determine the order (i.e., which representative will go first, second, etc.).

Representatives take turns selecting a case history card, reading it aloud, and attempting to provide the correct *specific* diagnosis (e.g., unipolar depression instead of mood disorder). A correct diagnosis earns the team 1 point. If the diagnosis is incorrect, the next team's representative gets the chance to diagnose.

Once a correct diagnosis is made, the team can earn an additional point by having its representative name or explain an effective treatment and the perspective with which it is associated. As the instructor, you will judge whether the explanation merits the point. If you rule that the treatment suggested is inappropriate, the next team's representative gets the chance to suggest a proper treatment.

An extra point is awarded if a team representative provides an appropriate treatment from the perspective (determined by the card drawn at the beginning) it represents.

Once an appropriate treatment is suggested, the case history card is discarded. Team representatives who have participated return to their teams, with different representatives taking a turn up in front.

The game continues with the next team (following the previously established order) representative choosing a case history card.

How to Play: Bonus Round

One volunteer from each team is named the "client." Each client selects one of the face-down disorder cards, and has 45 s to describe the symptoms of the disorder to her or his team members. The team's goal is to guess the disorder being described. During the 45-s period, team members may interrupt and ask questions.

A correct diagnosis of the disorder within 45 s is worth 2 points.

After each team has participated, the game is over. The team with the most points wins.

How to Play: Additional Notes

As the instructor, you must use your own judgment regarding specificity of correct treatments. For instance, I would not accept "drugs" as a treatment for schizophrenia. Students must specify a type of drug (e.g., phenothiazines), but I do not require the name of a specific drug.

Stress to students that they are not prepared to diagnose those with psychological disorders. Also stress that clinicians do not diagnose clients on the basis of a brief description. Finally, alert students to the impact of labeling people as mentally ill.

Of course, explain to students that cheating (e.g., providing a team representative with an answer) will result in a point deduction.

DISCUSSION The students' level of game performance will indicate how well they have mastered the subject matter. Interrupt the game as necessary to dispel confusion. Also, the game may be shortened or extended.

Use the following questions to facilitate the discussion at the game's conclusion:

1. What kinds of therapy are best for what kinds of disorders?
2. In selecting a therapist, what are the advantages and disadvantages of choosing one who is a strict adherent to a particular perspective versus a more eclectic practitioner?
3. Clients often have symptoms of more than one disorder. How may this fact affect the treatment process?

WRITING COMPONENT

Create a dialogue (two to three typed pages) among B. F. Skinner, Sigmund Freud, Carl Rogers, and Albert Ellis regarding treatment for George, the character on the television show, *Seinfeld*. Give the following description of George, noting that he has sought help for his depression:

> George is a balding, overweight, unmarried, middle-aged man who has difficulty with women. He is unfulfilled in his career and feels that even his friends make fun of him behind his back. George has a difficult time motivating himself to do anything and feels generally despondent.

Students find this writing exercise enjoyable and worthwhile, as it allows them to be creative while forcing them to understand and express the main tenets of the behaviorist, psychoanalytic, humanistic, and cognitive perspectives.

SUGGESTED READING

Corsini, R. J. (1991). *Five therapists and one client*. Itasca, IL: Peacock.

Davidson, G., & Neale, J. (1994). *Abnormal psychology*. New York: Wiley.

Ellis, A. (1984). Rational-emotive therapy. In R. J. Corsini (Ed.), *Current psychotherapies* (3rd ed.). Itasca, IL: Peacock.

Freud, S. (1935; reprinted 1960). *A general introduction to psychoanalysis*. New York: Washington Square Press.

Myers, D. G. (1995). *Psychology* (4th ed.). New York: Worth.

Rogers, C. R. (1951). *Client-centered therapy*. Boston: Houghton-Mifflin.

Skinner, B. F. (1974). *About behaviorism*. New York: Knopf.

Spitzer, R. L., Skodol, A. E., Gibbon, M., & Williams, J. B. W. (1983). *Psychopathology: A case book*. New York: McGraw-Hill.

Appendix A

Case Histories

Cut out, separate, and paste the following descriptions onto 3- by 5-in. index cards:

Ken is plagued by constant worries that what he has planned will not occur as scheduled. He makes hundreds of to-do lists each day and often checks these lists to make sure they are correct. Ken incessantly reminds his colleagues of upcoming deadlines, sometimes 15 or 20 times each day.

One day, Karl, a native of Hawaii, wakes up in Nebraska, with no memory of who he is, how he got there, or from where he came.

Julio believes he is an alien who has been left behind on Earth by his "pod." He is often difficult to understand, because he speaks frequently in rhyme and makes up his own words.

Brian appears to be a mild-mannered 20-something, but he sometimes believes he is a teenage female named Suzy who is a member of a high school dance team. At these times, he dresses in various matching outfits, carries pom-poms, and practices various dance routines. Brian is confused about why he sometimes awakens dressed in strange clothing.

Driving back from a concert, Gerri fell asleep at the wheel and crashed her Jaguar convertible. Her best friend perished in the crash. Ever since, although doctors can find nothing physically wrong, Gerri has been paralyzed in the arm with which she was steering.

Keshona is terrified of speaking in public. Although highly knowledgeable and competent, whenever she has to address a gathering of adults her heart pounds and her mouth gets dry.

Tuan has been arrested on numerous occasions for disturbing the peace and for illegally producing and selling alcohol and drugs to minors. Although a number of his clients have died from overdoses, he feels no remorse.

Trent was raised in a rural, isolated area. Interactions with members of the opposite sex were minimal. Now Trent can be sexually aroused only by llamas.

While on a visit to the Midwest, Samantha's residence was demolished by a tornado. Ever since, she has been plagued by terrible nightmares and occasional flashbacks.

Don goes through periods when he feels he just can't lose. He goes on gambling sprees, launches new get-rich-quick schemes, and engages in promiscuous behavior. At other times, he feels so down that he can't even get out of bed. Life seems purposeless.

No matter what he is doing, Ikimba always feels a little tense; the apprehension has no apparent cause. Even during weekends and vacations, he experiences constant uneasiness.

INDEX